When Things Don't Fall Apart

With warm regards,
Ilene Grabel.

When Things Don't Fall Apart

Global Financial Governance and Developmental Finance
in an Age of Productive Incoherence

Ilene Grabel

The MIT Press
Cambridge, Massachusetts
London, England

This book was set in Stone Serif by Westchester Publishing Services.

Printed and bound in the United States of America.

Library of Congress Cataloging-in-Publication Data

Names: Grabel, Ilene (Ilene J.), 1963– author.
Title: When things don't fall apart : global financial governance and
    developmental financial in an age of productive incoherence / Ilene Grabel ;
    foreword by Dani Rodrik.
Description: Cambridge, MA : MIT Press, [2017] | Includes bibliographical
    references and index.
Identifiers: LCCN 2017020443 | ISBN 9780262037259 (hardcover : alk. paper)
    9780262538527 (pb.)
Subjects: LCSH: Development economics. | International finance. | Financial
    crises. | Financial institutions. | Corporate governance. | Hirschman, Albert O.
Classification: LCC HD87 .G717 2017 | DDC 332/.042—dc23
LC record available at https://lccn.loc.gov/2017020443

Contents

Foreword

It happens only rarely and is all the more pleasurable because of it. You pick up a manuscript that fundamentally changes the way you look at certain things. This is one such book. Ilene Grabel has produced a daring and delightful reinterpretation of developments in global finance since the Asian financial crisis of 1997–1998.

The book addresses, and resolves, a long-standing puzzle: Why has our present model of financial globalization been so resilient, despite an abysmal track record that includes the most severe global financial crisis since the Great Depression, recurrent sovereign debt crises (in Latin America, East Asia, Russia, and Turkey), and many other disappointments (such as capital flowing "uphill" from poorer to richer nations)? How is it that we have not jettisoned this model for something that is more sensible and works better?

Professor Grabel's insight is that those of us who were looking for signs of change have had the wrong idea about how real reform often happens. We have been mistaken in searching for evidence of wholesale, programmatic reconsideration of the rules of global finance. Systems of governance rarely change through established blueprints, a master plan, or radical reforms. And besides, such a reform path would suffer from the same kind of hubris that the neoliberal playbook produced.

Instead, she suggests, it is the cracks in the consensus, the local heresies, and the small departures and innovations that matter and lead us in an altogether novel direction. Inconsistency, ambiguity, and incoherence are useful and productive—they are a feature, not a bug.

Thus, Professor Grabel builds a case for a gradual, evolutionary change in the global financial system and argues that there is at least as much evidence for this alternative thesis as there is for the regime-continuity thesis. The Asian financial crisis may have given the IMF new powers, but it also set in motion defensive moves on the part of developing countries, such as

self-insurance through reserve accumulation and mutual swap arrangements. The G-20 and Financial Stability Board may have been largely
ineffective to date, but there are signs they can evolve into experimental,
networked forms of global financial governance accommodating greater
developing-country influence. The IMF itself has not been overhauled, but
it has changed: it no longer treats capital controls as taboo, has distanced
itself from austerity, and pays increasing attention to social safety nets. And
look at the new institutions that have been created—regional reserve pooling arrangements, development and infrastructure banks—and the forum-
shopping benefits they confer to client states.

Put all of this together and we have what Professor Grabel calls a move
toward "a more complex, fragmented, and pluripolar direction" in international financial governance, "driven in large part by initiatives from
below rather than from above." The evolving system is one that provides
greater policy space, enables "unscripted innovations," and makes "pragmatic adjustments not dictated by an overarching scheme of economic
organization."

The book's deeper argument about how regimes really change is as
interesting as the specific details of the case of international finance. Here
looms the large figure of Albert Hirschman. As Professor Grabel is happy to
remind us at every turn, her argument is very much a Hirschmanian one.
Hirschmanian motifs—the advantages of improvisation, surprise, incrementalism, and pragmatism—are all over the book.

But to say that the book owes a debt to Hirschman is to undersell it. The
Hirschmanian perspective has rarely been deployed so well and to such
great effect. The reason Hirschman never developed a school of thought,
as he himself well recognized, is that his thinking did not lend itself to
emulation and replication. The flashes of brilliance, the unexpected turn of
argument, and the relish of paradox that characterized his style spawned
admirers but not followers. But we have all of those in this book. Professor
Grabel has produced not only an extensively researched book but also one
that is tremendously fun to read.

My colleague Roberto Mangabeira Unger likes to say that universal orthodoxy cannot be defeated solely by local heresies; overcoming it requires a universalizable heresy. Professor Grabel disagrees, as would Albert Hirschman.
She would be the first to acknowledge that the incremental innovations
she discusses in the book do not, in her words, "come close to displacing
neoliberalism from top to bottom." But the neoliberal consensus is gone,
the institutions that uphold it have become more agnostic and flexible, and

new arrangements have sprung up. We do not yet know where the international financial system will end up. Professor Grabel says this is as it should be: enjoy the Hirschmanian moment, and keep your fingers crossed that sanity and common sense will prevail.

Dani Rodrik
March 2017

Preface

In January 2010, I presented a paper at a conference in Muttukadu, India. The event brought together heterodox development economists to discuss the implications of the unfolding global financial crisis across the global south and east. This was to be a friendly audience—like me, most speakers had spent much of their academic careers as resolute critics of the global neoliberal model, the neoclassical model that sustains it, and the Bretton Woods institutions (BWIs) that enforce it.

I took the opportunity to present what was then, admittedly, a somewhat underdeveloped understanding of events emerging haphazardly at the BWIs themselves and across the so-called developing world. I argued that there were signs of meaningful though entirely inchoate change in aspects of global financial governance and, more specifically, in some of the institutions, norms, and practices that bore on policy space for development. As exhibit A, I cited what, just a few years into the crisis, appeared as surprising changes around the use of capital controls. As exhibit B, I cited the emergence of what appeared to be discontinuities and inconsistencies inside the International Monetary Fund (IMF) and in its relationships with some of its former clients. I argued that the developments before us were inconsistent with each other—for instance, that for every step away from neoliberalism one could find evidence of a return to it—that these discontinuities and inconsistencies were limited in scope, ad hoc in their evolution, theoretically uninformed, and that some appeared to have greater rhetorical than practical force. But I argued that we should nevertheless pay attention to them. I suggested that we were witnessing cracks in the neoliberal edifice, even though no compelling alternative vision or locus of power had arisen to replace it. I speculated that we were entering a new period—indeed, a new kind of period, an interregnum, if you will—marked by incoherence and aperture in global financial governance.

Rather than treat emergent incoherence as debility, I argued that we should view it as productive. I proposed the concept of "productive incoherence,"[1] the organizing theme of this book, to convey the idea that the absence of an overarching, compelling theoretical narrative to drive policy and institutional innovation should be recognized as a virtue insofar as it permits the flourishing of experimentation and problem solving, learning by doing and from others, and pragmatic institutional and policy adjustment in the face of unending challenges and obstacles confronting developing economies. The neoliberal era was marked by severe ideational and practical constraints on experimentation, as states in the developing world were induced to pursue a singular, idealized economic model despite its repeated failures and despite their diverse institutions, histories, cultures, historical paths, capacities, and the preferences of politically weak domestic interest groups. In contrast, and in the context of what appeared to be the emerging productive incoherence of the global crisis, policymakers in *some* countries of the global south and east were now enjoying increased space to chart pragmatic innovations. And in the face of enduring epistemic insufficiencies, unscripted innovations and localized experimentation seemed to me a better and more autonomy-enhancing path.

Suffice it to say that I had misjudged my audience. The talk induced anger and dismissiveness among the other participants and audience. Speaker after speaker rose to tell me that my analysis was at best naïve and at worst obfuscating. Didn't I realize that fundamental transformation in the power, practices, and ideas associated with neoliberalism was impossible in the face of entrenched interests, doctrines, and the myriad and inescapable vulnerabilities of developing economies? Didn't I realize that the aperture and changes that I identified amounted to little more than window dressing as institutions like the IMF sought to insulate themselves from failure and protect a franchise that was being restored by the global crisis? Couldn't I see that the crisis was creating conditions that enabled the reproduction of global neoliberalism and that, in the absence of a fundamental, systemic global challenge to neoliberalism, the prospects for meaningful change or even meaningful aperture in global financial governance and policy space were nil?

The hostile reaction proved extraordinarily beneficial. It convinced me of the need to clarify, sharpen, and develop my central arguments and, most importantly, to think through the essential matter of how to understand economic, social, and political change. The exploration of change ultimately drew me to the work of Albert O. Hirschman, whose insights and voluminous oeuvre have proven to be both invaluable and excellent company in this journey. The continued unfolding of the crisis gave me ample opportunity to broaden my gaze across the landscape of financial governance. Over the next few years, I continued to follow closely and write about the IMF and capital controls. At the same time, I began to follow developments associated with informal financial governance networks. More importantly, I also became a close student of the proliferation and transformation of liquidity support and project-finance institutions based in the global south and east. An invitation by the United Nations Development Programme to write a background paper on this subject in conjunction with the 2013 Human Development Report (on the theme of the "Rise of the South") provided me with the opportunity to extend the empirical scope of my earlier work. Fortunately I have had several opportunities to speak with officials of many of these institutions and to attend meetings that have brought officials together, namely, meetings hosted by the Union of South American Nations (UNASUR) and the Argentine Ministry of Economic and Public Finance in 2012; the Global Economic Governance Initiative of the Frederic S. Pardee School of Global Studies at Boston University in 2016; and a meeting organized by the United Nations Conference on Trade and Development (UNCTAD), UNASUR, and the Technical Commission for the New International Financial Architecture of the Ministry of Foreign Affairs and Human Mobility of the government of Ecuador in 2016. In these encounters, too, I have been struck by the gap between the achievements and dynamism of these institutions and the emerging networks among them, and the skepticism of many academics and civil society actors about their significance. The predominant view is that these institutions do not mark a significant break in the old order, dominated as it is by the BWIs, United States, U.S. dollar, and the global financial elite. I have now been told many times that these institutions are trivial when compared with the material and social power of the central authorities and actors that have dominated global financial governance over the past several decades.

As the global crisis has evolved, events have moved in directions that substantially strengthen the productive incoherence thesis. Since 2010, I have explored provisionally in a series of papers aspects of the argument that now come together in this book in a more developed, theoretically grounded, and empirically substantiated form. Stated simply, I advance two claims in the book. The first claim is positive. The global crisis has occasioned meaningful though disconnected, ad hoc, and experimental discontinuities in several dimensions of global financial governance and developmental finance that are of particular salience to developing countries. The empirical story is not one of wall-to-wall change. Nontrivial continuities are also readily apparent, and these should not be dismissed. The second claim is normative. The conjunction of discontinuities and continuities is imparting incoherence to global financial governance and developmental finance, but this incoherence is productive for development. This insight can be understood most fully within the context of what I term a "Hirschmanian" mindset.

Why the resistance to accounts such as my own? The easy answer is that I am wrong. An alternative answer is that social scientists and civil society advocates share a narrow conception of change. In this view, meaningful change must be fundamental, abrupt, systemic, coordinated, and informed by a consistent and overarching theoretical framework that gives direction to and unifies all of the moving parts. Moreover, change must derive from a worldview that encompasses a comprehensive, complementary set of core beliefs, values, and a utopian vision. Absent these features, any changes that do occur are insignificant, inconsistent, unviable, and distracting. In the instant case, this view holds that the discontinuities that emerged after the East Asian financial crisis and then deepened during the global crisis lack the character of meaningful advancement. After all, the innovations lack every feature that we tend to associate with epochal change. Innovations have been local (or at best regional, and occasionally transregional), inconsistent, sometimes fleeting, and out of step with the major competing economic worldviews—be it liberalism, Keynesianism, statism, or any other model. Indeed, there seems to be no model at all.

Throughout the book, I reject this notion of change as romantic and otherwise mistaken. The vision presumes that we have sufficient knowledge of the policies, institutions, norms, and practices that promote just, stable, and sustainable development. But by now we should be skeptical of that claim. It would be far better to accept that we just don't know enough and that, in that context, we are better off pursuing a course of action that is rich in experimentation, learning by doing, and ad hoc adjustment. This perspective leads us to recognize that in comparison with its neoliberal predecessor, the current period is marked by increasing policy space, room for unscripted innovations, and pragmatic adjustments not dictated by an overarching scheme of economic organization. Hence, the incoherence of the period is productive—holding within it the potential for the achievement of important economic and human development goals.

Productive incoherence is not without risks, and I explore these later in the book. Indeed, as of this writing, we look out at a world where incoherence and aperture appears everywhere. In some South American countries, neoliberals have replaced left-leaning populist governments. Some of the rising powers in the global south and east are stumbling, and all face a macroeconomic environment that is fraught with risk. At the same time, China is taking the lead in promoting a managed yet ambitious form of global financial (and broader economic) integration and is revitalizing the landscape of (what I term) developmental finance. Moreover, the financial governance architecture of the developing world is marked by increased density stemming from institutional innovation. Finally, there is a movement toward "deglobalization" propelled by the complementary forces of a backward-looking Trumpian agenda, British prime minister Theresa May's decision to pursue a "hard" (rather than a partial) "Brexit" from the European Union (EU), and the real possibility that neonationalist leaders in Europe will tally more wins at the ballot box in the coming years.

I must emphasize in this context that the argument advanced here about the virtues of the centrifugal tendencies in global financial governance now under way—which entail inter alia the emergence of national and regional loci of financial regulation and developmental finance—by no means represents a call for or support of deglobalization. The argument on offer concerns *transformations in the nature of international integration*, not a romanticized return to some idealized state of financial autarky or any regime that features neonationalist economic or political tendencies. The best outcome is that this interregnum of productive incoherence makes space for *reintegration* of a sort that provides developing countries with more room to maneuver than they enjoyed during the stultifying neoliberal era.

I began *When Things Don't Fall Apart* in 2013. As I write now (in February 2017), things still (fortunately) have not "fallen apart" for the developing world as they had in the 1980s and during the numerous crises of the neoliberal era. None of my arguments should be interpreted as suggesting that things won't fall apart—of course they always can. But the discontinuities that I explore throughout the book enhance the degree of resilience and provide opportunities to pursue multiple pathways when things inevitably do fall apart.

My friend Mark Blyth suggested the title of this book. He offered me insightful and characteristically pointed advice, for which I am most grateful. The book's title is a play on lines in the opening stanza of W. B. Yeats's 1919 poem "The Second Coming" ("Things fall apart; the centre cannot hold"). The poem was written in the aftermath of World War I, and it both reflects the anxieties of the period and anticipates the horrors that lay ahead. Novelist Chinua Achebe not only borrows these lines but also invokes the spirit of this poem in his 1958 novel *Things Fall Apart,* which focuses on upheavals caused by European colonization in Africa. Turning for a moment to personal matters, I note here that the title of my book came to have a particular resonance for me. I started, stopped, restarted, stopped, and then ultimately finished the book after things came dangerously close to falling apart completely—twice—owing to ultimately successful cardiac surgeries endured by my husband, George DeMartino. I will always be grateful to Drs. Daniel Lumian, John Carroll and his team, Simon Maltais, and Charanjit "Chet" Rihal for their collective brilliance and compassion.

Turning to more conventional debts, my thinking on matters that culminated in this book and my work on the book itself have benefited greatly from conversations and reflections offered by many friends and colleagues at various stages. Among the many (and at the risk of a failing memory), I thank Rawi Abdelal, Leslie Elliott Armijo, Philip Arestis, Diana Barrowclough, Günseli Berik, Albert Berry, Jacqueline Best, Patrick Bond, José Carlos Braga, Sasha Breger Bush, Miriam Campanella, Ben Clift, Eugenia Correa, Jim Crotty, Roy Culpeper, Christine Desan, David Ellerman, Sakiko Fukada-Parr, Jamie Galbraith, Randall Germain, Jayati Ghosh, Alicia Girón, Fred Gonzaga Jayme Jr., Stephany Griffith-Jones, Bill Grimes, James Heintz, Gerald Helleiner, Micheline Ishay, Jomo K. S., Alex Kentikelenis, David Kotz, Bill Kring, Noemi Levy, Wesley Marshall, David Martin, Arturo O'Connell, Isabel Ortiz, Matthew Paterson, Kari Polanyi Levitt, Chiara Piovani, Elizabeth Ramey, Martin Rhodes, Luis Rosero, Malcolm Sawyer, Mario Seccareccia, Rogério Studart, Matias Vernengo, Yongzhong Wang, and Richard Kozul-Wright. Chris Brown and Jack Donnelly, both University of Denver colleagues, were extremely generous with their time. I thank Jack for discussions of international relations theory and also for serving as my personal "Geek Squad." I thank Chris for his willingness to respond to my numerous queries.

I owe deep debts to colleagues who provided me with specific feedback on my work at critical moments. I thank particularly Michele Alacevich for his careful review of my treatment of Hirschman; and I thank Jim Boyce, Ha-Joon Chang, Greg Chin, Jim Crotty, Jerry Epstein, Kevin Gallagher, Eric Helleiner, Jonathan Kirshner, José Antonio Ocampo, Esteban Pérez Caldentey, and Robert Wade for discussions of numerous matters. My friends and mentors Jim Crotty, Jerry Epstein, and the late Kim and Matt Edel taught me so much, and I hope that I become half as good at being a human being and a scholar as they are (and as the Edels were). George DeMartino and

Jerry Epstein took on the task of reading the final manuscript, and this was both invaluable and exceedingly generous.

My four years as a coeditor of the *Review of International Political Economy* taught me a great deal, particularly about the pleasures of Hirschmanian trespassing. In this connection, I thank my colleagues at the journal, especially Wes Widmaier. I am also grateful to unnamed officials of many of the institutions that I discuss in chapter 6. On publication matters, I benefited from the sage advice of Mark Blyth, Kevin Gallagher, Joe Jackson, Jonathan Kirshner, David Kotz, José Antonio Ocampo, Scott Parris, Bob Pollin, Jonathan Wight, and Rick Wolff. It was a pleasure to start this process at MIT Press with Jane McDonald and then to conclude it under Emily Taber's extraordinarily able and thoughtful direction. I am also grateful to Laura Keeler, Jim Mitchell, and others at MIT Press, Mikala Guyton at Westchester Publishing Services, and Hal Henglein for their attentive work on my behalf. I benefited from the financial support of a University of Denver Professional Research Opportunities for Faculty grant during the final push to complete the book.

My intellectual debts to George DeMartino are particularly deep, not least in the realm of epistemic and normative issues and what they imply for the hubris and ethics of social engineering. Those who know his work will see signs of his influence here. In the case of this book, a series of conversations with George at the outset of my research proved to be pivotal. He urged me to consider the potential of the inconsistent developments in global financial governance as an incubator for progressive reform. Those conversations led to the concept of productive incoherence and the turn to Hirschman that inform this book. For those intellectual insights—and for his persistent encouragement—I am terribly grateful.

I am thankful to friends and family for their support, encouragement, and love during the writing of this book. I thank particularly in this regard Sara and Tommy Butler; Amelia, Amy, and my dear goddaughter Margo Cramer; and Katy Donnelly, Kathy Fabiani, Craig Freedman, Rob Garnett, Doreen Isenberg, Micheline Ishay, Paul Perasso, Chiara Piovani, and Elizabeth Ramey. Kathy and Paul swooped in to offer support in Rochester, Minnesota, for which I'll be forever grateful. Thanks go as well to my great students at the Josef Korbel School of International Studies. They have long inspired me to do research relevant to their commitments and aspirations, and I continue to learn a great deal from them. I have benefited from the work of many wonderful research assistants in the course of this project. Among them, I thank Kyle Barker, Brooks Bourland, Art Chambers, Ryan Economy,

Jesse Golland, Ann Job, Alex Knopes, Alison Lowe, Denise Marton Menendez, Norbert Steinbock, and my most recent and tireless team of Jeff Chase, Meredith Moon, Nyambe Muyunda, and Brooke Snowden.

Finally, I dedicate this book to George, who has supported me throughout this process, and in all things. His intellect inspires and nourishes me; his commitment to do for others never ceases to amaze me; and there is simply no one who loves me better. I'm proud to be a member of the Gray Team.

Denver, Colorado
February 2017

Abbreviations

AEs	Advanced Economies
AfDB	African Development Bank
AIIB	Asian Infrastructure Investment Bank
ALBA	Bolivarian Alliance for the Peoples of Our America (Spanish acronym)
ALBA-TCP	Bolivarian Alliance for the Peoples of Our America—Peoples' Trade Treaty (Spanish acronym)
AMF	Asian Monetary Fund
AMRO	ASEAN+3 Macroeconomic Research Office
ArMF	Arab Monetary Fund
AsDB	Asian Development Bank
ASEAN	Association of Southeast Asian Nations
ASEAN+3	Association of Southeast Asian Nations plus China, Japan, and South Korea
BDS	Bank of the South (Spanish acronym)
BIS	Bank for International Settlements
BNDES	Brazil's National Economic and Social Development Bank (Portuguese acronym; commonly referred to as Brazilian National Development Bank)
BRICs	Brazil, Russian Federation, India, China
BRICS	Brazil, Russian Federation, India, China, South Africa
BWIs	Bretton Woods institutions
CAF	Development Bank of Latin America (formerly known as Andean Development Corporation [Corporación Andina de Fomento]) (Spanish acronym)
CDB	China Development Bank
CMI	Chiang Mai Initiative
CMIM	Chiang Mai Initiative Multilateralisation

COFER	Currency Composition of Official Foreign Exchange Reserves
CRA	Contingent Reserve Arrangement (of the BRICS)
EBRD	European Bank for Reconstruction and Development
EC	European Commission
ECB	European Central Bank
EFSD	Eurasian Fund for Stabilization and Development
EFSF	European Financial Stability Facility
EIB	European Investment Bank
EMDEs	Emerging Market and Developing Economies
ESM	European Stability Mechanism
EU	European Union
FCL	Flexible Credit Line
FDI	Foreign Direct Investment
Fed	(U.S.) Federal Reserve
Finance G-20	Group of Twenty finance ministers and central bank governors
FLAR	Latin American Reserve Fund (Spanish acronym)
FSB	Financial Stability Board
FSF	Financial Stability Forum
G-7	Group of Seven countries (Canada, France, Germany, Italy, Japan, the United Kingdom, and the United States)
G-8	Group of Eight countries (G-7, plus Russia)
G-11	Group of Eleven at the World Bank and IMF
G-20	Group of Twenty (G-7, plus Argentina, Australia, Brazil, China, India, Indonesia, Mexico, Russia, Saudi Arabia, South Africa, South Korea, Turkey, and the European Union)
G-24	Intergovernmental Group of Twenty-Four on International Monetary Affairs and Development
GDP	Gross Domestic Product
IADB	Inter-American Development Bank
IBRD	International Bank for Reconstruction and Development (of the World Bank)
IDA	International Development Association (of the World Bank)
IEO	Independent Evaluation Office (of the IMF)
IIF	Institute of International Finance
ILO	International Labour Organization
IMF	International Monetary Fund

IMFC	International Monetary and Financial Committee (of the IMF)
MRDBs	Main Regional Development Banks
NAB	New Arrangements to Borrow
NAFTA	North American Free Trade Agreement
NDB	New Development Bank (of the BRICS)
NIEO	New International Economic Order
ODA	Official Development Assistance
OECD	Organisation for Economic Co-operation and Development
PBOC	People's Bank of China
PCL	Precautionary Credit Line
QE	Quantitative Easing
RCT	Randomized Control Trial
RMB	Renminbi (currency of People's Republic of China)
SAFE	State Administration of Foreign Exchange (of China)
SAP	Structural Adjustment Program
SBA	Stand-By Arrangement
SDDS	Special Data Dissemination Standard
SDGs	Sustainable Development Goals (of the United Nations)
SDR	Special Drawing Right
SOE	State-Owned Enterprise
SUCRE	Unitary System for Regional Compensation (Spanish acronym)
SWF	Sovereign Wealth Fund
TPP	Trans-Pacific Partnership
UN	United Nations
UNASUR	Union of South American Nations (Spanish acronym)
UNCTAD	United Nations Conference on Trade and Development
WDI	World Development Indicators
WTO	World Trade Organization

I   Crises, Change, and Productive Incoherence

1   Introduction: Contesting Continuity

The East Asian financial crisis of the late 1990s focused attention on the limitations of the Bretton Woods institutions (BWIs), the International Monetary Fund (IMF) and World Bank, and the broader inadequacies of global financial governance. The crisis catalyzed calls for a "new global financial architecture."[1] The global financial crisis that began in 2008 induced similar diagnoses and remedies. As the global crisis unfolded, prominent economists and other experts proposed radical, systemic reform. For instance, a United Nations (UN) commission chaired by Joseph Stiglitz ("the Stiglitz Commission") called for rebuilding the international monetary system from the ground up (UN 2009, chaps. 4 and 5). In a widely discussed March 2009 essay, Xiaochuan Zhou, governor of the People's Bank of China (PBOC), derided the dollar's privileged status as the world's global reserve currency and advanced the idea of a "super-sovereign reserve currency," a role that he argued could be played by the IMF's Special Drawing Right (SDR) (Chin 2014b; Zhou 2009). In addition, leaders of the Group of Twenty (G-20) nations signaled at the outset of the crisis the need for a "New Bretton Woods" to promote bold new thinking and international coordination (Parker, Barber, and Dombey 2008). Finally, representatives of the BRICS (Brazil, Russia, India, China, and South Africa) cited the global crisis as evidence that the U.S. financial model was irrevocably flawed and should be abandoned as a global ideal.[2] BRICS leaders also argued that the legitimacy of the BWIs was undermined by outdated, biased, and dysfunctional practices and that those institutions were out of touch with the dispersal in global economic power that was associated with the rise of the global south and east (Leahy 2011; Giles 2012).[3]

The most ambitious proposals for architectural reform faded quickly in the face of opposition from powerful political and economic interests and institutional and ideational inertia. In this respect, the fate of the reform campaigns inaugurated by the global crisis mirrored that of the more radical

New International Economic Order (NIEO) agenda of the 1970s (see Golub 2013) and also the less extensive proposals for a new global financial architecture that followed the developing-country debt crisis of the 1980s and the crises of the 1990s. In all of these instances, hopes for radical transformation in the global financial governance architecture were roundly defeated. Recurrent failures of the reform agenda have led many observers to emphasize continuity in global financial governance up to the present. What I will call the *continuity thesis* claims that the opportunity for meaningful reform created by the global crisis has been lost and that nothing of significance has changed in terms of global financial governance architecture, especially concerning emerging market and developing economies (EMDEs).

Is the continuity perspective correct or, minimally, largely adequate as an interpretation of the recent past and contemporary developments? In fact, it is neither. It is substantively mistaken in critical respects. The East Asian and especially the global crises induced a series of disparate, disconnected innovations in the world's financial governance architecture. The crises precipitated significant and sustained, though uneven, discontinuities across several dimensions of global financial governance. I argue that these discontinuities matter deeply from the perspective of EMDEs. They bear on national policy autonomy and policy space for economic and human development, financial stability and resilience in the face of disturbances, and financial inclusion. Recent initiatives carry the potential to contribute toward attainment of the UN's newly adopted Sustainable Development Goals (SDGs), particularly the goals that focus on sustainable and inclusive economic growth, infrastructure development, sustainable industrialization, and the realization of multistakeholder partnerships in pursuit of more just and inclusive development. This is not to say that the global crisis has occasioned an abrupt shift from one regime of global financial governance to another. It hasn't. As we will see, continuities today are as salient as the discontinuities. But then, how are we to make sense of the current conjuncture?

Purpose of Book

The chief purpose of this book is to present and defend one principal thesis—what I have called elsewhere the *productive incoherence thesis* (Grabel 2011; 2013a; 2015a; 2015b; 2017). It can be summarized simply. The emerging constellation of financial governance institutions and policies are not reducible or faithful to any overarching "ism," be it neoliberalism,

Keynesianism, dirigisme, or any other old or new model. When judged against the standards of any of these visions, which defined economic policy and institutional formation through much of the twentieth century, the changes we confront today appear variously as inconsistent, contradictory, redundant, ad hoc, and meager. The system (such as it is) that has emerged is at loose ends.[4] In the vacuum created by the absence of a unifying vision, a multiplicity of undertheorized, fragmented, overlapping, tenuous, and tentative interventions have emerged. It is in this sense that global financial governance, taken as a whole, is today "incoherent." This is the central positive claim advanced in the book.

This much might be apparent (and even disturbing) to many observers. But I will also contend, more ambitiously and provocatively, that this incoherence presents a welcome rupture, a break from totalizing visions (such as neoliberalism) that were intended to provide strict guidance on institutional design and policy choice and have sought to impose institutional harmonization globally over an irreducibly diverse world, as utopian schemes generally do. For the first time in a generation, many EMDEs have escaped the straitjacket of a commanding theoretical orthodoxy and the associated straitjacket of a narrowly prescribed menu of appropriate institutional forms and policy practices. Today EMDEs enjoy increased space to experiment pragmatically with new institutional forms and practices. Ideational and structural constraints that forced EMDEs to adopt strategies that were derived axiomatically on the blackboards of foreign and home-grown development experts are breaking down, and as of now no peer "ism" has emerged to replace them.

What is remarkable about the present conjuncture, but denied by continuity theorists, is the extent to which states that were for so long constrained under an encompassing global financial governance architecture are now enjoying development and financial policy autonomy. An unruly pragmatism has broken out in institutional design, governance, and policymaking. The new spirit entails learning from experience and learning from both the successes and failures of others, adjusting as necessary and in response to new challenges. The result so far has been the emergence of an increasingly dense, "pluripolar" set of fledgling institutions of financial governance and a diversity of institutional and policy practices. I purposely avoid the more commonly referenced "multipolarity" because the term is often associated with claims about the rise of one or perhaps two new hegemons or blocs that serve as a counterweight to the dominance of the United States and the international financial institutions that it dominates and that hold sufficient power to impose an alternative economic model.

Pluripolarity, as I will use it here, does not entail the claim of a rising hegemon, a unified theoretical or practical model, or displacement capacity but refers instead to increasing diversity, heterogeneity, and even inconsistency within the landscape of global financial governance. A critical test of the resilience and capabilities of emerging arrangements will occur in future crises, as states rely on and adjust fledgling institutions, practices, and policies in hopes of dampening instability and otherwise managing turbulence better than they had been able to do during previous crises.

My central normative contention is that the aperture that has emerged in the space between competing overarching models—the one we are leaving behind and the one that has not as of yet emerged to replace it—is to be taken not as a handicap but instead as an opportunity. The incoherence of the present system is, in a word, productive rather than debilitating.[5]

The Continuity Thesis

The continuity thesis, which denies notable change in the contemporary era, is not to be dismissed lightly. Its advocates comprise some of the most astute observers of global financial governance. And so we should pause to take stock at the outset, even if only briefly, of the underlying logic and empirical findings that sustain claims of continuity.

The East Asian crisis had a lasting imprint in EMDEs. Particularly notable in this regard was the proposal for an Asian Monetary Fund (AMF). Though the proposal failed, the crisis ultimately bore fruit in the region and beyond. Not least, it yielded the creation of a reserve pooling arrangement among the members of the Association of Southeast Asian Nations plus Japan, China, and South Korea (ASEAN+3). More broadly, the Asian crisis stimulated in other regions of the developing world an interest in regional mechanisms that could deliver countercyclical liquidity support and long-term project finance through institutions that are, to some degree or other, independent of the BWIs.

The legacy of the East Asian crisis is also reflected in the rise of reserve accumulation strategies across EMDEs—strategies that were driven largely by a desire to secure a degree of independence from the IMF in view of its overreach in the crisis countries and its myriad failures prior to and during the East Asian crisis. Reserve accumulation was enabled by fortuitous global economic conditions during the decade and a half following the East Asian crisis. These included but were not limited to sustained commodity demand and rising commodity prices through 2011 and net capital inflows through 2013 (propelled in part by low interest rates in the advanced economies, or

AEs). Reserve accumulation facilitated the growing assertiveness of larger EMDEs vis-à-vis the BWIs prior to and especially during the global crisis, and played a role in their ability to navigate the most dangerous early years of the global crisis relatively well. In some cases, reserves supported countercyclical fiscal programs, a response that was not available during previous crises (Grabel 2015b; Wise, Armijo, and Katada 2015; Ocampo et al. 2012). The insulation offered by high reserves, along with large international capital inflows in the years after the East Asian crisis and during the global crisis, also allowed EMDEs to deploy capital controls without fearing the reaction of investors, the IMF, or credit rating agencies. Reserve-rich EMDEs were not only able to retain a degree of autonomy from the IMF during the crisis but also in 2009 and 2012 took on the unprecedented role of funding the institution instead of borrowing from it.

How significant are these and the many other developments we will examine throughout the book? Continuity theorists are largely unimpressed (e.g., Akyüz 2013; 2016). We will probe these matters in some detail later in the book, but here a quick overview must suffice. Many observers recognize the emergence of a vast (bilateral) central bank swap network that sustained liquidity as an important legacy of the crisis. But they see this network as having limited political and economic implications for the international monetary system (Henning 2016; McDowell 2017). For others, evidence of continuity is found in the prevalence of unilateral and bilateral over coordinated multilateral or (outside of Europe) regional responses to the global crisis. In regard to the EMDEs, many cite the "institutionally light" nature of regional crisis response frameworks (Chin 2010).[6] Continuity theorists also emphasize the prevalence of U.S.-centered responses to the global crisis (Helleiner 2014b; Prasad 2014).[7] Indeed, the crisis strengthened the role of the dollar and underscored the importance of accumulating the currency in the form of reserves while also revealing the relative power and centrality of the United States even vis-à-vis the IMF (Akyüz 2016).[8] Further evidence of U.S. power in the global financial arena was provided by the ability of the U.S. Congress until late 2015 to block implementation of the modest IMF governance reforms agreed to in 2010 by IMF governors representing 95% of the institution's voting power (Vestergaard and Wade 2014). Relatedly, those arguing for continuity at the IMF highlight the continued enforcement of the "gentleman's agreement" on leadership, overrepresentation of key member states in the institution's decision making, consistency between recent and earlier conditionality programs (which feature austerity and reflect the neoliberal worldview and interests of key stakeholders), and at best a modest shift on capital controls (Gabor 2010; 2012; Güven 2012;

Kentikelenis, Stubbs, and King 2016; Nelson 2014a; 2017; Vestergaard and Wade 2015; Wade 2013a; Weisbrot 2015).

Several prominent observers are skeptical of claims about emergent pluripolarity in international financial governance (Akyüz 2013; Vestergaard and Wade 2013a; Wade 2011).[9] Some argue that the United States and other key countries within the Group of Eight (G-8) continue to dominate policy discussions in the emerging networks of economic governance (Helleiner 2014b). For instance, some observers dismiss the G-20 as little more than a larger, more unruly G-8 (Helleiner 2014b; Mittelman 2013; Ocampo 2010b; 2010c; Vestergaard and Wade 2012b). Worse yet, the inclusion of some EMDEs in the G-20 divides EMDEs and gives those fortunate few with a seat at the table an incentive not to rock the boat (Wade 2013b). Advocates of continuity also dismiss the significance and potential of various institutional innovations in EMDEs, particularly the arrangements associated with the ASEAN+3 countries and the BRICS, while others dismiss the collective significance of these and a range of other institutional innovations by what are often termed the "rising powers."[10]

Continuity theorists highlight the continued power of the financial sector. This is exemplified by the financial community's capture of the post-crisis Dodd-Frank legislation in the United States (D'Arista and Epstein 2011) and by the exploitation of the Eurozone crisis by the IMF and the European Union (EU) to advance neoliberal reforms that reflect powerful financial interests and ideas about financial liberalization that should have been discredited by earlier policy failures (Weisbrot 2015). Many advocates of continuity have argued that neoliberalism remains firmly entrenched and that the economics profession itself remains stuck in its commitment to neoclassical theory (Blyth 2013b; Hodgson 2009; Mirowski 2013). Finally, some have argued that the global financial system remains as fragile and crisis prone as ever, and that EMDEs remain as vulnerable to crises today as they have been over the past several decades (UNCTAD 2016, chap. 1).

The continuity view entails important and undeniable insights. Certainly in comparison with the clarity and scale of the Bretton Woods–era transformations and the heroic NIEO vision, contemporary changes are disconnected, piecemeal, paltry, and even contradictory. But the dismissal of aperture and real and potential change comes too easily. Defeatism reflects a prevalent expectation that meaningful change must be dramatic, systemic, coherent, and unambiguous. I reject this view because it both lacks sufficient theoretical nuance and is empirically inaccurate. Instead of that kind of change, the global crisis has induced ambiguous, evolutionary, uneven, modest, and cross-cutting initiatives that are reflected in continuities, discontinuities, and ambiguities in nearly equal measure. In the continuity view, these kinds of changes are chimerical and distracting rather than adequate or even notable.

Heroic Transformations in the Bretton Woods and Neoliberal Eras

Why do continuity theorists overlook and even deny the significance of contemporary events? A key aspect of the problem derives from largely unspoken but nonetheless deeply held conceptions about the nature of institutional transformation and about how social change is to be understood more broadly. The archetype of institutional change that many observers have in mind when assessing contemporary events is the "Bretton Woods moment." Surely, the emergence of the BWIs (and the associated Bretton Woods order) in the closing moments of World War II marked a fundamental change in global financial governance—one that featured a new international architecture that facilitated postwar reconstruction, shared prosperity, and financial stability. Although the Bretton Woods system is primarily understood in connection with the influence and needs of AEs, it also influenced economic conditions and strategies in EMDEs.

The sharp discontinuities associated with the creation of Bretton Woods were enabled by a unique confluence of national and international economic, political, geostrategic, and ideational conditions. As Eric Helleiner (1994; 2010a) has argued, these conditions include the common experience of World War II; the unique position of the United States in the world after the war, which gave it both the moral authority and the power to shape global economic institutions; and the economic devastation and political turmoil in postwar Europe and Japan. While the war and postwar crisis could have spawned a profound ideological contest about economic governance, a common ideational environment provided by an ascendant Keynesianism directed the pursuit of a new model of domestic economic management and international economic integration. The new Bretton Woods model was characterized by a (sufficiently) coherent model of economic mediation that was to be centrally administered and directed by powerful interests that shared a common worldview. The transformation was enabled and directed by decisionmakers who embraced a commitment to Keynesian "embedded liberalism" (Helleiner 1994; 2010a). Under these conditions, the Bretton Woods negotiators and other key political actors were afforded a once-in-a-century opportunity to design and implement a new economic order.

The neoliberal revolution of the 1980s and 1990s marks another fundamental turning point, a radical transformation in global financial governance and development policy that filled the vacuum introduced by contradictions internal to the Bretton Woods system and the Keynesianism that supported it. In a remarkably short period, the Keynesianism of the Bretton Woods era was displaced, wall to wall (or so it seemed), in domestic economic policy formation, development policy, economic theory, and in the institutions of international economic integration. The markers of this transformation comprise the emergence of the Washington Consensus, financial liberalization in the global north and south, and, more generally, the substitution of market mediation for state direction of economic flows (DeMartino 2000; Harvey 2005). In the view of many observers, the shift was as dramatic and consequential as the transformations signaled by the postwar initiatives.

In the case of the neoliberal revolution, there was no Bretton Woods moment—no summit of leading government officials gathering to bang out the next institutional architecture, directed in that effort by a new economic and political model. Instead, the change was enacted in the context of a fairly radical displacement of Keynesianism in the economics profession by the triumphant Chicago school of thought. The shift occurred against the backdrop of economic crises (stagflation, unsustainable developing-country debt, and other economic problems), which the existing Keynesianism was ill prepared to explain, let alone manage. Very quickly, neoliberal economists (such as Anne Krueger) were appointed to leadership positions at the BWIs—just as those institutions came to increase their activism in shaping domestic institutions and policies across the global south and (parts of) the east. Neoliberalism was also propelled by the increased economic and political influence of financial and industrial interests, which sought to escape the constraints of Keynesian statism (while of course holding onto Keynesian-inspired state subsidies and protections of all sorts). These and myriad other factors conspired to turn the tide and shape preferences toward market liberalization. The change in regime spread across the global north, though it faced stiff opposition there from well-organized civil society constituencies that were able to sustain state-provided protections from the market. Matters were different in the global south, where neoliberalism was installed under crisis conditions that provided the BWIs and domestic elites (and, in some cases, authoritarian leaders) with a historic opportunity to engage in radical economic reengineering. Though there was no Bretton Woods moment, the neoliberal revolution yielded a dramatic and extensive transformation in theory, ideology, and practice away from explicit state management of economic affairs in the EMDEs (DeMartino 2000).

The Global Crisis—The Continuity View

Against the standard of these epic transformations, history is littered with failed initiatives that leave no meaningful legacy other than the apparent futility of attempting institutional innovations that challenge dominant economic and political interests. Isn't this the legacy of the failed NIEO movement and of the failed reform efforts driven by the East Asian crisis and the crisis of 2008? Surely, contemporary adjustments in global financial governance pale in comparison with the two archetypal transformations of the twentieth century and fall far short of the most ambitious proposals of critics of global neoliberalism. As continuity theorists rightly claim, today we find neither a planned, expansive, abrupt, or coordinated displacement of neoliberalism nor a new, adequate, coherent theoretical model to ground ongoing innovations. We also cannot locate today any new oppositional interests that are sufficiently well organized and influential to counter neoliberal impulses and to direct architectural reform. Instead, the most ambitious proposals for reform in the immediate aftermath of the global crisis faded quickly in the face of opposition from entrenched interests and institutional and ideological stickiness. As in the past, hopes for radical transformation in global financial governance were roundly defeated.

What do we find in place of institutional, policy, and ideational revolution? At best, a series of fairly prosaic, mundane, localized, and disconnected adjustments to the crisis tendencies of neoliberalism, often driven by the champions of neoliberalism itself (such as finance ministries, and even the BWIs). *In short, they involve evolution, not revolution.* The initiatives undertaken appear at best to be ameliorative. Certainly, they can't begin to amount to a frontal challenge to neoliberal prescriptions, institutions, or practices.

In contrast to the continuity advocates, those who identify discontinuity in the present period tend to focus narrowly on isolated (though not unimportant) aspects of global financial governance. The clearest case of discontinuity is found in the reversal among EMDEs and even AEs, and within the international financial institutions and the economics profession, regarding capital controls. In addition, a few careful observers have argued that some changes at the IMF are indeed consequential. Others have highlighted the significance of innovations in the financial architectures of EMDEs in the creation of a multilayered global financial architecture, or what Stuenkel (2016b) terms a complementary "parallel order." To date, however, the dissent against the continuity thesis has largely failed to provide an expansive assessment of the aperture, discontinuities, and possibilities of the postcrisis period or to make the case for far-reaching, fundamental discontinuity.

It needs to be repeated here that the chief problem with the continuity analysis is its inappropriate notion of economic regime identity, stability, and change. Regime change is viewed either as systemic, enduring, and fundamental or as local, ameliorative, fleeting, and thin. Central to this vision is the notion of *displacement* as the test of the significance of change. Either neoliberalism has been or is in the process of being displaced in toto or it remains largely intact and unaffected by the diverse innovations under way. The IMF either has or has not shed its identity as the enforcer of neoliberalism. Liquidity support arrangements and development banks based in EMDEs either displace the BWIs, are trivial in relation to them, or are just a "poor man's" replica of the BWIs, guilty of the same sins (such as promoting extractivism and the dominant role of the U.S. dollar in global finance). At the moment, since there is no coherent challenger to neoliberalism in the domain of theory or practice, neoliberalism remains in charge, constraining the efficacy and significance of any institutional or policy innovations that might arise *within* it. For critics of neoliberalism, a romantic view of systemic change generates pessimism and dismissiveness toward institutional and policy experiments. All are domesticated by the neoliberal regime that sets the limits to what can be achieved and dictates what does and does not matter.

An Alternative Change Framework: Productive Incoherence

Is this the best or even the only way to understand social change—such as change in global financial governance? A central claim of this book is that it is neither. Change—real, meaningful, deep change—is unscripted. It can and does occur in diverse ways and takes diverse forms. An abrupt systemic regime shift is just one kind of change—and one that is historically atypical. Unfortunately, stylized accounts of the emergence of the Bretton Woods system continue to be the standard against which many judge institutional reform. I say "stylized" because over the intervening decades we have lost sight of the complexity of the birth of that system. As Helleiner demonstrates, the Bretton Woods vision unfolded over considerably more time than most observers tend to appreciate. The Bretton Woods system emerged through a contested process, not as a result of a decisive moment. It was the outcome of a slow, incremental series of developments that predated Bretton Woods and that influenced subsequent events. Design and implementation were fraught with difficulties and were challenged within and across nations (Helleiner 1994; 2010a; 2014a; 2016a).[11] Thus, postwar transformation is best understood as the outcome of a complex of uneven, incremental, and even contradictory developments rather than arising from an immediate, decisive shift from one regime to another. From a vantage point of seventy years on, the changes of the postwar era seem much cleaner and coherent than they appeared at the time. The lesson is that we need to be cautious about holding to an oversimplified account of the Bretton Woods era as the standard by which we judge contemporary events. Against that mythic standard, ongoing transformations must fail to register as noteworthy.

In contrast to heroic visions of change, I will suggest that organized institutional innovation of this sort is not always available. That much should be uncontroversial. More controversial is a second claim: that this kind of coordinated, coherent change is not the best model for promoting economic development, particularly inclusive and autonomy-enhancing development. Systemic institutional rupture can and often does induce overwhelming unintended consequences, the extent and depth of which mirror the extent and depth of the revolution that induces them, and generates much avoidable harm. Moreover, the success of abrupt systemic redesign depends on historical contingency and luck as much as on the prescience of its architects. Most often, history does not furnish us with the resources needed for the successful design and implementation of systemic revolution. What it does furnish us with in every moment is a surplus of hubristic experts who believe themselves sufficiently capable and knowledgeable about the world they inhabit to engineer utopia. When those experts achieve power, much damage is done (see DeMartino 2011; 2013a).

As should by now be clear, in my view it is an analytical, normative, and empirical mistake to impose the expectation of a grand, coherent plan as the standard against which to assess the significance of change. The romanticized view on the left and the right holds that institutional Armageddon followed by theoretically scripted, comprehensive, and coordinated transformation is the only way to effect meaningful, progressive change. I argue not only that this view fails to capture the diverse ways in which change actually occurs but also that it celebrates a form of economic and political change that is under most conditions decidedly suboptimal. Decentralized and evolutionary innovation and experimentation—disjointed, uneven, minimal, inconsistent, and chaotic as it may be—represents a better alternative. Strict policy and institutional harmonization is unsuitable in a world marked by ineradicable diversity. Moreover, while grand, unified strategies can induce massive harm in the event of failure, the harms associated with the failure of piecemeal reforms are apt to be localized, contained, and even reversible (DeMartino 2011; 2013a).

The alternative vision that I embrace here recognizes that fundamental change can and even should come about through the proliferation of partial, limited, and pragmatic responses to particular concrete challenges that arise. This vision is predicated on the idea that meaningful change often emerges as a consequence of disconnected, erratic, experimental, and inconsistent adjustments in institutions and policies as actors seek to manage the challenges and opportunities they face in an evolving world. This conception of change turns our attention away from epochal ruptures of the sort that occur infrequently but that receive disproportionate attention among scholars and other observers and toward the much more prevalent but mundane, prosaic, small-scale, evolutionary, and even insignificant as the wellspring of what can turn out to be meaningful transformation. To the degree that development itself is to be recognized as a series of transformations, each of which amounts to a social experiment that permits learning from error and success, the alternative vision on offer here also bears on how we think about development theory and practice. Recognizing our inescapable epistemic limitations, good development practice ought to embrace tentative steps of varying scope covering manageable terrains, from which can be inferred valuable lessons without pretension that these lessons are globally applicable.

Productive Incoherence and the Hirschmanian Mindset
The concept of productive incoherence concedes the absence of a consistent, unified disciplinary plan or theoretical narrative driving contemporary reform, but it emphasizes the opportunities afforded by the absence of a new unifying "ism." In this and other respects, the book takes explicit theoretical inspiration from the work of Albert O. Hirschman, one of the most thoughtful intellects ever to work in the field of development economics and social science more broadly. Hirschman's work is largely overlooked today by scholars and development practitioners. Chapter 2 attempts to repair this omission. Hirschman understood far better than most of his contemporaries the harmful effects of blueprint economics. Taking a Hirschmanian view, I argue that, freed from the straitjacket of a commanding theoretical orthodoxy, financial policymakers and other political actors in EMDEs for the first time in decades are enjoying a degree of freedom to experiment with new institutional forms and practices. What is remarkable about the present conjuncture is the extent to which states that were for so long constrained under the global financial governance architecture are now enjoying a degree of policy autonomy, which they are exploiting to create new structures and practices in pursuit of economic development, state capacity,

resilience, and financial stability. Pragmatic policy making and institution building of the sort Hirschman advocated entails experimentation in the small, learning by doing, learning from others, open-mindedness, humility, and adjusting as necessary and in response to new challenges. From this perspective, we should recognize the present period as one of extraordinary significance—one that holds substantial promise for meaningful reform via the creation of valuable knowledge and linkages that are overlooked by those holding to all-or-nothing change narratives.

The Hirschmanian view, which identifies promising discontinuities and pragmatic adaptation in global financial governance, emphasizes the fracturing not just of the neoliberal vision but of something more fundamental. What has disintegrated, and not a moment too soon, is the coherence that marked the neoliberal era—or, more accurately, the theoretical and ideological coherence that drove the era, even if the degree of coherence of actual institutions was far less than advocates or critics recognized. Today's "postneoliberal era" is not at all free of neoliberalism—indeed, aspects of neoliberalism are being restored with each recent national election—and it is not characterized by an alternative coherent doctrine or a corresponding set of institutional and policy arrangements.[12] It bears emphasis that its central feature is *incoherence* in the theory and practice of financial governance. But I will argue—and this is the key point—that this incoherence is *beneficial* for development insofar as it dramatically expands the possibilities for policy and institutional experimentation among the EMDEs. Productive incoherence captures the proliferation of ideas, institutional innovations, and policy responses that have been given impetus by the crisis, and the ways in which the crisis has helped to erode the stifling neoliberal consensus that prevented innovation and constrained policy space in EMDEs over the past several decades.

Features of Productive Incoherence

What does it mean to say that the current conjuncture is marked by productive incoherence? One caveat is in order on the way to a definition. First, the claim here is not that previous economic eras were in fact internally consistent or all-encompassing. Despite the best efforts of the most committed neoliberal ideologues, for instance, nothing like the neoliberal ideal could or ever did emerge in practice. That said, the neoliberal ideal acted as a deadweight around the ankles of less powerful actors who sought to pursue economic initiatives that were significantly inconsistent with its dictates. To say that the neoliberal project ultimately failed in its grandest ambitions is hardly to say that it was ineffective. On the contrary, economic arrangements from the local to the global level were substantially revamped owing to the intellectual force and economic power that were joined in the neoliberal campaign. When we compare the current period against its immediate predecessor, then, we are not comparing a fragmented system against a watertight one. Incoherence emerges to some degree or other in every regime as agents look to manage economic affairs and advance causal narratives that would be deeply imperiled by fidelity to any overarching, simplifying regime. The presence of incoherence itself does not distinguish the present from the immediate past. What does distinguish the present is the relative absence of a consensus around any particular unified theoretical ideal toward which the institutions of financial governance are to hew.

We might say, tentatively, that global financial governance features productive incoherence when some combination of these features emerges:

• The existing central economic authorities are incapable of exerting or sustaining deep influence over the behavior of state and key nonstate actors and, at a minimum, do not exert consistent effective veto power over these actors.
• The existing central authorities do not speak with one voice—they are instead internally disunified over their mandate, intellectual grounding, and scripts to enact when problems of various sorts emerge or critical decisions must be made.
• Key epistemic communities (including elite economic theorists and policy entrepreneurs) and other interests are characterized by substantive disagreement about relevant economic theory and practice rather than by consensus.
• Not just the most powerful states but EMDE states as well face a set of opportunities for economic, institutional, and/or policy innovation that are not clearly constrained by the ideologies or policy preferences of other key actors, such as central authorities or key states.
• The center of gravity of economic policy innovation disperses across states, such that the key states and central institutions of financial governance do not exert a monopoly over, or even leadership in, pursuing such innovations. Those historically deprived of policy autonomy or the willingness to innovate in ways that contradict established norms and practices abroad find increasing space for institutional and policy experimentation.
• Economic forces and interests do not compel conformance to any one systemic ideal but instead provide some degree of aperture that permits divergence from that ideal.

- As a consequence of some or all of these features, financial governance and economic development practice become increasingly heterogeneous, disconnected from central mandates and intellectual currents, and feature some degree or other of proliferation, fragmentation, pragmatism, learning by doing, or, more evocatively, what some theorists (following Lindblom 1959; 1979) call "muddling through."

All of these features are in evidence today. Rather than being unsettled by this state of affairs, I maintain that a world featuring productive incoherence is a better world to inhabit than many worlds characterized by high degrees of institutional and policy coherence. But I don't mean to overstep. The presence and impact of these features are unevenly distributed across the globe. Some EMDEs now enjoy enhanced institutional and policy autonomy, which they are able and willing to exploit. Others remain hobbled by political, economic, and ideational constraints. The hope is that the stragglers, too, will find in this period of increasing incoherence the space necessary to begin to chart alternative economic trajectories.

As we will see, Hirschman provides analytical clarity and direction as we try to make sense of contemporary developments. Hirschman broke with the predominant approach to development economics and social science of his day, which featured high theory and deduced policy prescriptions from Walrasian general equilibrium theory on the one hand and Keynesian theory on the other. The approach entailed identifying and eliminating what were taken to be the chief obstacles to the proper functioning of the market mechanism within EMDEs. Hirschman objected to textbook-driven development practice on several grounds while emphasizing the naiveté of his peers who believed that axiomatic-deductive reasoning could provide an adequate road map to necessary economic transformation. There is much more to be said about Hirschman's perspective on development. The richness of his oeuvre will emerge through an extended engagement with his work in chapter 2.

Discontinuities, Productive Incoherence, and the Global Crisis

The years leading up to the global crisis, and the crisis itself, precipitated significant and sustained change in the conditions facing EMDEs. Most important among these are an emerging attitude of intellectual uncertainty, pragmatism, and empiricism in the economics profession; a new landscape within which the BWIs operate, where they must negotiate to achieve and sustain influence that now seems precarious, and where they confront demands for governance reforms from increasingly assertive former clients, and potential and actual competition from and cooperation with EMDE institutions; the lack of recovery in Europe, and the fragility of the recovery in the United States; the serious and deepening financial fragilities and slowdowns in growth in EMDEs; and the tarnished image of the Anglo-American financial model. The discontinuities that have emerged in the financial governance landscape can only be understood in the context of these unique circumstances.[13]

The global crisis spurred expansion in the membership and scope of existing transnational financial governance networks. The Leaders' G-20 replaced the Leaders' G-8 in 2008, and the mandate and membership of the Financial Stability Forum (FSF) was broadened (and the body was renamed the Financial Stability Board, or FSB). It is true that these networks have proven to be unimaginative, timid, and impotent, even if they are more inclusive than their predecessors (Helleiner 2014b; Blyth 2013a; Payne 2010; Vestergaard and Wade 2012b).[14] Nonetheless, these groups should not be dismissed prematurely, since their future is not foreordained. Indeed, they may emerge over time as forums in which EMDE policymakers are able to promote serious dialogue, build relationships and coalitions, learn from one another, and refine their capacities to maneuver on the international stage and within multilateral institutions (Woods and Martinez-Diaz 2009).

Both the continuity and discontinuity views of the G-20 and FSB (and financial governance more generally) are represented in Helleiner's work. *The Status Quo Crisis* (Helleiner 2014b) sustains the continuity view. Helleiner argues there that the central roles of the U.S. Federal Reserve and the U.S. dollar have not just been unchallenged but have actually been strengthened by the crisis. In this account, formation of the G-20 and the FSB (and other initiatives) has not altered the global financial governance architecture to any appreciable degree. Helleiner's book nevertheless concludes with brief speculation about the potential for transformation over the medium term. In other work, both prior to and following his 2014 book, Helleiner speculates that the pressures unleashed by the crisis could ultimately result in more decentralized and fragmented international financial governance. Not least, he and Pagliari argue that current trends in financial regulation point in the direction of "cooperative regulatory decentralization" (see Helleiner 2009; Helleiner and Pagliari 2011). More recently and less equivocally, Helleiner (2016b) argues that policymakers are in fact "stumbling incrementally" toward such a regime—one that involves both increased multilateral cooperation and deepening decentralization—and that the G-20 and the FSB have begun to make more meaningful commitments.

The global crisis has had more immediate and significant effects on the IMF. These effects have been complex and uneven (Grabel 2011). On the one hand, the crisis has restored the IMF's relevance, coffers, and central role as first responder to financial distress, just when long-standing critics might have hoped for new institutional arrangements to manage crises that would have displaced or demoted the Fund. In important respects, IMF assistance to countries in distress has followed its well-rehearsed script: many conditionality programs continue to stress contractionary macroeconomic policy adjustments, privatization, and liberalization (Gabor 2010; Kentikelenis, Stubbs, and King 2016; Nelson 2014a; Weisbrot 2015). Moreover, EMDEs have secured only very modest commitments for increases in their IMF voting shares. Today the United States and Europe continue to exercise disproportionate influence at the institution (Lesage et al. 2013).

The other side of the ledger is not blank, however. Today there are promising signs that the neoliberal ideas and prescriptions of important economists and departments at the Fund are being challenged by the global crisis in ways that most observers did not anticipate. In response, IMF economists are learning to live with significant departures from the old script. Most notable in this regard, Fund leadership, research staff, and staff working with countries in distress have moved further and more consistently in the direction of normalizing the use of controls over capital inflows, and even on outflows (Grabel 2011; 2015b; 2017; Chwieroth 2015; 2014; Gallagher 2014; Moschella 2014). There is also evidence of change—uneven and inconsistent though it may be—concerning the IMF's approach to fiscal policy during the crisis (Ban 2015; Grabel 2011). Fund economists have developed conditionality programs that, while still harsh, display greater flexibility than was the norm during previous crises. While the Fund continues to advocate fiscal retrenchment, it also now routinely emphasizes the need for "pro-poor spending" to protect the most vulnerable during crises. The IMF's crisis response strategy is marked by ad hoc measures that reflect important ambiguities within the institution. Strikingly absent here is the unyielding attachment to a global strategy of neoliberalism that marked its interventions over the past several decades.

The IMF's geography of influence during the global crisis has been transformed substantially as well. Some of its former clients have emerged as important lenders. At the same time, the institution's client base has largely shifted to the European periphery, and in Europe the IMF appears to be the weakest leg of the European "Troika." Indeed, there is substantial evidence of tension between the IMF and European authorities over important matters such as debt sustainability in Greece—which became particularly evident during the summer of 2015, when a third assistance package for the country was being negotiated—and the most severe forms of austerity in peripheral European economies.[15] In a different vein, but in keeping with the idea of discontinuities at the IMF, in 2015 China achieved a long-sought goal of having the IMF include its currency in the SDR. In addition, though the formal voice of EMDEs at the IMF has increased only trivially, the crisis has opened channels for several of these countries, particularly China, to increase their informal influence. Moreover, we find increasing inconsistency between the rhetoric coming from the institution, its research, and its actual practice. As we will see, the rhetoric-research-practice gap reflects something more than public relations imperatives. The gap reveals increasing contestation and even confusion within the Fund.

Of equal if not greater importance, productive incoherence is also evidenced in the emergence of a far more heterogeneous financial governance architecture. As noted, the East Asian crisis renewed interest in the creation of alternative institutions of financial governance. The drive toward institutional innovation was given far greater force during the global crisis, while the resources necessary to sustain such experiments only became available to rapidly growing EMDEs following the Asian crisis. New innovations have now emerged at the transregional, regional, subregional, bilateral, and national levels. Today we encounter a range of new and expanded reserve pooling arrangements and development and infrastructure banks. Existing institutions evolved in significant ways during the global crisis and have continued to do so (as we will see in the discussion of the Chiang Mai Initiative Multilateralisation, the Arab Monetary Fund, the Development Bank of Latin America, the China Development Bank, and Brazil's National Economic and Social Development Bank). At the same time, new arrangements have arisen to rectify perceived failings in the global financial architecture, particularly the shortage of infrastructure financing. The new arrangements are exemplified in twin BRICS initiatives, the New Development Bank and the Contingent Reserve Arrangement, and also in the Eurasian Fund for Stabilization and Development and in the China-led Asian Infrastructure Investment Bank and the One Belt, One Road Initiative/Silk Road Fund. These and other innovations are emblematic of developments and aspirations across EMDEs. The new willingness and ability to undertake innovation in financial governance may turn out to be one of the most important legacies associated with the global crisis, especially when compared with prior crises.

The new arrangements do not coalesce around a singular, grand global architecture that might replace the BWIs. Instead, we are observing productive incoherence in the expansion of disparate and, in some cases, overlapping and interconnected institutions that complement the BWIs. Taken together, they are "thickening" and diversifying the financial landscape in EMDEs and introducing the possibility of a transition to a more complex, decentralized, multitiered, pluripolar global financial and monetary system (Armijo and Roberts 2014; Chin 2010; Grabel 2013a; 2013b; Huotari and Hanemann 2014; Mittelman 2013; Riggirozzi and Tussie 2012). The expansion of these initiatives is widening policy space for development. They also generate opportunities for experience-based learning and the creation of new partnerships and coalitions, and in turn enable EMDE "forum shopping." In sum, the initiatives are substantially complicating the terrain on which the BWIs operate. We might also understand these institutions, however small in scale, in terms of their potential to increase robustness and even what Nassim Taleb (2012) terms "anti-fragility" of the global financial governance architecture. This would involve a collection of institutions that enjoy some degree of autonomy from each other, where crises are less likely to generate contagion across countries, and where each crisis might allow for learning that induces new innovations that are better able to prevent and limit the scope of future crises. What I call the *productive redundancy* that is a feature of the emerging financial governance landscape is central to the achievement of these goals.

A final dimension of productive incoherence concerns capital controls. Changes in ideas and practices around capital controls emerged during the 1990s. The changes deepened and extended during the global crisis. Of the many extraordinary developments that have occurred during the crisis, the successful "rebranding" of capital controls is among the most notable (Grabel 2011; 2015b; 2017; Chwieroth 2015; Gallagher 2014; Moschella 2014). Formerly denigrated as a policy tool of choice of the weak and misguided, capital controls have now been normalized as a legitimate tool of prudential financial management, even within the corridors of the IMF and the credit rating agencies.

The rebranding of capital controls has occurred against a messy backdrop of uncertainty and economic, political, and ideational change that reaches far beyond the IMF. Productive incoherence surrounding controls is reflected in the proliferation of responses to the crisis by governments, multilateral institutions, rating agencies, and the economics profession that have not yet congealed into a consistent approach. Instead, we find a proliferation of strategies that defy encapsulation in a unified narrative. The collapse of a consensus around capital controls has widened policy space to a much greater degree than in the years following the East Asian crisis

(Abdelal 2007; Chwieroth 2010; Moschella 2010). As with most rebranding exercises, there is uncertainty about whether the new framing will prove sufficiently sticky, especially in the context of tensions and countervailing impulses at the IMF and elsewhere, a resilient bias among many economists against state management of economic flows, and new attempts to assert outflow controls in times of distress that would run counter to the interests of powerful financial actors. For now, though, there seems to be substantial momentum propelling increasing use of and experimentation with the flexible deployment of controls, in some cases with IMF support and in most other cases without IMF resistance.

Assessing the Significance of Change: A Hirschmanian Perspective

The institutional aperture, innovations, and policy changes examined in this book may not persuade those analysts who are committed to dramatic narratives of systemic change. They should. From my perspective, recent crises might be best understood as crucial turning points in a contested, uneven, and long-term process of pragmatic adjustment in global financial governance.

No one has made the case for the value of studying experimentation, diminutive changes, heterogeneity, and aperture more effectively than Hirschman. Hirschman argued for "possibilism"—the idea that small-scale, messy, disparate innovations revealed what could be; what reforms might be available. Central to his view is an emphasis on fundamental uncertainty—on deficient knowledge of what is and what could be. He counterposed possibilism with the predominant "futilism" in the social sciences (and especially in development economics)—the view that any initiatives that were not entirely consistent with the precepts of received theory were bound to fail (Hirschman 2013[1971]).

Hirschman's epistemic and normative views informed his understanding of social change in profound ways. He rejected the omniscient pretension that allows analysts to pass judgment ex ante on the significance of particular innovations, and the related tendency of social scientists to define change as either "fundamental" or "superficial." He despaired of the skeptical mindset that needs to dismiss most changes as superficial, a tendency that reflected both the futilism and the epistemic certainty that dominated social science in his time and indeed continues to infuse much scholarship today.

Following Hirschman, we can recognize the crisis and postcrisis periods as an extraordinary moment of institutional and ideational innovation that both reflects and contributes to a new degree of autonomy in financial governance in the EMDEs. Many of the innovations that I examine in the book might come across as prosaic and even trivial. But that's the central Hirschmanian point that must be kept in view—that the small, the disparate, the seemingly trivial, or the experimental must not be discounted in advance because they do not amount to much, because they are not the embodiment of some overarching plan, because they are not scalable, or because they are paltry when compared with the magnitude of the problems confronting EMDEs as they try to finance and sustain development.

The potential for change—meaningful, lasting change that can provide a basis for a more robust, participatory, sustainable development—is located here, in the disparate, the unplanned, and the experimental, rather than in a new "ism" to replace the now besieged neoliberal vision. Drawing on Hirschman's seminal work, I argue that the present era features practices that are far better suited to development than institutional fidelity to a disciplinary, coherent doctrine that serves as the blueprint for a new economic system. In this perspective, the absence of a new "ism" to replace neoliberalism is in fact expanding the terrain of policy and institutional experimentation. For those social scientists who cannot live without a new "ism," I propose *Hirschmanian Possibilism* as the new organizing system of thought. This doctrine rejects a coherent theoretical framework from which to deduce the singly appropriate institutional structure of the economy. Hirschmanian possibilism asserts instead the value of productive incoherence as a framework for creating a deeper, more resilient, more inclusive, and more developmental global financial governance architecture.

It needs to be reemphasized one last time before concluding this introductory chapter that the myriad innovations that I examine in subsequent chapters do not come close to displacing neoliberalism top to bottom. They do not sufficiently counter the power of the global financial community. Nor do they displace the IMF, the World Bank, or leading national governments as central actors in global financial governance or in shaping development policy. The innovations also do not inoculate EMDEs against economic downturns, capital flight, currency instability, or financial crises. Nor do they imply the emergence of financial multipolarity by 2025, as the World Bank predicted a few years into the global crisis (World Bank 2011). But the innovations do amount to *something*—to the evolution of a system of financial governance that encompasses both neoliberal and decidedly non-neoliberal features, and that is altering the geographic reach, influence, and internal governance of key actors. The transformations are generating pluripolar, multilevel arrangements that, to varying degrees, provide EMDEs with a degree of policy space that they have found it difficult to achieve during the neoliberal era. Rather than view the incomplete and improvisational aspects of the emerging non-neoliberal elements of the system—or the lack of a unifying, overarching model of global economic integration and financial governance—as debilities, we should recognize them as virtues. A noncoherent system, I argue, is one that is better able to promote the policy and institutional diversity and experimentation that are necessary to support economic development. In place of the pursuit of fidelity to a constraining model, the current era features pragmatic problem-driven responses and experimentation in response to pressing problems. After several decades of neoliberal coherence, this is a welcome deviation.

Related Literature, Caveats, and Risks

Hirschmanian possibilism requires patience regarding the realization of change. In this and other respects, scholars in international political economy will recognize affinities between Hirschman and contemporary "constructivist" scholarship in political science. Constructivism, too, emphasizes the importance of understanding change as inherently uneven, slow, and contested, often involving small, disconnected steps that have uncertain outcomes. We will return to constructivist contributions in chapters 5 and 7. For now, it bears noting that constructivist accounts emphasize subtle drivers of unscripted change that tend to be overlooked in reductionist accounts that focus on presumably more determinant factors such as the inexorable force of material interests. Hirschman would approve of this and related constructivist insights. For example, Campbell (2004, chaps. 3 and 5) speaks of change in political and economic institutions in terms that Hirschman himself might have used: as the outgrowth of pragmatic and ultimately uncertain processes of "bricolage."[16]

Per the Hirschmanian commitments that inform this book, I resist the temptation to label the innovations examined here as wholly "positive" or "negative." The book's organizing theme of productive incoherence suggests, of course, that on balance I am encouraged rather than discouraged. In my view, these changes hold within them the potential to generate a more heterogeneous, stable, and resilient financial architecture that is better positioned to promote development, financial stability, and financial inclusion. I speculate that this kind of architecture, in part because of the absence of a constraining, unified theoretical and political center, might enhance the autonomy of EMDE policymakers. For instance, the proliferation of forum shopping by EMDEs increases their leverage at the BWIs while providing smaller countries with opportunities that are potentially more favorable than those offered by the BWIs (on "competitive pluralism," see Culpeper 1997). Productive redundancy associated with a more heavily populated financial architecture enhances the adequacy of the global safety net and is central to the promotion of antifragility in global financial governance. These developments, in my view, are best seen as potentially transformative. At the same time, increasing policy space regarding capital controls is affording EMDEs the means to navigate disruptive capital flows better than they were able to do during the crises of the neoliberal era.

It would be terribly irresponsible, however, not to emphasize also the potential dangers associated with incoherence. I return to this matter in the conclusion to the book. Not least, in a world lacking universal rules of engagement backed by sufficiently influential authorities that can punish, or at least shame, disruptive behavior, countries may deem it advantageous to pursue beggar-thy-neighbor strategies. This concern, already expressed by the IMF in regard to the competitive use of capital controls and by EMDEs in connection with the spillover effects of monetary policies in AEs, should be taken seriously. In addition, incoherence and redundancy could breed uncertainty in times of crisis, just when questions such as who is in charge and who can and will offer assistance need prompt and dependable answers. But I will argue that these concerns should not authorize the premature short-circuiting of the new kinds of policy and institutional experimentation now under way. With Hirschman, I argue that protecting space for policy and institutional experimentation must be a central feature of any new multilateral initiatives to regulate what are seen to be harmful national financial practices.

Worrisome events in 2016 and signposts leading into 2017 are causing particular alarm among scholars and EMDE policymakers, and rightly so. EMDEs are now being damaged by uncertainty inaugurated by rising nationalism in the United States and several European countries, the fallout from Brexit, and the prospect of sustained monetary tightening and a chaotic policy environment in the United States. Today, EMDEs face a poisonous cocktail of macroeconomic and financial risks, including a sharp decline in commodity prices (through 2015), slowing economic growth, high levels of corporate and sovereign debt (a great deal of which is denominated in the U.S. dollar), instability of international capital flows, and tightening conditions in credit markets (see UNCTAD 2016, chap. 1). Any intensification of these crisis triggers in the coming year or two will surely test what are still very new and even fragile EMDE institutions and practices. Nothing that follows in this book should be taken as a guarantee that the EMDEs will be able to ward off economic disturbances. What we can hope for is that the initiatives examined here will allow these economies to do somewhat better than they have in the recent past, and that any new shocks will provide opportunities for new institutional and policy experiments that yield learning, cooperation, and enhanced robustness. These are precisely the kinds of opportunities that neoliberal coherence precluded.

Clarification of Terms

My principal professional interest is at the intersection of financial governance, economic development, policy space, and macroeconomic performance. In particular, I am concerned with the architectures and practices of global financial governance, especially as these bear on the prospects of EMDEs. Throughout the book, I use the term *global financial governance* to refer to institutions, arrangements, and policy practices, while *financial governance architecture* refers more narrowly to institutions and networks.

The term *development finance* is often used to refer to the provision of funding for long-term projects, such as infrastructure projects, provided by what are usually termed development banks. When I speak of *developmental finance*, I have in view those activities but also other financial flows that cushion the economy, private firms, and public entities from the effects of economic shocks and downturns of domestic or external origin. Beyond project finance, I emphasize the centrality of forms of financial governance and types of financial flows that can reduce the incidence of crises while ensuring liquidity, working capital, and trade finance during periods of distress and that can allow countries to reduce the depth of and/or ameliorate the effects of crises while protecting national policy autonomy. These are usually referred to as liquidity support arrangements, and they often involve the pooling of currency reserves among groups of nations. Developmental finance, as I use the term, therefore refers both to project finance and liquidity support. Defined in this way, developmental finance focuses attention on state actors and multilateral institutions that are charged with providing these services—not on private sector actors (such as investors) or nongovernmental organizations. But this sector is complex. The relevant institutions engage in the direct provision of finance of various sorts but also regulate private sector actors and financial flows that affect development prospects. Sometimes, the two activities are intertwined, so the focus here must be both on developmental finance and on financial governance.

Little more can usefully be said at the outset about what falls within and what falls beyond the scope of the book. I trust that my focus on developmental finance and financial governance will emerge clearly in the context of the discussion that follows.

For expediency, I have often, but not always, chosen to rely on the now commonly used term advanced economies (here AEs) to refer to wealthy countries and the equally common term emerging market and developing economies (here EMDEs) to refer to the developing and former socialist countries—what some analysts refer to as the countries of the global south and east. Nothing of significance is intended by that terminological choice.

I sometimes refer to the IMF and World Bank as the BWIs, and sometimes refer to the individual institutions as the Fund and the Bank, respectively. When speaking of the regional and multilateral development banks that are in fact a part of the broader architecture of the BWIs, such as the African Development Bank (AfDB), Asian Development Bank (AsDB), and Inter-American Development Bank (IADB), I refer to these individually by name.

Following common practice, I use the term global financial crisis to refer to the crisis that began in 2008.[17] Hereafter I often use Asian crisis to refer to the East Asian financial crisis. The dollar refers to the U.S. dollar, and I often use Fed to refer to the U.S. Federal Reserve. Finally, I use the terms policy space and policy autonomy to refer to a government's ability to select policy instruments and institutional forms free from external constraints, such as those imposed by the fear of triggering capital flight, or censure by the IMF or credit rating agencies.

The Book in Brief

Subsequent chapters provide a wide-ranging examination of important institutional and policy adjustments that have unfolded since the Asian crisis and especially during and since the global crisis. In chapter 3, I examine the Asian crisis itself since it is a key driver of innovations and reforms that deepened during the global crisis.

In chapter 4, I briefly explore the G-20 and the FSB, often taken by continuity theorists as exhibit A in the case against meaningful reform. I accept the claim that these networks have not achieved much of what had been hoped for them, but I contend that the verdict is more ambiguous and even promising—that these bodies are best seen as opportunities for learning, capacity building, and coalition building.

I turn to the IMF in chapter 5 and demonstrate at length the extent and diverse dimensions along which the institution has and has not evolved since the Asian crisis. The IMF can no longer be depended on to champion uncritically the neoliberal cause in the AEs or the EMDEs. Indeed, it has recently but certainly not always pushed back against the most strident neoliberal interventions in crisis situations.

The global financial governance architecture beyond the BWIs has been the site of extraordinary innovations over the past decade or so and especially during the global crisis. As we will see, institutions that provide liquidity support and those that provide long-term development and/or infrastructure finance at the national, bilateral, subregional, regional, and transregional levels are transforming the landscape of financial governance. The survey in chapter 6 is extensive but by no means comprehensive. Indeed, it has proven very difficult to keep up with institutional adjustments during the writing of this book, so rich and diverse are the innovations now under way.

Capital controls were central to the Bretton Woods era but were sharply stigmatized as desperate and ultimately self-defeating measures of the weak under the neoliberalism of the 1980s and 1990s. The consensus surrounding the indictment of capital controls began to crack in the years following the Asian crisis. Today, capital controls are back—they have been rediscovered and rebranded as a vital instrument of macroprudential management. This development is fundamental, so we explore it in depth in chapter 7.

In the concluding chapter of the book I examine the opportunities, lessons, risks, and mandates that arise in a pluri-polar, incoherent, and Hirschmanian world.

As the foregoing suggests, the argument that follows is largely empirical. I go to great lengths to sustain the case for pluripolarity, and for institutional and policy innovation that is not driven by any coherent economic doctrine. The empirical record can be overwhelming. A central question of the book is how to interpret these developments. If judged by the traditional standards of social science, the answer I offer is novel and even peculiar, so, before turning to empirical matters, I will take time in the next chapter to investigate carefully the work of Albert Hirschman to discern what he has to offer us in our engagement with contemporary events. Hirschman's central insights and commitments serve as both the analytical backdrop and the inspiration for this book. I will try to demonstrate why we should replace commonly held views on economic development and institutional and policy change with an alternative that features the productivity of incoherence.

2 Productive Incoherence: A Hirschmanian Perspective

How are we to come to terms with the emerging inconsistencies in global financial governance and developmental finance? The seminal work of Albert O. Hirschman provides extraordinary insight into the current conjuncture. Hirschman was a scholar and practitioner who, as much as anyone else, recognized the potential importance of mundane, fragmented, inconsistent initiatives.

Drawing on Hirschman's work, I argue that the present era is characterized by a quality of permissiveness that is far better suited for development than institutional fidelity to an overarching, coherent doctrine that serves as the blueprint for a new economic system. Central to this perspective is the Hirschmanian idea that the absence of a new "ism" to replace neoliberalism might not be a source of despair but instead should be recognized as a historic opportunity that is already expanding the terrain of ideational, policy, and institutional experimentation that is central to social and economic development.[1]

A Hirschmanian School of Thought?

The global crisis, especially in its early phase, burnished the legacy of John Maynard Keynes and other Keynesians, such as Charles Kindleberger and Hyman Minsky. Keynes's biographer Robert Skidelsky seized on the crisis to argue for the salience of Keynes in *The Return of the Master* and related work (Skidelsky 2010; 2011). Previous upheavals, particularly the fall of the Berlin Wall and the traumatic transition to market liberalization in Russia, led to the rediscovery of another classic work, Karl Polanyi's *The Great Transformation* (2001[1944]). The salience of Polanyi's book to understanding these events was underscored in Joseph Stiglitz's foreword to the 2001 reissue of the book (e.g., p. xii). Around the same time, Blyth (2002) used Polanyi's work, particularly its central conception of the "double movement," to make sense of the interaction between significant institutional transformations and changes in economic ideas during the 1930s and 1970s, while Harmes (2001) deployed the same work to make sense of the Mexican financial crisis of the 1990s.

These events have not had the same effect on the fortunes of Hirschman. Certainly, publication of two recent books by his biographer Jeremy Adelman (2013a; 2013b) and work by Michele Alacevich (2014; 2015; 2016) have begun to generate some interest in Hirschman's work. The occasion of Hirschman's death in December 2012 at age ninety-seven also inspired several thoughtful and broad-ranging reflections on the importance of his intellectual legacy.[2] Today a small number of public intellectuals, economists, and other social scientists are recognizing the salience and originality of his insights, even if their appreciation is necessarily selective in relation to Hirschman's vast and diverse oeuvre.

How wide were Hirschman's professional interests and competencies? Though formally trained as an economist, Hirschman's writings extended over a remarkable range of disciplines and subdisciplines as diverse as economic theory, development economics, Latin American studies, political science, public administration, industrial organization, political philosophy, intellectual history, and rhetoric. On many occasions, he reflected on his tendency to cross paradigmatic and disciplinary borders. The title of one of his best-known essay collections, *Essays in Trespassing*, perhaps best captures his embrace of intellectual wandering.

Nonetheless, while Hirschman is held in high esteem by leading scholars, there is no Hirschman school of thought or paradigm. Dani Rodrik (2007a) notes correctly and with regret that students of development economics no longer read Hirschman, a view also expressed by Taylor (1994). For too many, Hirschman is taken to represent outdated thinking that might be acknowledged respectfully in passing but that does not warrant careful scrutiny.

Why has Hirschman been disposed of so readily? A number of factors bear on his legacy.[3] Since the 1960s, appreciation of Hirschman's work has been constrained by factors connected to the sociology and norms of contemporary, specialized, professionalized social science. What Adelman (2013b, 3) terms Hirschman's distinct "brand of social science"—his discursive, literary, nuanced, and often witty style, his interdisciplinarity, and the sheer breadth of his interests and writing—places him in the tradition of the great social theorists of the eighteenth and nineteenth centuries, when intellectuals were broadly educated and their work was widely read by nonacademics. Their work eschewed the "specialization-induced intellectual poverty" that later defined the social sciences (Hirschman, cited in

Fukuyama 2013) and made it difficult for modern social scientists to engage with it. Better, it seemed, to avoid what one was not well trained to digest.

Hirschman flouted what would become central norms in the social sciences. Hirschman rejected simplistic paradigm-based thinking and grand claims. Moreover, he insisted on questioning the prevalent assumptions that enabled the predominant approach to social science. He was at least partially aware of his tendencies toward professional marginalization, referring to his proclivities as a "propensity to self-subversion" (the title of his 1995 book). Yet these were also surely among his greatest strengths as an original thinker (Gladwell 2013). His propensity to self-subvert was, in his view, a hard-won virtue—one that required the humble, inquisitive observer to perpetually subject his own beliefs to scrutiny. "In a time in which people were driven by strong ideological faiths and nothing seemed to work without the pre-defined guidance of a weltanschauung, Albert persisted in living outside of and without any weltanschauung," Nadia Urbinati (2015) said of Hirschman.[4] These commitments, in addition to the sheer breadth of his oeuvre, have sabotaged his standing and influence among contemporary scholars. As Drezner (2013) notes, Hirschman's rejection of paradigm-based thinking may help to explain why there is no Hirschmanian school of thought. On this point, Hirschman replied to a World Bank director who had sent him a paper referring to the "Hirschman Doctrine" in the following manner: "Unfortunately (or, I rather tend to think, fortunately), there is no Hirschman school of economic development and I cannot point to a large pool of disciples where one might fish out someone to work with you along those lines" (Hirschman, cited in Gladwell 2013).

Hirschman's profound rejection of the scientific pretensions, hubris, and grand narratives of development economics certainly limited his reach among scholars and development practitioners, who came increasingly to adopt reductionist models and epistemic certainty that facilitated their achievement of authority and influence in policy circles. On more than a few occasions, Hirschman himself reflected on what he—at his most charitable—termed a "difference in cognitive style" that distanced him from others in the field, particularly as social science evolved beginning in the 1960s (Hirschman 2013[1970], 143).

Hirschman's Legacy and Contemporary Development Economics

In 1994, Paul Krugman took stock of the state of development economics. Krugman argued that the field had only recently been rescued from the likes of Hirschman, Gunnar Myrdal (1957), and other like-minded thinkers.[5]

Krugman (1994, 39) acknowledges that he knows little of Hirschman's work beyond his 1958 book *The Strategy of Economic Development*, but this does not deter him in the least from passing judgment on Hirschman's legacy. Krugman calls the book brilliant, persuasive, but ultimately destructive.[6] In Krugman's view, the publication of the book marked the end of what he terms "high development theory"—the sweeping development theories of the 1940s and 1950s, as exemplified by the "big push" approach of Paul Rosenstein-Rodan (1943). Krugman (1994, 40) argues that Hirschman resisted and indeed rejected "the pressures to produce button-downed, mathematically consistent analyses and adopt[ed] instead a sort of muscular pragmatism in grappling with the problem of development." Hirschman's book appeared just when development theory was facing a methodological crisis, and it had a profound effect on the work of other development theorists and practitioners. In Krugman's rendering, Hirschman "did not wait for intellectual exile: he proudly gathered up his followers and led them into the wilderness himself. Unfortunately they perished there" (ibid.).[7] Krugman denigrates Hirschman's stylistic and methodological stance as "vain" and a "dead end" that led to the marginalization of high development theory and development economics until the field emerged from the desert in the late 1980s and 1990s with its new disciples adopting the supposed rigor of formal modeling (ibid., 47, 52).[8] One cannot help but note that Krugman's essay exemplifies the certainty and cognitive style that Hirschman so strongly rejected.

Is the rescue of development economics from Hirschmanian sensibilities that Krugman celebrates complete? Contemporary research in development economics tends toward one of two methodological poles, both empirical in nature: randomized control trials (RCTs) and "large N studies" by micro- and macro-development economists, respectively. Fukuyama (2013) suggests that the current fascination with RCTs in development economics is moving the field toward small ideas and away from Hirschmanian impulses. In his words, "It is hard to imagine that all the work being done under this [RCT] approach will leave anything behind of a conceptual nature that people will remember fifty years from now" (ibid.). He argues that Hirschman "operated at the opposite end of the spectrum. . . . His legacy is not data collection or micro results, but rather some very big concepts that continue to shape the way we think about not just development but public policy more generally."[9]

Others take a different view of the evolution and state of development economics. In a reflection on the state of the field, Rodrik (2009a) is largely optimistic. While expressing mild worries about RCTs, noting in particular limits to the generalizability of their findings, Rodrik argues that advocates of this approach are forcing macro-development economists to think more seriously about "evidence." Rodrik identifies evidence that micro- and macro-development economics are coming together in a "new development economics" that is more pragmatic, less self-certain and universalistic, and more encouraging of policy and institutional experimentation. Rodrik embraces two distinct forms of development trial and error: China's policy pragmatism on the one hand, which is consistent with Hirschman's emphasis on experimentation and learning by doing, and the positivist science of RCTs on the other, about which Hirschman might have been much less enthused (discussed later). Notwithstanding this point, Rodrik's reading of the state of development economics suggests that the field is becoming more "Hirschmanian," which he sees as an altogether positive step (see also Rodrik 2015a).[10]

Irrespective of whether Rodrik is correct about the state of development economics (and the discipline of economics more broadly), one can certainly see a clear Hirschmanian thread running through a great deal of his own work. Indeed, and in recognition of this connection, Rodrik was awarded the inaugural Albert Hirschman Prize by the Social Science Research Council in 2007, and from 2013 to 2015 he was the Albert O. Hirschman Professor in the School of Social Science at the Institute for Advanced Study at Princeton University. In the lecture occasioned by the 2007 prize, Rodrik reflects directly and admiringly on Hirschman's intellectual legacy (Rodrik 2007a; 2007c; 2007–2008). In that context, he draws a sharp distinction between Hirschman's work and his own on the one hand and the uniform, self-certain policy prescriptions of the Washington Consensus on the other. Rodrik (2007–2008) credits Hirschman for his embrace of pragmatic learning by doing and for his appreciation of the importance of "opportunism"— which refers to taking advantage of available spaces for innovation rather than insisting on a comprehensive home-grown or imported plan. Rodrik also highlights Hirschman's search for novelty and uniqueness, his appreciation of sequential and cumulative change, his insistence on the need to have a deep knowledge of local contexts, and his associated suspicion of naïve efforts to transplant policies and institutions from one context to another. Rodrik also celebrates Hirschman's "bias for hope" and his unrepentant embrace of the possible.[11]

Hirschman's insights appear in other contemporary scholarship. More than any other contemporary development economist, David Ellerman (2004; 2005) credits Hirschman for shaping his own thinking, and his work draws broadly and deeply on Hirschman's oeuvre. Gerald Helleiner

(2010) uses Hirschman's seminal work on exit, voice, and loyalty as a lens through which one can understand the relationship between EMDEs and the BWIs (as we will discuss). One also finds a clear (and acknowledged) debt to Hirschman running through the work of a small number of other contemporary development economists.[12] Several contemporary political scientists also draw productively on some of Hirschman's insights.[13] On balance, however, Hirschman's work remains terribly underappreciated, with just a few insights attracting the attention of most contemporary scholars.

Hirschmanian Themes

The failure to appreciate Hirschman's work is consequential and damaging. Hirschman's work offers a fresh and extraordinarily useful lens through which to make sense of the discontinuities and productive incoherence of the global financial crisis.

Which Hirschmanian themes provide guidance to observers of and participants in unfolding developments in the field of financial governance and developmental finance? For ease of exposition, I corral these themes under the categories of agent reactions to organizational failure; asymmetric economic relations; epistemic presumptions; failure of grand theoretical narratives and social engineering, and the related centrality of the diminutive, complex, and experimental; linkages and side effects; theoretical and ethical failures of development experts; and associated ideas around possibilism, futilism, and rhetoric. I begin with the best known of his insights and then move directly to themes that are most fertile for the task at hand.

Agent Reactions to Organizational Failure

Hirschman's *Exit, Voice and Loyalty: Responses to Decline in Firms, Organizations and States*, published in 1970, is among his best-known books, and it retains influence among academic economists, political scientists, and policymakers.[14] Hirschman extended its central insights in several later works, including his 1978 essay "Exit, Voice, and the State" and his book *Essays in Trespassing* (1981, 209–284). Exit and voice refer to the two ways in which individuals can respond to their dissatisfaction with the performance of business enterprises, nonbusiness organizations, states, and other institutions of all sorts. The two strategies can curb or even reverse institutional decline. Exit involves "voting with one's feet" (i.e., finding a replacement), relying on the mechanism of competition to ensure adequate performance.

Voice involves "staying put" and mobilizing within an institution to bring about change. The exercise of voice depends on some degree of loyalty and trust. Loyalty constrains the propensity to exit and can thereby create the trust and the space necessary for performance improvements. Excessive loyalty, however, can suppress both voice and exit, and can consequently perpetuate poor performance.[15]

Hirschman notes that economists elevate exit over voice, presuming the former to be more efficient. He cites Milton Friedman's advocacy of vouchers and competition in public schools as a "near perfect example of the economist's bias in favor of exit and against voice" (Hirschman 1970, 17). Hirschman (1981[1978]) later acknowledged that exit could sometimes occasion states to pursue productive reform. Nevertheless, his work on exit, voice, and loyalty can be read as a warning about the "cult of exit" among economists.[16] Hirschman argued that exit can undermine performance by eliminating the incentive to improve and weakening the effectiveness of voice, particularly since opportunities to exit are not randomly distributed. It is generally those possessing the greatest number of options, those who are most efficacious, mobile, and/or wealthy, who are able to exit poorly performing entities such as states or private institutions. In practice, this means that those with little leverage are left behind. Thus, authoritarian governments or poorly performing managers in public or private enterprises generally prefer to have their harshest critics exit. In typically elegant prose, Hirschman (1970, 59, emphasis in original) described this dynamic as "an oppression of the weak by the incompetent and an exploitation of the poor by the lazy which is the more durable and stifling as it is both *unambitious and escapable.*"

Asymmetric Economic Relations and the Molding of National Interests

Among political scientists working within international relations, Hirschman's first book, *National Power and the Structure of Foreign Trade* (Hirschman 1980[1945]), is regarded as a classic. Hirschman examines German trade and foreign policy in the interwar period to illustrate the ways in which economic policy can be used as an instrument of statecraft. He shows that asymmetric international economic relations carry the potential for coercion. In a bilateral trade relationship involving countries of disparate size, for example, the larger, more powerful state has influence over the smaller, weaker state since the opportunity costs of terminating the relationship are greater for the weaker state. Hirschman's argument appears uncontroversial today. But at the time it challenged the traditional liberal idea that greater economic integration promotes fairly dispersed benefits and hence cooperation among nations (Adelman 2013b, 213). Hirschman also broke with the standard mercantilist view that running a trade deficit necessarily undermines economic power. Instead, he showed that a state can exert coercive power over another with which it runs a trade deficit as its trade partner grows dependent on the foreign market (Drezner 2013). These arguments shed light not only on trade arrangements in the interwar era but also on trade and financial relations in a variety of national and historical contexts, including the contemporary conjuncture. Hirschman's insights are also useful for understanding the coercive power inherent in other types of asymmetric economic relations, such as those involved in North-South trade and investment agreements and the provision of support by large actors (such as the IMF) to states in crisis.

A less widely appreciated, though more innovative and useful, thesis appears in Hirschman's *National Power and the Structure of Foreign Trade* (see Abdelal and Kirshner 1999–2000, 120–121, 156; Kirshner 1997, chap. 4; 2014a). The thesis concerns the power to mold perceptions of national interest. Hirschman demonstrates that the economic incentives available in asymmetric relations can have profound political consequences in smaller, weaker states by shifting the domestic balance of power. Asymmetric relationships can reconfigure foreign policy choices and reshape the perception of national interest by "conditioning" smaller states. Such conditioning is evident in the creation of a "friendly attitude" in the smaller state vis-à-vis the larger state's priorities. Foreign policy decisions in the smaller state may come to reflect the growing influence of domestic interest groups that perceive an alignment between their country's national interests and those of the larger state.

As with Hirschman's argument about coercion, his perspective on the malleability of national interests sheds light on the subtle yet powerful effects of a number of bilateral and multilateral trade and financial arrangements (see cases in Abdelal and Kirshner [1999–2000] and Kirshner [1997, chap. 4]). In addition, and as Kirshner (2014a) argues, Hirschman's notion of preference and interest malleability is relevant to understanding the conditioning effects of American monetary power. For instance, the concept helps to explain the diffusion of capital account liberalization and the U.S. model of light touch financial regulation prior to the global crisis. "Conditioning effects" have since contributed to the emerging recalibration of national interest across EMDEs toward China and other rising financial powers and away from the United States and the IMF. These insights might also be useful for understanding whether and how the expansion of existing financial arrangements and the creation of new ones in EMDEs might ultimately reshape perceptions of national interest on the part of smaller (and poorer) states (see chapter 6).

Linkages and Side Effects

Hirschman's work on "backwards and forwards linkages" has had some influence in development economics and in discussions of economic development policy. He introduced these concepts in *The Strategy of Economic Development* and elaborated them in later works (e.g., Hirschman 2013[1981a]). The basic idea is straightforward: certain economic activities can create the propitious conditions for new upstream or downstream economic, political, or social capabilities. The idea of linkages grew out of Hirschman's view that growth should be thought of as an unbalanced process and that strategies should focus around targeted rather than comprehensive, grand plans.[17]

Hirschman also highlighted the essential role of "side effects," which were far more than the unintended ramifications of a project. Side effects are *"inputs essential to the realization of the project's principal effect and purpose"* (Hirschman 1967a, 149, emphasis in original, cited in Alacevich 2014). For example, a project might establish as an unintended consequence new networks that turn out to be vital to the project's success even though the centrality of the networks was not envisioned at its outset.

Epistemic Issues: Uncertainty, the Limits of Intelligibility, and the Power of the "Hiding Hand"

An important theme in Hirschman's work is the idea that knowledge is incomplete, tacit, partial, and dispersed. Like Keynes and Hayek, Hirschman took knowledge of the future to be fundamentally uncertain (Hirschman 2013[1970]). Following Knight (1971[1921]) and Keynes, he distinguished between probabilistic risk and (inherently) immeasurable uncertainty (Alacevich 2014). Hirschman likened the need for predictability—which entailed a scientist trend that embraced epistemic certainty and parsimony along with the search for general laws and grand paradigms—to neuroses that afflicted the social sciences (Hirschman 1967a, chap. 1; 2013[1970], 138; 2013[1971]; Adelman 2013a, introduction, 137; 2013b, introduction).[18] Hirschman identifies Amartya Sen as a fellow skeptic of overdone reductionism, and he endorses Sen's observation that much is to be gained by making things more complicated (Hirschman 2013[1986a], 249). In Hirschman's words, "let us beware of excessive parsimony!" (ibid., 262).

Hirschman called for appreciation of irreducible complexity (Adelman 2013b, 13). He asked, "Is it not in the interest of social science to embrace complexity, be it at some sacrifice of its claim to predictive power?"

(Hirschman 2013[1986b], 243). The commitment to complexity was both epistemic and practical. For Hirschman, the outcome of any intervention is unknowable in advance since it is always confounded by the *"balance* of the contending forces that are set in motion" and the totality of circumstances at the time of the intervention, neither of which was accessible to the researcher (Hirschman 2013[1970], 150, emphasis in original). In this and many other respects (discussed later), Hirschman anticipated a paradigm shift in economics, now just under way, toward understanding the economy as a "complex adaptive system" that features constant evolution and abrupt shifts, and, notably, the absence of sufficiently powerful equilibrating mechanisms (such as the Walrasian auctioneer) that can be relied on to bring an economy in a disequilibrium state back into equilibrium (Kirman 2016).

In Hirschman's view, attempts by social scientists to domesticate what was fundamentally uncertain, disorderly, contingent, and complex had troubling consequences for EMDEs. For Hirschman, as for Hayek (whom he drew on admiringly), there were "limits to 'intelligibility' of our complex world" (Adelman 2013b, 238; see Hayek 2014[1944], 181).[19] For Hayek, of course, the limits to intelligibility had determinant policy implications; namely, that it is impossible for any social planning agency to acquire the full range of information necessary to improve outcomes in a complex economy. Thus, for Hayek, it is only through the "'spontaneous order' of the competitive market that the diverse and ever changing plans of numerous economic actors, responding to unpredictable and complex shifts in the world, can be reconciled with each other" (Chang 2014, 101). For Hirschman, the failure of development economists and practitioners to appreciate complexity and the limits of knowledge led them to treat poorer countries as essentially simple systems that were analytically tractable. This epistemic error opened up EMDEs as fertile ground for model building, grand paradigms, programming, expert control, and quick fixes (Hirschman 2013[1970], 144).[20]

Hirschman's commitments to uncertainty, contingency, and complexity are a constant in his work.[21] His epistemic position was placed in particularly sharp relief in a project that he conducted for the World Bank during the 1960s. The project culminated in the 1967 book *Development Projects Observed*. The way in which Hirschman operationalized his epistemic views in the project led to an irreconcilable disagreement with the World Bank. The institution's staff ultimately ignored the work. This episode bears attention since it illustrates so well the nature of Hirschman's thinking and his break with the prevailing norms of social science in the 1960s and subsequent decades.[22]

In the spring of 1963, Hirschman proposed to the World Bank that he enter into what was then unchartered territory for the institution. This involved conducting extensive fieldwork for the institution in Asia, Africa, Latin America, and (after the advice of World Bank staff) southern Italy during 1964 and 1965. Hirschman examined the direct effects and the broad repercussions of various World Bank projects on the economy and society, with the ultimate aim of improving general elements of project appraisal, design, and management. The Bank's staff was expecting something akin to a manual that would provide concrete, generalizable tools for evaluation, such as ways to calculate the economic return on a project. But this is not what Hirschman submitted, either in a detailed, methodologically focused "Interim Observations" memo midway through the project or in the manuscript that was the project's final output. Instead, Hirschman urged a change in epistemic perspective at the institution, and in the interim memo he argued that it should avoid the "air of pat certainty" and work to "visualize the uncertainties," "the element of the unknown," and the "unexpected" that surrounds all projects.[23] Key uncertainties highlighted by Hirschman involve the ability to completely map out a project upon its launch, and the degree to which economic, social, and political change can interfere with project implementation. These uncertainties deflect projects from their anticipated course (Hirschman 1967a; Alacevich 2014, 150–151, 159).[24]

Hirschman's call for what amounted to a paradigm shift came several decades too soon. The profession was not yet ready to embrace the radical theoretical and practical implications of complexity. Hirschman's report was summarily dismissed (Alacevich 2014, 153–163). Some saw it as impractical; others saw it as simply incorrect—as a misrepresentation of what the institution was already doing. Still others dismissed it because of Hirschman's complete lack of interest in quantitative evaluations. Instead, he focused on developing qualitative analyses, comparing what he termed the "personal profiles" of projects, which included detailed historical reconstructions and consideration of their larger political and social contexts (ibid., 153–159).[25]

The first chapter of *Development Projects Observed*, "The Principle of the Hiding Hand," appeared as an essay in *Public Interest*. The essay is a particularly rich exemplar of Hirschman's epistemic commitments. Hirschman's clients, however, found it "thin," misspecified, and not useful as a guide to strategy (Alacevich 2014, 156).[26]

The Hiding Hand concept (the capitalization is Hirschman's) was of course a rhetorical play on Adam Smith's invisible hand, and it reflected Hirschman's recognition that actors always operate in a state of uncertainty and ignorance. But rather than inhibiting or distorting action, Hirschman saw uncertainty, ignorance, and error as potential drivers of productive action by policy entrepreneurs, just as Keynes emphasized the animal spirits that took hold among private investors and led them to risk adventures that were not warranted by the cold, hard facts. Underestimating problems (e.g., regarding a project's cost or the obstacles that could stymie it) propelled projects forward that would not be initiated in the presence of full information. In Hirschman's words, the Hiding Hand "beneficially hides difficulties from us. . . . People typically take on and plunge into new tasks because of the erroneously presumed *absence* of a challenge, because the task looks easier and more manageable than it will turn out to be (Hirschman 1967a, 12, emphasis in original). Once a project is initiated, project participants are challenged to develop creative solutions to the unforeseen problems that have arisen. The strategies they devise out of necessity can have positive and lasting spillover effects. Thus, predictive and other errors can breed success: actors can and sometimes do respond to crises creatively when they misjudge the nature of a task (ibid., 12). As Hirschman (1967a, 13) put it, "Our more lofty achievements, such as economic, social, or political progress, could have come about by stumbling rather than through careful planning, rational behavior, and the courageous taking up of a clearly perceived challenge."[27]

Hirschman's distinct vision of development followed from his epistemic commitments. In the words of his biographer Adelman, Hirschman's work is marked by the view that "the study of social change, if it is to be helpful, he felt, should rethink the typical reliance on predictions according to laws of change and consider instead the analysis of possibilities and alternatives for social change" (Adelman 2013a, 137). An essay Hirschman jointly authored with Charles Lindblom makes this point: "It is clearly impossible to specify in advance the optimal doses of . . . various policies under different circumstances. The art of promoting economic development . . . and constructive policymaking . . . consists, then, in acquiring a feeling for these doses" (Hirschman and Lindblom 1971[1962], 83–84).[28] Complicating matters further, beliefs can exert causal effects. In the contemporary vernacular, we might say that Hirschman viewed ideas as constitutive and not just reflections of the world. In the words of his biographer, Hirschman thought that "how we understand the world affects how we might change it" (Adelman 2013a, xvii).[29] For Hirschman, then, there was no uniform, timeless, context-independent set of factors (such as economic fundamentals) that determine the success or failure of a project. Societies are irreducibly complex, the future is fundamentally unknowable, economies are constantly in flux, and even efforts to know the world affect outcomes that arise within it (Hirschman and Lindblom 1971[1962], 83–84).[30]

The Failure of Grand Theoretical Narratives and Uniform Solutions

Hirschman's epistemic commitments underlay his critique of what he saw as "compulsive and mindless" reductionist theorizing in the service of easy causal explanations, quick fixes, and simpleminded solutions to complex challenges (Hirschman 2013[1970], 138).[31] In his view, ignoring the importance of uncertainty led economists to articulate excessively ambitious paradigms that not only oversimplified but also sought to domesticate the real world of messy, complex social environments in pursuit of predictability and order. Paradigm thinking often induced what Adelman describes as Hirschman's rejection of the "mindless overconfidence in the solvability of all problems or its twin, the fatalism that nothing can be changed willfully at all" (Adelman 2013a, xvi; Hirschman 2013[1971]).[32]

Hirschman's view of quick fixes and uniform solutions was also reflected in his rejection of what he termed the "obstacles to development" thesis (Hirschman 1965; 2013[1968b]; Adelman 2013b, 433–435). The obstacle thesis refers to economists' common tendency to search for and find a singular, new, fundamental obstacle to development (such as the shortage of capital) and to rewrite the history of development failures or successes based on the presence, absence, or elimination of this obstacle (Hirschman 1965; 2013[1970]).[33] Hirschman (1965) showed that certain commonly identified obstacles to development could turn out to be assets, that some were not obstacles at all, and that the elimination of certain obstacles could be postponed indefinitely. Attachment to the tradition of identifying obstacles necessarily led to simplistic, homogeneous prescriptions for development. Were Hirschman writing today, he could easily identify obstacle thinking in recent development fads that, for example, focus variously on property rights, social capital, microfinance, and, as of this writing, infrastructure.

Hirschman's impatience with grand narratives, the pursuit of perfection in ambitious utopian projects, and other forms of social engineering applied to plans from all political entrepreneurs—communists of the 1930s, advocates of "big push" and "balanced growth" models of the 1960s, and neoliberals of the 1980s and 1990s (Adelman 2013a, viii).[34] In place of social engineering, Hirschman advocated what he termed "immersion in the particular" (Alacevich 2014, 142; Hirschman 1967a, 2) and the need to liberate practice from the straitjacket of reductionist models that provided justification for encompassing, homogenous programs. The universalist approach "hindered rather than helped" since it precluded consideration of alternative or diverse paths to development (Adelman 2013b, 340; Hirschman 2013[1986a]).[35] Hirschman's approach instead was one of improvisation in pursuit of multiple development paths, not implementation of a pristine policy blueprint. He favored complexity, messiness, specificity, and contingency in contrast to what he saw as theoretically sanctioned, paradigm-based uniform solutions (Hirschman 1965; 1967a; 1969[1958]; 1973[1963]; 2013[1970]; 2013[1971]). In reflecting on his own work, Hirschman said, "With this conclusion I can lay claim to at least one element of continuity in my thought: the refusal to define 'one best way'" (Hirschman 1995, 76). This view was consistent with the work of economic historian Alexander Gerschenkron (1962), whose work illustrated the multiplicity and uniqueness of development trajectories in a variety of national contexts (Hirschman 2013[1981b], 58–59). As Alacevich (2014, 141) argues, Hirschman's focus on the particular and the complex was consistent with and helped to inspire the move away from grand theory in development economics in the late 1950s to mid-1960s.[36]

The Centrality of the Diminutive, the Complex, and the Experimental

Hirschman's epistemic and normative views informed his complex understanding of social change in other ways as well. As suggested, he rejected the common tendency to assess ex ante the significance of particular changes or innovations. He wrote of the tendency to dismiss reform, a tendency that reflected both a deep-seated skepticism and the epistemic certainty that dominated social science in his time, and indeed continues to infuse much work today. In this connection, he made an observation that is central to a proper understanding of the contemporary conjuncture, as I will demonstrate throughout this book:

> A distinction is often made between "real" and "apparent" or between "fundamental" and "superficial" changes: This device permits one to categorize as superficial a great number of changes that have, in effect, taken place and to assert in consequence that there has not yet been any real change. The decision to assert that *real* change has occurred is made to hinge on one or several tests. . . . But to set up such demanding tests is in itself an indication of a special difficulty and reluctance to concede change except when it simply can no longer be denied. (Hirschman 2013[1968b], 37, emphasis in original)

Hirschman's commitments led him to embrace the diminutive, which he argued could be the building block of meaningful, path-dependent reform and widespread change (Adelman 2013a, vii–viii; Hirschman 2013[1968b]; 2013[1970]; 2013[1971]). Hirschman viewed the task of the development intellectual and practitioner as finding "seams in even the most impregnable structures" in order to find "openings and prospective alternatives" (Adelman 2013a, vii–viii), a theme that resonates today with certain policy analysts (see Levin et al. 2012, and citations therein). This meant "challenging . . . the euphoric conviction that one could change everything at once—given the 'necessary conditions'" and led him to articulate an approach that "favored strategic focus over comprehensive breadth" (Adelman 2013a, vii–viii). In this connection, Hirschman said, "To look at unbalanced growth means, in other words, to look at the dynamics of the development process *in the small*" (Hirschman 1969[1958], ix, emphasis in original).

This view of change implied the need to be open to and welcome the unexpected (Hirschman 2013[1970]) and the related need for small-scale experimentation, or what Lindblom (1979; 1959) termed "muddling through." As Lindblom argues, "'Muddling through'—or incrementalism . . . is and ought to be the usual method of policymaking. . . . [Indeed] no more than muddling through—is ordinarily possible" (Lindblom 1979, 517). Hirschman and Lindblom (1971[1962], e.g., 77) explored this theme, arguing that policymakers should steer away from "integrated planning," meaning development models that focus on "big pushes," balanced growth, and so forth, and instead pursue piecemeal reform in a spirit of opportunism and open-mindedness.[37]

By now I hope it is clear that Hirschman was deeply suspicious of what I have termed coherence, which is predicated on the notion of the social world as a simple social system where everything fits and where the structure determines what can and cannot work, what is and is not possible. He believed that it was imperative to learn from small-scale, gradual initiatives and from multiple examples, to recognize uniqueness and the specificity of experiences, and to appreciate the possibility of a great many sequences rather than seek universal dictates in a reductive theory (Hirschman 1965; 1969[1958]; 1973[1963]; 2013[1970]; 2013[1971], 22).[38] As Fukuyama (2013) rightly notes, Hirschman's embrace of experimentation did not involve radical or revolutionary change. What Hirschman termed "reform mongering" involved gradualism and small-scale change by democratic governments. In *Development Projects Observed*, Hirschman (1967a, 19) argued that projects "should be developed as much as possible in an experimental spirit, in the style of a pilot project gathering strength and experience gradually, so that they may escape being classed and closed down as failures in their infancy." He further argued that "projects whose potential difficulties and disappointments are apt to manifest themselves at an early stage should be administered by agencies having a long-term commitment to the success of the projects" (ibid.). Elsewhere Hirschman wrote of the importance of the "propensity to experiment and to improvise" (Adelman 2013b, 323; Hirschman 1971[1957], 259).[39] In *Journeys toward Progress*, Hirschman (1973[1963]) demonstrated through careful case studies that slow reform mongering in Chile, Brazil, and Colombia eventually brought about significant progress, even though some well-intentioned reforms had negative effects and others were plagued by misperceptions and mistakes made by reformers and their foreign advisers (see Fukuyama 2013).

Taking a page directly from Hirschman, Ellerman (2004; 2005; 2014) asserts the importance of adaptive, pragmatic searching; horizontal (south to south) peer group monitoring; and a process of "social or open learning" in development. This involves fostering parallel experiments (which he sees as necessary for learning under uncertainty), pooling the experience of actual projects, seeing what works and comparing results, and promoting cross learning to ratchet up performance of the whole group (Ellerman 2005, 163–165, 234–239).[40] Ellerman offers the small-scale, gradual, incremental, and pragmatic adjustment of China's economic policies as an exemplar of a Hirschmanian approach (ibid., 196–197).[41] Rodrik's work (including his collaborative work on "growth diagnostics") is likewise characterized by an embrace of targeted as opposed to across-the-board policies, institutional innovation, and monitoring and evaluation as strategies to discover what does and does not work (Rodrik 2007b, especially chap. 2; 2007–2008; 2009a; Hausmann, Rodrik, and Velasco 2008; Hausmann, Pritchett, and Rodrik 2005).[42] Like Ellerman, Rodrik sees China as engaging in "experimental gradualism." He also notes that the case of China demonstrates that experimentation need not be limited in scope and can even extend to the national level (Rodrik 2009a, 43–45). Easterly's and McMillan's work has also been marked by an embrace of the "piecemeal" and a commitment to "searching" as opposed to grand, comprehensive, utopian plans (Easterly 2001; 2006; 2008; 2014; McMillan 2008; see discussion in DeMartino 2011, 17, fns1, 5, 141–150). These commitments impart a clear Hirschmanian flavor to Easterly's and McMillan's work, though their explicit intellectual inspirations are drawn from Popper (1957; 1971) and, in Easterly's case, Hayek (2014[1944]).

The Development Expert: Ethical Duties and Failures

Hirschman's epistemic and normative views bear directly on his conception of the ethical responsibilities of the researcher and development practitioner. Hirschman had an ethical commitment to the view that the people of the developing world could and should be the architects of their own unscripted future(s) (Adelman 2013a, 49; Hirschman 2013[1981b]). Hirschman wrote widely and dismissively of the "development expert" (e.g., Adelman 2013b, 323; Hirschman 1965; 1967a, chap. 1; 1969[1958]; 1971[1957]; 2013[1970]; 2013[1971]). This view reflected his embrace of the principles of autonomy and self-determination, in addition to his rejection of professional authority, epistemic certainty, and pristine blackboard planning.

Hirschman wrote often of the mutual distrust between the subjects and objects of development expertise. But his skepticism regarding the development expert was not limited to the foreign expert. He was equally skeptical of the reification of home-grown experts, particularly the nationals who return home after a period of study abroad with a sure cure for what ails their native country and with the arrogance to dismiss the ideas and experiences of those with longer historical memories (Hirschman 1973[1963], v).

Hirschman's distrust of experts stemmed from their hubris, reductionist sensibilities, and the associated fiction of expert control, which authorized them to devise sweeping plans and to oversell their benefits and discount the likelihood and costs of their failure (Hirschman 1967a; 2013[1970], 147; 2013[1971]; see Ellerman 2005). Hirschman's "Hiding Hand" essay masterfully dissects the rhetorical strategies that experts use to sell their reform plans (Hirschman 1967b, 19–23). These include what he terms the "pseudo imitation technique," pretending that a project is a straightforward application of a well-known technique that has already been used successfully elsewhere, and the "pseudo comprehensive program technique," dismissing previous reform efforts as piecemeal, and offering instead a comprehensive program without regard to the myriad uncertainties and risks that it entails. The latter strategy provides cover to experts in the event of program failure since it can always be claimed that failure resulted from not having followed the plan in full.[43]

These themes are echoed in what Hirschman (1973[1963], 247–249) terms his "Digression on the Semantics of Problem-Solving," where he takes on the practical power associated with labeling reforms as either "piecemeal" or "comprehensive." Nassim Taleb (2007, chap. 6) advances similar concerns in connection with what he terms the "narrative fallacy," or the tendency to oversimplify complex social phenomena via accounts that impose logical or causal links on sequences of events or facts. Such causal stories are dangerous to the extent that they are taken literally and induce overconfidence in the intelligibility and tractability of the world, and to the extent that they lead the expert to believe the world can and should be redesigned to conform to the elegant model that resides in his head. Long before Hirschman, Adam Smith and Henry Sidgwick had warned of the same conceits and errors (see

DeMartino 2011; Kirman 2016). Hirschman, of course, attributed the very same tendency to development experts and reformers. Easterly (2001; 2006; 2008; 2014) and Ellerman (2004; 2014) have also emphasized this concern. Like Hirschman, their views are informed by direct experience working in EMDEs and a Hayekian rejection of both the democracy-constraining and practical failings of social engineering.[44]

Hirschman's critical view of development experts also stemmed from his rejection of the idea that EMDEs were somehow simpler and more tractable than AEs (Hirschman 2013[1970], 144; Rothschild and Sen 2013, 367). This view of EMDEs, prevalent throughout Hirschman's career and too often in evidence today, founded the particular zeal and naïve optimism with which economists sought to tackle the "development problem." The idea that EMDEs and the behavior of actors therein are inherently tractable is a constant in development policy. One might consider the contemporary embrace of RCTs and conditional cash transfer programs that seek to modify the behaviors of the poor through small cash payments as indicators of the continued impact of old views about the simplicity of EMDE actors, structures, and practices.[45] That spirit was also in evidence with a vengeance in the postsocialist context of the 1990s, when leading economists converged on a simplistic, largely uniform reform package for the transition economies despite their distinct institutional frameworks, histories, assets, and cultures (see DeMartino 2011, chap. 9; McMillan 2008; Murrell 1995, 164, 177).

Possibilism, Futilism, and Rhetoric

The ethical responsibility of the development expert entails a commitment to what Hirschman termed "possibilism." Hirschman's possibilism entails the idea that small-scale, messy, disparate innovations reveal what could be, and what reforms might be available. As exemplified in the concept of the Hiding Hand, possibilism is grounded in faith in the demonstrated capacities of individuals, institutions, and societies to develop diverse, creative solutions to unforeseen challenges and development problems. Possibilism encapsulates the enduring bias for hope that infuses so much of Hirschman's oeuvre (see Sanyal 1994; Lepenies 2008).[46] Central to Hirschman's possibilism is his humility and his related emphasis on uncertainty—on imperfect, deficient knowledge of what is and what could be. He counterposed possibilism with the predominant "futilism" in the social sciences (and especially in development economics)—the view that any initiatives that were not entirely consistent with the precepts of received theory were bound to fail (Hirschman 2013[1971]). Hirschman wryly observed that development economists, particularly in Latin America, had a tendency to swing counterproductively between the poles of disaster and salvation, with no space for the intermediary state of purgatory (Hirschman 2013[1968a]; 2013[1970], 145–146). In contrast, and as examined earlier, Hirschman believed in the productive nature of ignorance, which often served as a condition of possibility for ultimately beneficial initiatives.[47]

Hirschman saw "possibilism" as an ethical compass that called for a "little more 'reverence for life,' a little less straitjacketing of the future, a little more allowance for the unexpected—and a little less wishful thinking" (Adelman 2013a, xii; Hirschman 2013[1970], 147).[48] Hirschman concluded his essay on "Political Economics and Possibilism" by identifying "the right to a non projected future as one of the truly inalienable rights of every person and nation; . . . [setting] the stage for conceptions of change to which the inventiveness of history and a 'passion for the possible' are admitted as vital actors" (Hirschman 2013[1971], 30; see also Hirschman 2013[1970], 147; Adelman 2013a, xii). Hirschman famously said of possibilism that "social scientists often consider it beneath their scientific dignity to deal with possibility until *after* it has become actual and can then at least be redefined as a probability" (Hirschman 1980[1945], xii, emphasis in original). In reflecting on his own work, Hirschman said that "the fundamental bent of my writings has been to widen the limits of what is or is perceived to be possible, be it at the cost of lowering our ability, real or imaginary, to discern the probable" (Hirschman 2013[1971], 22). Elsewhere he asked, "Aren't we interested in what is (barely) possible, rather than what is probable?" (Hirschman's diary, cited in Adelman 2013a, xii).

So deeply was Hirschman associated with the idea of possibilism that his *New York Times* obituary had the title "Albert Hirschman, Optimistic Economist, Dead at 97" (Yardley 2012). Some of Hirschman's contemporaries dismissed what they perceived to be the excessive optimism inherent in his case for possibilism. In a private letter, he responded to a negative review of his book *The Strategy of Economic Development* that focused on precisely this point. He wrote, "Perhaps I have overstated my case, but it seems to me that you in turn overstate the extent of my overstatement" (Adelman 2013b, 351).

Hirschman's possibilism was not simply a matter of disposition but rather reflected both his ethical commitments and his appreciation of the practical consequences of rhetorical choices. Hirschman's interest in the real political and economic consequences of what his biographer terms "how social scientists played with words" (Adelman 2013b, 6) was a theme that extended beyond his work on possibilism and futilism. In his view, the epistemic certainty that contributed to paradigm thinking made reality "appear more solidly entrenched than before" (Hirschman 2013[1970], 148) and diverted actors away from available opportunities and potentially productive courses of action (Hirschman 2013[1971]). He understood theorizing the solidity of obstacles to social improvement as a practice that could increase their practical salience. He famously said that "obstacles to the *perception* of change thus turn into an important obstacle to *change itself*" (Hirschman 2013[1968b], 43, emphasis in original; see also Hirschman 2013[1970]; 2013[1971]).

Hirschman's appreciation of the practical effects of rhetoric are on full display in his book *The Rhetoric of Reaction: Perversity, Futility, Jeopardy* (1991), his intellectual history of two hundred years of conservative rhetoric against progressive social policy (see also Hirschman 1973[1963], 247–249). Hirschman argues that conservative rhetoric fell into one of three categories, which he termed theses. The perversity thesis holds that well-intentioned actions have unintended negative effects that leave society worse off than before the intervention; the futility thesis holds that interventions will fail to produce any effects at all; and the jeopardy thesis holds that the costs of a proposed change are so great as to threaten other previous hard-won gains.[49] In developing these theses, Hirschman by no means denied the likelihood of unintended negative effects of interventions (Fukuyama 2013); indeed, he counted on them. Rather, he challenged the tendency to make the discovery of unintended negative effects a reason for opposing all deliberate efforts at reform—the tendency to allow the perfect to impede the good.[50]

Lamentable Evaluative Criteria

This selective Hirschmanian tour provides substantial, useful guidance when considering contemporary developments in financial governance and developmental finance. Indeed, one can tease a method out of Hirschman's madness—incomplete, to be sure, but good footing nonetheless for engaging irreducibly complex changes in an irreducibly complex world. The methodological prescriptions take the form of *pro*scriptions—as injunctions against deep-seated academic habits and sensibilities that today infuse the social sciences, especially political science and economics. Most simply put, along with Hirschman, *we should refuse to know too much, and we should refuse to rush to judgment.*[51] This imperative requires us to reject evaluative criteria that purport to determine ex ante or even ex post whether particular policy or institutional innovations are coherent, viable, sufficient, scalable, and significant.

Coherence

We should not vet new initiatives by reference to coherence criteria, adjudicating their viability based on the degree to which they "fit" into an overarching system. We should instead presume that any observed institutional innovations within and across countries will conflict to some degree or other with established institutions, just as existing institutions conflict with each other. This is equally true of innovations that are dictated by a coherent theoretical vision and those that are not. Seamless, coherent systems are neither possible nor ideal. Indeed, they are inherently risky. Similarly, we should not be concerned with whether they are redundant or duplicative in some way, in violation of some efficiency norm, or whether they are consistent with a generalized, universal theory, plan, or "ism." Tensions between seemingly inconsistent endeavors might be more apparent than real, and even real tensions might yield unforeseeable adaptations and innovations that serve to solve important problems.

Viability

We should not presume to know whether proposed or existing innovations can exist and survive over the long term or whether some or all of them are unviable in the context of pressures emanating from the global economy, the power of global financial actors, or fragilities in EMDEs. Even those that fail may impart useful lessons (provided we are open to them) that benefit other initiatives. Hirschman reminds us that learning happens through confrontation with obstacles and failures and not just or primarily through successes. Moreover, new capacities, knowledge, networks, and coalitions may be built in the context of institutional innovations even when particular policy or institutional arrangements fail to survive. These Hirschmanian linkages or side effects may bear fruit in unexpected and unpredictable ways over the medium and long terms. Finally, full exploitation of positive and negative events for learning purposes requires a break with paradigm thinking that constrains what lessons we can take away from the rich experiential record that presents itself. Following Hirschman, we need to aspire to be Isaiah Berlin's foxes rather than hedgehogs (Tetlock 2005).

Sufficiency

We should not be concerned with whether the observed innovations are adequate in the sense of addressing the full range of needs for developmental finance. They can't. But then, what can? Those who apply the sufficiency test are almost invariably drawn to paradigmatic accounts that

confer the status of sufficiency only to innovations that fit into their theoretical schemes. It bears emphasis that finding any innovation (or web of
interconnected innovations) sufficient requires utopian thinking where all
unintended consequences, contradictions, and perversions are eliminated
by theoretical fiat. That is not Hirschman's way, and with good reason.

Scalability
We should not judge innovations against the standard of whether they are
scalable and even universalizable (rather than contingent or context dependent) or speculate as to whether they are doomed to remain small, barely
surviving, and even then only in the specific environments where they have
arisen. We should presume instead that scalability is always in part illusory
and aspirational—it is a standard that is often imposed by grand narratives that require homogeneity and universality on reiterated yet context-
specific, diverse constructions. Replicability but with significant variation is
a less ambitious but more achievable goal than scalability—but it may be a
valid objective only if we recognize that replication is a story we employ to
make sense of what may be internally heterogeneous developments.

Significance of Change
Finally, we should not attempt to discern whether innovations represent
fundamental or superficial changes. We must not impose a "test" of fundamental change, such as whether any particular institutional endeavor dis-
rupts the structural power of the IMF or the United States. In addition, we
should not dismiss change on the grounds that what appears to be a new
development is simply a repeat of past practices in a new guise. We should
presume instead that significance is always context dependent—that a reiterated construction always represents novelty owing to the unique circumstances in which it occurs. In addition, we should presume evolution rather
than fixed identities and realize then that significance is revealed only over
time in the process of institutional adaptation. Moreover, we should recognize the need to parse reforms as significant or insignificant as an urge
driven in part by our professional training and the long tradition of futilism
and epistemic certainty that marks it—one we would do well to suppress as
we engage a world that is so much more complex and richer than we can
capture adequately through our various paradigms and predictive models.

Along with Hirschman, we might recognize that each of these criteria
reflects the drive of social scientists to repress uncertainty in the pursuit of
understanding and, ultimately, control. Each constrains our appreciation of
the possible, the nonsensical, the ad hoc, and the unscripted, and blinds us

to the significance and potential of piecemeal, small-scale initiatives that are now proliferating in EMDEs. It would be far better to intervene in ways that acknowledge the possibility that each might evolve with the effect of addressing pressing development problems and deepening capacities, provided they are not strangled by scientific closed-mindedness that deprives them of recognition, legitimacy, and support.

The Hirschmanian Method: Its Nature, Promise, and Risks

How might we make sense of the developments that I will examine in subsequent chapters from a Hirschmanian perspective? A central point is that the developments are not to be taken as universally good or bad, progressive or regressive, rational or irrational. Instead, we are encouraged by Hirschman to take them on their own terms, as context-specific gestures toward problem solving. This requires avoiding the kinds of evaluative criteria that predominate in much social science. In this sense, we must keep in mind the negative nature of Hirschman's intervention—to reject approaches to social science in general and the study of change in particular that presume to know in advance what developments are and are not possible, viable, and beneficial. We must avoid not just prediction but prenarration of the institutions and practices we encounter. If we learn just this much from Hirschman, that we are not authorized or competent to tell the history of institutional evolution and social change in advance, we will be much better able to appreciate and contribute to projects of economic reform.

Even if Hirschmanian possibilism has much to offer, the approach is hardly watertight or complete. As the foregoing suggests, no particular "method," no set of techniques, falls neatly out of the approach. To the degree that the approach can be reckoned a method, it is one that will not appeal to many social scientists. It may be encapsulated simply as a *rejection of dismissiveness*, as *observation without (premature) judgment* that at once takes account of the apparent limitations and risks associated with incoherence while refusing to dismiss new initiatives as dead ends, internally contradictory, ephemeral, inefficient, or necessarily damaging to development. The method calls for a particular attitude, addressing the researcher's sensibilities as she encounters unfolding events rather than addressing her techniques per se. Hence, the approach is consistent with quantitative and qualitative methods, and with empirical and analytical inquiry. Moreover, the approach is equally open to the study of state and nonstate actors and to investigations of local, national, regional, and global developments.[52] If Hirschman himself was often more apt to emphasize the salience of the small and disparate, that might be taken as a corrective to what he recognized as a misplaced disregard among his peers for this level of analysis. As his oeuvre demonstrates, he was equally comfortable engaging matters of state behavior and interstate dynamics. Nothing was off the agenda, but neither was any one domain, level, or factor taken to be the key to development. We find instead a profound rejection of a simplifying reductionism that, in Hirschman's view, could only generate illusions of understanding and control.

It would be irresponsible to end our survey of Hirschmanian themes, however, without attention to certain ambiguities and risks that we will encounter in applying this framework to contemporary events. First, observation without premature judgment can be taken as a thorough retreat away from the difficult but necessary task of assessing initiatives in terms of their contributions to goals that the development economist advocates. Does Hirschman leave us in a debilitating relativist morass? The answer—perhaps more a hope—is that he does not. At issue here is not our ability to apply normative criteria, theoretical insights, and empirical techniques to the initiatives unfolding around us—something we can't escape doing—but the certainty with which we cling to our normative assessments, theoretical conclusions, and empirical findings. Hirschman implores us over and over to recognize the *productivity of doubt*—including doubt in our own deepest convictions, theoretical priors, methods, and findings. We are urged to push back against the internal and external pressures to rush to judgment, giving space and time for initiatives to evolve and for events to play out before we dot all the i's and cross all the t's in our analysis.

But how long is long enough? When can we break into the never-ending sequence of events and begin to render judgment? Is it too soon, for instance, to evaluate the present postcrisis period, since so many of the initiatives that we will examine in later chapters are in their infancy (and some are not yet even born)? The answer, I think, is that Hirschman would have us render tentative judgments at each and every moment, all the while recognizing that what we are assessing is incomplete, unfinished. Since there is no ending to the drama, there is no natural point at which we can pass final judgment. Hence, there is no contradiction in avoiding premature judgment while at the same time grappling tentatively with the events under way around us. Hirschman's possibilism asserts that in this tentative grappling we should foreground existing and emerging potential and opportunities rather than limitations and failures.

This book's central claims can now be reframed in light of Hirschman's extraordinary contributions. The positive claim is that we are today immersed in a Hirschmanian moment, one marked by productive incoherence in terms of global financial governance and developmental finance. The normative claim is that the emergent Hirschmanian world is a good world to inhabit—one far better attuned to development than a fully coherent system. But it bears repeating a concern broached in chapter 1 and that will be revisited in chapter 8: that there is a grave risk that a global economic policy environment marked by incoherence may come to feature beggar-thy-neighbor initiatives in which efforts to insulate powerful constituencies at home from economic turbulence might offload risk and economic hardship onto others—especially the relatively powerless and vulnerable. This is not just an academic concern. For instance, many observers have called attention to the problems created for EMDEs by loose monetary policy in AEs during the global crisis, and have called for strategies that mitigate harmful spillover effects, including involvement by the IMF and other bodies (see chapter 7).[53] At the same time, and as we will also investigate in chapter 7, the IMF has expressed worry about the negative spillovers resulting from the proliferation of the competitive use of capital controls. It can reasonably be argued that these risks can only be managed adequately within an internally coherent global policy regime, one with mechanisms to ensure compliance among national governments. In this view, an incoherent regime is terribly risky and on that account unsustainable.

We will return to this matter in the concluding chapter of the book, once we have explored the range of initiatives now under way and as a consequence can examine the risks of incoherence more concretely than we can here. Some of these initiatives might indeed plausibly threaten economic welfare abroad even as they promote economic security at home. The question that will emerge is whether the imposition of policy and institutional conformity in line with some model or other is the best or even the only viable response to this threat. The global neoliberal vision answered that question in the affirmative, of course. But it must be emphasized that in practice that regime provided ample opportunity for powerful countries and elites to adjust the rules in non-neoliberal directions as circumstances warranted. Fidelity to the model was routinely sacrificed to protect those interests having sufficient influence. The range and extent of departures from the neoliberal ideal—such as state interventions in financial markets through lender of last resort activities and bailouts of private financial institutions—reveals that *coherent* systems are inherently risky and on that account unsustainable (Polanyi 2001[1944]). The Hirschmanian sensibilities that animate this work urge us toward an alternative answer. We are encouraged to recognize the risks of incoherence while avoiding the deep-seated fastidiousness (among economists and policymakers) that values order and consistency for their own sake. Legitimate concern over risk should drive the pursuit of a new mindset that focuses on managing policy diversity rather than enforcing policy conformity. In a Hirschmanian world, the mandate of global institutions (such as the BWIs) must be to enable arrangements that expand policy space for valued national economic objectives. It is of course not obvious just how this might be done. Hirschman would encourage us to look for the answer through application of the same strategies that he thought were productive for development—inaugurating a perpetual chain of experimentation, trial and error, learning by doing, and persistent policy and institutional adjustment to an ever-changing world.

In chapter 3, we turn to the Asian financial crisis, an epoch-shaping event that set in motion developments that prepared the way for the Hirschmanian impulses that have deepened and spread during the global crisis and that persist today.

II Setting the Stage

3   The East Asian Financial Crisis and Neoliberalism: The Beginning of the End of a Unified Regime

The East Asian financial crisis erupted in Thailand in May 1997, and through the summer and fall it swept through some of the most important and stable economies in the region—Malaysia, Indonesia, and the Philippines. By late October, the crisis had reached Brazil and Russia. Soon thereafter, the crisis destabilized South Korea. Aftershocks of the crisis further destabilized the region and other EMDEs in early 1998. In its scope and depth, the crisis of 1997–1998 proved to be far more disruptive and less tractable than prior crises in other regions, such as the crisis that engulfed Mexico in December 1994.

The Asian crisis took investors and IMF officials completely by surprise. Up until the eve of the crisis, IMF reports and business accounts were uniformly bullish about economic prospects in the region. Indeed, through 1996, four of the countries involved in the crisis were among the world's top six recipients of private capital flows. Moreover, the crisis occurred *after* the IMF had implemented a new set of information-based safeguards in the wake of the Mexican crisis that were intended to prevent financial instability. With the exception of Malaysia, the governments of the countries most deeply affected by the crisis approached the IMF for assistance. As a condition of assistance, the IMF demanded stringent neoliberal reforms, including severe austerity policies.[1]

The East Asian financial crisis laid the groundwork for consequential shifts in several dimensions of global financial governance and developmental finance that deepened during and since the global crisis. Here we explore inter alia the responses of EMDEs not just in East Asia but also far beyond the epicenter of the crisis, and the impact of these EMDE strategies and the crisis itself on the IMF.

The Solidification of Neoliberal Reform

Had the East Asian financial crisis not intervened, the IMF almost certainly would have modified Article 6 of its Articles of Agreement to make liberalization of international capital flows a central purpose of the Fund and to extend its jurisdiction to capital movements. A chief effect would have been to dismantle existing capital controls and preclude future ones. The proposal reflected the neoliberal tenor of the times and the related power of financial interests. During the long neoliberal era, the majority of leading academic economists, policymakers, and IMF staff advocated capital flow liberalization as a key to development along the lines of what Hirschman derided as the simplistic tendency to identify obstacles and universal quick fixes.[2]

Capital Flow Liberalization and Conflicting Interpretations of the Crisis

In the neoclassical canon, liberalized international capital flows were predicted to benefit the EMDEs in several mutually reinforcing ways. Liberalization would give the public and private sectors access to capital and other resources (such as technology) that were not being generated domestically, and consequently would increase the nation's capital stock, productivity, economic growth, and income. Capital flow liberalization would ensure policy discipline via the threat of capital flight and the attendant incentives for governments to maintain international standards for policy design, macroeconomic performance, and arm's-length forms of corporate governance. Liberalization would also ensure that finance would be allocated by markets rather than by governments, with the effect of directing capital to those projects that promised the greatest net contribution to social welfare (i.e., those projects that promised the highest rates of return).

In view of the impressive set of expected benefits, neoclassical academic economists and like-minded policymakers zealously promoted capital flow liberalization in EMDEs (and beyond) during the long neoliberal era. With notable exceptions to be explored later, the drive to liberalize finance marked the periods both prior to and following the Asian crisis. The case for liberalization was damaged by the Asian crisis, but the damage was scattershot. We will consider this matter in depth in chapter 7 since the pushback against capital liberalization that begins with the Asian crisis gathered strength during the global crisis.

Rejecting the neoclassical view, observers from Europe and Asia identified unrestrained capital flows as a key culprit in the Asian crisis (Wade

1998–1999). The Keynesian-inflected narrative focused on the intrinsic instability of financial markets and the way in which instability is amplified by the removal of regulations over domestic and especially international financial flows. The Keynesian narrative was quickly defeated by a far less threatening, non-Keynesian diagnosis that deflected attention from financial liberalization and the deficiencies of the global financial architecture.[3] Federal Reserve chairman Alan Greenspan and first deputy managing director of the IMF Stanley Fischer consistently rejected the view that financial liberalization contributed to the Asian crisis (Kirshner 2014b, 229–230). In a seminar at the IMF shortly after the first signs of crisis emerged, Fischer argued forcefully for the (by then) doomed effort to amend Article 6, arguing that capital account liberalization is an "inevitable step on the path of development, which cannot be avoided and therefore should be adopted. . . . [Liberalization ensures that] residents and governments are able to borrow and lend on more favorable terms . . . financial markets will become more efficient . . . [there will be a] better allocation of saving and investment. . . . Almost always these swings [in market sentiment] are rationally based" (Fischer 1997, points 9, 15).

The domesticated and ultimately dominant Asian crisis origin story reinforced the drive toward neoliberal reforms. According to this narrative, the roots of the Asian crisis were to be found in deficiencies in information, transparency, and market discipline, and in pervasive and damaging—though somehow previously unnoticed—cronyism, corruption, and institutional and political pathologies.[4] Taken together, the deficiencies came to be seen as the product of poor domestic policy choices and weak regulatory and supervisory practices in the crisis countries (Kirshner 2014b, 230; Helleiner 2014b, 95). These were broadly classed as features of a misguided "Asian model of development."

The Asian crisis narrative mirrored in key respects the official understanding of the Mexican crisis of 1994–1995 (Grabel 1999a; 1999b; 2002; Helleiner 2014b, 95). IMF crisis prevention efforts in the period after the Mexican crisis focused entirely on providing investors with accurate and timely information about the EMDEs. Indeed, the main message of the June 1995 Group of Seven (G-7) summit in Halifax was that accurate and timely information could dampen crisis tendencies. Summit participants urged the IMF to encourage prompt publication of economic and financial statistics and to identify countries that did not comply with the institution's new information standards. The standards eventually became the IMF's Special Data Dissemination Standard (SDDS), which was launched in April 1996 and became operational in September 1998.[5]

After the Asian crisis, the IMF continued to promote the SDDS and other measures to increase transparency and the availability of information to market actors (see Best 2006; Grabel 2003d; Mosley 2003). In 1999, the G-7 also created the FSF, an effort that was guided by the view that future crises could be avoided if a network of key financial regulators and actors shared information, engaged in dialogue, and coordinated actions (as we will discuss in chapter 4).

Neoliberalism and the Market-Perfecting Agenda

Given the dominant interpretation of the Asian crisis, it its unsurprising that in its aftermath the IMF and G-7 leaders, especially the United States, promoted reforms through a variety of forums that focused on regulatory and institutional harmonization around Anglo-American norms. Initiatives comprised greater dissemination of information and increased transparency; increased but light touch monitoring and surveillance; the adoption of universal, market-friendly standards and codes; arm's-length corporate governance; political independence of the technocrats that regulate financial markets; and an enhanced role for market liberalization, discipline, and private actors (such as credit rating agencies) in economic and financial governance.[6] Transparency became the "new golden rule" (Kahler 2000; Best 2005, chaps. 6 and 7). Greenspan argued that the benefits of measures that promoted transparency, discipline, and competition would naturally take hold in Asia as crony capitalism in the region receded (Cumings 1999). He was adamant about the broader implications of the Asian crisis for the victory of neoliberal capitalism. In triumphalist testimony before the Foreign Relations Committee of the U.S. Senate that was intended to overcome congressional resistance to increasing support to the IMF during the Asian crisis, Greenspan argued:

> We saw the breakdown of the Berlin wall in 1989 . . . and the massive shift . . . towards free market capitalist . . . structures. Concurrent to that was the . . . very strong growth in what appeared to be a competing capitalist-type system in Asia. And as a consequence of that, you had developments of types of structures which I believe at the end of the day were faulty, but you could not demonstrate that so long as growth was going at 10 percent a year. [But in the last decade or so, and particularly because of the Asian crisis, there has emerged] a consensus towards the . . . Western form of free-market capitalism as the model which should govern how each individual country should run its economy. (Quoted in Sanger 1998, D1)

While Greenspan was correct in attributing tremendous significance to the Asian crisis, he failed to note the coercion that facilitated the move to a more neoliberal form of capitalism in the crisis countries. The IMF's stand-by arrangements (SBAs) with countries in crisis conditioned assistance on stringent austerity policies; market liberalization and privatization; economic openness that provided foreign investors with access to formerly protected areas, such as banking; and a strengthened commitment to export-led growth.[7] The Asian crisis thus amplified pressures toward neoliberal conformance in the crisis countries through a variety of policy and ideational mechanisms, even in countries whose own development experiences shared little with this model.[8]

The "market-perfecting" reform agenda quickly drowned out concerns in Asia and beyond about premature, ill-advised financial liberalization and deficiencies in the global financial architecture. Instead, the new dominant discourse focused on opening markets and speeding the reform of policies and institutions so that they were consistent with Anglo-American norms (Chang 2000; Chang, Park, and Yoo 1998; Noble and Ravenhill 2000). A handful of countries, most notably China, were able to resist pressures for neoliberal conformance. Nevertheless, reform in the post–Asian crisis environment in both AEs and in most EMDEs cohered in the direction of enhancing neoliberal, market-led, private financial governance.[9]

The IMF in the Aftermath of the Asian Crisis

Paradoxically, despite its success in pushing a neoliberal agenda, the IMF emerged from the Asian crisis a greatly weakened institution. In the years that followed, the IMF faced a crisis of credibility and suffered from a decline in its financial resources, the size of its staff, and the geographic reach of its programs. Following the Asian crisis, academics and activists from across the intellectual spectrum called attention to the institution's domination by the U.S. government and private financial interests; its mission creep into areas that were historically the province of domestic policymakers; its ideological capture by market fundamentalists; its myriad failures in East Asia prior to and following the crisis; and its politically intrusive, overly expansive, and excessively harsh "one-size-fits-all" procyclical conditionality programs.[10] Conservative foreign policy analysts also denounced the IMF's handling of the Asian crisis. Former U.S. secretary of state Henry Kissinger (invoking a quip by the chief economist of Deutsche Bank in Tokyo) likened the IMF to "a doctor specializing in measles [who] tries to cure every illness with one remedy" (Kissinger 1998). Criticisms of the Fund's performance came even from its sister institution, the World Bank (Sanger 1999; Noble and Ravenhill 2000), and from inside the U.S. Treasury (Kristof and WuDunn 1999).

Many observers criticized the role of U.S. business and especially financial interests in driving the terms of the SBAs in crisis countries, especially in South Korea and Indonesia.[11] Concern about the role of private interests was driven home by the jubilance of then deputy U.S. Treasury secretary Lawrence Summers, who at a conference said that "the IMF has done more to promote America's trade and investment agenda in East Asia than 30 years of bilateral trade negotiations" (quoted in Hale 1998). In the same vein, former U.S. trade representative Mickey Kantor said, "Troubles of the tiger economies offered a golden opportunity for the West to reassert its commercial interests. When countries seek help from the IMF, Europe and America should use the IMF as a battering ram to gain advantage" (quoted in Weisbrot 2015, 132). The then managing director of the IMF, Michel Camdessus, referred to the Asian crisis as a "blessing in disguise" (ibid., 134). The United States and the IMF had been pushing to open financial markets in East Asia (and other countries) prior to the crisis (Kirshner 2014b), but the crisis provided precisely the leverage that earlier efforts lacked.

The U.S. government distanced itself from the IMF after the Asian crisis despite Greenspan's reading of the event and its tacit benefits to the domestic business community. U.S. criticism intensified after a congressionally appointed commission chaired by Alan Meltzer, a prominent conservative academic economist, issued a sharp indictment of the Fund's performance (International Financial Institution Advisory Commission 2000). The so-called Meltzer Commission, formally named the International Financial Institution Advisory Commission, indicted the IMF on many of the same grounds as other critics had done.

Downsizing the Institution and Its Geography of Influence

The IMF was hobbled by the events in Asia. The institution lost its sense of purpose and standing. Most observers came to view the IMF as increasingly irrelevant. Barry Eichengreen described the IMF in 2005 as a "rudderless ship adrift on a sea of liquidity" (quoted in Nelson 2014a, 156). A year later, Mervyn King (then governor of the Bank of England) had this to say: "Certainly, the Fund's remit is unclear. Its lending activities have waned, and its role in the international monetary system is obscure" (King 2006, 3). But King went on to explain that this was not a cause for worry since there was little need for the institution anymore: "From time to time, there may well be financial crises when it would be appropriate for the international community to provide temporary financial assistance. . . . But [it] has not been the role for the IMF vis-a-vis any developed economy for many years.

Moreover, nor is it likely to be true of many important emerging market economies in the future" (ibid., 10).

In contrast, Dominque Strauss-Kahn, then managing director of the IMF, worried about the IMF's loss of purpose in 2007: "What might be at stake today is the very existence of the IMF as the major institution providing financial stability to the world" (quoted in Weisman 2007, C1).

The scope of the IMF's loan portfolio contracted dramatically after the loans associated with the Asian crisis were repaid. Those EMDEs that could afford to do so deliberately turned away from the institution. The IMF's decline was reflected in many ways. Prior to the global crisis, demand for the IMF's resources was at a historic low. Major borrowers, including Argentina, Brazil, Ukraine, and Indonesia, had repaid their outstanding debts to the institution (Kapur and Webb 2007).[12] In fiscal year 2005, just six countries had SBAs with the Fund, the lowest number since 1975 (ibid.). From 2003 to 2007, the Fund's loan portfolio shrank dramatically: from US$105 billion to less than US$10 billion, with just two countries, Turkey and Pakistan, accounting for most of that debt (Weisbrot, Cordero, and Sandoval 2009). Indeed, with few exceptions, the Fund's portfolio after the Asian crisis primarily comprised loans to extremely poor countries that had no choice but to seek its assistance since they were not able to self-insure against crises through reserve accumulation (Chorev and Babb 2009). These trends radically curtailed the IMF's geography of influence.

The curtailment of the IMF's loan portfolio was also reflected in the institution's bottom line. By 2007, interest payments on outstanding loans to the IMF had nearly disappeared, and in the face of declining resources its executive board announced plans to trim staff by 15%, cut the administrative budget by US$100 million, and sell some gold holdings (IEO 2014, Annex 1; Kapur and Webb 2007; Nelson 2014a). The downsizing, which began in April 2008, constituted the largest reduction in staff in the institution's sixty-five-year history (IEO 2014, Annexes 1 and 2; Rozenberg 2007). But, as we will see, the downsizing at the IMF proved to be short lived.[13]

Institutional Reinvention
The IMF's role has evolved substantially over time.[14] Its original mission was to provide offsetting financing to states confronting exchange rate shocks under the Bretton Woods system of pegged exchange rates. The IMF adjusted its mission when that system collapsed in the early 1970s. The debt crises of the 1980s provided the IMF with new purpose, especially in Latin America. A reinvigorated IMF participated in sovereign debt negotiations and worked with private creditors, conducted surveillance over member

country policies, and enforced structural adjustment programs (SAPs) in indebted client economies. Later, the IMF served as a reputational intermediary in the post-Soviet states following their transitions to capitalism (Broome 2010), joining the World Bank in what Rodrik terms the campaign to "stabilize, privatize, and liberalize" (Rodrik 2006a, 973).

The aftermath of the Asian crisis posed a more demanding challenge to the IMF's mission than had earlier crises. Fallout from the crisis left the IMF casting about as it sought to restore its legitimacy.[15] Its efficacy and privileged role in financial governance were threatened by the lack of a widely recognized purpose, broad customer base, and resources. The crisis also amplified long-standing concerns about governance and voice at the institution (Best 2007; Holroyd and Momani 2012; Seabrooke 2007). At the same time that the IMF faced strong backlash from the United States, many of its former clients had begun to walk on their own. The Asian crisis also deepened divisions between the IMF and World Bank on important matters, particularly the IMF's precrisis advocacy of capital flow liberalization and the conditions attached to the Asian SBAs (Kristof and WuDunn 1999). Indeed, World Bank staff joined other critics in identifying the IMF's capture by private financial interests (Feldstein 1998; Noble and Ravenhill 2000; Wade and Veneroso 1998).

The Asian crisis induced the leadership of the IMF to appease critics more than it had in the past. Some concessions were more meaningful than others. In response to criticisms about IMF insularity and mismanagement of the Asian crisis, the IMF created an independent in-house unit charged with conducting analyses of its operations. This unit, the Independent Evaluation Office (IEO), was established in 2001. The IEO's second report, in 2003, echoed the by then widely advanced criticism that the IMF instrumentally used the SBAs in Korea and especially Indonesia to press some reforms that were orthogonal to crisis resolution but that served the interests of key stakeholders (IEO 2003; Crotty and Lee 2002; 2004).

In 2006, the IMF made a modest gesture to those demanding that EMDEs should be granted more voting power at the institution. Minor governance changes, known as the "Singapore reforms," gave China and South Korea slightly greater voting weight. Other IMF initiatives followed. New directives from the IMF leadership emphasized the reduction of poverty and inequality (Momani 2010), "country ownership" of Fund programs (Best 2007), and limits on the scope and content of conditionality (Momani 2005).[16] These policy directives largely failed to influence the institution's practices when it came to working with individual countries (see chapter 5),[17] but they nonetheless provided outside observers and even IMF staff with new standards, sanctified by the IMF itself, to hold the institution accountable.

Although few expected it at the time, the IMF's tepid steps during the early twenty-first century prepared the way for much deeper and more consistent changes in thinking and practice around capital controls during the global crisis. We return to this matter in chapter 5 and especially chapter 7 (see also Grabel 2011; 2015b; 2017).

Escaping the IMF: The Rise of National Self-Insurance

The IMF is often portrayed as having been the sole driver of the painful and politically unpopular reforms in East Asia following the region's crisis. Certainly it played a key role in advancing and enforcing the reforms. But that story is incomplete. Various domestic actors that had long felt themselves disadvantaged prior to the crisis instrumentally used the IMF to promote reforms that they previously had been unable to secure (Crotty and Lee 2002; 2004; 2005; Noble and Ravenhill 2000). Notwithstanding this point, the powerful role that the IMF played in advancing and enforcing neoliberal reforms during the crisis helps to explain the force with which EMDE policymakers sought to escape the institution after the crisis.

The race to escape the institution's orbit after the crisis complicated the IMF's search for a new mission. Policymakers in a number of Asian countries and in other successful EMDEs (particularly in Latin America) sought to insulate themselves from the hardships and humiliations suffered by Asian policymakers.[18] Policymakers achieved this insulation by relying on a diverse array of strategies. Countries that enjoyed strong trade performance and/or were attractive to foreign investors were able to self-insure against future crises through the overaccumulation of foreign exchange reserves. Some began to rely on trade finance, foreign direct investment (FDI), lending, and official development assistance (ODA) from fast-growing EMDEs, such as China and Brazil (Ghosh, Ostry, and Tsangarides 2012; Kapur and Webb 2007). In addition, some countries established bilateral swap arrangements among central banks (ibid.). We might think of these protective strategies collectively as promoting resilience and even antifragility, or the ability to learn from periods of instability and to adjust in ways that dampen the severity of future crises (see Taleb 2012).

The dramatic decline in the IMF's loan portfolio after the Asian crisis indicates the degree to which escapist strategies proved successful. During the global crisis, EMDEs did their best to avoid IMF oversight. Indeed, Korea would have been a good candidate for the (precautionary) Flexible Credit

Line (FCL) that the IMF introduced during the global crisis. But it did not apply for assistance, presumably because of its prior experience and to avoid the stigma of being one of the IMF's clients (Wade 2010, fn10). Instead, the Bank of Korea negotiated a reserve swap of US$30 billion with the Federal Reserve in October 2008 and a swap with the PBOC for US$29 billion in December of that year (Jiang 2014).[19]

The experience of the Asian crisis and IMF intervention had powerful behavioral effects that extended well beyond the region. Not just China, whose reserves have attracted much attention, but also Brazil, Turkey, South Korea, Argentina, South Africa, Russia, and other rapidly growing EMDEs were able to amass massive foreign exchange reserves in the years after the Asian crisis. The strategy is often referred to as the "precautionary" or "self-insurance" motivation for reserve accumulation. Large reserve holdings reduce the likelihood that speculators will identify the national currency as vulnerable to depreciation. Reserves give policymakers the means to protect the national currency if a speculative attack is nevertheless initiated, thereby reducing the probability that it will be necessary to turn to the IMF during economic turmoil. As we will see, the protective effects of reserve accumulation strategies were validated in the global crisis.

Foreign exchange reserve overaccumulation is also intended to facilitate and protect export-led growth strategies, which continued to be important to many EMDEs after the Asian crisis. Reserve holdings facilitate market intervention (e.g., "sterilization") that is necessary to maintain an undervalued exchange rate.

How extensive were the increases in foreign exchange reserves in the period after the Asian crisis? EMDEs (with reserves of just over US$7 trillion in 2015) accounted for 68% of the increase in global reserves between 2000 and 2015 (IMF 2017; author calculation) (see table 3.1).[20]

Reserve holdings relative to gross domestic product (GDP) have also increased dramatically over the last three decades. In the 1980s, reserves held by EMDEs were equal to about 5% of their GDP. This figure has doubled every decade since then, reaching about 25% of GDP by 2010 (Ghosh, Ostry, and Tsangarides 2012, 3). The ratio held steady through 2015, when EMDEs held reserves equal to about 24% of their GDP (IMF 2017; World Bank *World Economic Outlook*; author calculation). These trends are in stark contrast to developments in OECD (Organisation for Economic Co-operation and Development) countries, where reserves had grown to just US$3.4 trillion, or 8.1% of GDP, by the start of 2011 (Dadush and Stancil 2011). This figure barely changed through 2015, when AEs held reserves equal to about 9.5% of their GDP (IMF 2017; World Bank *World Economic*

Table 3.1

Official Foreign Exchange Reserves: Advanced versus Emerging Market and Developing Economies (US$ Billion)

	2000	2005	2008	2010	2015
AEs	1,331.3	2,177.8	2,606.9	3,420.6	4,252.5
EMDEs	733.9	2,256.1	4,854.2	6,274.7	7,066.6
World	2,070.3	4,439.4	7,466.9	9,701.1	11,323.7

Notes: AE=Advanced economies; EMDE=Emerging market and developing economies. AE and EMDE classifications from the IMF.
Source: COFER database (IMF 2017).

Outlook). Reserves are highly concentrated within EMDEs, however. In 2015, reserves held by China accounted for 47% of total EMDE reserves, while 15 EMDEs, including China, held 86% of total EMDE reserves (World Bank World Development Indicators; author calculation).

The overaccumulation of reserves in the post–Asian crisis context was facilitated by a variety of fortuitous circumstances: the boom in commodity prices during much of this period; the ability of some countries to maintain current account surpluses; the persistent appetite for imported energy, low-cost consumer goods, and capital goods in AEs (itself a consequence of many factors, such as deindustrialization, energy policy, income inequality, and wage stagnation); and the need to find an outlet for the vast pools of liquidity created during the long boom that preceded the global crisis. Though reserve accumulation enhances financial resilience and policy autonomy, it nevertheless entails opportunity costs since resources held in reserves might be more productively deployed; for example, to support public investment (Rodrik 2006b; Gallagher and Shrestha 2012).[21] But we must be careful to weigh the opportunity costs of holding large reserves against the beneficial effects of resilience and enhanced policy autonomy (Taleb 2012).

As with reserve holdings, the assets of EMDE sovereign wealth funds (SWFs) grew significantly in the period following the Asian crisis. As of December 2016, EMDE funds held 75% of global SWF assets—US$5.5 trillion of the US$7.4 trillion held globally in such funds (SWF Institute; author calculation).[22] SWF holdings are highly concentrated: as of December 2016, six EMDEs (namely, and in rank order, China, United Arab Emirates, Saudi Arabia, Kuwait, Qatar, and Russia) held 90% of the SWF assets held by all EMDEs. These six countries held 67% of global SWF assets. Though the explicit function of SWFs is not to promote financial stability or policy autonomy, a speculative attack against a country's currency is far less likely to occur when governments have signaled that reserves are so large as to justify cleaving off substantial resources to capitalize a fund.[23]

Large reserves played a key role in the ability of many EMDEs to navigate the global crisis relatively well. They also contributed to the increasing assertiveness of larger EMDEs vis-à-vis the BWIs prior to and especially during the crisis. EMDEs used excess reserves to expand their policy space. In some cases, reserves supported countercyclical fiscal programs, which were not within reach during previous crises (Grabel 2015b; Wise, Armijo, and Katada 2015; Ocampo et al. 2012). Reserve-rich countries were also able to experiment with capital controls and to deepen existing development banks and reserve pooling arrangements and create new ones.

The reserves accumulated by larger EMDEs not only allowed them to withstand the crisis but also created the conditions to reverse their historic dependence on the IMF. For the first time in history, EMDEs provided financial support to the Fund (see chapter 5). The ability of EMDEs to pursue strategies that were previously unattainable shrank the IMF's reach. Equally important, the behavior of those states that have achieved autonomy from the IMF and their economic success have served as examples for weaker states with less autonomy, some of which, in turn, reacted to the crisis in ways that would have been unimaginable in the recent past.

The Asian Monetary Fund and the Seeds of Architectural Innovations

The Asian crisis also turned attention to the creation of a new institution that could serve as a counterweight to the IMF. Interest in an Asian alternative to the IMF emerged in the summer of 1997, as the crisis was unfolding. Japan's Ministry of Finance proposed that an AMF provide emergency financial support quickly—absent IMF conditions—to countries in the region that were ensnared by the crisis.[24] Though the proposal was never fully articulated, it was to be capitalized with an initial US$50 billion contribution by Japan and another US$50 billion from other Asian nations.

The AMF proposal grew out of frustration in Japan and elsewhere in the region with economically harsh and politically intrusive IMF conditionality in the crisis countries.[25] The proposal also reflected concern over the limited voice of Asia at the IMF, dominated as it was by U.S. interests and priorities. The AMF proposal was eventually scuttled by tensions between Japan and China. The tensions were adroitly exploited by the IMF and especially by the U.S. government, both of which strongly opposed the AMF. Eisuke Sakakibara, Japan's vice minister of finance for international affairs during the Asian crisis, claims that "Larry Summers was furious" when the initiative was first proposed by Japan at the annual meeting of the IMF and World Bank in 1997 (quoted in Holroyd and Momani 2012, 206). The Chinese government was not unhappy with U.S. opposition to the AMF; in fact, Chinese leaders supported U.S. efforts to shelve it (Cumings 1999). Chinese and U.S. officials were concerned that the AMF would entail an increased role for the yen and, more broadly, for Japan in the region's complex power politics (Cohen 2012, 52).

We will revisit the failed AMF initiative in chapter 6. As we will see, the spirit of this initiative reemerged in an initiative of the ASEAN+3 countries and has been given new force by the global crisis. We will also see that new reserve pooling arrangements in EMDEs share a common ancestry in the Asian crisis experience.

Summing Up and Looking Ahead

The Asian crisis had paradoxical effects on the global neoliberal regime. On the one hand, it solidified neoliberalism through the leverage granted to external and domestic actors who had been unable to secure liberal reform prior to the crisis. Although the crisis halted efforts to make capital liberalization a central purpose of the IMF, the institution was nevertheless able to use SBAs to open the financial markets of client economies. But the Asian crisis also inaugurated a gradual, uneven rethinking of capital liberalization. In addition, the crisis had paradoxical effects on the IMF. It gave the institution a vast new client base, the economies of which were opened and liberalized in ways that were impossible prior to the crisis. But the crisis was ultimately costly to the IMF insofar as its crisis response led EMDEs to implement strategies to escape its orbit. The combination of a curtailed geography and widespread condemnation of institutional performance undermined the IMF's standing and the material resources at its disposal. Although the AMF vision catalyzed by the crisis failed to materialize, it had powerful effects in the region and across EMDEs more broadly. As we will see, the Asian crisis marked the beginning of a shift away from neoclassical "optimal" or "efficient" policy, regulation, and institutions. We find in the post–Asian crisis context an increased appreciation in EMDEs of policy and institutional innovation, experimentation, and strategies that promote redundancy, robustness, and learning by doing and learning from others.

In chapter 4, we consider the evolving role of two informal networks—namely, the G-20 and the FSB. Both have their roots in the Asian crisis, and both continued to evolve during the global crisis. The G-20 and FSB have the potential to create greater inclusion in global financial governance and provide the space for like-minded EMDE policymakers and technocrats to learn from one another, build coalitions that can be mobilized in other forums, such as the IMF, and leverage their voices—provided they choose to do so.

III The Global Crisis and Innovations in Financial Governance and Developmental Finance

4 Planting Seeds, Bearing Fruit? The Group of 20 and the Financial Stability Board

One might be forgiven if the mind runs immediately to the IMF when thinking about global financial governance in the postwar era. The IMF is now and has been for many decades the preeminent and arguably the most powerful institution in the global financial system. It would therefore not be unreasonable to begin and end an examination of global financial governance with the Fund, despite its diminished (and transformed) geography of influence since the Asian crisis. But we would be remiss were we to overlook the emergence of new transnational financial governance networks during the Asian crisis and the expansion of their membership and scope during the global crisis. These networks are part of an increasingly heterogeneous architecture of global financial governance, or what Slaughter (2004) more generally describes as an increasingly "disaggregated world order." Though the BWIs (especially the IMF) and the U.S. Federal Reserve unquestionably remain the central players, we should recognize newer networks as part of an evolving, fragmenting financial governance landscape.

Finance Networks

An important feature of global governance over the last two decades entails the creation of informal groups that constitute ad hoc "clubs of common interest" or "networks of networks."[1] These informal groups, consisting of what Pauly terms loose "networked governance," contrast with traditional, formal intergovernmental organizations and binding treaty-based arrangements of nearly universal membership established after World War II, such as the BWIs (Pauly 2010, 17–18). Networks seek to facilitate informal cooperation among policymakers. Implementation of agreements, recommendations, or guidelines that derive from these groups is typically left to the discretion of national authorities.[2] Networks among finance officials emerged at the multilateral level partly in response to the challenges of governing increasingly complex financial systems, and to the IMF's failure to identify ex ante risks and the limitations of its crisis management.

The most important finance networks began their lives as clubs for representatives of AEs.[3] But they have increasingly come to include EMDE representatives. This is true of many networks, including the two most important finance networks—namely, the G-20 and the FSB, which are the subjects of this chapter. There are also an increasing number of finance networks among EMDE officials (on these networks, see Woods and Martinez-Diaz 2009).

Neither the G-20 nor the FSB even remotely approach the IMF in terms of influence, not least because of their informality, lack of authority, and restricted membership. The global crisis provided an opportunity to test the efficacy of these two networks, and they both failed to live up to the expectations of their architects.

Critics are correct to emphasize their deeply disappointing performance. To date, despite somewhat broader membership, they have proven unimaginative, timid, and weak.[4] They did not advance innovative ideas precisely when they were needed most, and even today they remain largely on the sidelines (despite the headlines generated by the G-20 at critical points) and lack the degree of inclusiveness that would be necessary to facilitate coordination among financial officials. They also lack institutionalized means to bring about reform or compliance with recommendations, and they face difficulty reaching consensus on matters of central importance. Finally, the structure of these networks lends itself to capture by powerful member states and financial interests within them.

Nonetheless, the networks should not be dismissed entirely. There are already signs that these bodies might emerge over time as forums in which EMDE policymakers are able to promote serious dialogue, build relationships and coalitions, and refine their capacities to maneuver on the international stage (as per Woods and Martinez-Diaz 2009). From a Hirschmanian perspective, the networks can be understood as experimental forms of governance that cultivate new capacities. Critics overreach, then, when they dismiss these bodies as impotent and permanently irrelevant. Their principal features, such as their informality and lack of authority, certainly limit their immediate impact. But those same features might allow for a greater degree of flexibility and maneuverability over time than is available within the formal institutions of financial governance. In part for these reasons, their importance might require decades rather than years to realize.

By now, many observers have documented the disappointing performance of the G-20 and FSB. For this reason, we need not examine the
failures in depth here but instead will simply quickly survey the critics'
findings. It is altogether more difficult to speculate as to the broader potential of these networks, at present or in the future, but failing to do so would
be to commit the common intellectual error of premature foreclosure on
the promise of fledgling, imperfect innovations.

The G-20: A Brief History

Several years into the East Asian crisis, G-7 leaders created the "Finance
Group of 20" (hereafter the Finance G-20).[5] The Finance G-20 began meeting regularly in 1999; it was a technocratic body that brought together the
finance ministers and central bank governors of the G-7 nations (Canada,
France, Germany, Italy, Japan, the United States, and the United Kingdom)
and their counterparts from Argentina, Australia, Brazil, China, India, Indonesia, Mexico, Russia, Saudi Arabia, South Africa, South Korea, Turkey, and
the EU.[6] The Finance G-20 was envisioned as an informal forum to promote discussion of and cooperation on economic and financial policies, as
well as oversight and "agenda setting" on matters of central importance to
policymakers.

The Finance G-20 was formed out of recognition that the IMF and the
G-7 had overlooked the potential of large EMDEs to function as independent sources of systemic financial fragility in the years leading up to the
Asian crisis. Key finance officials from what were deemed "systemically
significant" EMDEs were brought together with their G-7 counterparts to
address a blind spot in G-7 and IMF oversight. The creation of the Finance
G-20 was also driven by recognition that a body was needed to oversee,
maintain a comprehensive view of, and informally coordinate the increasingly complex and densely populated international financial regulatory
architecture. This architecture was, by then, composed of a growing group
of institutions, committees, and organizations, such as the Bank for International Settlements (BIS), the Basel Committee on Banking Regulations
and Supervisory Practices, and the International Organization of Security Commissions. Despite the expansion of its membership, the Finance
G-20 continued to reflect the influence of dominant countries within
the G-7.

The early moments of the global crisis provided impetus for further evolution of the Finance G-20. On October 22, 2008, U.S. president George W.
Bush called a meeting of heads of G-20 member states. The goal of the

meeting was to create a plan to stabilize the financial system and contain the crisis. Viola (2014, 117) describes the G-20 Leaders' Summit (as the meeting was termed) as "a permanent and significant institutional adaptation to the financial crisis, as it shifted decision-making and policy co-ordination efforts to the highest levels of leadership." The institutionalization of the Leaders' G-20 (hereafter G-20) was reinforced at the group's 2009 meeting in Pittsburgh, Pennsylvania, in the United States, when member states declared it the "premier forum" for global economic discussions and cooperation, thereby largely displacing the Leaders' G-7/G-8 (G-20 2009b, 3). With this announcement, the group promoted itself from the world economy's "crisis committee" to its "steering committee" (Vestergaard and Wade 2012b, 481).

Notwithstanding the group's ambitions, its authority and achievements remain largely aspirational (Vestergaard and Wade 2011; 2012b). It has no enforcement capacity, and its decisions are not legally binding. The informality of the group is reflected in the absence of a charter and permanent staff.[7]

A Bold, Inclusive Model of Governance?

Early in the global crisis, some observers praised the G-20 for its quick and decisive action (Guerrieri and Lombardi 2010; Heinbecker 2011; Smith 2011).[8] G-20 members themselves celebrated their role in saving the world from another Great Depression through timely and bold coordination of macroeconomic stimulus programs that galvanized US\$1.1 trillion in support for the world economy. At the same time, several observers emphasized the inclusiveness of the G-20 and viewed it as a powerful, leading new player in global financial governance (see Carin et al. 2010; Rana 2013; Smith 2011). For G-20 optimists, the group's meetings signaled the emergence of a new global financial architecture that was more pluralist and inclusive than its predecessor, which had been dominated by the traditional powers. G-20 meetings were understood to give leaders of countries such as Brazil, Argentina, China, India, Saudi Arabia, and South Africa a seat at the table, alongside the usual cast of AEs.[9]

Most observers, however, were disappointed (Payne 2010).[10] Initial expectations for the G-20 rightly gave way to frustration among those hoping for change in global financial governance. On this matter, for example, Ocampo (2011; 2010b; 2010c) argues that the G-20 still reflects an "elite multilateralism"; for Mittelman (2013), it is a form of "mini-multilateralism that 'summitizes' global problems by "G-shopping"; for Vestergaard and Wade (Vestergaard and Wade 2011; 2012b; Wade 2011), the group is unrepresentative; lacks legitimacy, transparency, and accountability; has failed to accomplish what it set out to do; and has even failed to accomplish what its spokespeople claim that it has achieved. Similarly, Rachman (2010) views the body as "divided, ineffective and illegitimate."[11] Soederberg (2010) advances what is perhaps the broadest criticism of the G-20. She argues that the body "naturalized" and "depoliticized" the global crisis by legitimating a narrow technical response while substantially overselling the capabilities of its management efforts and its representativeness.

Though the group claims to involve systemically significant EMDEs, it has never set out an explicit criterion for membership. Indeed, the composition of the group suggests that the criterion remains ad hoc (Vestergaard and Wade 2012a). It would be imprudent and naïve, then, to claim that replacement of the G-7/G-8 by the G-20 represents a significantly more inclusive mode of financial governance.

A Brief Keynesian Flirtation

Optimism regarding the G-20 Leaders' Summits was particularly high in its early days, when its chief spokespeople called for ambitious measures to counter the crisis and curb the power of the financial community. It appeared that the new G-20 leaders' meetings just might serve as incubators for bold thinking. For example, the positive response to the International Labour Organization's (ILO) Jobs Pact at the 2009 G-20 summit in Pittsburgh bolstered the perception that the G-20's pro-growth orientation differed starkly from that of the austerity- and competitiveness-minded G-7 (G-20 2009b). The sense of early promise around the G-20 was also fueled by the triumphalist declarations of its leaders in 2009 regarding the "death of the Washington Consensus," their commitment to forge cooperative solutions to the crisis, and their agreement to triple IMF lending resources and increase the voice and vote of EMDEs at the BWIs.[12]

The G-20's flirtation with Keynes was but a brief one, spanning roughly from the fall of 2008 through late 2009.[13] By June 2010, the G-20 had returned to positions associated with its predecessor. The communiqué from the June 2010 Toronto meeting marks the end of the G-20's Keynesian awakening.[14] The Keynesian moment gave way to a strict orthodox reading of events. The shift in perspective is apparent in the June 2010 G-20 communiqué, which called for an end to reflationary spending under the guise of a new, oxymoronic embrace of "growth-friendly fiscal consolidation" (Blyth 2013a, preface, 59–62).

The spirit of international cooperation and coordination that marked the initial Keynesian-inflected response to the crisis quickly fell away. The

G-20 was thereafter beset by conflict among members on a variety of fronts, including the global spillover effects of successive rounds of quantitative easing (QE) by the Federal Reserve. Other conflicts centered on the role of the IMF in overseeing capital controls, the imposition of taxes on financial transactions, and the possibility of including China's currency in the IMF's SDR (Prasad 2014).[15]

The G-20's weak, informal structure seems to have facilitated institutional capture. Powerful member states frustrated pursuit of financial reforms that could have increased the resilience of the financial system. For instance, the G-20 failed to deal effectively with the shadow banking system, commodity market speculation, sovereign debt restructuring, and bailout-strained national budgets through imposition of new taxes on the financial sector (among other matters).[16] The G-20 considered but ultimately rejected at its Seoul Summit in November 2010 a South Korean proposal that would have expanded, institutionalized, and multilateralized a central bank swap regime once the Federal Reserve's vast and critically important ad hoc bilateral swap agreements with many central banks expired in February 2010 (Helleiner 2014b, 45–52; Henning 2016, 129–130). The Korean proposal involved a central role for the IMF, in which the institution would determine eligibility and provide liquidity to qualifying central banks (Henning 2016). EMDEs strongly supported this proposal; AEs, especially the United States, opposed it. The proposal disappeared from the global reform agenda after the Seoul summit (Helleiner 2014b). In passing on the proposal, the G-20 foreclosed on a reform that might have provided a permanent, less U.S.-centric support structure for the global economy since Korea's swap proposal would not have staked responses to future crises on goodwill or bilateral, ad hoc decisions by individual central banks. But just a few years later, a new and restricted version of the proposal emerged. In late 2013, the central banks of the United States, Canada, England, Japan, and Switzerland and the European Central Bank (ECB) agreed to make their "temporary swap arrangements permanent standing facilities via bilateral arrangements with the 5 others, comprising a network of 30 agreements" (Henning 2016, 130).

The G-20 and Infrastructure—The New Key to Development

The G-20 has discussed infrastructure and infrastructure financing since the launch of what it termed its "development agenda" in 2010. The new emphasis continued to mark subsequent summits in 2012–2016. The body's interest in infrastructure is reflected in communiqués and several reports, such as the 2011 report of its "High Level Panel on Infrastructure

Investment" (HLP 2011). Beginning in 2012 and continuing through China's tenure as G-20 chair during 2016, the body emphasized the links between infrastructure (and the connectivity thereof), cooperation among multilateral lenders, and sustainable development (e.g., G-20 2016c). In 2012, the G-20 began to highlight the importance of private sources of infrastructure finance, such as SWFs, pension funds, and insurance companies.[17]

Returning to a Hirschmanian theme from chapter 2, inadequate infrastructure and related finance is seen as one of today's chief development obstacles. Overcoming constraints in this domain has come to be seen as a magic bullet for development.[18] Following a familiar pattern, the G-20's interest in infrastructure has not resulted in meaningful action, though with customary fanfare the body announced in 2014 a vague "Global Infrastructure Initiative" and a poorly funded "Global Infrastructure Hub" (G-20 2014).[19] The latter draws together information and data with the goal of developing a pipeline of quality "bankable" projects. The hub idea represents a return to themes that dominated the G-7 agenda after the Mexican and Asian crises. Emphasis is therefore on correcting information inadequacies while privileging private actors and private financial flows in the development process. In September 2016, the G-20 announced the "Global Infrastructure Connectivity Alliance," for which the World Bank will serve as secretariat (G-20 2016d). In all likelihood, G-20 infrastructure initiatives will lag behind the infrastructure initiatives and institutions that are being driven by EMDEs, particularly China (see chapter 6).[20]

Learning to Maneuver?

The record of G-20 accomplishments is then, in a word, sparse. But the G-20 has distinguished itself in one venture. It has emerged as an important advocate of the right of countries to utilize capital controls. The G-20 has gone beyond the IMF in advocating national autonomy in this domain. As we will see in chapter 7, in 2011 the G-20 issued an expansive statement on capital controls. It came about as a consequence of Brazil's successful maneuvering within the G-20 and the IMF and the insistence of its representatives that the G-20 affirm the right of nations to utilize controls of their own design (Gallagher 2014, chap. 6; Grabel 2015b). Given the conflict about this matter within the G-20, it is not surprising that its statement of support equivocates. The episode is nevertheless worth noting since it signals growing EMDE influence within the G-20 and might portend increased EMDE efficacy in the future. The G-20 is still fairly new, and those EMDE member states that are inclined to challenge business as usual are learning how to exercise influence in this disparate and fractious body.

During its time as G-20 chair, China was expected to revive dormant discussions of global financial governance and capital controls. Reform in these domains has long been a preoccupation of China's officials, and was most famously given life in the 2009 essay by PBOC governor Zhou (2009). But China largely punted on these matters; in the end, its leadership was not marked by significant reform initiatives (see chapter 7). This was partially a result of the political and economic turbulence of 2016. The year was marked by Britain's decision to withdraw from the EU ("Brexit"), political volatility and uncertain electoral outcomes in many member states, and financial volatility induced by capital outflows and economic slowdowns in EMDEs, including China. Under China's leadership, G-20 members agreed only to inform one another of all major changes in currency policy to avoid surprises that could destabilize global financial markets, while reaffirming an earlier commitment not to devalue currencies at the expense of other member states (G-20 2016a; 2016b; 2016c).[21]

It is not surprising that to date this informal and heterogeneous body has failed to be a force for meaningful change in global financial governance. The G-20 does not possess the power to enforce policy change, even if its members were to forge consensus on reform. EMDE member states themselves hold disparate views on central questions of financial governance. Some, such as Mexico and Colombia and now Brazil and Argentina, are quite closely aligned with the neoliberal perspective and financial interests that have traditionally predominated in the United States and Germany. The neoliberal voices within the G-20 may be amplified in the coming years if right-leaning political parties displace social democratic or left-leaning governments in member nations. On the other hand, the recent success of nationalist and deglobalizing movements in leading AEs might make G-20 deliberations much more fractious than they have been up until now.

The History of the Future Is Not Yet Written

It bears repeating that the G-20's timidity is just part of the story. Some analysts see it as part of a process of longer-term structural change in global governance that reflects an emergent diffusion of global economic power. Armijo and Katada (2015), for example, see the G-20 (Leaders' Summits) as a breakthrough in regard to more inclusive global financial governance since, for the first time, the meetings provide space for major EMDEs to participate in global economic discussions. Among G-20 enthusiasts, Woods et al. (2013) advance perhaps the most subtle, restrained, and ultimately useful view of the body. They are heartened by the emergence of the G-20 as what they term the "world's emergency committee" during the global crisis. They see EMDE participation in the G-20 and other informal governance bodies (particularly the FSB) as sowing "the seed of a process of change" in global governance that began after the Asian crisis (ibid., 4).

More broadly, Ngaire Woods and Leonardo Martinez-Diaz (2009) argue that the G-20 is just one among many new and evolving informal networks that involve EMDE policymakers. They acknowledge the possibility that the G-20 may turn out to be nothing more than a larger G-7. However, they emphasize the potential for change embodied in these new networks, which they term "networks of influence." In this view, the networks increase the opportunity for dialogue, capacity building, influence, and coalition building among like-minded EMDE leaders and technocrats.[22] As such, informal groups provide space and opportunities for EMDE policymakers to enjoy more power and influence in setting agendas over the medium and long terms. Over the last decade, EMDE representatives have used G-20 meetings to learn how to function in such forums, and have grown more confident and assertive in them. China, in particular, has demonstrated that it takes G-20 summits very seriously, and, for the last several years, the BRICS group (despite its own internal tensions) has been holding its own summits, at which members coordinate the positions they advocate at the G-20 (Woods and Martinez-Diaz 2009).

It would be a grave intellectual and political error to dismiss the G-20 so as to sustain the strongest version of the skeptical or, to invoke Hirschman again, the futilist case. That there are obstacles to EMDE influence at the G-20 is not in doubt. But along with Hirschman we should recognize those obstacles as potential drivers of innovation and learning. A fair-minded reading of the evidence and appreciation of the aperture inherent in new networks points us toward inconsistency, incoherence, and uncertainty rather than toward continued lockstep advocacy of global neoliberalism through the monopoly power over global financial governance long enjoyed by the United States and the IMF.

Financial Stability Board

The story of the FSB parallels that of the Finance G-20 and the Leaders' G-20. Unlike its better-known cousins, the FSB attracted little attention during the global crisis. Since there is no FSB Leaders' Summit, the body is rightly understood to have considerably less authority than the G-20. Far less hope has been vested in the FSB, and it has consequently generated less disappointment. Few, if any, observers see it as an independent vehicle for meaningful reform in financial governance.

The FSB is the successor to the FSF. The FSF was created in April 1999 following the release of a G-7-commissioned report prepared by German Bundesbank president Hans Tietmeyer (Tietmeyer 1999).[23] The Tietmeyer report called for the creation of a coordinating body that would bring together representatives of key institutions in the global financial system in what Drezner termed a "club of clubs" (Drezner 2007, 136). The FSF was charged with taking the pulse of the system by identifying and warning national and transnational authorities about emerging risks.

The FSF brought together a far larger set of players than did the Finance G-20, something that might explain the greater difficulty that the FSF (now FSB) has in responding to crises. The FSF brought "together . . . representatives of the most important standard setting bodies that had emerged . . . since the 1970s (Basel Committee on Banking Supervision, International Organization of Securities Commissions, Committee on Payment and Settlement Systems, International Association of Insurance Supervisors, International Accounting Standards Board, Committee on the Global Financial System), as well as representatives of more formal international organizations (BIS, IMF, World Bank, OECD). Moreover, the design of the FSF also included national representation from central banks, finance ministries, and regulatory and supervisory authorities from the G-7 countries" (Pagliari 2014, 144). Over time, the FSF added representatives from Australia, Hong Kong, the Netherlands, Singapore, and Switzerland.

The global crisis induced the G-20 to expand the membership, mission, mandate, and coordination functions of the FSF. Expansion was accomplished at the April 2009 G-20 summit in London. The broadened mandate was signaled by modification of the group's name from the FSF to the more authoritative FSB. The FSB's network was broadened by extending membership to all G-20 members, the European Commission (EC), and Spain.[24] At about the same time, EMDE representation in other financial bodies (such as the Basel Committee on Banking Supervision) was also expanded modestly (Helleiner 2014b, 137–138). Nevertheless, the FSB, like the G-20, remains strikingly noninclusive of EMDEs. Criteria for inclusion remain opaque, and decisions concerning invitations appear to be ad hoc. The FSB announced in 2014 that the five EMDEs that already had a seat on its governing council (namely, Argentina, Indonesia, Saudi Arabia, South Africa, and Turkey) would each be granted a second seat in the interest of increasing their voice (FSB 2014).

During the global crisis, the FSB's mandate was expanded to include the promotion of financial stability. Its institutional base and governance structure were strengthened, and unlike either the Finance G-20 or the Leaders' G-20, it was given a formal charter (G-20 2009a; Pagliari 2014). But the FSB lacks legal standing, has a small staff, and possesses no ability to enforce regulatory or policy change (such as through sanctions) or compliance among either its members or the far larger group of nonmember nations. It is restricted to soft law mechanisms such as peer review and monitoring (Helleiner 2014b; 2010b).

Despite its engineered weakness, U.S. Treasury secretary Timothy Geithner described the FSB at its founding in grandiose terms, calling it a "fourth pillar" in global economic governance alongside the IMF, World Bank, and WTO (U.S. Treasury 2009). On this he was proven wrong. The FSB's nonuniversal membership poses a challenge to its legitimacy, as does its uncertain relationship to these three institutions of global economic governance. Pauly draws an apt parallel between the weak FSB and the informality of the League of Nations in the days prior to the IMF (Pauly 2010, 149). Helleiner (2014b, 14–15) characterizes the FSB as "remarkably toothless" and simply "a reformed version of an ineffectual body that the G-7 had created a decade earlier" (see also Helleiner 2011a).

The FSB achieved little during the global crisis, and even less than the G-20. But, as with the G-20, it may be more reasonable to think of the FSB as part of a long-term process of network formation that brings EMDE policymakers into dialogue with one another and with their G-8 country counterparts. It remains to be seen whether this interaction ultimately enables coalition and capacity building among like-minded policymakers, as well as pressure for meaningful changes in financial regulation and governance. But it is inconceivable that the experience of EMDE participants at the FSB—the learning, networking, and increased capacity formation that their engagement promotes—will not carry over into other institutions. Even abject FSB failure, Hirschman reminds us, presents opportunities for learning that cannot be achieved in any other way.

Conclusion

The Mexican and the Asian financial crises catalyzed policymakers to create new types of informal networks that, it was hoped, would provide useful oversight and coordination across an increasingly complex global financial terrain. The new networks brought together financial policymakers and technocrats from an important subset of AEs and an ad hoc, small assortment of EMDE counterparts, along with representatives of key institutions and informal groups of financial actors. The global crisis galvanized a broadening and deepening of the informal architecture of global financial governance through an expansion of the membership and mandate of these networks.

The networks that were born of each crisis have precious little to show for themselves. They have failed to identify important financial risks before they culminated in a crisis; they have been unable to overcome internal conflicts among members, or capture by their most powerful member states and the financial lobbies within them; and they missed the opportunity to press for and implement regulation and oversight, financial taxes, or reforms that might reduce the likelihood or severity of future crises.

The skeptics claim nothing has changed, and they have substantial evidence to marshal in defense of this view. In this view, the G-20 amounts to an utter failure. It has remained peripheral on matters of macroeconomic adjustment and financial regulation and governance. The same can be said of the FSB, though from the start expectations for it were far less ambitious than for the G-20.

The disappointment is warranted. But it is better to take a more balanced, patient, and modest view of the G-20 and FSB. These networks are not independent drivers of change but rather exemplify the disconnected and piecemeal nature of evolution now under way in the world's financial governance architecture (cf. Helleiner 2016b on emergent cooperative decentralization).[25] Though their performance has underwhelmed, we should recognize their potential to become seedbeds in which new networks might emerge.

This view incorporates Hirschman's possibilism and recognition of the open-endedness of history. The optimistic view pushes back against the urge to rush to judgment. Inspired by Hirschman, we might consider these networks as experimental forms of governance, in which learning happens: learning *about* and learning *how*—about the nature and risks associated with financial flows and how to intervene effectively to manage financial flows within and across national borders. This experimentation should be understood in the broader context of the disparate innovations in financial governance and developmental finance explored throughout this book. These innovations will undoubtedly generate important side effects and linkages that take the form of enhanced capacity, the development of voice, and coalition building among heads of state and finance officials in EMDEs. Indeed, EMDEs have already begun to leverage their membership in the G-20 to secure greater influence at the BWIs over governance reform and over IMF adjudication of the appropriateness of capital controls (see chapters 5 and 7, respectively).

Next, we turn to the IMF. We will find confounding evidence of unevenness, ambiguity, and contestation within the IMF and in its relationships with other actors during the global crisis. Taken together, developments at the IMF substantiate the central positive thesis of the book—a combination of continuity, discontinuity, ambiguity, and inconsistency signal the fracturing of the global neoliberal regime despite the absence of a coherent institutional or ideational model to replace it.

5 IMF Stewardship of Global Finance

For over three decades, the IMF served as the chief institution for managing financial crises in EMDEs. In this domain, it had no competitors, leading a prominent student of the Fund to remark that it is "the most powerful international institution in history" (Stone 2002, 1). This was an apt description—certainly up to and through the Asian crisis, when the IMF exerted extraordinary influence over policy and institutional formation over a large swath of the globe.

But the Asian crisis marked a fundamental turning point for the IMF. For better or worse, the declining influence of the IMF after the Asian crisis was not associated with the rise of alternative institutions with sufficient resources, expertise, and legitimacy to respond to national, regional, or global financial crises. It is therefore unsurprising that the global crisis led to the resurgence of the IMF, restoring it to its leading position in crisis response—directing assistance to ailing economies, conducting surveillance, and disciplining clients.

Those arguing on the side of continuity in the global financial governance architecture marshal substantial additional evidence to support a univocal reading. They claim that the crisis has induced only trivial adjustments in IMF governance and practice. But continuity is only half of the story—and by no means the most interesting half. A more adequate reading concludes that the crisis has had complex, contradictory, and uneven effects on the institution. If we look carefully inside the Fund and at the external environment in which it operates, we can glean evidence of substantive discontinuities, inconsistencies, and, in deference to the best analyses of the matter, what I will refer to as ambiguities across various dimensions of the institution.[1]

Continuities at the IMF during the global crisis entail replenishment of its financial resources and reinvigoration of its central mission; stability in its formal governance practices, leadership selection, and overrepresentation of key member states; and continued reliance on politically intrusive austerity policies in client economies despite a fleeting embrace of counter-cyclical policy during the earliest days of the crisis.[2] Discontinuities entail substantial shrinkage in and transformation of the IMF's geography of influence; the nature of its partnership with European institutions; financial support to the institution from EMDEs, which extends opportunities for informal influence over IMF practices; the institution's practical and rhetorical support for capital controls; and the new architectural context within which the Fund is entering into new kinds of complementary and competitive institutional relationships. Key ambiguities entail inter alia a widening gap between IMF rhetoric and research on the one hand and its operations on the other. Ambiguity is most apparent in the scope of IMF conditionality; its attention to social spending targets and vulnerable groups during crises; and its practices regarding austerity, inequality, and fiscal consolidation. These assertions are summarized in table 5.1 and elaborated in what follows.

A Conceptual Note for Economists: Constructivist Accounts of Ambiguity, International Organizations, and Institutional Change

A word is in order, especially for an economics audience, on the matter of institutional practice and change. Within political science, constructivism refers to a broad school of thought that refuses to reduce institutional behavior to geopolitical or economic imperatives or to self-interest (see Abdelal, Blyth, and Parsons 2010). In the words of leading constructivists, "The central insight of constructivism is that collectively held ideas shape the social, economic, and political world in which we live" (ibid., 2). The constructivist approach examines existing and emerging tensions among stakeholders and the myriad fluid factors that bear on their influence over institutional practice. Constructivist accounts emphasize the centrality of shared ideas and norms not because these are seen to cancel economic and material power but because those imperatives are always mediated by the ideational framing that agents engage to make sense of the world. Critical questions for constructivists, then, are how the diversity of ideas and norms that permeate institutions and epistemic communities, and that are held by clients and other external actors, affect institutional practices; how, when, and why ideas and norms change; how actors within institutions and in epistemic communities demarcate standards of appropriateness and legitimize particular understandings of rights and obligations; and how changes in these domains ramify at the level of institutional and policymaker behavior.

Table 5.1
Continuities, Discontinuities, and Ambiguities at the IMF during the Global Crisis

Institutional Attributes	Continuity	Discontinuity	Ambiguity: New Rhetoric, New Research, Old Practice
IMF identity and influence	• Resurrection of its role in crisis management and restoration of its financial vitality	• New and constrained geography of influence • IMF in the Troika • Institutional complementarity or competition on the horizon?	
IMF governance	• Gridlock on formal governance reform, 2010–2015 • Resilience of the "gentleman's agreement" on leadership selection • Lack of independence from key member states	• New lenders, rising powers, new (informal) channels of influence	
IMF practice	• Austerity and politically intrusive policy adjustment in support packages • Restoration of traditional discomfort with countercyclical policy	• Support for capital controls, particularly on inflows but also on outflows	• Narrower scope of conditionality • Attention to social spending targets, the poor, and the vulnerable in support packages • Growing inconsistency on austerity, inequality, and fiscal consolidation

Source: Author's analysis.

As this discussion suggests, constructivist accounts often stress processes that are complex, slow, and incremental and that involve layering of new ideas and practices over old.[3]

Constructivism peers into the black box by examining the internal culture of international organizations with an eye toward illuminating the diverse influences on their identities and changes in practices over time. The concept of ambiguity emerges within this context and is deployed in diverse ways. Jacqueline Best (2005; 2012) advances a sophisticated set of arguments about the fuzziness of rules within (complex) international organizations. Rather than impeding institutional performance, ambiguity is theorized as functional and even necessary to institutional viability and success. Fuzziness promotes cooperation among actors with diverse and even conflicting understandings and interests. It facilitates institutional expansion and the exercise of staff discretion, rather than the paralysis and turmoil that would arise in an organization with unambiguous rules. Ambiguity also helps to explain the divergences that arise routinely between institutional mission statements and actual practice. In Best's account, ambiguity arises not as a deliberate organizational strategy (even though internal actors may prefer it) but rather as a consequence of unresolved conflicts among major principals.[4]

Alternative constructivist accounts of the BWIs emphasize "strategic ambiguity" (Van Gunten 2015) or "organized hypocrisy" (Weaver 2008).[5] Strategic ambiguity arises as a form of productive avoidance in the presence of conflict among and between societal norms, multiple political masters with heterogeneous preferences, divergent interests and norms of internal staff, and in the absence of professional consensus. Under these circumstances, the organization may purposely enact vague policy and permit ceremonial rather than literal conformity to adopted policy as ways of managing. Organizational hypocrisy is apt to deepen when the interests of critical stakeholders diverge dramatically and/or when there is a breakdown in the professional consensus among an organization's staff members and among outside professional experts. Such moments generate "escalating hypocrisy" (as per Kentikelenis, Stubbs, and King 2016)—a dynamic layering process that can sustain the myth of organizational cohesion in the face of division, or organizational reform in the face of continuity. In their account, Kentikelenis, Stubbs, and King argue that, as the global crisis progressed, the IMF came to be marked by institutional schizophrenia. In this view, the Fund has come to cloak itself in multiple and increasing layers of rhetorical appeasement, becoming increasingly adept at using ceremonial reforms in order to mask the growing gap between its new rhetoric and the retention of its standard practices.

As the foregoing suggests, constructivism has little difficulty accounting for gaps between institutional rhetoric, research, and practice. Ambiguity speaks directly to this issue, of course, and serves as an important counterbalance to analyses that reduce inconsistencies in IMF practice to alleged dishonesty, callousness, failures of management oversight, or institutional self-promotion.[6] To be sure, these motivations figure into gaps between IMF policy and rhetoric. But this is just part of the story. The use of a blunt, reductionist approach to examine international organizations (as some analysts are wont to do) diverts attention from internal policy debates, tensions, pressures by diverse stakeholders, subtle changes, and contradictions, all of which can ultimately culminate in fundamental change even in the most hidebound institutions.[7]

Research on an organization's staff members (as opposed to its leadership) illustrates the ways in which space emerges between top-level decision making and ground-level application.[8] Recent analyses of the IMF, for instance, have demonstrated the degree to which staff economists shared a powerful worldview over the past several decades. The consensus around the virtues of market liberalization was sustained by recruitment and hiring practices that emphasized shared educational backgrounds, expertise, and normative commitments, socialization practices within the IMF, and a technocratic culture that yields professional authority to the IMF's economists. These factors contributed to a shared vision in which applied economics is seen to be driven by solid objective analysis. The technocratic presumption provided IMF economists considerable leeway to operate in ways that ultimately frustrated directives or contradicted rhetoric from the organization's leadership (Barnett and Finnemore 2004, 22–27). Momani (2010) explains what she sees as the IMF's "split institutional personality" in these terms—as the consequence of the institution's rigid organizational and technocratic culture and the narrow disciplinary and paradigmatic training of IMF staff economists. In this account, IMF staff economists possess neither the intellectual breadth nor the will to change their practices, even when the institution's leadership articulates new commitments that may even be embodied in policy directives.[9]

Institutional Change

Constructivism also has much explanatory power with respect to institutional change. The emphasis on the relative influence of shared ideas and norms helps to round out alternative materialist accounts that reduce institutional behavior and change to economic or other "objective" factors. Constructivist accounts combine the subjective and objective domains. Hence, exogenous shocks like economic crises may induce—though not dictate the content of—ideational transformations, which in turn bear on institutional behavior (see Blyth 2002). Crises may permit the flourishing of previously latent or subordinate ideas and norms, alter the balance of power within an organization among advocates of contending ideas, or create the ideological space for the generation of new ideas altogether.[10] Ambiguity facilitates normative adjustment when the stakes are high for internal actors. But since in the constructivist view ideational change is underdetermined by objective factors, change is theorized as messy, contingent, and contested, reversals are likely and perhaps even inevitable, and there is no stable ideational equilibrium.[11]

In recent work, Best (2014; 2016) has explored postcrisis transformations at the IMF. She finds that the overconfidence of staff members during the neoliberal era has been shaken by the series of financial crises, and especially by the global crisis. Today, IMF staff members operate with an appreciation of the risk of failure. This is to the good, since hubris combined with authority can be dangerous (DeMartino 2011; 2013a). In Best's view, there has been a pronounced shift at the IMF and other international organizations toward tentative policy advising, experimentation, and new metrics for assessing success and failure. But the pursuit of fail-safe policy entails a paradox, especially to the degree that decisionmakers seek to insulate themselves from the consequences of failure. As Best (2016, 6) puts it, "Ironically, this move towards more cautious policy responses may actually produce more failures in the longer-term: a development program that is limited to those initiatives whose outcomes can be quantified will avoid tackling many crucial challenges; and a system of financial regulation that continues to act as though systemic uncertainties are reducible to micro-level risks will be more [failure] prone."

We now turn to the primary focus of this chapter, which is to chart the degree to which the IMF evolved during and since the global crisis. As will be apparent in what follows, constructivist (and other) insights inform the analysis and sustain the major conclusions, which are read through a Hirschmanian lens.

IMF Identity and Influence

As with G-20 leaders, officials at the BWIs recognized the need and opportunity for fundamental reinvention in the early days of the crisis. As World Bank president Robert Zoellick put it in 2009: "The old order is gone. . . . Today we must build anew" (Zoellick 2009, 19). IMF managing director Dominique Strauss-Kahn echoed that, calling "2010 . . . a year of transformation" (Strauss-Kahn 2010a). But reality was far more complicated than the claim of wholesale reinvention suggests.[12]

Continuity
The global crisis has been good to the IMF. It rescued the institution from the irrelevance that followed the Asian crisis. The demands of the crisis reversed the short-lived downsizing of the institution during spring 2008

and spring 2009. More than one hundred economists were hired by the end of April 2009, and the IMF's workforce rose in size by about 20% between the end of fiscal year 2009 and 2012 (IEO 2014, 42).

The Crisis and the Resurrection of the IMF
The IMF's loan portfolio had shrunk dramatically by the time Strauss-Kahn was appointed managing director in November 2007. Total outstanding loans were then US$17 billion, compared with US$110 billion four years earlier (Weisbrot 2015, 156). By the time Strauss-Kahn resigned in May 2011, out-standing loans had risen to US$125 billion, and agreed-upon loans were at least two times greater (ibid.). Nonconcessional lending by the IMF was almost nil before the crisis; it stood at US$400 billion in 2008–2013 (IEO 2014, 2). The institution approved 17 SBAs for more than SDR50 billion in the first year of the crisis, and an additional 20 SBAs for SDR50 billion between September 2009 and the end of 2013 (ibid., 26).

Relative to borrowers' quotas, the size of loans during the global crisis was the largest in the institution's history (Nelson 2014a, 161). The aver-age size of the 84 loans that the IMF extended between 2002 and 2007 was 94.6% of country quotas; the 92 loans extended after 2008 and through 2012 averaged 398.3% of quota (ibid.). The largest of the IMF's programs after 2008 ranged from 10% to 16% of the recipient country's GDP (Rein-hart and Trebesch 2016, 12). By contrast, the median IMF program dur-ing the EMDE debt crises of the 1980s reached just 4% of GDP (ibid.). The Mexican and Indonesian loan programs of 1995 and 1997, respectively, made headlines at the time because the loans were almost six to seven times their quota, but they amounted to just over 5% of GDP (ibid., 11, table 1).

The maximum amount of cumulative access for IMF members was raised from 300% to 600% of quota in March 2009 (Boughton 2012, 752). The IMF also provided what it terms "exceptional access" to borrowers whose needs exceeded the official limit. It had done so in the past for "systematically impor-tant" countries, such as Mexico, Brazil, Argentina, Turkey, Indonesia, and Korea (Nelson 2014a, 161). From March 2009 to 2011, over half of approved arrange-ments exceeded 300% of quota (Edwards and Hsieh 2011, 80). Between 2008 and 2012, there were six IMF programs above 1000% of member quota (Rein-hart and Trebesch 2016, table 1). Greece's 2010 loan amounted to 3212% of its quota (and its 2012 loan, 2159%), Ireland's 2010 loan was 2322% of quota, and Portugal's 2011 loan was 2306% of quota (ibid.).

The IMF's reempowerment was driven by several factors. It enjoyed monopoly status by virtue of its expertise in responding to financial distress. As Nelson (2014a, 156) observes, "Aside from perhaps one state (the USA) and one supranational organization (the EU), there is no other governmental or intergovernmental player that can match the IMF in terms of command of material resources," let alone social power and experience in crisis response. Events on the periphery of Europe also had a significant impact on the IMF. European officials perceived a need for the IMF's expertise, financial resources, and authority. The IMF responded by inserting itself into the European rescues, and even in countries like Ukraine that are far from the heart of Europe (Lütz and Kranke 2014).

The IMF's resurrection was facilitated at critical moments by key member states. In November 2008, the G-20 announced the need to ensure the adequacy of the IMF's resources (and those of other multilateral financial institutions) and its readiness to increase them as necessary (Lesage et al. 2013). Though the matter received little attention, the Japanese government's decision to lend US$100 billion to the IMF in November 2008 came at an important moment, helping to catalyze financial support from the United States, EU, China, and others (Grimes 2009c; Holroyd and Momani 2012; Jiang 2014, 173).

Prior to the April 2009 G-20 Leaders' Summit in London, U.S. Treasury secretary Timothy Geithner primed the pump for IMF recapitalization by calling for a tripling of its lending capacity and for rapid progress on long-promised governance reforms (Beattie 2009). G-20 leaders responded by reconfirming IMF leadership in crisis response efforts. The significance of the G-20's decision was not lost on Strauss-Kahn, who, at the end of the meeting, said that, "Today is the proof that the IMF is back" (Landler and Sanger 2009). The decisions not only restored the IMF's mandate but also yielded massive new funding commitments (though a portion of what was announced as *new* funding turned out not to be) (Woods 2010; Helleiner 2014b, 51). G-20 leaders committed US$1.1 trillion to combat the crisis, with the bulk of the funds, US$750 billion, to be delivered through the IMF. The commitment permitted the tripling of the IMF's lending capacity called for by Geithner. It boosted the institution's lending resources by US$500 billion through what are called the New Arrangements to Borrow (NAB) and a new general allocation of SDRs equivalent to US$250 billion (Lesage et al. 2013).[13]

The use of the NAB as a vehicle for increased support has consequences for the IMF, as I discuss later. The NAB provides the IMF with a temporary funding source to supplement the standard mechanism of quota subscriptions paid by member nations. The NAB provides support to the IMF through bilateral credit arrangements between the Fund and 38 countries and institutions, such as central banks. Loans under the NAB were to be reaffirmed every six months, and were intended to provide temporary support until the permanent increase in IMF resources called for in a 2010 reform agreement was put in place.

The G-20 gave the IMF a second tranche of new funds in June 2012 as the Eurozone crisis expanded. At the G-20 Leaders' Summit in Los Cabos, it was announced that the IMF would receive a new infusion of US$456 billion, to come from 37 EMDEs and AEs, though the United States would not be contributing. Geithner argued that the Eurozone's problems should be solved in-house. He articulated this view as early as mid-March 2012, when he said that the Treasury Department had "no intention to seek additional US resources for the IMF" (quoted in BWP 2012), a position that was important for the administration of President Barack Obama leading up to the 2012 election insofar as opponents were eager to target him as wasting taxpayer resources on Europe.

The global crisis reinvigorated not only the IMF but also other multilateral institutions, such as the World Bank and the Inter-American Development Bank (IADB).[14] The activism of these institutions was facilitated by the G-20's April 2009 decision to devolve a portion of the new financial commitments to the IMF to regional/multilateral institutions following a proposal by Indonesia (Chin 2010).

Did the United States Outgun the IMF?
Even while U.S. credibility was initially damaged by the crisis, its unilateral monetary power was reaffirmed early on as the Federal Reserve acted quickly to open currency swap lines with the central banks in countries of geostrategic importance. A currency swap is an agreement between two or more central banks that enables a central bank in one country to provide (via an exchange or swap) a certain amount of foreign currency liquidity to another central bank in the event of a sudden liquidity shortage. Swaps enhance financial stability by relieving pressures in short-term money markets. Swaps may also be used to stabilize a currency or maintain trade patterns with key trading partners.

During 2007 and 2008, the Fed opened vast, ad hoc, temporary swap arrangements with 14 central banks. The value of the swaps peaked at almost US$600 billion in November and December 2008; all of the swaps expired in February 2010 (Helleiner 2014b). In September and October 2008, the Fed extended swaps to major AE central banks, namely, the European

Central Bank (ECB), Bank of Japan, Swiss National Bank, and the Bank of England, and also to the central banks of Canada, Australia, Sweden, Denmark, Norway, and New Zealand. These were quickly followed by swaps with "diplomatically and economically" important EMDEs, namely, Mexico, Brazil, Singapore, and South Korea, each of which signed a US$30 billion agreement with the Fed. Mexico already had a standing swap agreement with the Fed, but the 2008 agreement extended the amount to which it had access. Notably, the global crisis occasioned the Fed's first swaps with EMDEs outside of Mexico. Swaps were "highly sought after and highly welcomed" since they were seen as an alternative to IMF support (Gallagher 2014, 75). Most of the central banks that had swap agreements with the Fed drew on them extensively. U.S. interests, including the exposure of U.S. banks to certain foreign markets, critically shaped decisions to extend swaps.[15]

Some IMF observers have concluded that the breadth and depth of U.S. bilateral swaps signaled to the BRICs and other EMDEs the necessity of committing new funds to the IMF as a means of offsetting U.S. influence. At the same time, however, the size and speed with which the United States opened swaps early on moderated the bargaining power that BRICs contributions to the IMF might otherwise have facilitated, and which the BRICs might have been able to parlay into IMF governance reform (Helleiner 2014b; James 2014; Lesage et al. 2013).

U.S. swaps raise the following question: does this exercise of monetary power imply that the IMF played a subordinate role during the global crisis? For some analysts, the answer to this question is largely "yes." Helleiner (2014b) argues that the Fed's swaps were the single most important type of stabilizing monetary cooperation during the global crisis, dwarfing the IMF's support. In his view, the swaps reflect and reinforce the vast unilateral monetary power of the United States (see also James 2014; Prasad 2014). A more nuanced response to the question suggests that IMF impact and agency cannot be so easily dismissed. While it would be wrongheaded to deny the continuity of U.S. monetary power, the IMF undertook critical stabilization efforts that U.S. officials could not have undertaken on their own. IMF assistance packages (especially relative to quotas and GDP) and the number of countries with Fund programs after 2009 enhanced the institution's influence during and following the crisis. The crisis also restored the IMF to its role in enforcing policy change in clients. It is best, then, to recognize the interdependence of U.S. and IMF power and influence during and since the crisis. The crisis response by the United States and other leading countries helped to restore the IMF to a central position in global financial governance.

It is important to note in this context that there were political limits on the willingness of the United States to serve as unilateral international lender of last resort and to increase its support to the IMF. The U.S. Treasury began to distance itself from Europe in late 2009. It also refused to join others in the G-20 in a second round of IMF funding in 2012. In this context, contributions to the IMF by the BRICS and other EMDEs became more important. These shifts help to explain why demands for IMF governance reform by the BRICS became more assertive in 2012—as was apparent in the war of words waged by BRICS representatives, particularly Brazil and India (Nogueira Batista 2012).[16]

The Fed was not alone in undertaking bilateral swaps. The global crisis induced the rise of ad hoc "swap diplomacy." Since 2008, more than 80 swap agreements have been signed, involving over 50 countries in every region of the world. At the start of 2015, swaps represented collectively US$1 trillion in lendable resources (McDowell 2017, 2, table 1). Swaps constituted a large, broad, ad hoc international liquidity network (ibid.). In April 2009, the Fed itself accepted swaps from the ECB, the Swiss National Bank, the Bank of England, and the Bank of Japan. The ECB also created small swaps with Poland, Denmark, Switzerland, Sweden, and Hungary. The PBOC and the Bank of Japan each expanded existing swaps to South Korea. The PBOC ultimately established swaps with more than 20 countries. The Danish and the Swedish central banks extended a small swap to Latvia in December 2008 as a bridge to its IMF loan. And the central banks of Denmark, Sweden, and Norway each extended small swaps to Iceland in May 2008 before the country received an IMF loan (Helleiner 2014b, 41–42, fn63; Henning 2016, 129).[17]

For advocates of continuity, the creation of an international swap network has had limited implications for the international monetary system (McDowell 2017). But this view employs a narrow metric for gauging significance. The cross-cutting swap network reflects the disorderly nature of the initiatives that emerged during the crisis. Central banks and the IMF scrambled to respond to a global crisis of uncertain proportions and borders. That central banks played a critical stabilizing role is undeniable. For now, it bears repeating that this melee provided the IMF with the means and opportunities to reestablish itself as a leading, if not the leading, institution of crisis management.

Discontinuities

The global crisis marked a sharp transformation in the IMF's geography of influence, with the institution no longer enjoying wall-to-wall influence across EMDEs. Most of the institution's clients during the global crisis—especially those that received its largest support packages—came from regions that it had rarely frequented in the past. The rise of relatively autonomous EMDEs, such as Brazil, China, South Korea, and India, has had dramatic impacts on the IMF's sphere of influence. Many EMDEs enjoyed the fiscal space to provide financial support to the IMF for the first time in its history. Equally important, their behavior served as an example for less powerful countries that were able to respond to the crisis in ways that would have been inconceivable during previous crises.

New Geography of Influence and the IMF in the Troika

The IMF has provided crucial assistance to EMDEs during the global crisis via SBAs and other programs. But Europe has been the IMF's chief preoccupation. The IMF has made loans to countries on the periphery of Europe, including Iceland, Ireland, Greece, Portugal, Cyprus, Central and Eastern European countries, and Ukraine. Iceland's 2008 SBA was the first for an AE in decades, and in 2010 Greece became the first country in the Eurozone to sign an SBA. Greece continues to be the most challenging of the IMF's new clients and its biggest failure (Mody 2016; Moschella 2016). IMF loans to Eurozone countries peaked in 2014 at US$92 billion (IMF 2016d). As of March 23, 2015, the IMF had arrangements with eight countries in Europe (including precautionary lines of credit, as with Poland), with commitments totaling about US$78.8 billion (IMF 2015c). By March 15, 2016, the number of loans to European countries had fallen. By then, five countries in what the IMF terms emerging Europe had outstanding loans (with commitments totaling around US$37.4 billion), and total outstanding credit to European members was around US$56 billion (IMF 2016d). Programs in Greece (2010 and 2012), Ireland (2010), and Portugal (2011) were record breaking in terms of loan size in dollars and loan size relative to GDP and quota (Reinhart and Trebesch 2016, 19, table 1).

   IMF loans had been regionally concentrated during prior crises. But the extent of the concentration and involvement in Europe was unprecedented in the organization's history. The IMF lent over US$200 billion from 2008 to 2015, of which around two-thirds went to AEs in Europe (Weisbrot 2015, 157; Reinhart and Trebesch 2016, 10). Greece, Ireland, and Portugal accounted for around 80% of total IMF lending during 2011–2014 (IEO 2016, 2). As of mid-February 2015, almost 85% of outstanding credit (plus a prospective US$10 billion disbursement to Ukraine in 2015) was extended to Greece, Ireland, Portugal, and Ukraine (Schadler 2015, 5). Programs in the European periphery place the IMF in a familiar role in a new neighborhood. The IMF is again promoting procyclical austerity policies, though mostly in high-income Eurozone countries and some middle-income countries in Eastern Europe and the former Soviet Union (Weisbrot 2015, 157).

The crisis in the European periphery brought the IMF into a partnership with two European institutions—the EC and the ECB—forming the "Troika." The Troika was formally launched on March 25, 2010, in connection with Greece, when euro area heads of state declared "their willingness to take determined and coordinated action, if needed, to safeguard financial stability in the euro area." They proclaimed themselves ready "to contribute to coordinated bilateral loans" as part of "a package involving substantial IMF financing and a majority of European financing" (quoted in Moschella 2016, 5). The Troika was a partnership of necessity. The IMF alone could not fill the borrowing gaps faced by European clients, and European institutions, while (at least initially) possessing sufficient financial resources for the assistance packages, needed to import the institution's expertise, authority, and credibility (Nelson 2014a).[18] The treaty establishing the European Stability Mechanism (ESM) does not legally require IMF involvement when precautionary financing is extended to member nations, though it does state that assessments "shall be conducted together with the IMF," "wherever appropriate and possible" (quoted in Henning 2016, 124).[19] As recently as winter 2016–2017, European creditor nations affirmed their strong preference to include the IMF in its programs (ibid.).

During earlier crises, the IMF worked with the G-7 and other multilateral institutions, especially the World Bank. The IMF had also previously been involved in discussions with European institutions—for example, around the formation of the European Monetary Union after the signing of the Maastricht Treaty (Moschella 2016, 5). Prior to the launch of the Troika, the IMF also worked with the EC on programs for EU members that were not part of the Eurozone, and worked with European actors in the case of (non–EU member) Iceland. But the IMF had not been involved as regularly and deeply with other institutions until the Troika. The arrangement has constrained the IMF in particular ways since "each participant was bound by the decisions of the group and the expectation that any concerns or disagreements would not be raised in public" (Bernes 2014, 12; IEO 2014, 7). As we will see, these expectations were not always fulfilled.

The IMF's Subordinate Position within the Troika
There is substantial evidence that the IMF has occupied a subordinate position in the Troika and that the relationship between the IMF and its European partners has been fraught with tension over fundamental policy decisions.

In the case of Latvia and Romania, the IMF attempted unsuccessfully to temper European demands for severe austerity (Lütz and Kranke 2014, table 3). In Estonia, Latvia, and Lithuania, the IMF initially favored external devaluation of domestic currencies, while European Troika members and Baltic governments themselves favored the painful strategy of "internal devaluation" involving downward adjustment of nominal wages and fiscal contraction (Kattel and Raudla 2013, fn13).[20] The IMF's IEO also takes note of tensions with the EU in the Baltics. In the summer of 2009, IMF staff apparently had doubts about the realism of Latvia's fiscal targets and the decision to maintain the currency peg, and mission staff reported that its negotiating position was weakened by EU action (IEO 2014, fns43, 46).

More broadly, European Troika members have generally been far more "hawkish" than the IMF on fiscal policy (Clift 2014). For example, in negotiations over Ireland's program, the IMF favored a fiscal adjustment that was half the size demanded by the EC and ECB—ultimately the Troika demanded a fiscal adjustment that represented a compromise between their respective proposals (ibid.).[21] Leaked reports on Cyprus reveal disagreement within the Troika. European Troika members in May 2013 pushed to impose a levy on insured and uninsured depositors in the country's solvent and insolvent banks, over the objections of the IMF (Evripidou 2013).[22]

Tensions within the Troika surfaced in negotiations around all three of Greece's assistance packages. Conflicts between the German government and the IMF also flared on several occasions. A leaked internal (German) Bundesbank report written after Greece's first SBA refers to the IMF as the "Inflation Maximizing Fund" (Evans-Pritchard 2010; Vary 2011). The report illustrates the depth of German fabulism on Greece and the IMF. Equally revealing is German finance minister Wolfgang Schäubel's April 2014 remark that "Greece could serve as a model for Ukraine" (Weisbrot 2015, 2).

The IMF's evaluation of Greece's first SBA reveals its relatively weak position in the Troika. In 2013, the IMF issued an "Ex Post Evaluation" of the first SBA in Greece (IMF 2013a). The assessment notes that European partners ruled out debt restructuring despite the fact that the IMF flagged the country's public debt as unsustainable (ibid., 29);[23] that Europeans demanded conditions that were too detailed and broad ranging, and were slow to make decisions; and that it was difficult to coordinate with European Troika partners (IMF 2013a; Whelan 2013).[24] Officials of the EU were disquieted by the IMF report, and an EU spokesperson announced that it "fundamentally disagrees" with its substance (*New York Times* 2013).[25]

The first SBA with Greece was replaced by another in March 2012 for €130 billion (not all of which was disbursed). Intra-Troika tensions flared again during the negotiations that culminated in the signing of the agreement. Conflicts within the Troika in the summer of 2011 centered on bank recapitalization, debt relief and sustainability, and fiscal policy (Moschella 2016). The IMF advocated swift bank recapitalization, whereas European lenders were hostile to the idea (Eichengreen 2012, 3; Moschella 2016). Greece was ultimately permitted to restructure its debts in early 2012 after European leaders found the case for a partial write-down too obvious to ignore (Moschella 2016). Banks and investors accepted a deal that paid them about half the face value of their bond holdings.[26]

In July 2015, conflicts between European and especially German officials and the IMF were apparent in a pitched battle over a third loan to Greece.[27] The IMF issued a "debt sustainability analysis" on July 2, just three days before a referendum that Greek prime minister Tsipras called to force a popular vote on the Eurogroup's austerity package.[28] Senior IMF officials (including IMF managing director Christine Lagarde and then chief economist Olivier Blanchard) announced that the institution could not participate in a new Greek program in which debt was unsustainable. Greek debt was then at 175% of GDP, above the 110% of GDP that the IMF had set as a sustainable target. The analysis indicated that Europe's officials needed to develop a plan for easing Greece's debt burdens via restructuring or sizable debt relief, something that the German government found unacceptable. U.S. Treasury secretary Jacob Lew reinforced the IMF's message. In commenting on the sustainability analysis, an IMF staff member said that "the EU has to understand that not everything can be decided based on their own imperatives" (Taylor 2015). Not surprisingly, Prime Minister Tsipras viewed the IMF's intervention favorably, and cited it in a televised appeal to voters before the referendum. European members of the IMF's Executive Board reportedly tried to stop publication of the sustainability analysis, and the EC responded to the IMF's analysis by producing its own, less pessimistic analysis. Undaunted, the IMF's message on debt sustainability was reinforced in a memo to EU authorities ahead of a summit on Greece. The memo stated that "Greece's debt can now only be made sustainable through debt relief measures that go far beyond what Europe has been willing to consider" (IMF 2015b, 1). The memo highlighted other points of contention between the Fund and European Troika members, such as the feasibility of a medium-term primary budget surplus target of 3.5% of GDP and the assumption that Greece would be able to borrow at AAA rates on international markets by 2018.[29]

In August 2015, Greece ultimately reached agreement with European officials on a third loan of €86 billion (US$94 billion). European negotiators pressed for and received from the government commitments to new, more severe austerity policies and a primary budget surplus of 3.5% of GDP by 2018. In addition, a Eurosummit statement that preceded the agreement with Greece included the provision that "the government needs to consult and agree with the Institutions [as European Troika members started to refer to themselves at that time] on all draft legislation in relevant areas with adequate time before submitting it for public consultation or to [the country's] Parliament" (EU 2015, 5).

During 2015 and the first half of 2016, the IMF continued to flag its refusal to participate in the third loan to Greece until Europeans agreed to significant debt relief (Lagarde 2015b). Lagarde said that the budget surpluses that were a part of the August 2015 agreement would require "heroic" efforts by the Greek population, and that maintaining such surpluses well into the future is "highly unrealistic" (Donnan and Giles 2016). The IMF's shift to persistent advocate of Greek debt relief rather than "persistent scold" surprised many observers (Thomas 2015), particularly since it had hardly played a positive role in earlier rounds of the Greek crisis (see Galbraith 2016).

In May 2016, the IMF walked back from confrontation with European officials. It signed off on a May 2016 deal to unlock $US11.5 billion in loans in a deal that commits Greece to greater austerity while putting off further discussion of IMF participation until late 2016, following a new analysis by the Fund of what the Eurogroup's vague commitments mean for Greece's debt (Varoufakis 2016). Prior to release of the formal analysis, IMF research director Maurice Obstfeld and director of the European Department Poul Thomsen noted on the institution's blog in December 2016 that assessment of the European plan revealed that it would deliver a primary budget surplus of 1.5% of GDP by 2018 and that additional austerity required to achieve a 3.5% surplus would prevent "the nascent recovery from taking hold" (Obstfeld and Thomsen 2016). Notwithstanding the absence of any signs of recovery in Greece (nascent or otherwise), the blog post triggered a new round of dueling public statements. Eurozone officials expressed disappointment that IMF staff published the blog post during negotiations with Greece, and they chided the institution for its breach of confidentiality norms. They stated that they "hope that we can return to the practice of conducting program negotiations . . . in private" (Reuters 2016a).[30]

The simple arithmetic of the assistance packages helps to explain the IMF's junior position.[31] There was a great deal of variability in the degree to which the IMF cofinanced European programs. It provided a relatively small portion of the financing toward many of the region's SBAs. Many of these programs had a complex financing geometry involving a number of European governments and support mechanisms. For instance, Greece's first package in 2010 involved an IMF commitment of €30 billion, in comparison with €80 billion in European assistance (though this amount was later reduced). The IMF contributed just €1 billion to a €10 billion combined financing initiative with the ESM in a May 2013 agreement with Cyprus and US$2.1 billion to Iceland's November 2008 SBA, while Denmark, Finland, Norway, and Sweden contributed US$2.5 billion, Poland US$200 million, and the Faroe Islands US$50 million. The IMF contributed US$17 billion to Ukraine's April 2014 program, while the United States, Europe, and World Bank contributed US$15 billion in additional lending. In May 2011, the IMF provided financing of €12.6 billion to Portugal, while the EU provided €25.2 billion in a three-year package. In the region's most complicated cofinancing arrangement, the IMF provided €22.5 billion of the total of €67.5 billion in assistance to Ireland in December 2010.[32] In the case of Latvia (2008) and Greece (2012), the IMF provided 20% or less of the total financing, whereas in Hungary (2008) and Romania (2009 and 2011) the IMF provided more than 60% of the support and the EU provided the balance (Miyoshi 2013, 19–21).

Notwithstanding intra-Troika conflicts, the IMF should not be viewed as the failed savior of Greece or other peripheral European countries. The IMF ultimately supported many European demands for greater austerity in Greece and elsewhere, and continues to do so. The IMF equivocated in its position on debt sustainability in Greece. The IMF also charges a much higher interest rate than European creditors (up to 3.9%, while Europe charges slightly above 1% on average); IMF loans have to be repaid on average in five to seven years, compared with up to fifty years for European loans; and the IMF has extracted more than €86 million annually in profits on European loans since 2013 (Gros 2016). Indeed, some observers emphasize cooperation rather than conflict within the Troika (Weisbrot 2015). A balanced assessment must conclude that there is ample evidence of both conflict and cooperation.

The IMF's decisions and recommendations in Europe are deeply influenced by the European governments on its Board of Governors and Executive Board, especially the larger and more powerful countries among them (Lütz and Kranke 2014; Weisbrot and Jorgensen 2013). European chairs have significant influence in program approvals, not least because they hold almost a third of IMF quotas (Mohan and Kapur 2015, 51). European overrepresentation facilitated not only IMF decisions to provide large amounts of support to the region but also decisions on exceptional access and systemic risk waivers (discussed later). Hence, Vestergaard and Wade (2015, 3) could argue that overrepresentation was "invaluable in securing the IMF's willingness to act as a junior partner of the eurozone politicians."

Increasing Complementarity or Competition on the Horizon?

Despite massive increases in lending capacity, the IMF by itself is nevertheless inadequate to the task of responding to crises in internationally integrated, highly liberalized, liquid, and increasingly opaque financial markets. This is apparent when we compare the IMF's still limited resources against the massive pools of capital held by money managers, and the resources in shadow financial markets, derivatives, and private equity and hedge funds, or even when we consider its resources against the collective size of the SBAs in relatively small countries on the European periphery (see Henning 2009b, 3).[33] Liquidity support from the IMF during crises will increasingly need to be augmented, and in some cases it may be supplanted by other institutions (see chapter 6 and Grabel 2013b). The IMF is now, and will continue to be, pressed into relationships of convenience during crises, in which it complements the resources of existing and new institutions, even when such arrangements dilute IMF autonomy.[34] The IMF's strained partnership with the Troika illustrates the importance of thinking carefully about the nature of any partnerships between the institution and liquidity support arrangements in EMDEs, and the importance of doing so outside the context of a crisis (see chapter 6).

Institutional substitution, or forum shopping, is emerging as a live possibility for countries in distress (see chapter 6). Today the IMF faces competition from China and even the World Bank. For instance, writing early in the crisis, Wade (2010, fn10) noted that the IMF lost new business to the World Bank outside of the European rescues. Even in Europe, Turkey broke off negotiations with the Fund in early March 2010 because of the severity of its conditions. A few weeks later, the country negotiated a US$1.3 billion loan with the World Bank (ibid.).

The case of Nigeria illustrates the new opportunities for forum shopping. In February 2016, the Fund called on policymakers to remove its currency peg and capital controls, a recommendation that the country's president rejected. Soon after, Finance Minister Kemi Adeosun announced that the country would not apply for IMF loans (Nwachukwu 2016). Instead, Adeosun announced that Nigeria would receive US$6 billion in FDI from China (*Premium Times* 2016), while also receiving support from the World Bank through its International Development Association (IDA), the unit at the World Bank that works with the poorest countries. In 2016, the government also applied to the World Bank and the AfDB for additional, larger loans (of US$2.5 billion and US$1 billion, respectively) (*Financial Nigeria* 2016).[35]

The government of Azerbaijan has also engaged in successful forum shopping. In July 2016, the country's finance minister highlighted both the continuing stigma on borrowing from the IMF and the high interest rates on its emergency assistance (Farchy 2016a). The government announced that it was pursuing lower-cost loans from the World Bank and possibly the Asian Development Bank (AsDB) and European Bank for Reconstruction and Development (EBRD). The same dynamic played out in a number of other country contexts during 2016. Indeed, as a consequence of increased demand, the International Bank for Reconstruction and Development (IBRD, the World Bank's main lending arm) lent US$61 billion in fiscal year 2016 (Donnan 2016c). By comparison, the previous peak of IBRD lending during the crisis was US$44.2 billion in 2010 (ibid.).

The increase in emergency budgetary support by the World Bank not only suggests a growing trend toward forum shopping. It also suggests the messiness in global financial governance as countries turn to other multilaterals for emergency support that would traditionally have come from the IMF. By now, IMF staff are certainly aware that institutional competition or opportunities for forum shopping are broadening. A key question going forward is how this awareness will affect IMF practices.

IMF Governance

Many IMF observers, myself included, hoped that the global crisis would create space for long-awaited governance reforms that would give EMDEs more voice and influence at the institution. Governance changes at the Fund could involve formal and informal adjustments. On the formal level, voting rights and decision-making procedures at the institution can be altered. On the informal level, there is the possibility of changes that bear on the relative influence of individual members over decisions, practices, and norms at the institution even in the absence of reform of formal procedures.

Continuities

Formal IMF governance processes have long been a point of contention among EMDE member states and civil society organizations. To date, progress on even modest formal governance reforms at the BWIs has been glacial.

After nearly twelve years of pressure, the Singapore reforms of 2006 embodied largely inconsequential changes in the voice and vote of EMDEs at the IMF. Under the agreement, the voting share held by the United States fell from 17% to 16.7% and that of high-income countries fell from 52.7% to 52.3%. China secured an increase from 2.9% to 3.6% in its voting share, and the shares held by the remaining 163 of the IMF's 185 member countries dropped from 37.1% to 36.6% (Weisbrot and Johnston 2009).

In 2007, Brazil's then finance minister Guido Mantega expressed frustration with stubbornly slow and insignificant progress on IMF governance reform. At the IMF's annual meeting in October 2007, Mantega maintained that absent serious governance reforms EMDEs "would go their own way. . . . We will seek self insurance by building up high levels of international reserves, and we will participate in regional reserve-sharing pools and regional monetary institutions. The fragmentation of the multilateral financial system, which is already emerging, will accelerate" (Mantega 2007, 3). These sentiments continued to resonate and deepen during the global crisis.[36]

Governance Reform and the Global Crisis
IMF quota subscriptions (hereafter quotas) are the funds that each member nation hands over to the IMF. They constitute a significant part of the Fund's capital and provide a secure permanent basis for its lending. Quotas largely determine how much a member can borrow and its share of voting rights, which translate into member countries' voting weights on the Fund's Board of Governors and Executive Board. Each country gets a "basic" vote, plus additional votes in proportion to its quota. The United States has always enjoyed unilateral veto power at the IMF since it holds over 17% of total quotas and over 16% of total votes. It is the only country holding veto power over important decisions, such as changes to the organization's Articles of Agreement, which require an 85% supermajority of member votes. U.S. veto power has been termed the "most important 'frozen asymmetry' of the IMF governance structure" (Lesage et al. 2013, 20). Given the voting shares held by the United States, it is not surprising that the institution "reflects US economic policy preferences more faithfully than perhaps any other international organization" (Henning 2009b, 1).

In late 2008, new quota negotiations began at the BWIs and in five regional development banks. In mid-March 2009 (in advance of the first BRICs Leaders' Summit in June 2009), the BRICs issued a communiqué that explicitly linked quota reform to an increase in their contributions to the BWIs (Armijo and Roberts 2014, 516). The first EMDE funding commitments to the IMF in April 2009 were not conditioned on implementation of specific governance reforms. Nevertheless, the institution's new funders, particularly Brazil and China, used the moment to emphasize the need to reallocate IMF quotas (and hence voting shares) to reflect more accurately the economic significance of large EMDEs in the global economy (Woods 2010). During the April 2009 discussions, senior Chinese officials announced that Beijing would be willing to increase its contributions if its quota reflected its economic weight; namely, by basing its quota on output per person (Landler 2009). In the fall of 2009, the BRICs countries and the Group of 24 (G-24) proposed a 7% increase in quotas in favor of EMDEs (Wroughton 2009; Reuters 2009a).[37] China proposed a far more ambitious goal: in September 2009, a finance ministry official called for establishment of a timeline to transfer 50% of the voting rights at the BWIs to EMDEs (Reuters 2009a; 2009b).[38]

At the time of the negotiations, the BRICs did not consistently present a united front on governance reform. The Russian government was particularly ambivalent. On various occasions, it aligned itself with critics of IMF governance, and it was among the most outspoken critics of the "exorbitant privilege" enjoyed by the United States (Johnson 2008). But Russian officials occasionally distanced themselves from positions taken by fellow BRICs countries. For example, during the fall 2009 meeting of the IMF and World Bank in Istanbul, a Russian central bank official emphasized that its purchase of IMF bonds was not conditioned on IMF governance reform (Reuters 2009b). Russia's ambivalence exemplifies what Jones (2011) notes is the fluid, uncertain relationship among the BRICs and between them and other EMDEs (see Ban and Blyth 2013, fns1, 2; Mittelman 2013).

In 2009, the G-20 announced with much fanfare that it had moved forward on its commitment to reform formal governance at the BWIs. Representatives agreed to redistribute quota shares by at least 5% from "overrepresented" members to what it termed "dynamic" EMDEs at the IMF, and by at least 3% at the World Bank by January 2011 (G-20 2009b). The language of the agreement was opaque, making it difficult to determine exactly which countries would gain votes and which would lose them. The lack of linguistic clarity reflected conflict within the G-20 (Wade 2011, 363). The G-20 also agreed in 2009 to reallocate some seats on the IMF's Executive Board to EMDEs by consolidating some European seats, and to increase the IMF's general quota so as to triple its lending capacity. The IMF's International Monetary and Financial Committee (IMFC) endorsed the G-20 agreement the following month (Lesage et al. 2013), continuing the vague language on quota redistribution. Negotiations on the governance reform components of the agreement then stalled for a year owing to conflicts between the United States and Europe and among European countries.

In October 2010, the Finance G-20 regained momentum on IMF governance reform when its members agreed to a number of proposals, including a shift of 6.2% in quota shares to dynamic EMDEs by October 2012 (G-20 2010). In November 2010, the IMF's Executive Board approved this measure, which was included in a broader package known as "The 2010 IMF Quota and Governance Reform Agreement" (hereafter the 2010 agreement). Specifically, the 2010 agreement involved several measures: a vast increase in the lending power of the institution by doubling IMF quota resources; an amendment of the IMF's Articles of Agreement to provide for an all-elected Executive Board;[39] and a shift of 6% in quota and voting shares away from AEs (principally in Europe) toward rapidly growing EMDEs, with an understanding that, in order to increase the representation of EMDEs, "advanced European" countries would reduce their representation on the 24-person Executive Board by two seats via a complicated arrangement involving sharing and rotation of seats and chairs within groups (Truman 2015; IMF 2010f; Lesage et al. 2013, 560–561; Wade 2011, 364–365).[40] Under the agreement, China would become the IMF's third-largest member country behind the United States and Japan. Moreover, the top ten shareholders at the Fund would henceforth represent the ten largest economies in the world, which now include China, Brazil, India, and the Russian Federation (Eichengreen and Woods 2016; IMF 2016b). (We will see that the headline figure of 6% overstates the degree of change.)

The IMF's Board of Governors ratified the 2010 agreement in November of that year. It was to be implemented in October 2012, following ratification by member countries. The majority of members approved the agreement. But approval by an 85% supermajority was required. Implementation of the agreement then stalled for five years because the U.S. Congress failed to approve it in late 2012 and again in January 2014, even though the government's executive branch had done so and despite repeated exhortations by the IMF.[41]

In the face of gridlock, the IMF was unable to secure the anticipated increase in its secure quota-based lending resources. It remained dependent on the willingness of its members to lend to it on a temporary bilateral basis through the NAB. The IMF was forced to rely on temporary borrowing for 70% of its credit capacity, with only 30% of lending capacity derived from stable country quotas (IEO 2014, 25). This left it vulnerable to sudden demands on its resources. The degree of dependence on temporary bor-rowed loans had no historical precedent: prior to the global crisis, member quotas provided more than 80% of the IMF's lending capacity (Mohan and Kapur 2015, 47; IEO 2014, 25).

Congress finally ratified the 2010 agreement in mid-December 2015, as part of an "Omnibus" spending bill. Congressional Republicans were ultimately won over because the language of the bill required the United States to take all necessary steps to repeal a systemic risk exemption that the IMF had introduced in 2010 (to be discussed) and that the U.S. exec-utive director at the IMF vote to repeal this exemption (U.S. Congress 2015, section 9004-5). The Treasury Department agreed to push to repeal the exemption to appease congressional Republicans (Calmes 2016).

Strauss-Kahn wrapped the 2010 agreement in hyperbole, calling it "his-toric" and calling the "landmark reforms" "the most fundamental gover-nance overhaul in the IMF's 65-year history and the biggest ever shift of influence in favor of EMDEs to recognize their growing role in the global economy" (IMF 2010f). In the view of critics, what Strauss-Kahn hailed as landmark change was better described as "microscopic" and even "mislead-ing" (Vestergaard and Wade 2014; 2015). The reforms shifted just 2.6% of voting shares from AEs to EMDEs, with the rest of the increase in dynamic EMDE shares coming from what were deemed to be overrepresented EMDEs. The G-7 countries as a group sacrificed just 1.8% of their aggregate vot-ing power (Vestergaard and Wade 2013b). The 2010 agreement made the shift in voting shares to EMDEs appear more significant by virtue of a new classification system introduced at the time, under which South Korea and Singapore were reclassified as EMDEs even though they continued to be grouped with AEs in the IMF's flagship publication, *World Economic Outlook* (Lesage et al. 2013). Civil society groups noted that the agreement did little to address Africa's effective disenfranchisement at the Fund (BWP 2010b). The agreement also maintained the unilateral veto power of the United States since its voting share fell (trivially) from 16.7% to 16.5%, whereas BRICs countries as a bloc hold 13.51% of voting shares and are therefore deprived of veto power (Lesage et al. 2013).[42]

Why Did the BRICs Governments Approve the 2010 Reforms?
It may seem puzzling that BRICs country governments ratified the 2010 agreement, given its serious shortcomings and the financial contributions to which their governments committed themselves.[43] After all, at the begin-ning of 2009, the BRICs together held more than ten times the amount of currency reserves that the IMF had at its disposal. Despite these holdings,

the group was in a relatively weak and sometimes divided position at the IMF. The bloc was not in a position in the short run to force governance changes that were more significant than those embodied in the 2010 agreement.

Approval of the 2010 agreement by the BRICs reflects several factors. Its members preferred to minimize default risk and to outsource conditionality by contributing to the IMF rather than engaging in bilateral assistance. Notwithstanding solidaristic rhetoric, BRICs leaders privileged increasing their own influence at the Fund over the broader matter of increasing EMDE influence. The incremental nature of the 2010 agreement was seen by BRICs governments to open the door for increasing their influence at the Fund over time. The BRICs also saw it as being in their interest to contribute to the IMF to reduce the likelihood that the United States would unilaterally inject massive amounts of liquidity into the global financial system, thereby undermining the value of the dollar-denominated investments that they held.

The "Gentleman's Agreement" on IMF (and World Bank) Leadership
Early in the crisis, critics raised another aspect of governance reform that centered on the process by which leaders of the BWIs are selected. EMDEs had long chafed at the Bretton Woods–era gentleman's agreement that has ensured that the IMF's managing director is a European and the World Bank's president an American. G-20 finance ministers agreed to end this practice at their March 2009 meeting in Sussex, England (Eichengreen 2009). In reality, the practice continued.

In April 2011, BRICS[44] representatives announced that they sought an end to the gentleman's agreement (Armijo and Roberts 2014, 514–515). It appeared that the first chance to act on this would be at the conclusion of Robert Zoellick's term as World Bank president in June 2012 (ibid.). But the arrest and resignation of Strauss-Kahn in May 2011 provided an earlier opportunity. IMF directors representing the BRICS quickly issued a statement calling for an open, merit-based selection process (ibid.). Some—though by no means all—EMDE leaders and representatives at the IMF used the opening in 2011 to press publicly for Mexico's Agustín Carstens. Lagarde and, very briefly, Stanley Fischer also emerged as candidates. Russia briefly promoted the candidacy of Kazakhstan's Grigori Marchenko, but quickly endorsed Lagarde (Armijo and Roberts 2014, 515). Old appointment patterns prevailed in July 2011 when the IMF's Executive Board, using the usual weighted voting that reflects country quotas, replaced Strauss-Kahn with Lagarde, a fellow European. Supporters of Lagarde's appointment justified the decision on grounds that a European was needed at the helm because of the Eurozone crisis. Critics rightly identified the hypocrisy of this view insofar as Europeans led the IMF through decades of crises in EMDEs. Lagarde was quietly reappointed to a second IMF term in February 2016, when she was the sole candidate for the position.

The commitment to the gentleman's agreement on leadership was also reaffirmed at the World Bank. In April 2012, it was announced that an American, Dr. Jim Yong Kim, would serve as World Bank president beginning in July 2012. Two highly qualified candidates had emerged early on as leading candidates for the World Bank post. Nigeria's former finance minister (and former World Bank managing director), Dr. Ngozi Okonjo-Iweala, was nominated for the post by South Africa. Colombia's former finance minister and former UN undersecretary-general for economic and social affairs, Dr. José Antonio Ocampo, was nominated by Brazil. World Bank governors in Europe interviewed candidates Kim, Okonjo-Iweala, and Ocampo and reportedly deemed the latter the best prepared, possessing the clearest ideas about where to take the Bank, and the most knowledgeable on economics (Wade 2012). Ocampo withdrew on April 13, 2012, to make space for Okonjo-Iweala's candidacy once it became clear that it was politically important that the World Bank's executive directors representing EMDEs—a group known informally as the G-11 inside the Bank—present a unanimous vote for one candidate (Wade 2012; Wroughton 2012b). Okonjo-Iwela withdrew shortly thereafter, once other EMDEs threw their support behind Kim and when it became clear that politics and bilateral relations with the United States rather than merit were driving the process.[45]

The fluid and sometimes conflictual relationships within the BRICS and between the BRICS and other large EMDEs created space for Kim's appointment.[46] The BRICS and other EMDEs did not offer unified support for either Ocampo or Okonjo-Iweala. Kim's candidacy was supported by Mexico and Russia; Ocampo by Brazil and not by the government of his country of origin, Colombia; and Okonjo-Iweala by South Africa. In addition, Kim's appointment was facilitated by the ability of the United States to exploit these fractures by offering leadership carrots to EMDEs, such as when Jin-Yong Cai, a Chinese national, was appointed chief executive officer of the International Finance Corporation (the private sector lending arm of the World Bank Group) in August 2012 and Kaushik Basu, an Indian national, was appointed chief economist at the World Bank in September 2012 (see Wade 2012).[47] Following the pattern with Lagarde, Kim was the only candidate put forward at the end of his first term, and he was unanimously reappointed in July 2016.

Lack of Independence from Key Member States

The circumstances surrounding the IMF's decision to grant exceptional access to Greece (and others in the Eurozone) and the introduction of the systemic risk waiver provide a window into the overrepresentation of key member states in IMF decision making.

In 2010, it was clear that Greece would either need to default on its debt, which largely comprised bonds held by private investors and banks in France, Germany, and Britain, or would need exceptional access to IMF loans beyond its quota to support debt service (Ellmers 2016, 11). French and German banks blocked debt restructuring (Blustein 2015, 11). U.S. banks were indirectly exposed to Greek debt through credit default swaps that insured European bank loans (Ellmers 2016). With restructuring off the table, the IMF granted exceptional access to Greece in 2010. The IMF's exceptional access policy allows nations to access funds provided that four criteria are met—namely, that there is a high probability that public debt is sustainable in the medium term; the country faces exceptional balance of payments pressures; it has good prospects for regaining market access; and it has a policy program likely to succeed. The Fund acknowledged that it violated the first of these criteria when lending to Greece in 2010. In order to approve the 2010 loan, the IMF introduced the systemic risk waiver. The waiver provides exceptional access to borrowers when there is "high risk of international systemic spillover effects," even if public debt is deemed unsustainable in the medium term (IMF 2010c, 20). The waiver did not require an upfront debt restructuring. Waivers were also invoked to justify IMF loans to Ireland and Portugal.

The decision to create the systemic risk waiver tarnished the IMF's credibility (Schadler 2014; Robertson 2015). As the IMF itself later acknowledged, the waiver aggravated long-standing internal concerns about governance. EMDE and other representatives criticized the exceptional treatment of Europe as another instance of the IMF's lack of evenhandedness, the imprint of Europe's overrepresentation on the Executive Board and managing directorship, and the specter of U.S. influence (IEO 2013, 25–26, 29; 2014, 7, 25; Blustein 2015, 2; Ellmers 2016). Representatives from EMDEs questioned whether the exceptional access granted to Europe would be available to them in future crises (IEO 2013, 25; 2014, 7, 25). The waiver was also controversial among the IMF's rank and file (Ellmers 2016). In January 2016, the IMF dropped the systemic risk waiver following horse trading in the U.S. Congress in late 2015 around the 2010 reform agreement.[48]

The IMF's lack of independence from European members is also apparent in the decision to support so many European rescues, to join Greek programs absent debt write-downs or extensions of payment periods, and to serve as a junior partner to European institutions. Mody puts the matter bluntly: "The IMF's subordination to its major shareholders became painfully clear when it parachuted into the euro crisis" (Mody 2016). In a similar vein, Rogoff argues that the IMF "sycophantically supported each new European initiative to rescue the over-indebted eurozone periphery, committing more than $100 billion . . . risking not only its members' money but ultimately its . . . credibility" (Rogoff 2011). Mody (2016) also sees the IMF's shift to a fiscal consolidation message in 2010 as consistent with (and reflective of) the sentiments of the United States and powerful European members.

The contents of IMF Article IV surveillance reports also reflect the substantial influence of key states.[49] They are often given a pass on macroeconomic conditions that induce a stern warning for less powerful states (IEO 2011, 25, 44; 2013, 25–26, 29). Powerful members exercise influence not just over what is in surveillance reports but also over what is removed. In a study of Article IV and other reports from 2012 to 2014, Eichengreen and Woods (2016, table 1) find that "deletion rates" are generally higher for advanced and emerging economies than for developing countries (see also IEO 2013, 26).

Discontinuities

The preceding discussion of IMF governance offers substantial evidence of continuity. But concurrent and continuing changes at the IMF (and World Bank) are beginning to reconfigure channels of informal and even formal influence of member states. These changes will no doubt accelerate in the coming years. One channel of evolution stems from the new roles that leading EMDEs are assuming at the institution.

New Lenders, Rising Powers, New Influences?

During the crisis, China was initially reluctant to contribute additional funds to the IMF. At the November 2008 G-20 meeting, the country's representatives argued that it had already fulfilled its quota to the institution. It emphasized that its voting power should increase if other countries wished it to contribute more. It also insisted that were additional funding to be forthcoming, it would be through modalities that minimized its risk (Jiang 2014, 172–173). As the crisis worsened, however, China saw fit to reverse its position.

Some of the Fund's former clients took on a new role at the April 2009 G-20 meeting that gave the IMF its first tranche of funding related to the global crisis. For the first time in IMF history, the institution issued its own bonds. This provided the vehicle for unprecedented financial support from EMDEs. The bonds were SDR-denominated, tradable in the public sector, and limited to a one-year maturity—conditions demanded by new EMDE lenders that were willing to commit funds only through instruments that would maintain pressure for governance reform while also offering them a safe alternative to bilateral support to distressed economies (Holroyd and Momani 2012, 208; Jiang 2014, 174).

Negotiations over new financial commitments and the means through which they were to be committed to the IMF were contentious. China was among the first at the 2009 G-20 meeting to commit new resources to the IMF (Chin 2014b, 194). In doing so, the country's policymakers broke new ground in emphasizing that their contributions would help to stabilize the global economy and protect poorer countries from the fallout of the crisis (ibid.). In Chin's view, equally notable is the fact that the country worked closely with the BRICs (and later the BRICS) and other East Asian governments to press for international monetary and IMF governance reform (ibid.).[50] China worked closely with Brazil and Russia to insist that new contributions would take place through purchase of the new SDR-denominated bonds and not through the NAB, since contributions through this channel do not translate into greater voting shares (ibid., 195). Indeed, all of the BRICs countries and South Korea made their contributions through the IMF's SDR bonds rather than the NAB, though most other countries committed new resources to the IMF through the NAB.[51]

China committed to purchasing US$50 billion of the new bonds, while Brazil, Russia, South Korea, and India each committed to purchasing US$10 billion. Thus, US$90 billion in new resources for IMF lending in 2009 came from EMDEs, some of which were past clients. The historical significance of this decision was not lost on Brazil's then president, Lula da Silva, who quipped, "Brazil is now a creditor of the IMF!" (quoted in Armijo, Katada, and Roberts 2015, 37).

In late 2011, Lagarde called on EMDEs for a second tranche of commitments while the IMF also sought new resources from AEs. Among the former, Brazil's government was initially most receptive. However, Brazilian president Dilma Rousseff refused to announce the precise nature and dollar amount of the country's second contribution until she was apprised of plans for IMF governance reform and until Eurozone leaders articulated a credible rescue plan. She also made it clear that the country's decision on new funding would be tied to a later meeting among BRICS leaders, an announcement that signaled solidarity among the often fractious group.

Never one to miss a chance to note historical ironies, Mantega stated during Lagarde's visit to the country, "It's a great satisfaction to us that this time the IMF did not come to Brazil to bring money like in the past but to ask us to lend money to developed nations" (quoted in Leahy 2011).

At the same time as Lagarde sought a second round of support from the G-20 in 2011, European policymakers appealed directly to the BRICS and other large EMDEs for contributions to the European Financial Stability Facility (EFSF). China, in particular, was targeted for support. The country bought EFSF bonds after French president Nicholas Sarkozy made an emergency call to China's president, Hu Jintao, in October 2011 (Jiang 2014, 167). About 25% of China's currency reserves might have been used to purchase European sovereign debt, which China viewed as advancing its commercial and political interests within the EU (ibid., 166–167). The other BRICS declined European requests for bilateral support. In September 2011, Mantega announced a BRICS bailout fund for the Eurozone but then dropped the initiative when China did not support it (Armijo, Katada, and Roberts 2015, 37).

Lagarde continued to seek additional IMF funding in 2012. G-20 finance ministers announced new commitments at their April 2012 meeting. As expected, the United States was unwilling to contribute. The specific contributions to be shouldered by EMDE members were not announced until BRICS representatives met informally on the eve of the June 2012 G-20 Leaders' Summit in Los Cabos (Chowla 2012). The BRICS pledged US$75 billion of the US$456 billion in new IMF funding committed by G-20 countries. China's share was US$43 billion, Brazil, Russia, and India each committed US$10 billion, and South Africa pledged US$2 billion.[52] The new BRICS pledges were made via temporary, bilateral standby credit lines under the NAB to be activated as needed, with the understanding that they were to be drawn on only after the IMF's existing resources had been substantially utilized (Wroughton 2012a). BRICS governments explicitly conditioned release of this second tranche of funds upon implementation of the stalled 2010 agreement (ibid.).[53] Mantega clearly articulated the quid pro quo involved in the BRICS position when he stated that the promise of additional funding was tied to "an understanding that the reforms of the Fund's quotas . . . will be implemented according to the timetable agreed by the G20 in 2010" (quoted in Giles 2012). China's President Hu also linked the announcement of new funding to implementation of the 2010 agreement (Jiang 2014, 174). Even after this second recapitalization by the BRICS, Lagarde continued to seek support from EMDEs. During a visit to

Colombia in December 2012, she noted "that (the country) is in a situation where it can offer support" (quoted in Stringer 2012).

What should we make of the BRICS and their potential to exercise their voice at the BWIs? Armijo and Roberts (2014, 519–520) put the matter well: "Instead of dismissing the BRICS as trivial for their limited achievements thus far, it makes more sense to conceptualize them as in the process of building capacity, adjusting to China's looming presence within the club itself, and working through common positions . . . ; the BRICS organization itself functions most readily as an 'outside option' for China to employ to exercise leverage within the major existing global governance institutions . . . ; BRICS' preferences, singly and jointly, for global governance turn on reform and evolution, not revolution."

What is most important about the commitments to the IMF by the BRICS and EMDE members of the G-20 is that they reflect the emergent power and autonomy of countries that weathered the global crisis relatively successfully. Long-standing frustrations with the BWIs and gridlock around the 2010 agreement contributed to the decision by the BRICS in July 2014 to make good on their promise-cum-threat to launch a new development bank and reserve pooling arrangement (Giles 2012).[54] The same frustrations contributed to new China-led initiatives as well (see chapter 6). There is every reason to expect that in the coming years continued frustrations with the IMF by increasingly efficacious actors will generate additional pressure on the institution to reform its formal internal governance procedures. Absent such reforms, we should expect increased forum shopping by a larger set of EMDEs.

Informal Channels of Influence

An examination of formal governance procedures—whether it concerns voting shares or leadership selection processes—does not address the fact that institutional decisions and practices are also influenced by myriad informal processes. As with any extensive, complex organization, the IMF comprises diverse constituencies that often disagree among themselves about fundamental matters pertaining to the institution's mission and strategies. Scholars whose research looks inside international organizations have documented the myriad fissures within these organizations, the diverse channels of formal and informal influence within them, and the complicated processes by which meaningful change within them may be facilitated or stymied.

There is by now an extensive, insightful body of literature on the various means by which countries seek to achieve greater influence in IMF affairs than is afforded by their formal voting rights. At the same time, internal staff members can sometimes exert greater influence than is codified within formal IMF procedures.

Nelson (2014a; 2017) finds that formal governance mechanisms at the IMF, including voting by the IMF's Executive Board, can be less important to the institution's activities than some outsiders recognize. On paper, many important decisions require a supermajority, which gives the United States effective veto power. But Nelson notes that Executive Board voting on lending programs is informal and is recorded on an up or down basis, with the board almost always unanimously approving staff proposals. In practice, the procedures provide space for internal and external actors to influence the terms of IMF agreements through informal back channels. Moreover, even when powerful countries use formal channels of influence at the IMF, staff may well reach decisions and take actions that stray from positions that key states communicate through formal voting mechanisms. For example, IMF staff extended a loan to Sri Lanka in July 2009 despite U.S. and U.K. abstentions from an Executive Board vote, by which they conveyed reservations about the loan (Nelson 2014a, 167).[55]

While the EMDE loans to the IMF and increasing EMDE assertiveness are certainly contributing to a gradual process that can be expected to result in significant changes in IMF practices over time, we must keep in mind that it is not generally possible to overhaul both formal and informal practices all at once. Stickiness in either domain may act as a temporary brake on institutional reforms that would seem to be warranted. Alternatively, dynamism in one domain might allow actors to circumvent enduring roadblocks in the other domain. Adjustments in voting shares, then, might be less important than many observers appreciate (as per Nelson 2017). Stagnation in formal governance processes may be overcome by new informal institutional norms and practices that result from changes in funding sources and instruments, personnel, ideologies, recognition of complementarities and/ or competitive threats from other institutions, and the changing economic fortunes of diverse members. In short, we should expect evolution in IMF governance to be messy and uneven, with at least some consequential changes occurring out of the public eye.

From this perspective, the support for the Fund coming from EMDEs represents a landmark event for the institution. It is implausible to assume that these changes in financial flows between member nations and the IMF will not ultimately bear on the ability of EMDEs to exert influence at the institution in ways that decisively alter its informal and even its formal practices. But it is easy to be skeptical about the influence of new lenders on the IMF. It took five years to implement the modest 2010 agreement, which was the most high-profile objective that they have sought. But the skeptical view fails to recognize that what we might call *offensive* influence, securing change that is detrimental to the interests of one's opponents, represents the highest level of influence. Lower down on the ladder is *defensive* influence, or the ability to block, derail, or veto initiatives by other parties that one views as detrimental to oneself. If we are interested in searching for evidence of changes in informal governance processes at the IMF, then we might look first for changes in EMDEs' defensive capacity at the IMF.

China's visibility on the global stage and its demonstrated commitment to creating new financial institutions exemplifies the potential that new lenders have to influence informal decision making at the IMF, even only gradually and primarily via defensive influence. The visibility and defensive assertiveness of the Chinese government is reflected in many other ways. For example, the country's policymakers have always pushed back aggressively when the U.S. Treasury has branded it a "currency manipulator."[56] China has always resisted U.S. efforts to enlist the IMF in containing or criticizing it.[57] For instance, the IMF announced in August 2007 that it would monitor global imbalances as per a plan advanced by the United States. Identification of imbalances would trigger an automatic audit and IMF staff recommendations to correct the problem. In response, China suspended Article IV consultations and presented a competing analysis that centered on the contribution of AEs, especially the United States, to persistent trade imbalances. China found support for this position among its BRICs partners in early 2009 as they were preparing for their first Leaders' Summit. In March 2009, BRICs finance ministers signed a formal statement that called on the IMF to extend surveillance to AEs. In June of that year, the IMF's new Article IV guidelines abandoned the language on exchange rate levels to which China had objected.

BRICS leaders pushed back a second time in April 2011, when the IMF again took up the U.S.-driven idea of providing data on trade imbalances. The communiqué of the fourth BRICS Leaders' Summit, in late March 2012, argued that it was "critical for AEs to adopt responsible macroeconomic and financial policies [and] avoid creating excess global liquidity . . . [while also noting that the BRICS were] concerned about the slow pace of quota and governance reforms in the IMF . . . [and calling] upon the IMF to make its surveillance framework more integrated and evenhanded" (BRICS 2012). These examples demonstrate the ways in which the BRICS, as per Armijo and Roberts (2014, 520), can amplify China's leverage and deflect criticisms advanced through the BWIs, G-20, and other arenas of global governance.

China's assertiveness is also reflected in the government's indictment of the role of the United States in the global crisis, its questioning of the continued viability of a dollar-denominated international monetary system, and the downgrade of U.S. government debt by China's credit rating agency in August 2011 and October 2013. The appointment in July 2011 of Min Zhu, former deputy governor of the PBOC, as deputy managing director of the IMF provides a channel by which China has already enhanced its influence over informal decision making at the IMF. It remains to be seen how China's growing influence will affect the voice of other EMDEs. Equally important, Zhu's succession by Tao Zhang (in August 2016), also a former deputy governor of China's PBOC, might indicate the emergence of a new norm in which the position is reserved for a Chinese official. In addition, in March 2012, Jianhai Lin was appointed secretary of the IMF and of its IMFC, and in 2008 "Justin" Yifu Lin was appointed chief economist and senior vice president of the World Bank. As Henning and Walter (2016, 9) argue, China's representation among senior staff at the BWIs demonstrates a substantial increase in its informal influence at the BWIs since 2008 (despite continued setbacks in formal governance reform). In November 2015, China also achieved a long-sought (though largely symbolic) goal of having the IMF agree to include its currency in the SDR basket alongside other currencies that the institution had long designated as having "global reserve currency" status; namely, the dollar, euro, yen, and British pound. The decision was operationalized in October 2016.

The now regular (once to twice a month) meetings of the BRICS executive directors at the BWIs have created an informal network of influence that facilitates broader changes at these institutions, notwithstanding tensions within the group (Wade 2011). These and other emergent networks among EMDEs are now laying the groundwork for more significant changes at the BWIs in the future (as per Woods and Martinez-Diaz 2009).

These developments are occurring at a time when the Trump administration in the United States is sending contradictory messages about its role in global institutions. Trump appointees at the Treasury Department are at once indicating that they intend to press to reduce the reach of the IMF in Europe and beyond and to revive failed U.S. efforts to involve the IMF in exchange rate surveillance (Donnan 2017; Mnuchin 2017). At the same time, however, they intend to reduce U.S. funding commitments to the IMF and World Bank, without recognizing that decreased funding will almost certainly reduce U.S. leverage over these institutions (Donnan 2017; *Economist* 2017b). China appears to be seizing the resulting opportunities for increased influence within the IMF (*Economist* 2017b).

The IMF discovered new vitality as first responder to economic distress at the same time as it has faced a diminished terrain over which it can dictate economic policy. Equally important, the institution became dependent on raising new resources from vibrant EMDEs while facing a closed door on contributions by the United States in 2012. Even if this new role for EMDEs does not translate into meaningful formal changes in the institution's governance in the near term, it cannot be dismissed as inconsequential since it reflects broader changes in economic power that are expressed within the IMF in other ways. It is too early to gauge the extent to which the EMDEs are ultimately able to use the emerging networks among their representatives to enhance their formal and informal influence at the Fund. It is also too early to know the degree to which the IMF must change course more than it has to date to maintain its absolute and relative influence in relation to competing institutions and increasingly autonomous EMDEs. But the fact that these are now pertinent questions, even with uncertain answers, indicates the degree to which the IMF confronts a dramatically altered landscape that poses significant challenges to its internal governance and external influence.

IMF Practice

We now consider the IMF's conduct during the crisis. We find evidence of both important continuity with and significant departures from past practice. The emphasis on practice and rhetoric allows us to identify important ambiguities and inconsistencies and, especially, notable gaps between the institution's public statements, research, and operations.

Continuity

As the global crisis emerged, the IMF's leadership initially seemed to renounce its traditional embrace of procyclical (austerity) policy responses. In 2008 and 2009, key officials publicly advocated the use of countercyclical macroeconomic policies (involving lower interest rates and increased government spending) to boost growth. Strauss-Kahn and Blanchard championed the dramatic expansion in government expenditures, in November 2008 going so far as to propose to the G-20 that AEs and EMDEs with fiscal space should participate in a global fiscal stimulus equal to 2% of world GDP (IEO 2014, 9; IMF 2008). In May 2009, Strauss-Kahn argued that "fiscal policies should counteract the crisis, not make it worse. . . . Many African countries have room on this front" (quoted in Reichmann 2013, 37; IMF 2009b). Farrell and Quiggin (2017, 16–17) note that what was remarkable was not so much Strauss-Kahn's proposal as the nearly complete "absence of dissent within the IMF, an institution which had until recently been associated with very different economic ideas." The IMF's rhetoric of countercyclicality tracked and reinforced the same powerful Keynesian resurrection in which the G-20 and many prominent and formerly anti-Keynesian economists suddenly found themselves (see Farrell and Quiggin 2017; Skidelsky 2010; 2011).

The early rhetorical embrace of countercyclical policy reflected the sensibilities of key IMF officials and foxhole Keynesianism. But it also served instrumental purposes. Strauss-Kahn and others saw in the early moments of the crisis not just the need but also an opportunity to regain the resources and standing that the institution had previously lost. The IMF's early embrace of Keynesian responses also distracted attention from the degree to which it shared responsibility for the crisis, not least by having reified light touch regulation for several decades and failing to flag fragilities that culminated in crisis.[58]

Austerity and Politically Intrusive Adjustment in Support Packages

Rhetoric and traditional IMF practice were realigned in June 2010 when the Fund began to advise major AEs to pursue "fiscal consolidation" while maintaining monetary expansion if needed.[59] The shift mirrored the pivot back to orthodox ways of thinking about fiscal policy on the part of most G-20 leaders and many prominent economists. Strauss-Kahn returned to the script of his predecessor, Michel Camdessus, when he said in June 2010 that he was "totally comfortable" with deficit cuts "even if it has some bad effect on growth" (BWP 2010a).

In reality, the conditionality programs advanced during and since the global crisis are in important respects similar in scope and content to those advanced during the Asian, Mexican, and other EMDE crises (see Grabel 2011). Nelson (2014a, 162–163) puts the matter well, arguing that "changes in the design of lending arrangements have been subtle (some might say nearly imperceptible) . . . [and that] the crisis of 2008 was not a breaking point in either the scope or content of conditionality" despite the IMF's public advocacy or use of countercyclical policy. Continuity should not be surprising since, in the view of many Fund staff, "many of its patients were suffering from the same disease" (ibid., 163), a disease that it had long treated in other patients.

Support Early in the Crisis
There is by now a vast amount of literature that shows that IMF assistance programs negotiated early in the global crisis featured its traditional austerity prescription and the associated portfolio of macroeconomic policy adjustments. IMF programs in Iceland, Latvia, Hungary, Romania, Greece, Portugal, Pakistan, Ukraine, and El Salvador included limits on or large cuts in fiscal outlays and tax increases (Grabel 2011, 821–822). A review by UNICEF (2010) of IMF programs in 86 countries found that the Fund advised two-thirds of their governments to reduce total public expenditures in 2010 and to further their fiscal contraction in 2011. Weisbrot et al. (2009) studied 41 countries with IMF agreements and found that 31 of these agreements involved tightening fiscal or monetary policy, or both. A study by Islam et al. (2012) of Article IV consultations from 2009 to 2010 in 30 low-income countries and 20 middle-income countries found that fiscal adjustment was a feature in 48 of the 50 cases.[60]

Assistance packages involving the Troika early in the crisis parallel IMF programs elsewhere. SBAs in Hungary in November 2008, Romania in April 2009, and Latvia in December 2008 looked a great deal like earlier programs in EMDEs (Gabor 2010, 822). An examination by Weisbrot and Jorgensen (2013) found that the 67 Article IV consultation reports prepared for 27 countries in the EU from 2008 to 2011 emphasize fiscal consolidation, reductions in social expenditures, measures that weaken the bargaining power and income of labor, and measures that make it more difficult for governments to promote growth and employment or reduce poverty and social exclusion. They also observe that a number of Article IV reports refer to the Eurozone crisis as an opportunity to make changes that would in other circumstances be politically difficult (see also Weisbrot 2015, chap. 1, especially 46–47).[61] The Asian crisis had previously provided similar opportunities for the IMF, the U.S. government and U.S. firms, and domestic liberalizing forces, such as opponents of Korean chaebols (see chapter 3 and also Weisbrot 2015, 132–134; Crotty and Lee 2002; 2009).

Support Later in the Crisis
One might argue that the sudden onset of the crisis left the IMF with little choice but to dust off the old playbook. Continuity might therefore have been expected early in the crisis. But IMF programs later in the crisis are also marked by continuity. In fact, the number of conditions per loan has increased in recent years, with widespread use of expansive, politically sensitive conditionality involving reductions in welfare programs (Griffiths and Todoulous 2014). A vast review of IMF "Country Reports" for 174 countries

from January 2010 to February 2013 by Ortiz and Cummins (2013) concludes that the IMF has contributed significantly to decisions to cut fiscal expenditures in EMDEs.[62] In their comprehensive examination of IMF conditionality in loan agreements involving 131 countries from 1985 to 2014, Kentikelenis, Stubbs, and King (2016) find unambiguous evidence of continuity in IMF conditionality across much of this period. They conclude that, despite its claims to the contrary, the IMF continues to advocate labor market liberalization and reductions in public sector employment and government wage spending. On this basis, the authors argue that the IMF has an "escalating commitment to hypocrisy."

Other research reaches similar conclusions. Ban (2013) found that in 2013 the IMF continued to demand fiscal constraint in Bulgaria, Romania, Hungary, Portugal, Lithuania, and Estonia. A September 2013 loan of US$6.7 billion to Pakistan includes provisions for privatization and reductions in the fiscal deficit, principally through extending taxation. Hanieh (2015) and Mossallem (2015) find strong evidence of continuity in loans to several countries in the Middle East and North Africa despite a shift in IMF rhetoric toward social inclusion after the 2011 Arab Spring uprising.[63] Loans extended in 2016 continue the pattern. A US$1.5 billion IMF loan to Sri Lanka in April 2016 highlights the need to curtail state-owned enterprises (SOEs) and subsidies and to liberalize trade; a US$613 million loan to Bosnia in May 2016 calls on policymakers to address SOEs, cut taxes, and improve the business environment; a US$2.9 billion loan to Tunisia in May 2016 emphasizes reduction of the fiscal deficit and subsidies, exchange rate flexibility, and SOE reform; and a US$478 million loan to Suriname in May 2016 targets the elimination of electricity subsidies and increased tax revenues. A loan package of US$12 billion to Egypt in November 2016 was conditioned on liberalization of the exchange rate, reduction in energy subsidies, introduction of a value-added tax, fiscal consolidation, reductions in the public sector wage bill, and a tightening of monetary policy.[64]

Several African countries have sought IMF assistance since 2014 as they grappled with commodity price weakness, capital outflows, and a slowdown of global and especially Chinese growth, FDI, and loans.[65] Some observers have suggested that African countries have returned to the IMF not just out of desperation but also out of a perception that it is less neoliberal than in the past (Pilling 2016). But the few recent agreements with African countries retain the IMF's usual focus on fiscal restraint and privatization. A US$918 million loan to Ghana in April 2015 followed a 2014 Article IV report highlighting control of the wage bill and enforcement of a "no subsidy policy" on fuel and utilities (IMF 2014b, 17).[66] A US$1.5 billion precautionary loan to Kenya in March 2016 followed a 2014 Article IV consultation that urged the government to contain the wage bill, widen the tax base, privatize SOEs, and reduce the number of parastatals (IMF 2014c).

Discontinuity

The most prominent discontinuity in IMF practices during the global crisis concerns its rhetoric and practice on capital controls. This matter warrants substantial attention and is explored at length in chapter 7. The IMF came to embrace controls on inflows but also on outflows. The change in IMF practice has contributed to the normalization of capital controls as a tool of prudential macroeconomic management. The revival of capital controls began haltingly after the Asian crisis. But it became far more significant and consistent during the global crisis. These changes are by no means irreversible, and indeed are a site of contestation. But, as we will see, the case of capital controls provides a window into the complicated dynamic of an IMF that has been racing to catch up with the policy decisions of increasingly autonomous EMDEs; changes in the material power of member states that hold diverse views on this instrument, some of which have worked through the IMF and/or the G-20 to press for greater policy autonomy in regards to capital controls; and changes in the ideas of prominent mainstream academic economists and some of the Fund's research staff.

Despite the studies cited regarding continuity in IMF conditionality, some observers find evidence of subtle discontinuities in its lending programs.[67] Early in the crisis, Broome (2010) found that while IMF loans to Mexico, Belarus, and Iceland in late 2008 and early 2009 featured the usual procyclical policy targets, he argues that the institution demonstrated a more flexible approach to crisis management, as evidenced by its differentiated treatment of borrowers, the provision of precautionary financing to Mexico, and its tolerance for short-term capital controls. This conclusion is cautiously echoed by Bird (2009). Later in the crisis, Broome (2015) finds evidence of both continuity and discontinuity across 93 SBAs from 1985 to 2012. He concludes that SBAs negotiated during 2008–2012 are characterized by the IMF's usual mix of procyclical adjustments, but he argues that the institution moved away from promoting the structural reforms that were features of earlier SBAs. Broome speculates that discontinuities in Fund practices may stem from endogenous change at the IMF and exogenous change on the country level insofar as structural reforms such as trade liberalization have already been "locked in."

Ambiguities: Discontinuities in Rhetoric and
Research, Continuities in Practice

Though the design of IMF assistance packages during the crisis reveals strong continuity with past practice, there are subtle departures in IMF rhetoric and less subtle departures in IMF research that bear noting. These gaps between practice on the one hand and rhetoric and research on the other can be dismissed as subterfuges designed to disarm critics. But a more nuanced reading highlights the tensions and ambiguities that are revealed by new rhetoric and research, and the potential that these gaps hold to expand policy space.

Narrowed Conditionality: Rhetoric versus Practice

Throughout the global crisis, the IMF intensively marketed the idea that it had narrowed the scope of conditionality. Toward this end, Fund reports and statements by key officials herald the "end of conditionality" and emphasize country ownership and national policymaker involvement in reform programs.[68] The IMF's Lagarde distanced the institution from conditionality in a 2011 press briefing in which she said, "Structural adjustments? That was before my time. . . . We don't do that anymore" (quoted in Kentikelenis, Stubbs, and King 2016, 2).

What the IMF signaled as a radical rethinking of conditionality in fact predated the global crisis. Disdain for the IMF after the Asian crisis led staff to review conditionality in 2001 and then to adopt streamlined conditionality guidelines in September 2002 (IMF 2014a). Real change proved illusory, however. A 2007 study of conditionality by the IEO found that despite the adoption of streamlining guidelines in 2002, the number of structural conditions on Fund programs remained steady, and the Fund continued to promote conditions that were not necessary to achieve program goals. Moreover, the IEO found evidence of inconsistency in IMF conditionality (IEO 2007; 2009). Scholarly studies of the scope and terms of conditionality prior to the global crisis corroborate the IEO's findings (e.g., Best 2007; Bird 2009; Momani 2005; Steinwand and Stone 2008).[69]

The global crisis provided the IMF with another opportunity to inaugurate and then trumpet changes in its approach to conditionality. The purported end of conditionality was marked by the announcement in March 2009 that the Fund had eliminated "structural conditions" in lending programs as "performance criteria" and demoted them to the more flexible status of "benchmarks." Structural conditions are generally nonquantifiable measures, such as privatization, that alter the economy's underlying institutions and practices in ways deemed necessary for achieving program

goals. They can be binding or nonbinding. Performance criteria are specific, measurable quantifiable conditions, often relating to macroeconomic
variables (Edwards and Hsieh 2011). They must be met in order for a borrower to receive installments of a loan beyond the first installment (Bird
2009). Violation of performance criteria automatically triggers program suspension unless the IMF's Executive Board approves a waiver. By contrast,
benchmarks are enforced at staff discretion.

As the first wave of SBAs was being signed in Europe, it seemed that the
IMF's forceful new rhetoric around conditionality would be matched by
its practice. But the same package of structural reforms that has long been
at the heart of IMF practice were essential features of European SBAs. The
Greek programs of 2010 and 2012 contained benchmarks involving privatization and restructuring of state-owned assets. For instance, the 2010 program was conditioned on privatization and restructuring of the national
railway, state holdings in road transportation, airports, ports, utilities, real
estate, and gaming (IMF 2010d, 50, 69, 80). In fact, the number of structural conditions increased over the course of Greece's first program (IEO
2016, 31). The 2012 program was conditioned on reductions in minimum
wages, changes in national collective bargaining arrangements, and measures that eliminate tenure and reduce employer contributions to social
security programs (IMF 2012c, 21–23; Traynor 2012). In March 2014, the
Troika insisted that the Greek government lower salaries for new public
employees, reduce salaries for other civil servants, and retain the previously
lowered minimum wage (Dabilis 2014). Many EMDE and European SBAs
call for pension system and public sector reforms and elimination of subsidy
programs. At the same time, SBAs continued to feature privatization as a
structural condition in those cases where prior programs left some SOEs
standing. Jamaica was one such case, and privatization of its national airline
featured in its February 2010 SBA.

By now it is clear that the scope and content of conditionality in IMF
assistance packages during the global crisis are consistent with those of previous crises (Grabel 2011, 821; Kentikelenis, Stubbs, and King 2016). Structural conditions remain central to the IMF's toolkit, even if some structural
conditions have been downgraded to benchmarks. Indeed, the use of
benchmarks has increased in recent years.[70] The IMF reincorporated and
widened the scope of many reforms, including structural reforms, as the
crisis progressed after 2008. Agreements in 2014 had the highest number of
benchmarks since this type of condition was introduced in the 1980s, and
the number of conditions on loans rose during the global crisis. The numbers contradict the IMF's long-standing claims regarding its streamlined

approach to conditionality, let alone its more dramatic claims about the end of conditionality.

More broadly, borrower experience with IMF conditionality has not changed in any meaningful way since the crisis (Nelson 2014a, 165). The IMF's own review of conditionality in programs signed between 2002 and September 2011 shows that "the number of conditions per program has fallen since peaking in 2004—but only back to the 2002 level" (Nelson 2014a, 162–163; IMF 2012b). Nevertheless, recent reports by the institution's staff emphasize discontinuity by highlighting the reduction in the number of structural conditions in the SBAs of the global crisis (e.g., IMF 2012a; 2012b).

The shift in rhetoric regarding conditionality hung over one of the new instruments that the IMF introduced during the global crisis. In March 2009, the IMF introduced the FCL. The FCL is essentially a precautionary (one- to two-year) line of credit designed for countries that meet a demanding set of preconditions.[71] To qualify, a country must demonstrate international capital market access and a sustainable external position; sound monetary, fiscal, and exchange rate fundamentals; a track record of sound policies and a credible commitment to their retention; the absence of bank solvency problems; and effective financial sector supervision. The criteria for policy soundness are so demanding as to render most EMDEs ineligible. Not surprisingly, few countries (namely, Mexico, Poland, and Colombia) have applied for and received FCLs.[72] The IMF was apparently disappointed that more countries did not apply (Henning 2016, 123). One observer characterizes the FCL as a "large insurance policy one never wishes to claim" (Güven 2012, 874). The IMF has cited the FCL as an example of its new, modernized conditionality. But the FCL transforms traditional structural ex post conditionality into a demanding ex ante conditionality that elevates precisely the same neoliberal policy and institutional agenda that the Fund has been promoting over the last three decades (Grabel 2011).

Social Spending Targets and Attention to Vulnerable Groups
in Support Packages

The IMF made much of its new commitment to social and pro-poor spending targets during the global crisis. Indeed, the support packages of the global crisis can be distinguished on paper from those of the Asian and prior crises by the IMF's new emphasis on social protection. This emphasis appears in many IMF reports—for example, one that surveyed 15 SBAs between July 2008 and September 2009 (IMF 2009d) and another that surveyed program packages in 19 low-income countries in the same period

(IMF 2009b, especially Annex 3; see also IMF 2014e). A 2009 report argues that social goals were supported in Fund programs and that social spending rose in some countries, such as Costa Rica (IMF 2009d). A 2011 IMF report goes further. It concludes that social spending as a percentage of total public spending rose in almost all program countries. More recently, the IMF has highlighted the ways in which its programs helped governments in EMDEs (including in low-income countries and countries in the Middle East) and in Greece to maintain or increase social spending and social assistance during the crisis (IMF 2015a; Clements, Gupta, and Nozaki 2013). The IMF has also claimed that program countries enjoyed increased spending on public health as a share of GDP (Clements, Gupta, and Nozaki 2014).[73]

One example of the IMF's increased attention to the most vulnerable during the crisis involves its stipulation that rather than eliminate the "13th month pension" in Hungary in response to fiscal difficulties, the government impose an income test to insulate poorer pensioners from the harshest effects of the crisis. A similar feature was incorporated into the SBAs with Latvia and Romania (Lütz and Kranke 2014).[74] In Greece, the IMF claims that it supported employment programs that target youth and jobless households and enhanced healthcare access for the uninsured via a voucher system, and that pension cuts targeted recipients of the highest pensions and supplemental pensions (IMF 2015a).

Critics contend that the ameliorative social policies that the IMF purports to have introduced have been inadequately or superficially incorporated into program design. For example, data from social expenditure targets in sub-Saharan Africa show that they have not been met half of the time, and that concerns regarding these targets remain secondary to the IMF's preoccupation with macroeconomic targets (Kentikelenis, Stubbs, and King 2016).

It is difficult to square the IMF's emphasis on protection of socially vulnerable groups with the severe fiscal constraints that are a key feature of so many of its recent programs. It is true that the decline in tax revenues and ODA has complicated the matter of financing social protection during the crisis. On the practical matter of where the funding for social protection is to come from, especially in the short run, the IMF has been largely silent. And in the case of Greece, for example, it is clear that IMF claims do not square with myriad indicators of severe social misery in the country during the crisis (Foy 2015; Galbraith 2016; Smith 2015). Its inconsistent opposition to the Troika's demands for Greek austerity pale in comparison with the extent of the dislocation that austerity has induced. Making matters worse, even when the IMF addressed the matter of financing social protection, its claims strained credibility. For example, a 2016 program in Egypt calls for a strengthened social safety net that includes increased spending on food subsidies and cash transfers to be financed by savings from fiscal consolidation (IMF 2016e).

The gap between IMF rhetoric and practice on protecting the vulnerable in recent programs tracks prior failures to change IMF practices on poverty and inequality (on prior failures, see Momani 2010). IMF critics are right to demand much more of the institution, but it is important to recognize that the new rhetoric on pro-poor spending is not strictly reducible to a public relations offensive, ceremonialism, or outright misstatements. The IMF's failure to incorporate social spending targets reflects in part the challenges of changing organizational cultures in institutions comprising diverse stakeholders, embedded interests, familiar scripts, and continuity in staff. In that kind of environment, the incorporation of new principles, norms, goals, and strategies cannot be orderly or seamless (Vetterlein 2010).[75] Changing practice to incorporate new aspirations is complicated and difficult, and can be frustrated by staff that are ill prepared, resistant, and that operate with some degree of autonomy, and by constraints imposed by external actors (as per Park and Vetterlein 2010).

Growing Inconsistency on Austerity, Inequality,
and Fiscal Consolidation
In 2010, and especially after the fall of 2012, the IMF's key officials, reports, and research began to highlight the costs of extreme austerity, inequality, and fiscal consolidation. These messages reflected self-assessments by IMF staff of the institution's work, new staff research, and intra-Troika tensions. The IMF's gentler rhetorical stance after 2012 also reflected proactive efforts to protect the institution's restored franchise, as well as broader zeitgeist concerns about inequality.

On the matter of austerity, in late 2012, Lagarde nudged European Troika counterparts and especially the German government toward a more flexible position. She called them to task for what she termed "wishful thinking" in the Greek program (Reuters 2012a), while also pressing to curtail the austerity program at the annual IMF–World Bank meeting in Tokyo in October 2012. At the same meeting, Germany's Schäuble publicly rejected this challenge. A senior IMF official involved in the negotiation of Ireland's November 2010 program highlighted intra-Troika tensions over austerity in remarks in 2013 (Smyth 2013).

IMF economists expressed unease with radical austerity and severe inequality during the crisis, arguing that they were counterproductive to growth. In

2010, Daniel Leigh and his colleagues provided empirical refutation of the "expansionary austerity" thesis for AEs, as offered by Alesina and Ardagna (2009) and former ECB chair Jean-Claude Trichet, which holds that slashing spending during crises creates jobs. The research of Leigh et al. (2010) was featured in the IMF's October 2010 *World Economic Outlook*. It reflected early evidence of the costs of austerity in some of the first countries caught up in the global crisis.

Research by Blanchard and Leigh in 2012 and 2013 concluded that the fiscal multipliers that the IMF (and other researchers) used had seriously and consistently underestimated the negative effect of fiscal tightening on European growth early in the crisis (see, e.g., Blanchard and Leigh 2013).[76] This work first appeared in the October 2012 *World Economic Outlook* (IMF 2012g, especially box 1.1), and led to tense exchanges between Lagarde and European critics at the IMF–World Bank meeting in Tokyo. The EC shot back quickly and released a report that downplayed the effect of austerity on European growth (Spiegel 2012; EC 2012). But despite the high profile of Blanchard and Leigh's work, it had no noticeable effect on the IMF's practices in Europe or elsewhere. And even the authors themselves seemed disquieted by their own findings. They inexplicably defended the Fund's work in Europe as "mostly right" (Blanchard and Leigh 2013; IMF 2012g, especially box 1.1). In 2015, Blanchard defended the IMF's work in Greece, saying that "fiscal consolidation explains only a small fraction of the output decline" (IEO 2016, fn5). And in statements to the press, Blanchard spoke against stimulus policies and reversals of austerity (Weisbrot 2015, 163), and he supported the IMF's insistence on further fiscal consolidation (Mody 2016).

Research and public statements by key IMF staff in 2012 raised questions about the strategy of "fiscal consolidation," especially "front-loaded" consolidation, which the G-20 and the IMF promoted in 2010 and 2011. In the foreword to the April 2012 *World Economic Outlook*, Blanchard argued that financial markets do not react to fiscal consolidation as conventional economic theory assumes. Blanchard wrote, "Markets appear somewhat schizophrenic—they ask for fiscal consolidation but react badly when consolidation leads to lower growth" (IMF 2012h, xiv). Clift (2014) notes that the IMF's growing skepticism about extreme fiscal consolidation was a point of contention within the Troika. But he also observes that from 2010 onward the IMF advocated only a slower, somewhat more mindful procyclical fiscal policy than the EU and ECB had recommended (ibid.).[77]

Internal assessment of the IMF's work in Greece and broader research by the institution's staff in 2013 and 2014 continued to reflect tensions within the Troika and discomfort at the IMF with radical austerity and inequality.

The April 2013 *World Economic Outlook* took a sidelong glance at the obsession with fiscal rectitude and inflation by the European Troika and some G-20 members (IMF 2013e). The *World Economic Outlook* refers to inflation as the "dog that didn't bark" (ibid., chap. 3). Other Fund research published around this time evidences unease with extreme austerity. One study concludes that Northern Europe would need to accept more inflation if Southern Europe is expected to adjust (Blanchard, Jaumotte, and Loungani 2013), a theme that is obliquely echoed in the April 2014 *World Economic Outlook* (IMF 2014d, 54–55). In addition, a widely cited study by Ostry, Berg, and Tsangarides (2014) examined the costs of inequality for growth, political and economic stability, social cohesion, and progress in health and educational outcomes. It concludes that some redistributive policies can have benign or even beneficial effects on growth.[78]

The IMF's views on austerity, inequality, and fiscal consolidation evolved inconsistently during the crisis. Research by the institution's staff and public statements by key officials remained largely orthogonal to the institution's practice with client states (Ban 2013; Gabor 2010; Güven 2012; Ortiz and Cummins 2013). Ban (2015) characterizes the IMF's stance on fiscal matters as "hybridized . . . editing . . . a very modest recalibration" in which precrisis orthodoxy is overlaid with mildly Keynesian themes in its research and public statements in 2008–2009 and again after 2012. The IEO takes note of the perception that the IMF's advice on fiscal policy matters is evolving modestly and gradually, even while it continues to emphasize the primacy of fiscal space when considering the viability of short-term fiscal stimulus (IEO 2013; Reichmann 2013). In summing up interviews and surveys, especially among EMDE representatives, the IEO reports that there is "a shift in perceptions. . . . [A] common view . . . was that the IMF . . . abandoned its emphasis on fiscal adjustment and was . . . more attuned to . . . social and economic development . . . [and that] the IMF became a strong proponent of short-term fiscal stimulus, wherever fiscal space was available, further dampening its preoccupation with fiscal discipline" (IEO 2013, 11). In mid-2016, Lagarde continued to speak of her desire to have the institution go "deeper and further" in its work on inequality, but at the same time she acknowledged skepticism about the matter by outsiders and some within the institution (Donnan 2016a).[79]

For some observers, the new framing of outdated policies represents a desperate attempt by the IMF to burnish its image. But it is better to see the gap between research, rhetoric, and practice as one among several ambiguities—resulting in part from the IMF's "silo-like" organizational culture (as per Nelson 2017, 205)—that reflect a contested, uneven, and ultimately uncertain process of change being negotiated within an extraordinarily complex international organization.[80]

This discussion sustains the following tentative conclusions. The IMF's response to the global crisis diverges in some respects from, and is less coherent than, its response to the Asian crisis and prior crises. IMF practice concerning macroeconomic adjustment evidences strong policy continuity with that of previous crises, despite new research by the institution's economists, a multifaceted rhetoric of change, and Keynesian-inflected concerns during the early moments of the crisis. The IMF continues to apply pressure to secure compliance with stringent fiscal policy targets and expansive conditionality.[81] To a limited extent, the Fund now emphasizes the need to protect social spending targets and the dispossessed while moderating the pace of fiscal consolidation and austerity. Although it has failed to move much beyond aspirations in these areas, the new rhetoric and research mark important breaks with the past that legitimize a concern for the poor and for the social costs of inequality and austerity. Though it is certainly not the IMF's intent to do so, the new rhetoric is empowering external actors to hold the institution accountable to IMF-sanctioned normative criteria and concerns that had largely been missing from the IMF platform. In addition, the rhetorical turn exposes the long-held neoliberal script to contestation from IMF insiders, such as IEO researchers who have proven themselves willing and able to indict the institution. Indeed, for the first time in decades, there is growing overlap between the insights of IMF insiders and outside researchers on IMF failures.

Conclusion

The question is not "do we have a new IMF?" as some observers, such as Weisbrot (2015, 160), have bluntly put the matter. For him, the question can easily be answered in the negative. Proof of concept is found in the scope and severity of conditionality, the influence of key member states and the failed ideas they advance, and IMF hypocrisy (ibid., 160, 163). Weisbrot presses the matter further in asserting, with equal certainty, that there will be no significant change in the future (ibid., 239). He predicts that the IMF will be less important to EMDEs as China gives countries more and better options (ibid.), but he doesn't recognize that this shifting landscape will alter IMF governance and practice.[82]

In my view, the matter is far more complex than other analysts will allow. The IMF has been and is evolving in ways that bear centrally on global financial flows and governance. In some domains, we find clear and compelling evidence of continuity. In others, especially as concerns capital controls, we find consequential discontinuities (see chapter 7). And in still others, we find mounting evidence of inconsistencies and ambiguities that involve substantive gaps between the rhetoric, research, and policy practice. As is clear by now, I treat change at the IMF in a manner that is in keeping with subtler treatments that emphasize unevenness, discontinuity, and incrementalism.[83] The conclusion to be drawn is that there has been partial and inconsistent though meaningful change at the IMF, despite evidence of continuity.[84] This finding is driven by the empirical record when read through a Hirschmanian lens—one that recognizes that institutional evolution is typically contingent, messy, and contested, and that though historical developments are path dependent, the future is fundamentally unscripted.

In seeking to come to some conclusion about whether the IMF has actually changed, many observers scrutinized a widely circulated 2016 essay in the IMF's *Finance and Development* magazine. The essay "Neoliberalism Oversold?" by IMF economists Jonathan Ostry, Prakash Loungani, and Davide Furceri (Ostry, Loungani, and Furceri 2016) reflects on the implications of their own and their colleagues' recent research on austerity, inequality, and fiscal consolidation. Some IMF watchers seized on the essay to support the case that the IMF had changed fundamentally. Others emphasized its affirmation of central doctrines of neoliberal policy as evidence that the change is more apparent than real. In reality, the essay exemplifies an internally contested, inconsistent, and still evolving process of change at the IMF during the global crisis. On the one hand, Ostry, Loungani, and Furceri state that "there is much to cheer in the neoliberal agenda" (ibid., 38). They affirm the IMF's traditional view in stating that many countries have little choice but to engage in fiscal consolidation because markets will not let them borrow, and they emphasize the benefits of privatization, trade expansion, liberalization, and FDI. But they also argue that aspects of the neoliberal agenda "have not delivered as expected" (ibid.). In making this case, they cite recent research that shows that countries with "ample fiscal space" would do better to live with debt; that expansionary fiscal consolidation has been discredited; and that the short-run costs of fiscal consolidation have been underplayed.[85] In a subsequent *Financial Times* article, Ostry notes the simultaneous wariness and new openness at the IMF, stating that the essay "did not reflect 'mainstream culture' at the IMF and would not have made it into a fund publication as recently as five years ago" (Donnan 2016b). In the same article, Rodrik quips, "What the hell is going on?" He notes that " 'there is definitely a gap' between the IMF's research arm and other parts of the institution. 'The operational side . . . is typically more orthodox. . . . There the change is slower and is lagging behind the thinking' " (quoted in Donnan 2016b). Rodrik also observes that the IMF's push for debt relief in Greece suggests that research by Ostry and others is influencing IMF policy. In an interview on the Ostry, Loungani, and Furceri essay, the IMF's Obstfeld describes the process of change at the IMF as "evolution not revolution" (IMF 2016b, 1). This seems a reasonable interpretation of how change occurs in a complex organization comprising diverse internal and external stakeholders with conflicting interests and competing views about prudent economic policy.

As events in Europe demonstrate, for the first time in decades, the IMF's role as the central driver of crisis response activities is in question. The centrality of the IMF will depend on its continued ability to retain the financial vitality and authority it regained during the global crisis, and on whether EMDEs are willing or are forced to turn to the IMF in the coming years. The latter, in turn, depends very much on the ability of EMDEs to navigate future global turbulence, and on whether emerging institutions in these countries develop the capacity to compete with the IMF or evolve in ways that create linkages with the institution that are distinct from those that characterize the Troika. For now, the IMF has many "unmet challenges," as Eichengreen and Woods (2016) have recently argued. These include addressing the content and lack of evenhandedness of conditionality and surveillance, addressing the long-identified absence of a sovereign debt restructuring mechanism, and making significant progress on governance (ibid.). Failure to take on these challenges will reinforce deep concerns about its competence, credibility, and legitimacy (Eichengreen and Woods 2016; Nelson 2014a).

That said, crisis-induced transformations in global financial governance provide the IMF with yet another opportunity for reinvention. One path entails an effort to reassert itself as the driver of institutional and policy coherence across the EMDEs (and those AEs that are unfortunate enough to face IMF conditionality). That path will be difficult to tread given increased EMDE autonomy and assertiveness during and since the crisis, and the erosion in confidence in the simplistic neoliberal script. The other path leads toward recognition of the legitimacy and necessity of policy autonomy, where the IMF coordinates activities with established and emerging EMDE institutions of financial governance to mediate institutional and policy diversity rather than imposing conformity (see chapters 6–8). This task is perhaps less appealing to economists trained during the latter decades of the twentieth century, who were socialized to theorize and engineer a globally coherent regime that infused national economies while spanning national borders. It may require a Hirschmanian shift in weltanschauung that encompasses a new vision of the role of economists in the development process.

If we widen our gaze beyond the IMF to consider the EMDEs themselves, we find widespread experimentation and an increased density in the landscape of institutions that provide liquidity support and development finance. Existing institutions have been given new life by the global crisis, and entirely new institutions have been created. Some of these initiatives, especially the largest, which feature China as the key driver, are already having significant impacts on the BWIs. In this context, some observers, such as Ocampo (2010c), have called for the IMF to take on new roles in coordinating or supporting the evolving, dense geometry of global financial governance. In the next chapter, we turn to the new emerging landscape.

6   The Changing Institutional Landscape of Financial Governance and Developmental Finance in Emerging Market and Developing Economies

The crises of the 1970s and 1980s generated demands for "South-South" development institutions that would be largely autonomous from the BWIs. In contrast, the Asian and the global crises spawned a new pragmatism reflected in the view that EMDE institutions could complement and, to a much lesser extent, substitute for the BWIs. EMDE institutions are evolving in ways that allow them to fill persistent gaps in the global financial architecture—such as by increasing their ability and commitment to provide long-term project and infrastructure financing and by expanding liquidity support during periods of instability. In short, we find institutional proliferation and expanding mandates that place the EMDEs at the center of an evolving landscape of what I have referred to throughout as financial governance and developmental finance.

As I have by now argued at length, the Asian and especially the global crises precipitated discontinuities in the global financial governance architecture. The willingness and ability of EMDEs to undertake ad hoc and uncoordinated innovation in financial governance in the absence of a theoretical and political consensus around a new paradigm is one of the most important legacies of the recent crises. The innovations are best understood as uneven, partial, experimental, contested, and incomplete. In this chapter, I focus on salient discontinuities—namely, the way in which crises have contributed to decentralized institutional innovations in the domains of reserve pooling and project and infrastructure finance in EMDEs. The innovations do not coalesce around a unified global architecture that rivals the BWIs. Instead, we find an expansion in the reach and mission of disparate institutions that pre-dated the global crisis, as well as the creation of entirely new ones. Taken together, they increase the heterogeneity and density of the financial governance landscape and seed the ground for a more complex, decentralized, and resilient global financial system (Chin 2015; Grabel 2013a; 2013b; Helleiner 2010; Huotari and Hanemann 2014; Mittelman

2013; Riggirozzi and Tussie 2012).[1] Equally important, the initiatives also promise to enhance policy autonomy and thereby widen policy space for development. At the same time, the emerging institutional landscape complicates the terrain in which the BWIs operate; affords EMDE policymakers greater voice than is available to them at the BWIs; increases EMDE exit options and leverage at the BWIs by increasing the opportunity for forum shopping; and creates opportunities for unscripted learning by doing and learning from others. When approached from this vantage point, the developments surveyed in this chapter emerge as enormously promising institutional experiments. The perspective on offer follows Hirschman in refusing to discount small, disconnected, ad hoc innovations for which the pedigree cannot be traced back to a grand, utopian scheme. Instead, these incremental innovations have taken root in the concrete demands facing policymakers, who are adjusting pragmatically to the changing circumstances and challenges they face.

Crises and Interest in Regional and Transregional Financial Architectures in EMDEs

Interest in regional financial architectures in EMDEs is rooted in the development models and economic crises of the past several decades (Ocampo 2006, chap. 1). In South America, a first wave of financial regionalism was associated with the "Grand Designs" of the 1950s and 1960s, a second with the "New Regionalism" or "Open Regionalism" of the 1980s and 1990s, and a recent wave with the "post-hegemonic, post-neoliberal" politics in countries that up until recent elections featured populist and left-leaning governments (Riggirozzi and Tussie 2012). In EMDEs and Europe, economic and financial crises spurred the creation of regional reserve pooling arrangements and safety nets (Rhee, Sumulong, and Vallée 2013). For instance, the creation of the European "currency snake," Arab Monetary Fund, ASEAN Swap Arrangement, and Andean Reserve Fund is connected to the instability associated with the collapse of the pegged exchange rate system, the oil shocks of the 1970s, and the Latin American debt crisis of the 1980s.

The Asian Crisis
The East Asian and other crises in the 1990s stimulated interest among scholars and practitioners in regional financial mechanisms to deliver liquidity support and long-term project financing through institutions that were to some extent independent of the BWIs. As discussed in chapter 3, the

AMF proposal was motivated by the Asian crisis. But the focus on regional financial architectures extended beyond the region. For example, Mistry (1999) argued for the expansion of regional crisis management capacities that would support national and global institutions; Agosin (2001) for a Latin American Fund capitalized by a modest proportion of the region's reserve holdings (possibly backed by contingency credits from the international banking system), which could supplement IMF initiatives and provide a degree of protection from regional financial crises; and, in the 2002 "Monterrey Consensus," the UN advanced a case for a multilayered financial architecture in which regional and subregional institutions play a greater role (UN 2002, para. 45).

The Asian crisis and subsequent global economic conditions played a pivotal role in the rise of reserve accumulation strategies by EMDEs. The success of this strategy provided the political confidence and material support for the institutional innovations of the global crisis.

The Global Crisis

The global crisis focused more attention than the Asian crisis on the role and capacity of regional and transregional financial arrangements in EMDEs. The UN's Stiglitz Commission and a second UN-appointed commission called for a new global monetary system built from the bottom up through a series of agreements among regional arrangements, echoing the embrace of financial regionalism that followed the Asian crisis (UN 2009, chap. 5; 2014). UNCTAD (2011, 115), too, emphasized the role of regional financial architectures. It usefully offered a vaguely articulated concept of "developmental regionalism" to frame discussions of South-South cooperation. Scholars such as Ocampo (2010c) argued that improving economic and social governance requires a multilayered network in which regional and subregional institutions mediate between global and national financial arrangements.[2] In a similar vein, Wade (2008) discusses institutional "middleware"—software that allows different families of operating systems to communicate with one another in one integrated platform—as an analogy for what is currently lacking in the global financial architecture.

Support for regional financial architectures also came from unexpected actors. In contrast to the hostility with which the IMF greeted the AMF proposal, Strauss-Kahn argued during the global crisis that the Fund should "look at ways to collaborate with regional reserve pools. We . . . do not see such funds as 'competitors' . . . collaboration could . . . include Fund resources . . . as a backstop to regional pools" (Strauss-Kahn 2010b).[3]

Statements released by the IMF's IMFC in October 2010 and April 2011 also highlighted the importance of IMF cooperation with regional arrangements (Rhee, Sumulong, and Vallée 2013, 227; Miyoshi 2013, 4). For its part, in April 2009 the G-20 promoted regional financial arrangements when it dispersed a portion of the IMF's new funds to the main regional development banks (MRDBs) to support new lending (Chin 2010). At the time, Indonesia proposed that a portion of the IMF's new resources be allocated to the AsDB (ibid.). In November 2010, the G-20 charged finance ministers and central bank governors with exploring "ways to improve collaboration between regional financial arrangements and the IMF," and a year later it endorsed a broad set of modest principles for cooperation (see G-20 2011b).[4] As we will see, under Lagarde's leadership, the IMF has continued to deepen its engagement with regional (and transregional) reserve pooling initiatives.

The global crisis has stimulated heterogeneous financial regionalisms across EMDEs.[5] Some observers, including myself, see the crisis as having even a broader effect on the financial landscape, moving it in the direction not just of more regionalisms but toward a more complex, fragmented, and pluripolar direction—driven in large part by initiatives from below rather than from above.[6]

Analytical Framework

The diverse institutions that I survey in what follows can be corralled under the following framework: institutional stasis; capacity expansion; hybridization; and institutional creation.

Institutional stasis refers to maintaining rather than expanding precrisis institutional activity and identity. *Capacity expansion* refers to enhancements in the scale of activity of existing institutions. It is most simply achieved through increased funding by participating governments but also through new revenue streams, expanded geographical reach, or the introduction of novel mechanisms or programs toward achievement of traditional or newly identified objectives.

Hybridization can occur purposely, when an institution decides to reach beyond its existing mission, but also unintentionally, when an institution seeks to maintain its traditional focus but its actions ultimately blur aspects of the institution's identity. For instance, a development bank that traditionally provides project financing might begin to provide countercyclical financial support during a crisis, or its project support might come to play an important countercyclical role during the crisis. Finally, *institutional creation* involves transformation of proposals or aspirations into concrete institutions by existing or new parties.

A Selective Survey of Architectural Innovations in EMDEs

There are far too many innovations to examine here, and I make no claim for comprehensiveness or even exploratory depth. Instead, I provide a view from 30,000 feet of a sample of institutions—transregional, regional, sub-regional, national, and multilateral—the evolution of which is emblematic of developments and aspirations elsewhere. I first consider arrangements that involve reserve pooling. I then turn to development banks that provide longer-term project and/or infrastructure financing. As discussed in chapter 1, these two forms of support constitute what I term developmental finance.

For reasons of space and also because I am focused on initiatives that take the BWIs as their critical point of departure, I do not consider two other types of financial architectural innovations, namely, payment systems and macroeconomic, monetary, and exchange rate integration schemes (on these, see Fritz and Mühlich 2014; 2015).[7] These, too, evolved considerably during the global crisis, reflecting other modalities of experimentation and discontinuity in the global financial architecture.

Tables 6.1 and 6.2 summarize the results of this survey and anticipate the discussion that follows. Table 6.1 highlights the chief goals and practices of the institutions and arrangements that I survey. Table 6.2 maps their stasis and change during the global crisis.

Reserve Pooling Institutions and Arrangements

Reserve pooling, also known as liquidity sharing, is initiated for the purpose of providing precautionary liquidity and/or countercyclical forms of support to members of a pooling arrangement in the event of currency, liquidity, and/or balance of payments pressure. Support is intended to stave off or mitigate stress in a member economy. It can also reduce the severity of a variety of contagion effects experienced by participating nations, while protecting policy autonomy, especially during periods of economic instability. Reserve pooling may take place through a formal institution or agreements among participating central banks. In some cases, participating central banks may physically transfer reserves to an institution that

Table 6.1
Chief Institutional Goals or Practices

Institution or Arrangement	Reserve Pooling	Liquidity/ Countercyclical Support	Precautionary Support	Development, Project, or Infrastructure Finance	Other Goals, Motivations, and/or Practices
CMIM	✓	✓*	✓*		• Support central banks by improving return on international reserve investments and facilitating public debt restructuring
FLAR	✓	✓	✓		• Support trade and financial integration • Prohibit trade conflict in balance of payments adjustment programs • Promote policy coordination
ArMF	✓	✓			• Support trade and financial integration** • Support monetary policy coordination and exchange rate stability** • Support eventual establishment of a common currency** • Support financial deepening**
EFSD	✓	✓		✓	• Grants to poorer member states to support social programs
CRA	✓	✓*	✓*		• Reflection of frustration with the IMF
CAF		✓***		✓	• Support regional integration and development of local currency bond markets
NDB				✓	• Support sustainability, including sustainable infrastructure • Reflection of frustration with World Bank and MRDBs

AIIB & Belt and Road Initiative/Silk Road Fund		✓	• Support China's geostrategic ambitions and economic needs, promote integration, focus on infrastructure with emphasis on sustainability • Reflection of frustration with governance of the World Bank and MRDBs (especially AsDB) and their failure to prioritize infrastructure
BNDES	✓***	✓	• Support the internationalization of and FDI by Brazilian firms • Offer trade credit and working capital to Brazilian firms operating abroad
CDB	✓***	✓	• Support the government's macroeconomic policies and development objectives
MRDBs	✓***	✓	• Poverty reduction, provision of public goods, and infrastructure investment

Notes: CMIM=Chiang Mai Initiative Multilateralisation; FLAR=Latin American Reserve Fund; ArMF=Arab Monetary Fund; EFSD=Eurasian Fund for Stabilization and Development; CRA=Contingent Reserve Arrangement; CAF=Development Bank of Latin America (formerly Andean Development Corporation); NDB=New Development Bank; AIIB=Asian Infrastructure Investment Bank; Belt and Road Initiative=One Belt, One Road Initiative; BNDES=Brazil National Bank of Economic and Social Development; CDB=China Development Bank; MRDBs=Main Regional Development Banks (including the African Development Bank [AfDB], the Asian Development Bank [AsDB], the Inter-American Development Bank [IADB], but excluding the European Bank for Reconstruction and Development [EBRD], and the European Investment Bank [EIB]).

* Arrangement established but no drawings to date.

** Stated secondary goal, but no action or evidence to support claims.

*** Provision of countercyclical support is not an explicit function of the institution, but some resources disbursed during crises have countercyclical effects.

Source: Author's analysis.

Table 6.2
Mapping Stasis and Types of Change during the Global Crisis

Institution or Arrangement	Institutional Stasis	Capacity Expansion	Hybridization	Institutional Creation
CMIM		✓		✓
FLAR		✓	✓	
ArMF		✓		
EFSD			Created as hybrid	✓
CRA				✓
CAF		✓	Project loans and "fast disbursement and contingent operations" played a countercyclical role	
NDB				✓
AIIB & Belt and Road Initiative/ Silk Road Fund				✓
BNDES		✓	Support played a powerful counter-cyclical role	
CDB		✓	Support played a powerful counter-cyclical role	
MRDBs		✓	✓	

Source: Author's analysis.

manages them in a common pool and disburses them following application by a member and evaluation of the member's request. Alternatively, central banks may self-manage their funds domestically and commit themselves legally to contribute funds to a common pool when circumstances warrant.[8]

Decisions by reserve pooling arrangements (and development banks) are made by boards that are either residential or nonresidential. Nonresidential boards are more cost-effective and are widely understood to be more agile and responsive to the particular needs of member countries.

Table 6.3 summarizes key aspects of the reserve pooling arrangements examined here.

Table 6.3
Reserve Pooling Institutions and Arrangements (US$Billions; 2016 Data Unless Otherwise Noted)

Institution or Arrangement	Fund Resources	Precautionary Support	Rapid Disbursals	IMF Link	Surveillance by	Conditionality or Adjustment Requirements
CMIM	240.0 pledged	Yes (not yet utilized)	No	Above 30% threshold for both lending facilities	AMRO; IMF involvement above 30% threshold	Qualification criteria under precautionary facility; IMF program under both lending facilities above 30% threshold
FLAR	3.9 subscribed	Yes	Yes, for some facilities	No	FLAR's Division of Economic Studies	Support tied to remediation plans and requires recipient to forgo trade strategies that are harmful to other FLAR members
ArMF	3.8 (2015) subscribed	No	Yes, for some facilities	No, but support under three facilities predicated on drawing reserves from other institutions (including the IMF)	ArMF	Yes, for support under all but two facilities
EFSD	8.5 subscribed	No	Yes, though evidence scant	No, but is "guided" by IMF in some matters	Eurasian Development Bank	Yes, for all "financial credits"
CRA	100.0 pledged	Yes (not yet utilized)	No	Above 30% threshold for both lending facilities	IMF involvement above 30% threshold (otherwise uncertain)	IMF program under both lending facilities above 30% threshold

Sources: Institutional websites, annual reports, financial statements, and investor presentations (and, where unavailable, news stories).

The Chiang Mai Initiative Multilateralisation

In 2000, the Chiang Mai Initiative (CMI) built on the failed AMF proposal and a 1977 bilateral currency swap agreement among five Association of Southeast Asian Nations (ASEAN) central banks.[9] The CMI ultimately involved the ten central banks of ASEAN and the ASEAN+3 countries. The CMI was conceived as "bridge financing and a supplement to IMF-led bailouts" (Grimes 2015, 149). The initial value of the swaps was US$30 billion, and the value of these commitments increased several times. Initially, and at the behest of creditor countries, disbursals in excess of 10% of the credits available to a borrowing country required that it submit to an IMF surveillance program. The threshold for IMF involvement was raised to 20% in 2005.

The global crisis induced the deepening and expansion of the CMI. The arrangement is now intended to address potential and actual balance of payments and short-term liquidity difficulties among its members. In 2009, ASEAN+3 finance ministers agreed to "multilateralize" the arrangement, an idea they had considered since 2005 (Cohen 2012, 44). The arrangement was accordingly renamed the Chiang Mai Initiative Multilateralisation (CMIM). Multilateralization entailed several things. Decisions on disbursing funds from a US$120 billion virtual currency pool would be made collectively. Members pledge reserves to CMIM, which are owned by and remain with member nations. Assistance under CMIM would be disbursed as dollar–local currency swaps among the ASEAN+3 and Hong Kong. Multilateralization was also reflected in the decision to establish an independent secretariat, the ASEAN+3 Macroeconomic Research Office (AMRO). After politically challenging discussions, AMRO was established in Singapore in 2011 and began to operate in January 2012. It is the regional surveillance unit of the CMIM. It "monitors and analyses regional economies and contributes to the early detection of risks [through preparation of quarterly reports on the macroeconomic conditions of the region and member countries], provides policy recommendations for remedial actions, and ensures the effective decision-making of the CMIM" (AMRO website). AMRO's mandate is more ambitious during crises. It is to provide a timely "analysis of the economic and financial situation of the CMIM Swap Requesting Country; to monitor the use and impact of the funds disbursed . . . ; and monitor the compliance . . . with any lending covenants to the CMIM Agreement" (Rhee, Sumulong, and Vallée 2013, 233).

The link between CMIM support and IMF surveillance has been a matter of controversy among members from the start. Initially some members, most notably Malaysia, opposed any IMF link (Sohn 2012). But China's and

Japan's representatives argued that the IMF link was essential to CMIM's credibility during its formative period. The link also allayed concerns about repayment and reflected the challenging politics of regional surveillance.[10] At the outset, China reportedly favored linking all CMIM disbursals to IMF conditionality (Amyx 2008, 121; Hamanaka 2016).[11] Japan also favored the IMF link, since it keeps the IMF (and hence the United States) engaged in the region (Cohen 2012, 52). Paradoxically, this link may have inhibited members from drawing on available resources, given their experience with the IMF during the Asian crisis (Sussangkarn 2011). For committed futilists, the link undermines the significance of CMIM. But to the extent that the threshold for IMF involvement has been raised several times, and that CMIM and AMRO continue to evolve and deepen their relationships with regional and transregional bodies, the significance of the IMF link can be expected to diminish over time.

As the global crisis worsened, CMIM members wrestled with and deepened the arrangement a second time. In May 2012, the size of the swap pool was doubled to US$240 billion, the maturity of the IMF-linked and delinked swaps was lengthened, and the arrangement's original crisis resolution facility was renamed the Stability Facility. Moreover, in a gesture that signified increasing CMIM autonomy, the threshold for IMF involvement (including for the new precautionary line of credit) was raised to 30% in 2012, with a plan to increase it to 40% in 2014, "subject to review should conditions warrant" (Grimes 2015, 150, fn8).[12] The move to 40% was deferred, and though raised in a speech by the finance minister of the Philippines during a May 2017 ASEAN meeting, no action was taken (Caraballo 2017). Observers suggest that the adjustment to 40% is ultimately likely since the governments of China and Japan reportedly will support it once CMIM's screening, surveillance, and conditionality are regularized (Katada and Sohn 2014). A new Precautionary Line was also introduced in May 2012. The Precautionary Line is intended as a crisis prevention facility available to members that are at risk of experiencing a funding crisis despite "responsible" macroeconomic and financial management. Precautionary support is to be extended without strict ex ante conditionality. However, members would have to meet a five-point qualification criterion that is based on the "Economic Review and Policy Dialogue Matrix" for all ASEAN+3 members. The indicators under this matrix focus on external position and market access, fiscal policy, monetary policy, financial sector soundness and supervision, and data adequacy (ASEAN+3 2016; AMRO 2016a). Disbursal criteria under the Precautionary Line are under development, as noted in the communiqué of a May 2016 meeting of ASEAN+3 finance ministers and central bankers, which states that the body was "looking forward to further development" of disbursal criteria (ASEAN+3 2016). The communiqué also notes that disbursal would be linked not just to criteria under the Review and Dialogue Matrix but also to reviews of the economic reports of the country and analyses by AMRO, AsDB, and the IMF. These measures indicate the institutional cooperation and complementarity that is an explicit part of the CMIM/AMRO vision.

China, Japan, and Korea provide 80% of CMIM resources, while ASEAN countries provide the remaining 20%.[13] Poorer countries have privileged borrowing access. Multilateralization also involves an agreement on voting weights, a matter that was contentious. Japan reportedly favored tying voting weights to contributions, mirroring the practice at the IMF and some regional financial institutions (Ciorciari 2011, 939–940). Negotiations ultimately yielded a compromise after smaller ASEAN members raised concerns about dominance by large members. Decisions regarding renewals and disbursals from CMIM are decided on the basis of a weighted two-thirds majority voting system in which each country receives 1.6 basic voting shares plus additional voting shares based on contributions. Reflecting the power and wealth dynamics of the region, China and Japan have the same voting weight, Korea half that weight, and ASEAN countries the residual. Despite China's and Japan's significant block of votes, neither alone can veto disbursals.

Despite the evolution of CMI/CMIM since 2000, its development has been described by some observers as "excruciatingly slow" and episodic, driven as it is by crises and irregular contact among officials (Cohen 2012, 61). Skeptics see it as mostly symbolic (Cohen 2012, 45; Grimes 2015, 150). For some, the 2012 decisions were disappointing (Grimes 2015; Haggard 2013). For instance, critics cited the paradoxical nature of the Precautionary Line. On the one hand, it represents a maturation of CMIM. On the other, it was seen to threaten the still limited regional political solidarity by creating two classes of ASEAN members—those with and those without responsible policies (Grimes 2015, 154, 157). It also potentially places China and Japan in the position of determining which countries fall into which category (ibid.).

Some analysts have suggested that great power rivalries, mutual suspicion, and regional security tensions run so deep that the IMF is viewed as a necessary "neutral third party" in the region, especially by China and Japan (Grimes 2011; 2015, 149; see also Cohen 2012). Historical and political mistrust among CMIM members compounds challenges within CMIM and is reflected in the tradition of noninterference in one another's affairs and in the cautious, institutionally shallow integration often referred to as the "ASEAN way" (Katada and Sohn 2014). Some see the IMF link as reflecting the dominant role of the United States and the IMF (Parisot 2013). Others note that CMIM's swaps have never been activated, and that as the global crisis emerged, members turned to bilateral swaps between their central banks and those of the United States, China, and Japan (Helleiner 2014b). Later in the crisis and after the CMIM's Precautionary Line was introduced, Japan, China, and Korea each became parties to large, new bilateral swaps with several ASEAN member states, and Japan and China each opened swaps with Korea (see Grimes 2015, table 1; Mühlich and Fritz 2016). These developments are taken as evidence that CMIM failed its first real test (Cohen 2012; Emmers and Ravenhill 2011; Grimes 2009b; 2009c; 2011; Ravenhill 2010). Others dismiss CMIM since larger members continue to stockpile reserves while the swap pool (especially the portion that is not linked to the IMF) remains small relative to the potential needs of larger countries during crises (Cohen 2012; Kim and Yang 2014).[14]

Several observers are also skeptical as to whether AMRO will ever evolve into a true regional surveillance body (Azis 2011; Brown 2011; Grimes 2011; Kawai 2010). Critics cite sensitivities among members, lack of clarity about how its autonomy might be ensured and how its analyses might be used, and what standards it will apply (Grimes 2015; Haggard 2013). Grimes concludes that "progress in AMRO seems to have stalled," though he also notes that participants in AMRO surveillance procedures report that they have been given privileged access to member economic data and that undisclosed discussions of economic policy have been productive (Grimes 2015, 153; Siregar and Chabchitrchaidol 2013).

Not all observers are skeptical about CMIM and AMRO. Chin (2012, 7) is cautiously optimistic; he sees AMRO's progress as a possible "second step" in a gradual loosening of the CMIM-IMF link. AMRO is in fact developing in notable ways. As of 2016, 25 members of its 46 person staff were on its surveillance team.[15] Its staff—though still small relative to its mandate of reviewing the economies of 13 member countries—is refining surveillance capabilities. AMRO completes a surveillance paper on each member country every year, though these are not yet publicly available. AMRO, the IMF, and national central banks and finance ministries are developing processes for working together in various ways. To date, the IMF has participated in all key AMRO meetings; AMRO has reached an agreement with the Fund to observe all of its meetings with individual countries; Fund staff have engaged in "outreach and dialogue" with AMRO (Miyoshi 2013, fn25); and central bank governors and finance ministers now meet at AMRO. These processes are likely to enhance the capabilities of AMRO staff to conduct surveillance independent of the Fund.[16] In the interim, this contact could render the IMF-CMIM link more palatable to CMIM members should AMRO represent member country interests with the Fund in an effective and vigorous manner. The maturation of AMRO's surveillance capabilities and authority could very well reduce or even eliminate the need for an IMF link (Sussangkarn 2011, 213–218). Finally, as an indication of the evolving character of CMIM, ASEAN+3 members signed an agreement in November 2014 to upgrade AMRO to an international organization. The agreement went into effect in February 2016.

It would be naïve to imagine that the CMIM will take the place of the IMF in the region. It is not intended to do so. But this hardly suggests that the CMIM is fated to remain a marginal or subordinate player. The key is to recognize complementarities that can enhance the CMIM's stature, influence, and relative autonomy over time in ways that promote regional financial stability. From this perspective, for instance, the large national reserve accumulation in CMIM countries, alongside CMIM's financial resources, increases the capacity and creates productive redundancy in the global and regional safety nets, with vast potential benefits to global financial resilience. Smaller CMIM members may also benefit from the opportunity for forum shopping during crises that CMIM affords. Moreover, IMF-linked swaps through CMIM might eventually be associated with adjustment programs that look substantially different from those negotiated in cases where AMRO officials do not have a seat at the table with the IMF. If, as some now worry, AMRO is unable to acquire influence over the IMF, CMIM and AMRO officials might very well continue to weaken the IMF link by further raising the threshold for IMF involvement in CMIM affairs.[17]

These concerns should be taken seriously, but if the global crisis reveals anything, it is that unexpected developments happen just when the need arises.[18] The decisions made in 2009 and 2012, and the ongoing discussions in CMIM and AMRO, underscore the dynamism of the arrangement and policymakers' commitment to push its institutional boundaries, even if just gradually. What some have described as a disappointingly slow process should be recognized as promising and productive when one considers the historical and geopolitical factors that would seem to doom the enterprise from the start. In any event, it is premature to conclude that CMIM and AMRO will fail to adapt as new demands are placed on them. Contrary to the view of skeptics, CMIM's limited resources in comparison with the potential needs of larger member countries or the vast resources of some of the region's central banks, or compared with China's vast crisis-response package of November 2008, does not indicate insignificance. CMIM is part of an evolving liquidity-support architecture within which its contributions could be consequential. It is not (yet) intended to substitute for other institutions, but the learning, trust, bargaining, and socialization by finance officials that takes place through CMIM may very well create the conditions for more significant cooperation and further institutional development in this and other regions during future crises. The point is that the identities and practices of fledgling institutions are not set in stone from the get-go and are not dictated once and for all by their charters. Instead, they often evolve and adapt in ways that were not anticipated by their founders, especially when they start at a manageable scale and develop in line with their expanding internal resources and the challenges they confront. There is no reason to think that CMIM and AMRO are incapable of that kind of development. In fact, they seem to be evolving along these lines.

The costs of the EU's failure to address regional surveillance and the Troika's heavy-handedness were certainly not lost on CMIM members as they gathered in 2012 to expand and deepen CMIM arrangements. That lesson continues to inform CMIM thinking and decision making. Indeed, in 2016, a study of "Troika Financial Assistance Programs in the Euro Area for CMIM's Future Reference" (ASEAN+3 2016) was completed under CMIM's auspices. In addition, in May 2016, CMIM and AMRO conducted "test runs" of the IMF delinked portions of CMIM funds under various scenarios, and later in the year conducted the first test run of the crisis resolution facility that is linked to an IMF program. The test revealed important inadequacies, which are now being addressed.[19] These initiatives indicate that CMIM and AMRO continue to deepen their capacities in the postcrisis context.

CMIM's structure and procedures have been watched closely by policymakers in Latin America (AsDB and IADB 2012), inspiring the 2014 decision to launch a similar initiative by the BRICS, as we will see. Moreover, representatives from AMRO, ESM, the Latin American Reserve Fund, the Arab Monetary Fund, the Contingent Reserve Arrangement of the BRICS, the Eurasian Development Bank, the G-20, and the IMF met for the first time on the sidelines of the fall 2016 meetings of the IMF–World Bank (AMRO 2016b). The meeting served as a forum to discuss views on cooperation among these regional and transregional bodies and with the IMF and regional financial arrangements. The decision was made to convene for further discussion annually (AMRO 2016b), suggesting increased cooperation, the deepening of networks, and the gradual emergence of an increasingly complex financial architecture across the globe.[20]

The Latin American Reserve Fund

Latin America has the longest history of regional integration efforts and the greatest number of regional and subregional financial arrangements in the developing world (Ocampo and Titelman 2012). The Andean Reserve Fund was founded in 1978. In 1988, the organization changed its name to the Latin American Reserve Fund (Spanish acronym FLAR) when it decided to admit non-Andean nations, the first of which was Costa Rica in 2000. Like CMIM, the FLAR is a regional reserve pooling arrangement that lends to member central banks.[21] It is designed to respond to transitory liquidity issues in member states. In the event of more enduring structural problems, the FLAR may provide what ultimately can be seen as "bridge finance" while a member seeks support from another institution, particularly the IMF (Perry 2015, 28).

The FLAR maintains five credit facilities, including balance of payments, liquidity, and contingency loan facilities. Contingency loans provide precautionary access to funds for up to six months (with possible renewals) to address internal or external shocks. Access is capped at twice a member's paid-in capital. There is no provision for prequalification under the contingency line. Balance of payments credits, which provide funding for up to three years and are capped at 2.5 times a member's paid-in capital, are the most frequently used of the FLAR's credit facilities, closely followed by the liquidity credit line, which provides resources for one year up to paid-in capital (Ocampo 2015a, 160).[22] Poorer FLAR members Bolivia and Ecuador have somewhat higher access to all of the FLAR's credit facilities (ibid., fn7). The FLAR also supports member central banks and other public institutions through assistance in managing reserves by improving the liquidity of and return on international reserve investments and facilitating public debt restructuring.

Headquartered in Bogotá, Colombia, the FLAR has eight members.[23] FLAR capital comes primarily from capital subscriptions by member central banks, though it twice issued bonds (US$150 million in 2003 and US$250 million in 2006). FLAR members deposit funds as capital contributions with the institution (in contrast to CMIM), which FLAR manages. As of June 2016, the FLAR had subscribed capital of US$3.9 billion, of which almost US$2.8 billion is paid-in. Four members (Colombia, Costa Rica, Peru, and Venezuela) account (equally) for almost 67% of its subscribed capital; the smaller countries account for 8.3% each.

The FLAR is older, has a broader mandate, has a larger permanent staff, but is less well capitalized than CMIM.[24] The FLAR is not hampered by some of the leadership and governance issues that plague CMIM. Each

FLAR member is assigned one vote. A supermajority of 75% of those present is required for key decisions, such as disbursal of funds. The supermajority scheme becomes more demanding when decisions involve modification of credit limits, terms, and existing agreements. The institution's straightforward and equitable governance is vital to its ability to respond rapidly and flexibly to support requests, particularly in comparison with more cumbersome IMF support procedures (Ocampo and Titelman 2009–2010, 262; Rosero 2014). The average FLAR approval time for balance of payments and external debt restructuring is 32 days (Carrasquilla 2015). However, the institution's voting system has at times delayed decisions. The selection of the last few executive presidents, for instance, took several years (Rosero 2014).

FLAR lending decisions appear markedly evenhanded despite stark differences in country size and political ideologies among members (Rosero 2014). Lending is not linked to the IMF. This fact and the FLAR's equitable voting system contribute to its legitimacy among members. There has never been a default on a FLAR loan despite the absence of traditional conditionality, even though some members have been in arrears to the IMF or have defaulted on commercial loans (Kawai and Lombardi 2012). The extraordinary repayment record reflects the effectiveness of peer pressure among members and their ownership of the institution (Rosero 2014, fn9). FLAR members treat the institution as a preferred creditor. These factors have resulted in a sterling credit rating (indeed, the best in Latin America, not including the IADB) (Ocampo 2015a).

The FLAR has deepened its surveillance capabilities over time. Since 2011, the FLAR has had a macroeconomic monitoring unit, the Division of Economic Studies, which reviews and monitors member performance and economic prospects. A central bank seeking balance of payments support or external debt restructuring is required to present to the FLAR executive president a written report on how it will mitigate the problem that motivates the support request through monetary, credit, exchange rate, fiscal, and/or trade measures. A decision on whether to grant support is then made by the nonresident Board of Directors following consideration of the remediation program by the Division of Economic Studies. To this point, the FLAR has not denied support on the basis of the plans presented, and has generally not required additional adjustment measures beyond those proposed by a central bank requesting support (Velarde 2015, 150).[25] Hence, there is no conditionality in the traditional IMF sense.[26] But as part of its loan contract, the borrowing country agrees not to impose measures that affect the imports from another FLAR member as part of its balance of payments restructuring process (Rosero 2014, 46). Division of Economic Studies staff assess the balance of payments situation and repayment capacity of countries receiving support (Titelman et al. 2014, fn28). Staff may also make technical visits to the country's institutions and require reports to the FLAR's executive president and board (ibid.). The review is expedited in the case of short-term support, such as liquidity and contingency credits. The executive president is authorized to approve these requests without involvement of the Board of Directors (Rosero 2014, 65).[27] The streamlined approval process permits very rapid short-term support disbursement.

Over its lifetime (and through September 2016), the FLAR has made 47 disbursements, amounting to roughly US$6.4 billion (Mühlich and Fritz 2016). The FLAR has lent to all of its members except Uruguay and Paraguay. In some cases, the FLAR contributed stabilizing resources when the IMF did not, or when members declined to engage the Fund (Ocampo and Titelman 2012). The FLAR has disbursed balance of payments loans to members during crises (namely, during the debt crisis of the 1980s, the period that followed the Asian crisis, and during the global crisis) in amounts that exceed IMF disbursals to FLAR members (with the only exception being the period 1989–1993) (Ocampo 2015a, 164). Prior to the global crisis, FLAR lending was significant in comparison with IMF lending; indeed, from 1978 to 2003, FLAR loans of US$4.9 billion were almost 60% of the size of the US$8.1 billion in loans from the IMF to countries in the Andean Community (Chin 2010, fn41). Excluding Venezuela, the FLAR disbursed 22% more than the IMF to FLAR member countries from 1978 to 2013 (Ocampo 2015a, table 1). Though FLAR resources are relatively small in the aggregate, they are significant relative to the needs of smaller member states, and lending has been redistributive subregionally (Ocampo and Titelman 2009–2010, 262). The institution's main direct beneficiaries have been Bolivia and Ecuador (Ocampo 2015a, 163). But mitigation of crises in smaller members induced by balance of payments issues has also benefited the region's other economies by stabilizing trade flows (Kawai and Lombardi 2012), as has the commitment required of borrowing countries not to take measures that interfere with intra-FLAR trade. For instance, Colombia, an important trade partner, has gained indirectly from repeated FLAR support to Ecuador (ibid.).

The FLAR's presence reduces the pressure on smaller countries to accumulate reserves and hence the opportunity cost of doing so (Eichengreen 2010). The FLAR has provided important savings to members by making funds available at better terms than are available on international markets to countries under stress (Rosero 2014). In some instances, FLAR resources have been leveraged as part of broader support programs.[28] FLAR member-ship has also been beneficial to members since reserves committed to it have yielded greater returns than those maintained in national reserve portfolios (Perry 2015, 27).

In terms of lending, the FLAR largely maintained rather than expanded its role during the global crisis. Compared with the tumultuous period of 1978–1991, there has been a sharp falloff in the number of loan requests and loans granted (Rosero 2014). The decline reflects Latin America's relative vitality during the crisis rather than any failure on the part of the FLAR.[29] During the global crisis, the FLAR received and acted on requests for assistance to support balance of payments or liquidity from only two members. It provided support to Ecuador on four occasions, for a total of US$1.8 billion, and it approved a loan of US$482.5 million to Venezuela in July 2016.

Looking beyond lending as a metric of change, we find evidence of gradual FLAR evolution during the global crisis and up to the present. Membership broadened, with Uruguay joining in 2009 and Paraguay in 2015. In 2015, Guatemala and the Dominican Republic were formally invited to begin the process of accession (FLAR website, annual report 2015, 25). FLAR members approved a 40% increase in subscribed capital in 2012 (Titelman et al. 2014, fn9). Uruguay and Costa Rica prepaid their entire subscribed capital in 2011 and 2015, respectively; Paraguay increased its paid-in capital in 2015, and in the same year, Costa Rica doubled its subscribed capital (Ocampo 2015a, 160). In recent years, the FLAR has begun to play a more important role in improving the investment conditions of members' reserves, giving it a role as a regional financial intermediary (Ocampo 2015a, 160). In addition, after more than a decade of dialogue, the FLAR and the IMF agreed to allow a portion of the capital paid in to the FLAR to count toward their international reserves with the IMF (FLAR website, annual report 2015, 27). This double counting reduces the cost of FLAR membership for new (especially small) economies.

The FLAR is insufficiently capitalized to respond on its own to the needs of larger economies, especially during crises that affect several members simultaneously. The FLAR's potential to expand its capacity is limited by the absence of some of the region's largest economies, including Brazil, Mexico, Chile, and Argentina. Observers have consequently argued for broadening its membership and deepening its resources (Ocampo 2015a; Titelman et al. 2014). The recent inclusion of and invitations to smaller economies is indicative of an interest in membership expansion. Observers have also argued for instituting larger paid-in quotas for members (Eichengreen 2010; Rosero 2011); establishing contingent credit lines with member central banks and private banks; intermediating funding from or cooperating with the IMF (Rosero 2011; 2014); and connecting it with other subregional, regional, and multilateral institutions (Ocampo and Titelman 2012).

Broadening FLAR membership and capitalization poses challenges. It is difficult to cultivate and sustain ownership in an institution as its membership increases. A larger institution might risk loan defaults with consequent effects on the institution's credit rating, and may require both new forms of monitoring and even some type of prenegotiated ex ante conditionality (Titelman et al. 2014, 21, fn23). This could be politically challenging. For this and other reasons, Titelman et al. (2014) argue that any prenegotiated conditionality should not involve the IMF or any other outside entity. It may also be difficult to maintain the institution's governance structure, particularly if larger countries maintain higher paid-in quotas. On this point, Ocampo (2015a, 168–170) argues that the FLAR should introduce new membership categories for the largest and smallest countries and move to weighted voting for larger loans.[30]

Even if expanded, institutions like the FLAR should be viewed as complementary insurance mechanisms that are part of a global patchwork of financial cooperation. In extreme cases, the IMF could leverage FLAR capital to mobilize a larger pool of resources, or the FLAR could take action in conjunction with other regional institutions (Titelman et al. 2014, 17). We might envision a capacity-based division of labor in which regional mechanisms like the FLAR provide support to small- and medium-sized countries and act independently during localized economic disturbances—something it has already done—while the IMF provides support to large countries and partners with the FLAR during large-scale crises, though without IMF-driven conditionality (as per Ocampo 2006, chap. 1; 2015a, 170).[31]

The FLAR has pursued "strategic alliances" with a range of other institutions, including AMRO, the Development Bank of Latin America, and the BIS. The result is an emerging cross-cutting network of cooperation that stands to enhance the capacity of these partners while generating cross-institutional learning. Connecting FLAR more directly to the IMF, on the other hand, may be politically unpalatable to some members, particularly those few that still have populist governments (Armijo 2012). Cooperation between the FLAR and the IMF to date has involved the participation of FLAR officials in IMF training programs (Miyoshi 2013, 21), the decision to count a portion of FLAR commitments as part of their IMF reserves, and participation (as previously noted) along with other institutions in an October 2016 meeting at the IMF, now to be held annually. More generally, the relationship between the IMF and regional financial arrangements has always been uneasy and complex (Eichengreen 2015, 133–134), as Europe's recent experience underscores. There is no reason to expect that this would not be the case with the FLAR.[32]

The Arab Monetary Fund

The Arab Monetary Fund (ArMF), headquartered in Abu Dhabi, United Arab Emirates, was founded by central bankers from the Arab world and began operating in 1977.[33] It began as the monetary arm of the Arab League. Today it has 22 members and a small amount of subscribed capital, approximately US$3.8 billion as of the end of 2015.[34] As with the FLAR, the ArMF takes deposits from member central banks. The ArMF can borrow from members and from Arab and foreign institutions and markets, and can issue securities. Like the FLAR, the ArMF has a broad developmental and financial stability responsibility. ArMF policy mandates include the provision of financial support to members experiencing balance of payments problems; the promotion of exchange rate stability, monetary policy coordination, financial market deepening, intraregional trade, and current account liberalization; and the eventual establishment of a common currency (an early, unrealized political goal of the Arab League).

The ArMF has several lending facilities. Four of its facilities focus on balance of payments needs, three on supporting particular sectors (viz., government finance, the financial system, trade, and oil), and, since 2009, a facility supports countries facing short-term liquidity problems caused by difficulties accessing international financial markets. ArMF loans have varying access limits and are disbursed with varying degrees of oversight. The institution appears from the one relevant study to be extraordinarily nimble. McKay, Volz, and Wölfinger (2011, 21) report that some types of loans, such as those available under the new short-term liquidity facility and what are termed automatic balance of payments loans, are disbursed very quickly and carry no requirement of a country mission or conditionality. Management makes a decision following rapid preparation of an internal report, with later notification to the Executive Board (see also Mühlich and Fritz 2016, 15). Other types of loans are generally approved in one to six weeks and require an adjustment program agreed to by the member state and the ArMF (McKay, Volz, and Wölfinger 2011, 21). For example, loans under the extended loan facility support structural balance of payments problems, provide the largest amount of support, and have a repayment period of up to seven years. Extended loans involve consideration by the Executive Board and require a mission, an adjustment program, conditionality and monitoring by the ArMF, and supplementary support from other regional and multilateral institutions, such as the IMF (Corm 2006; McKay, Volz, and Wölfinger 2011, 21). Conditions on ArMF loans tend to be less stringent than those associated with the IMF (Corm 2006, 309; UNCTAD 2007,122; UNCTAD 2015b, 74).

The ArMF has a technical staff that observers consider highly competent (McKay, Volz, and Wölfinger 2011; Miyoshi 2013).[35] Staff members conduct reviews of member country economic conditions and financing needs (ibid.). However, some analysts question whether monitoring is sufficiently stringent (McKay, Volz, and Wölfinger 2011), though loan arrears remain small and are associated with countries facing particularly difficult political and social conditions (e.g., Somalia, Syria, and Sudan).

The ArMF's governance structure is not unlike that of the BWIs (and the MRDBs). Decisions of the eight-member Executive Board are by absolute majority, with votes weighted by size of member contribution. Three countries (Saudi Arabia, Algeria, and Iraq) together hold 38.5% of the votes. That these countries are overrepresented underscores the point that governance of EMDE regional institutions is not inherently more egalitarian than that of the BWIs.

From its establishment through the end of 2015, the ArMF has made 174 loans to 14 member nations, totaling US$8.2 billion (ArMF website, annual reports).[36] Average drawing volume tends to be very small, and smaller, oil-importing members have been the most frequent users of lending facilities (especially in the 1980s) (Mühlich and Fritz 2016). About 63% of the loans were related to balance of payments pressures. The ArMF was faced with growing demands on its resources stemming from the challenge of the global crisis, the Arab Spring, and rising food and falling oil prices. During 2009 the ArMF made five loans totaling US$470 million via its new short-term liquidity facility. Between 2009 and 2015, the institution approved a total of 33 loans to eight countries, totaling US$3.5 billion. Moreover, the dollar value of loans extended during each year of the period 2009–2013 exceeded that for any other year (except 1988) since the institution began to operate. The US$800 million in loans extended in 2015 represents a new peak for the institution.

The ArMF has no formal relationship with the IMF. The IMF has provided technical assistance to the ArMF on domestic bond market development (Rhee, Sumulong, and Vallée 2013). The ArMF also coordinates with the IMF on technical workshops (ArMF website, annual reports, table B-2) and took part in regular meetings of the IMF and World Bank during 2015. The institution's Articles of Agreement charge it with providing "complementary" lender of last resort financing for some types of loans. Borrowers are expected first to withdraw their reserve tranche from a regional organization, the IMF, or another multilateral body before seeking support from the ArMF's ordinary, extended, and structural adjustment facilities (Miyoshi 2013, 31–32). This explicitly complementary role is necessitated by the ArMF's small capitalization and is reflected in the frequent parallel use of the IMF and ArMF. Since its creation, parallel use has occurred on 22 occasions, mostly during the Arab Spring (Mühlich and Fritz 2016, 23). The ArMF's resources and lending could obviously be increased significantly to provide more support to its poorer members, given the vast assets possessed by some of its oil-exporting members.

The Eurasian Fund for Stabilization and Development

The member countries of the Eurasian Economic Community created the Eurasian Fund for Stabilization and Development (EFSD) in June 2009.[37] Until 2015, it was known as the Eurasian Economic Community Anti-Crisis Fund. Since its founding, the Fund has operated as a hybrid that involves features of reserve pooling and development banking. The EFSD serves as a regional safety net that extends what it terms financial credits to governments to offset the effects of the global crisis; funds stabilization programs by supporting budgets, balance of payments, and currencies; and ensures the long-run economic stability of member nations. The EFSD also provides what it terms investment loans to governments and firms for large interstate projects that support regional integration or national investment and has a new program of grants aimed at supporting social programs.

The EFSD was established with subscribed contributions of US$8.5 billion by six countries.[38] It has paid-in contributions of US$2.8 billion, most of which comes from Russia, its largest member.[39] Paid-in contributions to the EFSD come from pooled member resources via budget contributions. At present, it has no capacity to issue bonds or to otherwise tap financial markets (Rhee, Sumulong, and Vallée 2013). Votes at the EFSD are weighted by capital contributions (as per the ArMF, the BWIs, and the MRDBs). Russia holds 85% of the votes and consequently holds veto power.

The Eurasian Development Bank manages EFSD resources and conducts surveillance of EFSD borrowers (Rhee, Sumulong, and Vallée 2013, 224).[40] There are no automatic disbursals of financial credits from the EFSD, and all disbursements are tied to a heavily and regularly monitored adjustment (i.e., conditionality) program. Financial credits are followed by consultations intended to determine the likelihood of borrower success in implementing reforms or stabilization programs that are funded by the EFSD. Recipients are not required to work with the IMF, though the EFSD claims that it is "guided" by the IMF in matters relating to financial credits. It also uses IMF benchmarks when assessing various matters, such as corporate governance. Indeed, an EFSD annual report notes that the manager "consulted with the IMF on a regular basis regarding economic policy guidelines for Armenia, Belarus, Kyrgyz Republic, and Tajikistan" and that EFSD officials have been discussing coordination initiatives with the AsDB, World Bank, and IMF since 2014 (EFSD website, annual report 2014,12). The EFSD does not extend financial credits to countries that are in arrears to the IMF, other multilateral institutions, or EFSD members. However, in the case of Belarus, the EFSD extended a financial credit to the country when the IMF declined to do so. Decisions on financial credits by the EFSD are rapid—available evidence suggests that internal decisions on loan disbursements are made in two to eight weeks (Mühlich and Fritz 2016, 15).

To date, the EFSD has extended only four financial credits, totaling almost US$3 billion (to Tajikistan in 2010 and 2016, Belarus in 2011, and Armenia in 2015). Its largest extension of financial credits to date was to Belarus—its support package of US$2.6 billion was equal to almost 6% of the country's GDP.[41] The 2010 support package of US$70 million to Tajikistan was equal to about 1% of its GDP. The case of Belarus suggests that EFSD surveillance has teeth: disbursal of a sixth tranche of funding was postponed from 2013 to 2015 because the country missed stabilization targets established in its agreement with the EFSD. Support was reestablished in 2016.

The Contingent Reserve Arrangement of the BRICS

The BRICs acronym was developed in 2001 by Goldman Sachs' Jim O'Neill, who saw Brazil, Russia, India, and China as having broadly similar characteristics. O'Neill predicted that these countries would have higher levels of economic interaction with one another (O'Neill 2001). The marketing label had performative force: it is credited with spurring coalition building, the creation of networks of influence inside and outside the group (e.g., within the IMF and the G-20), and institutional innovations (Ban and Blyth 2013).

Beginning in 2006, Russia promoted informal meetings of diplomats from the four countries.[42] The first recorded meeting among the group's policymakers took place when their foreign ministers met on the fringes of the UN General Assembly in the fall of 2006. Since 2006, BRICs officials have deepened, broadened, and formalized discussions of financial governance. The first BRICs leaders' meeting was held in Japan on the eve of the 2008 G-8 summit, and the first stand-alone BRICs Leaders' Summit took place in Russia in 2009. Since then, leaders have been meeting annually at the group's Leaders' Summits and informally on the sidelines of international meetings, while heads of ministries have also met regularly. BRICs executive directors at the BWIs also meet informally. Intensified intra-BRICs cooperation in international finance after 2009 led to broader dialogue and the development of structures to institutionalize cooperation among officials in other policy areas, such as agriculture, national statistics institutes, and foreign policy. South Africa was invited to join the group at the third Leaders' Summit, in China in 2011, and the group has since been known as the BRICS.

Since 2011, the BRICS has moved rapidly to develop plans and launch initiatives to create new financial institutions. The first BRICS-level financial initiative was the announcement in mid-2011 of plans to establish joint listing of one another's stock index futures and other derivative indices on their respective stock and securities exchanges. This came to fruition in March 2012, when the five founding members of the BRICS Exchanges Alliance began cross-listing benchmark equity index derivatives. In 2011, BRICS leaders promised to strengthen cooperation among their national development banks. Plans for financial cooperation became more ambitious in 2012, when the group began to discuss formation of a development bank that would supplement existing institutions. In 2012, BRICS finance ministries also agreed to encourage trade between members, denominated in bilateral currencies.

Intra-BRICS cooperation took a step forward at the July 2014 Leaders' Summit in Fortaleza, Brazil. In what became known as the Fortaleza Declaration, the group announced that it had reached agreement on two initiatives—the founding of a reserve pooling arrangement called the Contingent Reserve Arrangement (CRA) and the New Development Bank (NDB) (the latter will be discussed later). Long-standing frustration with the BWIs was explicit in the Fortaleza Declaration, which stated that, "International governance structures designed within a different power configuration show increasingly evident signs of losing legitimacy and effectiveness" (BRICS 2014b). Notwithstanding these frustrations, the declaration also made clear that both the CRA and the NDB were to be complements to, and not substitutes for, the BWIs.

The CRA is a reserve pooling arrangement meant to provide liquidity protection (including precautionary support) through currency swaps to members during balance of payments crises.[43] China has pledged US$41 billion to the CRA's US$100 billion pool; Brazil, India, and Russia have each pledged US$18 billion; and South Africa has pledged US$5 billion. Pledges by China, Brazil, India, and Russia to the CRA are nearly equal to each of their IMF quotas. At this point, most CRA capital is callable. No single member is to have effective veto power over fundamental changes in the CRA. As of this writing, the criteria to be used in decisions pertaining to qualification for support under both the liquidity and the precautionary facilities are still under development. Support decisions will be made by a "Standing Committee" comprising five directors appointed by each of the member country central banks. Countries applying for support from the CRA (including for precautionary support) in amounts above 30% of their eligibility must be in compliance with the surveillance and disclosure obligations of the IMF's Article IV (sections 1 and 3) and Article VIII (section 5), and they may not be in arrears to BRICS nations or to regional or multilateral institutions (Henning 2016, 125–126; BRICS 2014c, Article 14(b)(v)). The most controversial aspect of the CRA rests precisely in the decision to replicate the CMIM-IMF link.

It is unrealistic to treat the BRICS as a serious challenge to the roles of the United States and the IMF in global financial governance.[44] Instead, it should be seen as a group that occupies an "intermediate space" in global interstate power (Armijo, Katada, and Roberts 2015; Armijo and Roberts 2014) and as creating a "parallel order" rather than one that rivals the United States and the BWIs (Stuenkel 2016a; 2016b). The group's ability to cooperate is rooted in part in its potential to serve as a counterweight to traditional powers.

That said, important sources of tension that sometimes yield conflict persist among BRICS members (Chin 2014a). The BRICS group has often had to overcome or, more accurately, work around important differences and persistent fissures to reach consensus on some matters of global financial governance. The Russian government, in particular, has not always or easily fallen into line with positions taken by other members, and it has used its membership in the BRICS instrumentally in its conflicts with other powers (e.g., as a way to insulate itself from clashes with the United States and Europe over its policy in Ukraine). Indeed, China and Russia oppose adding the other BRICS to the permanent membership of the UN Security Council because this would reduce their own influence (Bond 2016, 615).

The launch of the CRA triggered an avalanche of commentary that broke down along the lines of Hirschman's possibilists and futilists. Futilists dismissed the "empty symbolism" of the CRA, emphasizing the decision to replicate the CMIM-IMF link, the small size of CRA resources relative to potential demands, and the dollar-based funding commitments to the CRA that reinforce the currency's dominant global role.[45] More broadly, skeptics emphasize what they see as fatal internal tensions that will continue to disrupt the group's cohesiveness and its potential to transform financial governance.[46] Others emphasize the "sub- or neo-imperial" tendencies of the BRICS, while still others dismiss the significance of the BRICS because their growth prospects have slowed.[47]

Possibilists are not persuaded. In the possibilist view, the CRA (warts and all) is part of an evolving, fragmenting global financial landscape in which institutional experimentation is becoming the "new normal." From this perspective, the CRA is understood to complement existing institutions and advance the growing disbursal of economic power while holding the potential to increase the voice of EMDEs in the global financial governance architecture either directly or through the leverage associated with forum shopping.[48] For possibilists, the CRA is one among many parallel experiments that provide opportunities for learning, problem solving, and deepening networks of influence.

Possibilists insist that it is premature and unhelpful to dismiss in advance the CRA and other BRICS initiatives. It is of course true that the impact of the BRICS and their various initiatives will be uneven and even contradictory, reflecting enduring tensions within each of its member states, among its members, and between those members and other actors (states and institutions). But that is equally true of all complex institutions and their endeavors—they are not adequately described by exclusive reference to their formal mission statements or just one aspect of their practice. It is also true that critical issues must be addressed before the CRA begins to disburse funds. China's economy is larger than all of the other BRICS combined (Chin 2014a). It will be important for China's voice at the CRA not to dominate those of other members, something that may be complicated by the size of its contributions (Chin 2014a; Desai and Vreeland 2014). In addition, the CRA (like the CMIM) will have to address the difficult issues of surveillance and its relationship to the IMF.[49] But these obstacles are not insurmountable, and the motivation to overcome them is high given the degree to which the CRA promises results that are not presently achievable elsewhere. There is good reason to expect that the CRA will ultimately develop independent, well-resourced, and technically competent surveillance capacity over time, and as that occurs, the IMF link may lessen or be eliminated. For these reasons, the CRA carries significant potential to catalyze widespread change through its own internal performance, through competition or cooperation with other pooling arrangements, and through the example it sets for other institutions (Griffith-Jones, Fritz, and Cintra 2014).

Development Banks

Development or infrastructure banks are specialized financial institutions that channel large sums of long-term financing for investment in capital-intensive projects, and public and private enterprises and particular sectors (such as infrastructure) that generate positive externalities but that are likely to be underfunded by private banks.[50] Development banks are generally mandated to provide credit at terms that would render industrial and infrastructure investment viable. They also perform other functions, such as providing technical assistance to borrowers. Development banks differ in many ways. For example, they diverge in terms of the size of their assets, overall significance in the economy, source of funds, types of projects that are funded, and whether they focus on long-term lending to large industries and infrastructure or on realizing special policy mandates.

Development banks in EMDEs and the MRDBs were created over fifty years ago to address the shortage of project and infrastructure finance. EMDEs host the majority of development banks. A recent study found that as of 2015 there were over 250 national development banks across the world, holding at least US$5 trillion in assets (Gallagher and Sklar 2016). The Asia and Pacific region hosts the largest number of national development banks (119), followed by Latin America and the Caribbean (63), Africa (61), the Middle East (45), and Europe and North America (15) (ibid.).

In the 1950s and 1960s, over 70% of the World Bank's IBRD and IDA operations were directed toward infrastructure. But by 1999 only 19% of IBRD and IDA operations targeted infrastructure (Humphrey 2015a, 3). The shortfall in infrastructure spending and financing emerged and widened in the 1980s and 1990s as Western bilateral donors and the MRDBs focused instead on social and policy-related lending (e.g., poverty alleviation) (Chin 2014a, 368; Humphrey 2015a; 2015b). Over the last decade, IBRD and IDA lending for infrastructure rebounded to 30%–40% of activity (Humphrey 2015a).[51] Despite this rebound (from a low level), the exigencies of the global crisis and the freezing of private markets aggravated the infrastructure financing gap (Chin 2014a). In the crisis context, the World Bank, MRDBs, and some national, subregional, and regional development banks based in EMDEs took on roles that we traditionally associated with institutions that focus on liquidity support, such as the IMF and FLAR. Development banks introduced and, where such facilities previously existed, significantly increased disbursements of shorter-term loans and other forms of financing (such as trade credits) that had countercyclical effects. Indeed, a recent World Bank survey of 90 development banks across the world highlights the important and often overlooked countercyclical impact of these institutions (de Luna-Martínez and Vicente 2012).

The inadequate provision of infrastructure financing remains a critical deficiency of the global financial architecture (Chin 2014a). A widely cited study of the infrastructure investment gap in EMDEs estimates it at US$1–1.5 trillion per year over the next twenty years (Bhattacharya and Romani 2013).[52] Other studies suggest that by the 2020s EMDEs will need US$2–3 trillion annually to support sustainable infrastructure investment that would be sufficient to achieve the SDGs (Bhattacharya, Oppenheim, and Stern 2015; Bhattacharya and Holt 2017).[53] To put the infrastructure investment gap into context, note that in fiscal year 2014 the World Bank Group spent US$24 billion on infrastructure, which represented an increase from US$16.7 billion in the previous year (UNCTAD 2015b, 172). The recent creation of two new development banks that focus on sustainable infrastructure and a range of other infrastructure-focused initiatives led by China can only be understood in the context of the infrastructure gap.

The world of development banking has its own terminology. Authorized capital represents the maximum amount of capital that an institution can raise, as determined by the maximum number of shares that it can issue, as set forth in its Articles of Agreement. Member nations commit callable capital to the institution as a guarantee in the event that these resources are needed. The World Bank introduced callable capital as a feature of multilateral development bank operations, and today the World Bank (and the IADB) has a higher share of callable capital than do regional development banks based in EMDEs. This allows the World Bank to issue bonds at some of the lowest rates in the world, for sovereign or nonsovereign issuers (Humphrey 2014). Paid-in capital is the amount of up-front capital actually contributed by member nations. Subscribed capital is composed of paid-in and callable capital. Paid-in capital, together with reserves that are built up as a consequence of the institution's operations, constitutes the institution's equity. Finally, the ensuing discussion sometimes refers to the World Bank Group, which includes all five of the institution's organizations, and sometimes to the IBRD or IDA, the World Bank Group's two main lending arms, which together constitute the World Bank. We use the less cumbersome and more common term World Bank in cases where the lack of precision is not consequential to the discussion.

The terrain of development banks is vast, and hence the discussion of particular institutions in what follows is intended to be illustrative rather than comprehensive. Table 6.4 summarizes key aspects of the development banks examined here.

Table 6.4
Development and Infrastructure Banks and Initiatives (Selected, US$Billions, Unless Otherwise Noted)

Institutions	Resources	Capital		Loans	
	Assets	Authorized	Subscribed	Approved	Disbursed
EMDE Development Banks and Initiatives					
CAF	32.5 (CY2015)	15.0 (CY2015)	5.0 (CY2015)	12.3 (CY2015)	5.9 (CY2015)
NDB	N/A	100.0 (2016)	50.0 (2016)	1.5 (first loans, 2016)	N/A
AIIB	N/A	100.0 (2016)	85.9 (July 2016)	1.7 (first loans, 2016)	N/A
Belt and Road Initiative;	N/A	N/A	N/A	Unreported	Unreported
Silk Road Fund	40.0 initial capitalization (2016)	N/A	N/A	Unreported	Unreported
BNDES	291.0 (FY2016)	N/A	N/A	33.7 (CY2015)	41.8 (CY2015)
CDB	1700.0 (CY2015)	N/A	N/A	N/A	276.0* (CY2014)
BWs and related institutions					
World Bank Group	551.5** (FY2016)	N/A	N/A	64.0 (FY2016)	49.0 (FY2016)

IBRD	371.0 (FY2016)	2,307,600 shares*** (FY2016)	263.0 (FY2016)	29.7 (FY2016)	22.0 (FY2016)
IDA	180.5 (FY2016)	N/A****	245.4***** (FY2016)	16.2 (FY2016)	13.0 (FY2016)
MRDBs					
AfDB	32.5 (September 30, 2015)	94.0 (September 30, 2015)	91.8 (September 30, 2015)	8.8 (CY2015)	4.2 (CY2015)
AsDB	128.2 (FY2016)	147.5 (CY2015)	147.0 (CY2015)	15.4 (CY2015)	11.7 (CY2015)
IADB	116.5 (CY2015)	170.9 (CY2016)	170.9 (CY 2016)	11.1****** (CY2015)	10.2 (CY2015)

Notes: Data are most recent available. CY=Calendar year data for year ending as specified; FY=Fiscal year data for year ending June 30, 2016; N/A=data unavailable or not applicable; Bretton Woods and related institutions=World Bank Group (IBRD, IDA), AfDB, AsDB, and IADB (and excluding EBRD and EIB).

*CDB annual report for 2015 does not provide total loans extended in that year, but it does report that US$355.6 billion in loans were made across several sectors in 2015.

**Figure is the sum of IDA and IBRD assets.

***IBRD does not assign a dollar value to authorized capital, but each subscribed share has a value of US$120,635.

****IDA does not have authorized capital.

*****IDA subscriptions and contributions committed.

******Includes guarantees.

Sources: Institutional websites, annual reports, financial statements, and investor presentations (and, where unavailable, news stories).

The Development Bank of Latin America

The Development Bank of Latin America (formerly the Andean Development Corporation; Spanish acronym CAF) was created to support development and integration of the Andean Community countries. The renaming of the institution is consistent with its broadening reach throughout Latin America and the Caribbean.

The CAF was launched in 1970.[54] Its membership and the focus of its loan programs have broadened considerably over time. The CAF is a multilateral, regional development bank that focuses on mobilizing medium- and long-term lending for productive investment and fostering regional integration. It lends to governments, the private sector, and public institutions. The CAF raises funds from shareholder countries and through commercial paper activities in the United States and Europe. A large majority of its funds (69% in 2015) come from bond issues sold in international and member country capital markets. In 2015, the CAF raised US$3 billion from bond sales.

Today the CAF has 19 member countries from Latin America and the Caribbean, plus Spain and Portugal.[55] Its newest member, Barbados, became a shareholder in 2015, and Trinidad and Tobago completed the process of becoming a full member in the same year. The CAF is headquartered in Caracas, Venezuela, and has 12 other offices and a nonresident Board of Directors. Member countries are both clients and shareholders of the CAF. The CAF is owned almost exclusively by EMDEs. Members own most of its assets, which is in marked contrast to the ownership structure of other regional multilateral lenders. Borrowing shareholder countries hold nearly all of the votes at the CAF. By comparison, just 37% of the votes at the World Bank are held by borrowing shareholder countries (Humphrey 2014, 616). CAF administration has emphasized that AEs will never be allowed to hold more than 10%–15% of its shares to preserve its governance structure and mission (ibid., 620).

At year-end 2015, the CAF's total assets were valued at US$32.5 billion, an increase of 51% over 2011. Shareholders' equity in the institution increased by 50.7% over the same period (CAF website, author calculation). Authorized capital in 2015 was US$15 billion and subscribed capital US$5 billion. The CAF is among the most dynamic of all multilateral development banks in terms of lending volume. The CAF was relatively marginal in regional lending during the 1970s and 1980s, when the World Bank dominated lending to the region, followed by the IADB.[56] This began to change in the 1990s, as World Bank and (to a lesser extent) IADB shares of lending to the region fell. CAF lending grew fourfold between 1991 and

2007; during the same period, lending by the IADB doubled and World Bank lending to South America grew by only 40%. Between 2000 and 2011 CAF contributed 56% of total multilateral financing to Andean Community members.

The CAF lends broadly throughout its membership. Andean countries receive a substantial share of CAF loans. From 2011 to 2015, Bolivia, Colombia, Ecuador, Peru, and Venezuela received 56% of loan disbursals. In contrast to the FLAR, a significant percentage of recent CAF loans have gone to larger countries. From 2011 to 2015, for instance, 30.3% of its disbursed loans went to Argentina, Brazil, and Mexico (CAF website).

In 2015, the CAF funded almost as much infrastructure in Latin America as the IADB. At year-end 2015, 62.3% of the CAF loan portfolio was in infrastructure. In 2015, the CAF approved $3.3 billion in loans for infrastructure (which represented 27% of approved loans), whereas the IADB approved US$4.3 billion for infrastructure and environment (which they report as a combined category). Almost half of CAF-approved disbursements from 2010 to 2015 were in the form of medium- and long-term loans. Given the scarcity of medium- and longer-term finance in EMDEs, the CAF's role is significant. CAF lending was particularly important during the global crisis insofar as funds for longer-term project finance in EMDEs contracted severely, especially as private lenders fled these markets.[57]

CAF finance has important countercyclical and developmental impacts since it provides stable funding to members. CAF financing dampened instability during the EMDE financial crises of the 1990s and the global crisis, when CAF loans remained high. Annual loan approvals ranged from US$9.1 billion in 2009 to US$11.7 billion in 2014. During 2011–2015, the CAF averaged US$11.1 billion in lending annually, compared with US$8 billion from 2006 to 2010. In 2015, the CAF increased its countercyclical activity through what it called fast disbursing and contingent operations of US$2.4 billion. In 2015, the CAF approved a record volume of loans of US$12.3 billion (and disbursed US$5.9 billion), while the IADB approved loans of $US11.1 billion (and disbursed US$10.2 billion).

Despite CAF dynamism, it has by no means displaced the World Bank and the IADB in regional crisis response capacity (see Table 6.4). In 2008, 2009, and 2010, CAF loan approvals were US$7.9 billion, US$9.1 billion, and US$10.5 billion, respectively. By contrast, in the same years, the World Bank approved loans to Latin America of US$4.6 billion, US$14 billion, and US$13.9 billion, while the IADB approved loans of US$11.2 billion, US$15.5 billion, and US$12.4 billion (Ocampo and Titelman 2012, 15). Later in the crisis, the gap between CAF loan approvals and those of the World

Bank and the IADB to all of Latin America and the Caribbean narrowed. In 2012, for instance, the CAF approved US$9.3 billion, while the World Bank approved US$6.6 billion and the IADB US$11.4 billion in loans to the region (Humphrey 2014, 615).

As with the FLAR and some ArMF lending facilities, the CAF loan approval process is very rapid compared with that of the World Bank and the IADB.[58] The average time to loan approval by the CAF is usually under three months (Humphrey 2015a, 17). Rapid approval stems from the institution's streamlined procedures, in which loans and technical assistance up to fairly large limits are approved by the CAF's senior management rather than its full membership, following a rigorous project evaluation at several stages in the project life cycle. Agreed-on borrower commitments are designed during this process. However, failure to meet these commitments generally does not result in the suspension of loan tranches. Rather, failure may trigger additional technical assistance by the CAF. The CAF tends to emphasize those actions that can be implemented by a country's executive branch or that are likely to achieve legislative approval.

Also like the FLAR, country ownership (both literally and figuratively) in the CAF accounts for its very high loan recovery rate. During the financial crisis of the late 1990s, Ecuador's government continued to service its CAF debt while disappointing other creditors, and when Peru's government limited debt service payments to 10% of export earnings during the 1980s, it continued to service debt to the CAF in full (Griffith-Jones, Griffith-Jones, and Hertova 2008). Indeed, there were very few defaults on CAF loans from 1999 to 2003, despite the fact that the region faced severe difficulties. As a consequence, the CAF's credit rating is investment grade and is higher than those of its individual member countries. Moreover, the speed of loan approvals and the close relationship with borrowing countries accounts for the proclivity of Andean member countries to borrow from the CAF, even though its loans are somewhat higher in cost than those offered by the World Bank and IADB (Humphrey 2014, figure 1). The higher cost of CAF loans stems from the CAF's somewhat lower credit rating than the World Bank and IADB, which in turn derives from the fact that the World Bank and IADB have a high share of callable capital guaranteed by highly rated, nonborrowing AEs (ibid., 618). The CAF often cofinances loans with the World Bank and the IADB.

Member nations' commitment to the CAF is also apparent in the ease with which the institution raised capital from its members during the global crisis. One might have expected national policymakers to withdraw from multilateral commitments. Instead, early in the crisis, CAF officials were able to tap shareholders for additional paid-in capital contributions. Shareholders quickly and unanimously approved a US$2.5 billion paid-in capital increase in August 2009 (Humphrey 2014). A CAF Treasury official spoke of the ease of securing this capital increase: "We asked shareholders for US$1 billion . . . they gave us US$2.5 billion. We can increase the capital base whenever we need to, because the structure of our shareholders is so different. It's not like that with the IADB and the World Bank, where some shareholders contribute capital and others benefit by taking out loans" (quoted in Humphrey 2014, 628). Humphrey observes that "including paid-in capital from new members, CAF raised US$4 billion in paid-in capital following the 2008 crisis, almost as much as the vastly larger World Bank (US$5.1 billion) and more than twice as much as the IADB (US$1.7 billion)" (ibid.). In 2015, CAF shareholder countries again approved an increase in paid-in capital (of US$4.5 billion) (CAF website, annual report).

The CAF issues a large percentage of bonds in Latin American currencies, which are held by regional and international investors. For example, in June 2004, the CAF issued bonds in Colombian pesos (which was a first for Latin America), and it did so again in December 2008 and April 2009. More recently, it issued bonds in Peruvian, Mexican, Venezuelan, and Uruguayan currencies.[59] In 2007, 32.9% of CAF bonds were issued in Latin American currencies; in comparison, the IADB issued just 14.9% of its bonds in Latin American currencies in the same year (Ocampo and Titelman 2009–2010, table 2). During the global crisis, the CAF introduced and utilized two new financial products to support infrastructure finance, "Collateralized Infrastructure Debt Obligation," a securitized debt obligation for which infrastructure loans serve as collateral, and "Debt Funds for Infrastructure." The latter were used in Colombia in 2014 (issued in Colombian pesos and indexed to inflation) and Uruguay in 2016 (issued in Uruguayan pesos and dollars, and also indexed to inflation). Local currency bonds reduce exchange rate risk for the CAF and borrowing countries. More importantly, it promotes the development of local currency bond markets, something that has positive spillovers from the perspective of financial resilience, stability, and access to long-term credit. It also mitigates the locational mismatch that plagues so much lending to EMDEs. The CAF has also signed cooperative agreements with the Green Climate Fund and the Global Environment Facility, reflecting its increasing emphasis on sustainable financing.

The New Development Bank

The BRICS Fortaleza Declaration of 2014 also announced the launch of the NDB. As with the CRA, the NDB was motivated by deep frustrations with the governance of the BWIs.

The NDB is designed to finance investment in infrastructure projects and more sustainable development (including sustainable infrastructure) in the BRICS, with an eye toward allowing other low- and middle-income EMDEs to buy in and apply for funding in the future. It has authorized capital of US$100 billion and subscribed capital of US$50 billion (with each of the five founding signatory countries contributing US$10 billion); 20% of subscribed capital is paid in (and will be paid in over a seven-year schedule), and the rest is callable. The initial size of the NDB's resources is notable. By comparison, the IBRD had subscribed capital of US$263 billion as of June 30, 2016, of which only $15.8 billion is paid in. China's contribution of US$10 billion to the NDB is not much smaller than its contribution to the World Bank, and the contributions by each of the other BRICS to the NDB exceed their contributions to the World Bank.[60]

The NDB approved its first loans in May 2016. By year-end 2016, it had approved a total of seven loans, collectively amounting to US$1.5 billion. Each of its member nations was approved for one of its first five loans, and an additional two loans were approved later for China and India. The loans were extended to public sector entities in each of the countries to support small-scale renewable energy and transportation-related projects, and were financed by "green" renminbi (RMB)-denominated bonds issued in the Chinese market. As of November 2016, the institution reported that it had received approval from member governments to develop local currency bond offerings in the Indian, Russian, and South African markets (NDB 2016a; 2016c).

The five members of the NDB hold equal votes in the institution, and its presidency will be held for five years and will rotate among the five members. The first president is Indian; the chair of the Board of Governors is Russian; a Brazilian chairs the Board of Directors; the headquarters is in Shanghai, China; and Johannesburg, South Africa, will host the African regional center. There are also plans for a regional office in Brazil. The location of the NDB's headquarters in China was reportedly a matter of controversy, but the decision was reportedly made after China agreed to contribute a large share of the CRA's initial funds (Chin 2014a).

The Articles of Agreement of the NDB are in important respects similar to the governance model of the World Bank and the MRDBs. This is notable in light of what its founders identify as its break with prevailing norms (Humphrey 2015b, 23). For example, each capital share translates into one vote (ibid., 8). However, unlike the legacy institutions, the NDB has a nonresident board (BRICS 2014a, article 12(g)). The BRICS countries have assured themselves of a dominant position in the institution, even as new members join. Contributions by new members cannot reduce aggregate voting power by the BRICS to below 55% or provide any new member with more than 7% of aggregate voting shares (ibid., article 8). Nonborrowing members can never have more than 20% of total voting shares (ibid.). Moreover, the institution's president and vice president must be from the BRICS (ibid.). This governance structure may inhibit expansion of the institution's membership. So, too, might the likelihood that the NDB will not be awarded a AAA credit rating based on the bond ratings of the BRICS countries themselves and the fact that it does not have any AEs among its shareholders (Humphrey 2015b).[61]

Despite these obstacles, some analysts suggest that NDB loans could dwarf those of the World Bank in the next several decades, especially if membership is broadened and the institution cofinances loans with governments and private investors (Desai and Vreeland 2014). In terms of cofinancing possibilities, the NDB signed memoranda of understanding with the CAF and the World Bank in September 2016, and with BNDES in April 2017. The NDB's loan portfolio capacity is projected to reach about US$45–65 billion by 2025 (Humphrey 2015b, figure 5).

Along with the initiatives led by China, the creation of the NDB should be understood in part as a response to the vast need for infrastructure spending and finance. Taken together, these initiatives are apt to have catalytic effects on the World Bank and the AsDB (and other MRDBs). Certainly, the rush to create infrastructure finance facilities within the legacy institutions and the G-20 suggests that this is the case, particularly since attention has returned to the infrastructure gap as a central obstacle to development.[62] Chin (2014a), for example, suggests that the World Bank may have renewed its attention to infrastructure finance partly in response to the perceived threat posed by the NDB.[63]

Risk management is a key challenge for the NDB. The NDB must ensure that its loan portfolio is of high quality; that loans are carefully chosen and monitored for their developmental, social, and environmental impacts; that finances are sustainable; that the cost of borrowing from it is not prohibitively high; and that China's influence does not dwarf all others (Chin 2014a; Desai and Vreeland 2014). That the institution's first loans in 2016 were for renewable energy is notable; maintaining such a focus is essential to the institution's credibility and progressive impact. As of August 2016, the institution disclosed an "Environmental and Social Framework," though it was developed without civil society input or consultation. Civil society groups note that while the principles embodied in the framework document are commendable, the document does not advance sustainability criteria or robust social and environmental safeguards (Coalition for Human Rights in Development 2016). Moreover, the matter of incorporating new members into the NDB will have to be addressed. That is a lot to manage, and there is good reason to expect a series of failures and missteps as the NDB matures and expands. That is simply the nature of institutional development.[64]

Initiatives Led by China: The Asian Infrastructure Investment Bank and the Belt and Road Initiative/Silk Road Fund

Simultaneous with its involvement in BRICS initiatives, the Chinese government has created an ambitious new institution, the Asian Infrastructure Investment Bank (AIIB), the equally ambitious "One Belt, One Road," or simply the "Belt and Road" initiative, and at least 13 regional or bilateral funds that will radically increase Chinese development and infrastructure finance abroad (Gallagher, Kamal, and Wang 2016, 1). The Silk Road Fund is one of the 13 new funds. Taken together, the funds are projected to contribute up to US$116 billion in project financing. Three funds, totaling US$22 billion, are earmarked for Africa; four funds, totaling US$37 billion, for Latin America and the Caribbean; and two funds, totaling US$6 billion, for Eurasia. In addition, there is a Green Silk Road Fund and a China-ASEAN Fund (with the AsDB), totaling almost US$6 billion, a US$3.2 billion South-South Climate Fund, and a US$2 billion South-South Cooperation Fund (ibid., table 1). The funds express the foreign policy ambitions and economic objectives of China's leadership but also reflect frustrations with the governance of the BWIs, the dominance of the United States and especially Japan at the AsDB, and the failure of the World Bank and other MRDBs to respond to unmet infrastructure needs (Dollar 2015).[65] It is clear that China is "poised to be the largest development [and infrastructure] lender in the world" (Gallagher, Kamal, and Wang 2016, 1). In what follows, I discuss the AIIB and the Belt and Road/Silk Road Fund.[66]

In terms of capitalization and number of members, the AIIB represents the largest of China's contributions to the changing institutional landscape. It is to focus on infrastructure (and cross-border infrastructure connectivity), sustainable economic development, and the promotion of regional cooperation by working with bilateral and multilateral institutions (AIIB 2016b). China's leadership announced the AIIB in 2013, and it was founded in October 2014. The bank is headquartered in Beijing. During 2015, China invited 57 nations to join as founding members, and by December 2016 all had signed the organization's Articles of Agreement. As of May 2017, there are 77 approved members.

Among G-7 countries, only the United States and Japan are absent from the AIIB. In public statements, U.S. government officials expressed disappointment that some of its key European and Asian-Pacific allies, including the United Kingdom, Germany, South Korea, Australia, New Zealand, and India, joined as founding members (Parker, Chassany, and Dyer 2015). The U.K. government was singled out for what an unnamed senior U.S. administration official termed its "constant accommodation of China" (quoted in Perlez 2015). Chinese officials, along with those of the IMF, World Bank, and AsDB, have made it clear that they see the AIIB as complementary to legacy institutions (McGrath 2015). The decision by the United States and Japan not to join suggests that they see it differently. U.S. officials defended their decision on grounds that critics found hypocritical—that the AIIB would neither embrace norms around transparency and anticorruption nor adopt the social and environmental safeguards of the BWIs and AsDB.

The AIIB was established with an authorized capital base of US$100 billion, with initial subscribed capital by China of US$29.8 billion. As with the NDB, 20% of the subscribed capital is paid in. The AIIB will initially have US$20 billion of usable capital, which could sustain US$100 billion of total lending (Griffith-Jones, Xiaoyun, and Spratt 2016, 18). The size is significant: the AIIB's authorized capital amounts to almost 68% of the authorized capital base of the AsDB (US$147.5 billion) and is equal to 38% of the IBRD's subscribed capital. In its first year of operation, 2016, the AIIB approved nine projects across seven countries, totaling US$1.7 billion. All but one of these loans is to be cofinanced with legacy institutions (e.g., World Bank, AsDB, EBRD).[67]

By 2025, the AIIB is conservatively projected to have a loan portfolio capacity of US$70–90 billion (Humphrey 2015b, 15). Under less conservative scenarios, its loan portfolio could reach US$100–120 billion or more, making it the second-largest development bank in the world (Griffith-Jones, Xiaoyun, and Spratt 2016, 26). By comparison, US$120 billion was more than the individual lending by the AsDB, IADB, or AfDB in 2014, and almost as high as the total stock of lending by the IBRD in 2014 (which was US$140 billion) (ibid.). The AIIB will largely cofinance projects with other multilateral lenders in its first years of operation. With cofinancing, the scale of the infrastructure projects to which the AIIB contributes could reach US$240 billion by 2025 (ibid., 27). Many legacy institutions (namely, the AsDB, EBRD, EIB, and World Bank) have signed cooperative agreements with the

AIIB. With 16 of the world's largest economies as shareholders, the AIIB is likely to receive a AAA bond rating, lowering its cost of capital and making its loans attractive to middle-income countries (Humphrey 2015b). The AIIB's openness to membership, reflected in part in its permitting founding members to participate in negotiations over its statutes, distinguishes it from the NDB and gives the AIIB operational advantages (ibid.).

The AIIB reflects a widespread tension in the emerging financial architecture between continuity and innovation (as argued by Chin 2016). In terms of continuity, the first AIIB president is from China (the largest shareholder), while future presidents must be from a regional member nation. Voting shares at the institution depend on several factors, including GDP. Nonregional members of the AIIB are limited to 25% of the institution's aggregate voting share, ensuring the dominance of Asia's and particularly China's voice. China will hold 26.06% of the votes at the institution, providing it with de facto veto power on major policies and decisions that generally require a supermajority.[68] In terms of discontinuities, the AIIB has a dual nonresident board comprised of a large Board of Governors and a 12-person unpaid Board of Directors (nine from the region, three from outside the region). The directors will meet periodically during the year to supervise operations and management. The AIIB's structure is expected to speed decisions and lower operating costs.[69] The AIIB also has no branch offices in borrowing countries. Most importantly, the institution will almost certainly be a key actor in the emerging pluripolar distribution of financial power in the world economy.

The AIIB widely circulated a document for comment that outlines its "Environmental and Social Framework for Lending."[70] By February 2016, its Board of Directors had approved an "Environment and Social Policy." Many observers nonetheless raised concerns about social and environmental standards and the institution's support for coal-fired plants in places lacking access to power (He 2016, 13–15). In October 2016, the AIIB took on these (and other) matters in an "Energy Strategy" document that it presented for public comment.[71] The document notes that "coal and oil-fired power plants would be exceptionally considered if cleaner technologies are not available for well-founded energy security or affordability reasons" (AIIB 2016a). While that statement generates concern about its commitment to sustainability, it does introduce a bar that coal- and oil-fired plants will have to clear and opens the institution to close surveillance by environmental organizations.[72] In addition, it should be noted that many AIIB staff have extensive World Bank experience. This suggests that the new institution is informed by and has the opportunity and perhaps also the intent to draw on the World Bank's (and the AsDB's) safeguards in this domain (Chin 2016, 15). Not all observers are persuaded that the World Bank represents the best model of environmental stewardship, however.[73]

In 2014, at about the same time as it unveiled the AIIB, China launched another initiative focused on infrastructure (and energy). It involved the creation of two modern-day "Silk Roads"—the overland "Silk Road Economic Belt" and the "21st Century Maritime Silk Road."[74] The Belt and Road initiative has roots in ideas and practices that have existed at the national and subnational levels since the 1980s (Summers 2016). It will facilitate transportation and communications between China and some 65 countries across Central Asia, the Middle East, Russia, and Europe, and through investments in maritime infrastructure, it will speed access to East Africa, the Red Sea, and the Mediterranean. Anxious observers of China's rise see the Belt and Road as its most ambitious effort to extend economic diplomacy and its grand strategy through its own Marshall Plan. It promises to enhance the country's dominant role in Asia, buy influence, and secure privileged access to markets and resources (Clover and Hornby 2015).

The Silk Road Fund was created to support projects of the Belt and Road initiative, which will also be supported by the AIIB and the China Development Bank (CDB). The fund has an initial capitalization of US$40 billion. Support for the Silk Road Fund comes from four government agencies. In 2015, the PBOC transferred US$82 billion to three state-owned banks for Belt and Road projects (*Economist* 2016b). The State Administration of Foreign Exchange (SAFE, which is the PBOC unit that manages the renminbi) will hold a 65% stake, China Investment Corporation (a sovereign wealth fund) and the China Export-Import Bank will each have 15%, and the CDB will have the remaining 5% (Kozul-Wright and Poon 2015). The fund is open to investors from other countries as well (Gallagher, Kamal, and Wang 2016). Official figures indicate that 900 deals, worth US$890 billion, are planned or under way. By comparison, the postwar Marshall Plan was valued at US$130 billion in current dollars in 2015 (*Economist* 2016b).

Given the large environmental footprint of the energy-related loans made by China's older policy banks (such as the CDB), it is by no means certain that the new Chinese-led initiatives will have a greener footprint in practice than those of their predecessors (see Gallagher, Kamal, and Wang 2016; Tabuchi 2017). The first four loans made by the AIIB were for projects that prima facie do not ensure sustainability—an electricity grid, slum development, and highway and road construction—while the second batch of loans are for hydropower and a gas turbine. Nevertheless, these (and other) Chinese-led financial initiatives seem particularly fruitful in their "potential to transform multilateral lending more broadly" (Kozul-Wright and Poon 2015). As Kozul-Wright and Poon (2015) note, China's experience with experimental and incremental development strategies makes it particularly suited for this leading role in transforming the institutional landscape. China's initiatives also increase the possibility for forum shopping, with attendant effects on voice in existing institutions. The Chinese initiatives have already placed and will likely continue to place pressure on the private sector, the G-20, the World Bank, and the MRDBs to increase infrastructure spending.

National Development Banks: The Brazil National Bank of Economic and Social Development and the China Development Bank

Brazil's National Bank of Economic and Social Development (Portuguese acronym BNDES) and the China Development Bank (CDB) have been described as "mega banks" since they have assets of greater than US$100 billion, which distinguishes them from the over 50% of development banks with assets of less than US$10 billion (Chandrasekhar 2015b). The activities of BNDES and the CDB during the global crisis provide dramatic examples of the evolving nature of national development banking.

BNDES

BNDES was founded in 1952.[75] It was created as a public (federal) development bank to provide long-term and/or high-risk capital primarily to private Brazilian firms whose needs for capital were not being met by the country's private banks (Hochstetler 2014a, 361). BNDES is part of an extensive public bank infrastructure in Brazil, though we focus here on this institution only.[76]

In terms of its assets, BNDES eclipses all other national lending institutions in Latin America. As of June 30, 2016, its assets totaled US$291 billion (BNDES website). BNDES is significantly larger than the IADB (which had assets of US$116.5 billion in 2015 and subscribed capital of US$170.9 billion in 2016) and close to the size of the IBRD (which had assets of US$343 billion and subscribed capital of US$253 billion as of June 30, 2015). BNDES annual disbursements more than quadrupled during former president Lula da Silva's tenure in office (2003–2010), growing to three times the size of the World Bank's annual lending in 2010 (Hochstetler 2014a, 360). BNDES disbursed US$41.8 billion in 2015, which was a 15.6% reduction in disbursements compared with the previous year. BNDES disbursements for the first two quarters of 2016 totaled $11 billion, which suggests continuation in the downward trend in disbursements. But even with the reduction in disbursements, BNDES disbursements in 2015 still dwarfed those of the

IADB by a factor of over four to one, and were close to those of the World Bank Group, which disbursed US$45 billion worldwide in fiscal year 2015 (and US$49 billion in 2016). Indeed, the only development bank based in an EMDE whose assets and disbursements exceed those of BNDES is the CDB.

The activity of BNDES has varied as national development strategies have evolved, but it has consistently remained a central actor in Brazilian finance (Hochstetler 2014a). It has been so central to economic policy that Armijo (2017) termed it a symbol of the country's "new developmentalism."[77] The expanded mission that BNDES took on under President Lula after 2005 necessitated a dramatic increase in its resources (Hochstetler 2014a). New activities included supporting the internationalization of Brazilian firms by enlarging the export-financing programs established in the previous decade, supporting outward FDI of Brazilian firms, and offering trade credit and working capital to Brazilian firms operating abroad when traditional sources of financing dried up (Armijo and Echeverri-Gent 2014; Tavares de Araujo 2013). The internationalization of Brazilian firms induced modest internationalization of BNDES (Hochstetler 2014a). In August 2009, it opened its first branch office in South America, in Montevideo, Uruguay, followed by a holding company in London, and in 2013 an office in Johannesburg. As Hochstetler notes, international lending by BNDES should not be seen as a matter of "South-South" solidarity: "Brazil's President Luiz Inácio Lula da Silva [spoke of] . . . the link between BNDES' international lending and Brazil's foreign policy interests [as driven by its] . . . being a 'big country' promoting its strategic economic and political interests, along with those of its loan recipients" (ibid., 360–361).

BNDES rhetoric concerning internationalization overstates its practice. BNDES disbursements in South America are more qualitatively and quantitatively limited than both the bank's champions and critics contend (Hochstetler 2014a; Hochstetler and Montero 2013). Structural and legal factors restrict its international activities in ways that may keep many of the bank's resources inside the country and that tightly link finance to Brazilian firms and to employment generation at home (Hochstetler 2014a; Hochstetler and Montero 2013). Notwithstanding these constraints, 16% of the loans made by BNDES during fiscal year 2016 were denominated in foreign currency (on par with levels in the previous two years).

Under President Lula, BNDES began to provide countercyclical finance. During the global crisis, BNDES increased disbursements, coordinated actions with private banks to support distressed firms, and took other measures to channel liquidity to small and medium-sized banks that were under stress (Armijo 2017; Tavares de Araujo 2013; Torres Filho 2011). The government used the public bank infrastructure to orchestrate a rapid countercyclical response to the global crisis, but the majority of disbursals went through BNDES (Armijo and Echeverri-Gent 2014; World Bank 2013b, 106). Enabled by a generous capital injection from the government, in 2009 BNDES extended special credit facilities and loans at subsidized rates (World Bank 2013b, 106). BNDES accounted for a third of the growth in credit to the private sector during 2008 and 2009 (Hochstetler and Montero 2012). In 2010, annual lending by BNDES amounted to about 70% of long-term credit in the country (Chandrasekhar 2016). It played a critical role in providing financing when private domestic lenders in Brazil contracted their operations in 2008 and all but froze lending from September 2008 to January 2010 (Chandrasekhar 2016; Torres Filho 2011).

Countercyclical interventions by BNDES required an unprecedented increase in disbursements. BNDES disbursements averaged just over 2% of GDP from 2000 to 2007. They then ranged from 3% to 4.5% of GDP between 2008 and 2014 (Tavares de Araujo 2013, figure 5; Gottschalk 2016). As of late 2009, BNDES accounted for 19% of the stock of outstanding loans from the country's financial system to households and firms (Armijo 2017). By the end of 2011, the bank's loan portfolio was equal to 10% of GDP and its total assets represented about 15% of GDP (ibid.). The expansion of public credit was central to the country's ability to emerge from a recession after only a six-month downturn, and to the stability of manufacturing in the face of a 16% fall in exports from September 2008 to March 2009 (Hochstetler and Montero 2012). Notably, in December 2009, 67% of bank loans in the country with a maturity of over five years were made by BNDES (Torres Filho 2011). A 2016 report states that at present over 90% of loans with a maturity of greater than three years were extended by the country's three public banks, and BNDES is by far the largest provider of long-term finance in the country (Studart and Ramos 2016, 21). Under these circumstances, it is not surprising that BNDES is a key player in overall Brazilian infrastructure finance (ibid., 25).

Observers have long criticized BNDES on many grounds, including the damaging environmental footprint of the projects it supports and the concentration of its loans among a relatively small number of large firms and sectors, particularly electricity and gas (Armijo 2017; Hochstetler and Montero 2013).[78] However, research on BNDES also shows that it is almost the sole source of domestic funding of sustainable infrastructure (Studart and Ramos 2016) and that support for innovation went to smaller and newer firms (Hochstetler and Montero 2013). In addition, it developed new programs to assist micro, small, and medium-sized firms (Armijo 2017). In fact, 31% of total disbursements in 2014 went to small and medium-sized firms (Gottschalk 2016).

In recent years, BNDES has begun to cooperate with other multilateral and regional development banks. It has partnered with the World Bank; in 2011, it signed a Financial Cooperation Agreement with the presidents of development banks of China, India, Russia, and South Africa as part of its continuing engagement with the BRICS, and, in the fall of 2015, it signed a memorandum of understanding designed to strengthen cooperation with the NDB.

CDB

China has three major "policy banks"—the CDB, the Agricultural Development Bank of China, and the Export-Import Bank of China. These public banks were established in 1994 to provide financing to high-priority government projects. The CDB supports the government's macroeconomic policies and development objectives, and our discussion focuses primarily on this institution.[79] It is a primary source of long-term finance for infrastructure and large-scale investment in basic and heavy industry (UNCTAD 2015b, 169). In fact, US$1.5 trillion of CDB loans went to infrastructure and basic industry from 2006 to 2014 (Wang 2016, 4). As of year-end 2014, about 53% of the CDB's outstanding loans were allocated to infrastructure (ibid., 14).

The CDB is the world's largest development bank in terms of assets, which remained high and grew steadily during the global crisis. The CDB's assets were US$108 billion in 2001 and US$560 billion at the start of the crisis in 2008. By 2013, they had risen to US$1.3 trillion (Wang 2016). At year-end 2015, they stood at roughly US$1.7 trillion (a 22% increase over 2014), about five times the 2015 assets of the IBRD.[80]

The CDB undertook strongly countercyclical initiatives during the crisis by lending actively in the domestic market and providing important support for the country's export performance. Lending by the bank grew markedly: at year-end 2008, outstanding loans were valued at US$460 billion, and at year-end 2014, they stood at US$1.2 trillion. The loans extended in 2014 were valued at US$276 billion, which represented a 20% increase over 2013 lending (CDB website, annual report 2014, 12). As signs of an economic slowdown and financial fragility became apparent during the summer and fall of 2015, the CDB responded with new countercyclical support that supplemented other government measures.

During the crisis, China launched a variety of bilateral financial initiatives in Asia, Africa, Latin America, and the former Soviet bloc countries through its policy banks, especially the CDB, but also through the Export-Import Bank. Cross-border loans and lines of credit are driven by many of the same objectives as the country's currency swaps, particularly access to key resources and markets and support for SOEs and other firms. At year-end 2015, the CDB's foreign currency loans totaled US$276 billion, which represented 19% of its total loan portfolio and a ninefold increase in foreign-currency lending compared with 2007 (CDB website, annual report 2015, 60).[81] Many of these loans support infrastructure development in EMDEs and China's access to raw materials (UNCTAD 2015b, 169–170).

China committed around US$132 billion in financing to African and Latin American governments between 2003 and 2011, and more than 80% of this financing was committed since the start of the global crisis.[82] About half of these loans (US$75 billion) were resource secured, involving exports of oil, cocoa, and diamonds. Interest rates on loans from China's policy banks are not generally out of line with rates available on global markets, and interest rates on loans to Latin America are roughly comparable to those of the World Bank, IADB, and CAF (Gallagher 2016, 78). The lack of transparency around Chinese loans is cause for concern by policymakers in EMDEs. China's loans do not carry the same policy conditionalities as loans from the BWIs. But these loans are not without "strings," such as those that tie loans to the procurement of goods and construction services from Chinese firms. CDB conditionality illustrates that loans made by EMDE lenders are not always more advantageous to recipients than loans from multilateral sources. But the evidence on these conditions is not unequivocal. Contrary to popular perception, Bräutigam and Gallagher (2014) find no evidence that China's loans involve specific requirements to employ workers from the country or that they lock in low commodity prices. Moreover, they find that borrowers have room to negotiate on employment, training, and local content when this is seen to benefit the project from the perspective of its lenders.

Today, the CDB and the Export-Import Bank of China provide more financing to Latin American governments than the World Bank and the IADB, and more to Asia than the World Bank and AsDB (Gallagher 2015b). The CDB and the Export-Import Bank of China provided US$21 billion in finance to Latin American governments and state-run firms in 2016 (Myers and Gallagher 2017). China's cross-border loans dwarf those of BNDES. From 2008 to April 2015, the CDB extended loans to 40 countries, valued at US$233 billion (and representing 60% of the bank's total credit portfolio) (Wang 2016, table 3). The international holdings of the CDB and the Export-Import Bank are estimated to be about US$684 billion, which is very close to the combined US$720 billion in international assets held by the World Bank, IADB, AfDB, and AsDB (Gallagher, Kamal, and Wang 2016, figure 1). However, it is critical to note that the vast majority of the US$117 billion in energy-related loans made by the CDB and the Export-Import Bank to EMDEs in 2007–2014 are in oil and gas exploration, and even more are in power plants, 66% of which are coal fired (ibid.).[83] Thus, international loans by the CDB and Export-Import Bank of China cannot be seen as supporting the environmental concerns embodied in some of the SDGs (Tabuchi 2017). Moreover, this lending surge is not without other costs. The risks associated with overleveraging in China and overlending to (now) slowing EMDEs are only now becoming apparent.

The significance of lending to EMDEs by Brazil's and especially China's development banks (and those of the other BRICS as well) extends beyond the economic value of the loans.[84] Loans by China and Brazil enhance their individual influence and also enhance the collective international stature of rising powers vis-à-vis the AEs. In addition, lending by China and other emerging powers is imparting complexity to the traditional Bretton Woods–era architecture of project finance, when the line between AE lending and EMDE borrowing was clearly drawn.

The Main Regional Development Banks

The MRDBs are a type of multilateral development bank that deserves some attention here, though they are BWIs and not creations of the EMDEs. They, too, evolved, though modestly, during the global crisis. Among the MRDBs, I focus here on the AsDB, IADB, and the African Development Bank (AfDB).[85] Nonborrowing AEs are shareholders in these three institutions, and are the dominant decisionmakers in the AsDB and IADB since voting shares are allocated according to capital contributions by member nations. The AsDB and the AfDB are headquartered in EMDEs, whereas the IADB is headquartered in Washington, D.C.

Generally speaking, the MRDBs are vehicles for poverty reduction and the provision of public goods. The global crisis demonstrated the crucial countercyclical function that the MRDBs serve when private financial markets freeze. Prior to the global crisis, the AsDB was already lending more than the World Bank inside the Asian and Pacific region, and the IADB and FLAR were already providing more crisis-related financing in South America than the IMF (Woods 2010). The global crisis accelerated this trend. The MRDBs enjoyed an increase in their resources (thanks to the G-20) and accordingly became more active and introduced new countercyclical programs. The AsDB, AfDB, and IADB responded to the crisis in their regions in some cases more quickly and with larger loans than the IMF and the World Bank, and they introduced new temporary rapid financing programs and counter-cyclical lending facilities to support developing and low-income countries (Chin 2012; Woods 2010). The MRDBs as a group increased their lending commitments to EMDEs by 71% in 2009 compared with 2008, and their disbursements grew by 45% in the same period.[86]

With G-20 backing, the AsDB introduced a new countercyclical instrument, the Counter-cyclical Support Facility, to provide support of up to US$3 billion to economies in the region affected by the crisis. Between 2008 and 2009, AsDB's lending commitments grew by 42% and its disbursements by 33%. Other MRDBs quickly followed the AsDB's example, and they were granted a portion of the new funds committed to the IMF to establish new regional lending facilities to promote rapid countercyclical support within their regions (Chin 2012). The IADB established a US$6 billion rapid disbursal Emergency Liquidity Fund to support the countercyclical efforts of member governments. It also increased callable capital by US$4 billion, increased its commitments by 38% in 2009 (having already increased its disbursements significantly in 2008), and disbursed 60% more in 2009 than in 2008. The IADB approved loans of US$11.2 billion, US$15.5 billion, and US$12.4 billion in 2008, 2009, and 2010, respectively (Ocampo and Titelman 2012, 15). The AfDB established a US$1.5 billion Emergency Liquidity Facility during the crisis. Between 2008 and 2009, it increased its lending commitments by 137% and its disbursements by 125% (which is the largest increase in disbursements of any of the MRDBs).

The MRDB response to the crisis involved the launch of a large number of regional initiatives. In these efforts, individual MRDBs generally worked with other institutions, notably the World Bank (Ocampo et al. 2012, 65–69). The World Bank and the MRDBs have often competed with one another (ibid.). The massive needs generated by the crisis pushed the institutions to collaborate. There were nevertheless major failings in these responses. Both the World Bank and the MRDBs responded inadequately to the needs of low-income countries. In addition, despite rhetoric to the contrary, investment in infrastructure by the World Bank and the MRDBs fell as a share of total investment in recent decades (though more recently it has begun to rise modestly) (Humphrey 2015b, figure 2).

The World Bank and the MRDBs have long been criticized for the slow pace of their loan approval procedures, particularly in comparison with institutions such as the CAF, and even now in relation to the AIIB and

NDB. From initial project identification to first disbursement, the average loan approval time for the IBRD and IDA is 28 months (and for sovereign loans it is 14 months). For the AfDB, the average is 13 months; for the AsDB, 11 months; and for the IADB, 5.8 months (Humphrey 2015a, 13, figure 14).[87]

Despite expansion in the scale and scope of activity by the MRDBs during the global crisis, gross disbursements by the World Bank Group still outstrip those of the MRDBs. In 2015, the IADB disbursed loans of US$10.2 billion, the AsDB US$11.7 billion, and the AfDB US$4.2 billion. Those figures amount to 20.8%, 26.2%, and 9.4%, respectively, of the World Bank Group's disbursements.[88] In contrast, the IBRD approved loans of US$23.5 billion and US$18.6 billion in 2015 and 2014, respectively. Commitments by the IBRD exceeded its historical average of US$13.5 billion a year in loan approvals from 2005 to 2008, before the global crisis. In 2015, the IBRD approved what was a record level of financing for any year except at the height of the global crisis. Notwithstanding the expansion in activity by the MRDBs and especially the World Bank, these institutions appear stalled in comparison with China-backed initiatives, those of the BRICS, the dynamism of the CAF, and even that of a less expansive BNDES. This is particularly the case when one considers the inability of the Western-backed multilateral development banks to increase their paid-in capital despite much talk of the infrastructure finance gap and the challenges of the SDGs (Gallagher, Kamal, and Wang 2016).[89] The pivot of project finance away from the West is clear when one takes account of the full range of China's policy banks, the new family of multilateral development banks and funds financed and/or cofinanced by China, and its support for the NDB (ibid., 3).

A Caveat Regarding Africa and Two Initiatives Led by Venezuela

Neither the Asian nor the global crisis has had a major catalytic effect on reserve pooling and project finance institutions on the African continent. The only meaningful outcomes in this regard relate to South Africa's role in the CRA and the NDB, its membership in the AIIB, and the activism of the AfDB.[90] This stands in contrast to the effects of these crises elsewhere in the global south and east, as we have seen. This type of unevenness is to be expected—indeed, it is part and parcel of the overall inconsistency at the heart of the emerging financial architecture. Where we have seen more meaningful steps toward financial architectural innovations in Africa is in the realm of regional macroeconomic coordination and monetary integration, where several subregional initiatives are in the planning stages (see Fritz and Mühlich 2014, 29–40).

Two initiatives led largely by Venezuela are worth noting briefly because they contain elements of development banking and also because they illustrate the fragility of institutional experimentation. The Bolivarian Alliance for the Peoples of Our Americas (Spanish acronym ALBA) is a multifaceted project built around a vision of Latin American and Caribbean solidarity described as "post-hegemonic regionalism" and "regionalism without regions." ALBA encompasses a suite of financial, trade, aid, and social integration programs, one of which is a development bank, the Bank of ALBA.[91] The bank was established in January 2008, is headquartered in Caracas, Venezuela, and has a branch in Cuba. It is a development bank with a small portfolio (and subscribed capital of US$1 billion) and a mission of supporting ALBA's integration aims and its social, economic, and political programs.[92] At the 11th ALBA Summit, in February 2012, members committed to allocating 1% of their reserves to the Bank of ALBA. Loans made by the Bank of ALBA do not involve conditionality, and discussions are reportedly by consensus (Janike 2008).[93]

As of this writing, the prospects of the Bank of ALBA (and the other initiatives under ALBA's umbrella) remain uncertain, though dim, owing to the severe political and economic challenges confronting Venezuela.[94] But the experience with ALBA's many initiatives and the relationships involved in building them may lay the groundwork for future innovations that may arise as political and economic circumstances evolve and acute needs for new initiatives emerge. Failed initiatives, too, provide critical opportunities for institutional learning.

The other initiative led largely by Venezuela that bears mention is an ideologically related project to create a development bank, the Bank of the South (Spanish acronym BDS). The BDS was founded in 2007 and became a legal entity in 2009 (with US$7 billion in subscribed capital, though recent reports suggest that the figure has grown to US$10 billion).[95] The BDS project moved forward in late November 2016 after a long period during which it failed to advance beyond its legal existence. At a meeting at the headquarters of the Union of South American Nations in Quito, an executive board was installed (with representatives from Venezuela, Uruguay, Ecuador, and Bolivia). The board announced that the institution would begin its preoperative phase and that Uruguayan economist Pedro Buonomo would be the bank's first president (*El Telégrafo* 2016).

The initial BDS vision entailed the principles of equal voice among members and the rejection of conditionality. The BDS had stalled long before the loss of oil-fueled revenue and confidence and before many of the region's governments moved away from populism. The Venezuelan government turned its attention away from the BDS (and toward ALBA) once other BDS members, such as Brazil, succeeded in shaping the institution in the image of a traditional development bank rather than as a vehicle of popular socialism.[96] The announcement in 2016 that the BDS would nonetheless begin functioning was unexpected, not least because of political shifts in Argentina and Brazil, original signatory countries.[97] It has initial planned paid-in capital of US$90 million, and Bolivia, Ecuador, and Venezuela are reported to have paid in already.[98] Fundamental questions remain about where the institution's capital will come from. Other critical challenges include the weakness of the Venezuelan economy and leadership changes in Argentina and Brazil that could prove to be hostile to the institution.

Governance, Surveillance, Conditionalities, and Institutional Linkages

Many of the reserve pooling institutions and development banks examined here are characterized by governance structures that differentiate them from the BWIs, in which AEs (especially the United States) have disproportionate weight. Many of the institutions are organized to promote greater inclusiveness, though there is quite considerable divergence in the degree to which this is achieved by design or in practice. Indeed, some of the institutions considered here hew rather closely to the BWIs in terms of governance (when it comes to the influence of countries that contribute a large portion of the institution's capital, the role of a resident board, and other matters), whereas others have made a rather sharp break with these norms. The fact that the institutions surveyed have diverse and complicated decision-making structures reflects the necessary and real tensions between the demands of the larger countries that provide the bulk of financial support, recognition of the legitimacy of concerns about inclusiveness for smaller, poorer countries, and the complicated power politics that necessarily infuses regional and transregional initiatives.

Like governance, the matter of "getting conditionality right" continues to be a key challenge, which institutions are managing in diverse ways. Some institutions, such as the CMIM, CRA, ArMF, and FLAR, plan to or already do conduct surveillance (including country missions) and utilize conditionality or require some type of adjustment program, at least under certain circumstances. Others, such as the EFSD, require conditionality under all circumstances. Some, such as the FLAR and CAF, employ an approach to monitoring that works with borrowing governments in ways that are decidedly distinct from the top-down approach of the IMF and World Bank. Here, surveillance (and in the case of FLAR) adjustment programs are minimalist, highly country-specific, peer based, and exclude the BWIs. Some institutions are actively wrestling with these issues and involve the IMF explicitly under certain circumstances (e.g., the CMIM and CRA). In contrast, the EFSD involves the IMF implicitly through consultations and, like the CRA, abstains from lending to countries in arrears to it. The early design of the BDS and the Bank of ALBA renounced conditionality altogether. In the newest institutions, such as the AIIB and NDB, the matter of project selection and assessment is still evolving, as is the issue of how to handle nonperforming loans.

For the most part, the institutions considered here are more agile than the BWIs (and the MRDBs) inasmuch as they respond quickly to economic challenges in their field of operations. In several instances, this agility—coupled, critically, with a sense of country ownership and the appropriateness of surveillance procedures—has induced countries receiving support to treat the lending institutions as if they held preferred creditor status.

An obstacle facing reserve pooling arrangements in particular concerns the challenges posed by precautionary forms of support. Some institutions, such as the CMIM, plan to utilize prequalification criteria before support is disbursed. Others, such as the FLAR, have thus far successfully used their own forms of monitoring and dialogue to determine eligibility for precautionary support without resorting to prequalification criteria. For the CRA, the matter of qualification for both liquidity and precautionary support remains under consideration among member central banks, though at this point the CRA mirrors the link to the IMF that is a feature of the CMIM.[99] Precautionary support is always a complex matter, as we have seen in the case of the IMF's FCL. It often involves some sort of prequalification criteria, which may mean that the candidates that meet the criteria are those that are least likely to need support, and in the case of regional and transregional bodies, it may undermine the solidarity that is an intrinsic part of these arrangements.

Conclusion

As the foregoing makes clear, the institutions surveyed diverge from one another in many ways, such as their internal governance, aspirations, size and capacity, member buy-in, and the degree to which they are explicitly or implicitly linked to legacy institutions. They do not meld into any sort of new, coherent system of financial governance architecture or developmental finance. Not all are equally likely to survive, let alone thrive, in the years ahead. Indeed, the BDS was shipwrecked for many years on the shoals of the economic challenges and conflicting visions among member nations. Despite the recent resurrection of the project, its prospects are uncertain. The fate of the Bank of ALBA is similarly in doubt. Neither individually nor collectively do any of the reserve pooling institutions considered here promise or aim to challenge the IMF as the central institution of crisis response. In the realm of development banks, the institutions considered here should also not be considered against the standard of displacement of the World Bank or the MRDBs. That said, many have the firepower to play central roles in the provision of project and infrastructure finance across EMDEs. They do not amount to a new pole of financial power that will necessarily demote AE hegemony in financial affairs. Instead, the initiatives are fragmentary and heterogeneous, some are internally fraught with rivalry and suspicion, and many are no doubt marked by the same kinds of ambiguity as the IMF, where gritty, muddled day-to-day practice conflicts with coherent, pristine mission statements. Finally, the institutions may work at cross-purposes, especially during crisis moments, undermining each other's efforts and/or imposing cross-border spillovers that disrupt each other's economies.

I do not take these features as fatal flaws. Instead, guided by Hirschman, I recognize the present period of institutional experimentation, expansion, and hybridization as a moment of pragmatic innovation that just might yield institutions and practices that do better than their predecessors in promoting financial stability and resilience and, as a consequence of that, provide at least the possibility for development that is more stable, inclusive, sustainable, and protective of autonomy. With Hirschman, I place emphasis on the potential inherent in unscripted adjustments that are freed from the constraints imposed by hegemonic narratives that purport to demonstrate the single path to economic security and development.

At a minimum, the flourishing of heterogeneous EMDE institutions of financial governance and developmental finance generates new opportunities for exit from unresponsive institutions and for at least a degree of forum shopping among alternatives. As a consequence, it may increase EMDE resilience, bargaining power, and voice vis-à-vis the BWIs (Helleiner 2010). To the extent that opportunities for forum shopping are realized, the BWIs may face pressure to respond to long-held concerns by EMDEs. In any event, the leverage of larger EMDEs in global and regional financial governance is certainly increasing as several of the institutions surveyed here have come to play a more prominent role during the global crisis. Redundancy and the networks of cooperation that are already emerging among institutions may increase overall resilience and enhance antifragility in the global financial system. In this connection, I note that UNCTAD calls for "more diversified financial systems," by which is meant different institutions of different sizes and mandates (UNCTAD 2013, chap. 3), that Ocampo (2006, chap. 1) has long called for a denser financial architecture, and that Culpeper (1997) argues for the benefits of competitive pluralism among multilateral development banks on the grounds that overlap and rivalry encourage innovation and productivity.[100] Multiple layers and increased density have the potential to yield productive redundancy—which can reduce instability, contain and ameliorate crises, and increase opportunities to finance development. The emerging productive redundancy promises to disturb the apparent efficiency of the streamlined, top-down, centralized financial governance architecture that characterized the neoliberal era, which promised efficiency but in fact generated extraordinary risk and crisis contagion while starving most EMDEs of adequate developmental finance.

The new pluripolar landscape is already affecting formal and informal governance and decision making at the IMF, and consultations within the G-20, as we have seen. As we will see in chapter 7, the terrain on which capital controls are theorized and pursued has likewise shifted. Only the most unimaginative accounts can fail to recognize that the BWIs and leading AEs today must manage a jumble of newly empowered competing interests and that doing so is already altering and will continue to alter their rhetoric, research, and practice. When compared with the neoliberal era, the change is nothing short of extraordinary, not because neoliberal impulses and strategies have been subordinated to a comprehensive alternative but because the stifling uniformity of the neoliberal era is undermined by the proliferation of EMDE institutions that are, to varying degrees, relatively autonomous from the primary institutions of neoliberal authority.

There are no guarantees, of course, that the new opportunities afforded by institutional innovation, exit, and voice will necessarily generate a more just economic landscape. The increased aperture in financial governance may not survive as emerging powers attempt to assert hegemony over other EMDEs. Would a financial governance architecture dominated by China, say, necessarily provide greater breathing room in the long run for smaller, lower-income countries? But for now, at least, we should be attentive to the potential for progressive reform that has emerged as a consequence of the increased policy space that the evolving, incoherent system provides. Certainly in contrast to the neoliberal era, when financial governance structures, practices, and ideology represented a suffocating obstacle to innovation and experimentation, today's leaders look out on a more heterogeneous landscape that may very well prove to be much more congenial to unscripted, locally appropriate initiatives.

The new initiatives provide Hirschmanian opportunities—for learning by doing and learning from others, parallel experimentation, and providential problem solving that only comes about as a consequence of the Hiding Hand. Progress often happens when obstacles are initially underestimated so that new initiatives appear to be viable and when practitioners are then forced to search for solutions that were previously unimaginable. The next crisis may very well propel new initiatives and a deepening of embryonic institutions and partnerships that speak to challenges that now appear irresolvable. Moreover, the proliferation of institutions, even if they are not as credible, efficient, and experienced as the BWIs or the MRDBs, is vital to the creation of new networks within countries and across national borders that can enhance indigenous and widely dispersed capacity in areas that are fundamental to economic development. We should remember in this context that even experimental failures can and often do leave in their wake vital linkages and knowledge that may be available for and enable subsequent endeavors. In this vision, few successes and failures are final—they are more typically steps along branching historical paths as actors seek to confront the challenges they face. They are best able to do that, Hirschman also reminds us, when they are free to do so unencumbered by theoretical visions and institutional monopolies that attempt to prenarrate the future. Ad hoc, pragmatic adjustments rather than a tightly constrained choreography are what Hirschman put his faith in, messy though they may be. And that is just what is emerging across the new financial governance architecture.

"It was as if the Vatican had given its blessing to birth control." So begins an article on the resurrection and growing respectability of capital controls at the IMF (*Economist* 2013). Indeed, one of the most surprising effects of the global crisis has been its profound impact on thinking and practice around what was until recently a forbidden policy instrument.

Capital Controls: A Brief History

In the immediate aftermath of World War II, the IMF fully embraced capital controls. For several decades following the war, capital controls were utilized almost universally around the globe. Capital controls were widely understood by academic economists, policymakers, and IMF officials as necessary tools of prudential financial management (Helleiner 1994; 2014a; Pérez Caldentey and Vernengo 2012). Controls were implemented to enhance macroeconomic policy autonomy, promote financial and currency stability, protect domestic industries from foreign control or competition, and ensure the provision of adequate credit to favored sectors at the right price (Epstein, Grabel, and Jomo K. S. 2004).

John Maynard Keynes and U.S. Treasury official Harry Dexter White are widely credited with incorporating capital controls as a central feature of the emerging Bretton Woods system. They advocated controls on both the sending and receiving ends, and emphasized the need for cooperation between capital source and recipient countries (see Crotty 1983; Helleiner 1994; Horsefield 1969, 31, 65; Steil 2013, 134, 150). Keynes stated that "control will be more difficult to work by unilateral action . . . if movements of capital cannot be controlled at both ends." In the same vein, White argued that "almost every country, at one time or another, exercises control over the inflow or outflow of investments, but without the co-operation of other countries such control is difficult, expensive and subject to considerable evasion" (quoted in Horsefield 1969, 31, 65). Keynes's plan granted greater autonomy to individual states over the method and degree of controls. White's plan placed cooperation among capital sending and recipient governments at center stage, with an obligation on the part of recipients of foreign capital to cooperate in blocking inflows when other governments made such requests (Steil 2013, 134, 150).

Before Keynes and White, Raúl Prebisch advocated capital controls in peripheral economies. Prebisch maintained that controls were essential to manage cyclical fluctuations and to shift the composition of capital inflows away from short-term and toward long-term finance. Under his direction, the Central Bank of Argentina in 1943 introduced controls to promote financial stability and sustain economic development (Pérez Caldentey and Vernengo 2016, 1728).

The Neoliberal Era and the Asian Crisis

The stagflation of the 1970s inaugurated a paradigm shift in the economics profession away from traditional Keynesian thought and toward the Chicago School view of the virtues of market mediation. By the early 1980s, the IMF was firmly in the grip of neoliberalism. In that intellectual milieu, capital controls were largely derided as a vestigial organ of wrongheaded, dirigiste economic meddling.[1] The case for liberalizing international capital flows in EMDEs was nested in a broader neoliberal embrace of financial liberalization. Liberalization involved the deregulation of domestic financial flows and institutions, promotion of financial innovation, "light touch" financial regulation, and inflation targeting by politically independent central banks.[2]

Rather than shaking the IMF from its neoliberal commitments, recurrent crises during the 1980s and 1990s had the effect of recommitting the institution to financial liberalization. The Asian crisis is emblematic in this regard. When Malaysia introduced outflow controls in 1998, the IMF viewed them as retrogressive, calling them a "step back" toward outdated, self-defeating policies (Adam and Kate 2010). The IMF was not alone in excoriating Malaysian leaders. A representative article in the international business press stated that "foreign investors in Malaysia have been expropriated, and the Malaysians will bear the cost of their distrust for years" (cited in Kaplan and Rodrik 2001, 11). One commentator likened the country's outflow controls to a financial Roach Motel, observing that they "deeply frightened global investors" because "money can get in, but it can't get out" (Coy, Kripalani, and Clifford 1998, 37). Flagging the country's controls, Moody's, Standard and Poor's, and Fitch downgraded Malaysia's sovereign debt rating (Abdelal and Alfaro 2003).[3]

With notable exceptions, IMF staff and the economics profession remained largely intolerant of capital controls through the early twenty-first century. During the long neoliberal period, one had to look to the work of the Keynesian minority within the academic wing of the economics profession and to the world's heretical finance ministries for forceful, consistent support of the management of international capital flows.[4]

Ultimately, however, neither the IMF nor the economics profession could remain impervious to recurrent crises associated with financial liberalization or to EMDE practices that flouted the neoliberal prescription. In the late 1990s, just prior to the Asian crisis, the IMF was poised to enshrine capital flow liberalization in its Articles of Agreement (as discussed in chapter 3). The Asian crisis derailed that effort. Moreover, despite the neoliberal tenor of the times, some countries (such as China, Chile, and Colombia) stubbornly maintained controls, with notable success. Partly in response, the Asian crisis precipitated the beginning of a begrudging reevaluation of capital controls. Indeed, what now appears as the "new normal" (Grabel 2011) regarding controls resulted from a gradual process of legitimation that began slowly and unevenly after the Asian crisis (Abdelal 2007; Chwieroth 2010; Moschella 2009).

Early cracks in the neoliberal consensus following the Asian crisis appeared in the work of prominent neoclassical economists, such as Jagdish Bhagwati (1998) and Martin Feldstein (1998), who criticized the way in which powerful interest groups and the IMF used the crisis to press for capital account liberalization. They were soon joined by other leading mainstream economists, such as Maurice Obstfeld and Paul Krugman (Obstfeld 1998; Krugman 1998), who came to recognize the risks associated with unrestrained capital flows. Academic literature following the Asian crisis gradually reflected this evolving view. Notably, cross-country empirical studies offered strong support for the macroeconomic achievements of inflow controls (Chwieroth 2010, chap. 8; Epstein, Grabel, and Jomo K. S. 2004; Magud and Reinhart 2006). Evidence supporting the achievements of outflow controls was far less abundant, but nontrivial, as discussed in Epstein, Grabel, and Jomo K. S. (2004) and Epstein (2012). Research on Malaysia by Kaplan and Rodrik (2001), for instance, is strongly favorable regarding the achievements of Malaysia's outflow controls.[5]

IMF research economists began to adjust their views on capital controls in the context of this academic ferment. Early adjustments in IMF thinking were subtle, uneven, and inconsistent. Nonetheless, in the period following the Asian crisis, the center of gravity at the Fund shifted away from an unequivocal, fundamentalist opposition to any interference with the free flow of capital to a tentative, conditional acceptance of temporary, "market-friendly" inflow controls (Prasad et al. 2003).

As expected, the new pragmatism encountered pushback from many leading economists (e.g., Edwards 1999; Forbes 2005). The profession was clearly unwilling to shed its commitment to capital flow liberalization, and the new thinking failed to generate anything like a new consensus. Instead, the late 1990s and the years since have been marked by halting steps away from the orthodoxy on capital flow liberalization. The resulting unevenness is apparent in the work of the IMF itself during and following the Asian crisis, as illuminated in a 2005 study by the IEO of IMF practices from the Asian crisis to 2004 (IEO 2005). The IEO (2005, 48) acknowledges a discernible disconnect between IMF research on the one hand, which at best featured ambivalence toward capital controls, and the creeping tolerance for controls by the institution's economists when they worked with particular countries on the other.[6] The relative autonomy of different departments at the IMF, a lack of univocal leadership from the top, and the internal entrepreneurship of midrange staff when working in different contexts help to account for IMF inconsistency during the period (Chwieroth 2010; 2014).

Adding to the emerging confusion surrounding capital controls, policymakers from different parts of the world crafted competing etiologies of the Asian crisis. As discussed in chapter 3, those from the United States emphasized crony capitalism and overregulated banking systems, the solution for which was increased financial liberalization. In contrast, Asian and European analysis targeted radical financial deregulation (Wade 1998–1999). The divergent diagnoses generated conflict over the financial liberalization ideal and contending perspectives on the need for and nature of desirable reforms to global financial governance.

The Global Crisis: Rebranding Capital Controls

The global crisis occurred in the midst of the new aperture surrounding financial liberalization and transformed the landscape concerning the legitimacy of capital controls. Beginning in 2008, a large number of EMDEs and several countries on the European periphery implemented far-reaching, heterogeneous controls on capital inflows and outflows in response to diverse economic challenges. From an immediate precrisis vantage point, the range and creativity of the policy interventions across a significant swath of economies was audacious.

The impact of the crisis and the new capital management initiatives on economic thinking and practice is nothing short of stunning. Today there is appreciation among economists and policymakers of the channels by which unrestrained capital flows and high levels of liquidity can undermine macroeconomic and trade performance through their effects on the exchange rate and asset markets. The Asian and global crises together provided ample cross-national evidence that large, footloose capital inflows aggravate financial fragility by fueling spectacular, unsustainable asset bubbles and excessive leveraging by households and firms, including financing strategies that involve severe locational mismatches. Equally important, large-scale reversals of capital flows severely test the limits of financial resilience and reserve adequacy. On the political side, the crises underscored the connection between large, unmanaged capital flows and the rise of interstate tensions over policy spillover effects. They also highlighted the political tensions aggravated by creditor-mandated adjustment programs built on the myth of economic recovery through fiscal restraint. That the global crisis originated with the implosion of the highly liberalized, liquid, and internationally open financial system in the United States severely damaged the case that neoclassical economists had made for several decades: that the U.S. brand of financial liberalization was the ideal to which all other countries should aspire (Kirshner 2014a).

Keynesian-inflected ideas about the legitimacy and necessity of managing international capital flows now infuse the work of a broad set of economists in academia and in the policy community. Notably, the IMF evolved significantly during the crisis despite continuing signs of discomfort (Chwieroth 2014; Gallagher 2014; Grabel 2011; 2015b; Moschella 2010; 2014). The new, pragmatic IMF view recognizes that capital controls are a "legitimate part of the policy toolkit," to borrow a now oft-cited phrase from IMF research on the subject during the crisis (e.g., Ostry et al. 2010; 2011). Greater tolerance is also reflected in the statements of officials associated with other multilateral institutions, important figures in the world of central banking, analysts at credit rating agencies, and the recent research of economists who one would not have associated with Keynesian thought.

The complex processes of change around capital controls during and since the crisis can most accurately be understood as experimental, messy, uneven, contested, and evolving (in a word, Hirschmanian). Capital controls have been thoroughly "rebranded."[7] Earlier efforts to rebrand controls failed to stick other than among the already-receptive Keynesian minority in economics. For instance, in 2003 and since, Ocampo (2003; 2010d) argued consistently for "capital account regulations," meaning a family of policies that includes capital controls. In 2004, Epstein, Grabel and Jomo K. S. (2004) advocated "capital management techniques" involving two complementary, overlapping types of financial policies—capital controls and those that enforce prudential management of domestic financial institutions. Prior to the global crisis, these contributions attracted little attention among mainstream economists or practitioners. In contrast, the IMF today refers to capital controls matter-of-factly as "capital flow management" techniques (IMF 2011d; 2012f; Ostry et al. 2011). The new, innocuous term is suggestive of a neutral, technocratic approach to an instrument that had long been discredited as a policy mistake by backward countries.[8]

Rebranding has occurred against a broader backdrop of uncertainty and financial volatility; economic, political, and ideational aperture; and discontinuity in financial governance (Grabel 2011; 2017; Grabel and Gallagher 2015). The productive incoherence of this state of affairs is reflected in the proliferation of responses to the global crisis by national governments, multilateral institutions, credit rating agencies, and the economics profession that have not yet crystallized into a consistent vision or model.[9] In response to diverse economic challenges, we find a range of national experiments with capital controls and inconsistent practices by the IMF that are not adequately described by a simplistic narrative. This incoherence has widened EMDE policy space to a greater and more consistent degree than in the years following the Asian crisis (cf. Chwieroth 2015; Moschella 2014; Gallagher 2014).

The sheer scale of the crisis, the bold rhetoric around the need for new strategies to combat it, and the range of unorthodox policy responses pursued across the globe have provided broader validation for protective national policy responses in EMDEs.[10] The G-20's brief "Keynesian moment" in 2008–2009 opened space for experimentation with capital controls and countercyclical monetary and fiscal policy responses.[11] The IMF's rhetorical attention to pro-poor spending during the crisis also helped to legitimate countercyclical responses (Grabel 2011; 2013a). At the same time, expansionary monetary policies in the United States and other AEs contributed to the normalization of protective responses to the crisis in EMDEs. What the IMF's Lagarde (approvingly) termed the rise of "unconventional monetary policies" (i.e., negative interest rates) in a number of AEs provided cover for other unorthodox policies, such as capital controls.[12]

Winners, Losers, Spillovers, and Capital Controls

During the 2009–2014 period, EMDEs received net capital inflows of US$2.2 trillion (Stiglitz and Rashid 2016a). As a consequence, many EMDEs were confronted with surges of liquidity, asset bubbles, inflationary pressures, and currency appreciations. That the market capitalizations of stock exchanges in Mumbai, Johannesburg, São Paulo, and Shanghai nearly tripled in the years that followed the global crisis is just one indicator of the fragility induced by these inflows (Stiglitz and Rashid 2016a).

Expansionary monetary policies in AEs exacerbated the flood of capital to EMDEs. Investors and speculators were able to engage in profitable carry trade, borrowing at low interest rates in AEs and then investing in EMDEs, which were characterized by higher interest rates during much of the global crisis.[13] In a departure from the old script, capital controls were necessitated by the side effects of the relative success with which many EMDEs navigated the global crisis and of their own good fortune when it came to commodity prices and economic growth. This success, coupled with economic weakness and low returns on assets in AEs, drove investors and speculators to EMDE markets. The use of capital controls by what we might think of as "winning economies" contributed significantly to the legitimation of this policy instrument in the eyes of policymakers, the IMF, the international investment community, and the neoclassical core of the economics profession. Despite relative EMDE success, precious little of the capital inflows went to fixed investment, and hence could not be said to benefit the real economy (Stiglitz and Rashid 2016b). In addition, capital inflows facilitated increases in EMDE dollar-denominated corporate debt. The BIS reports that the debt of nonfinancial corporations in EMDEs went from approximately US$9 trillion at year-end 2008 to over US$25 trillion by year-end 2015, and doubled as a percentage of GDP over the same period (cited in UNCTAD 2016, chap. 1).

The tide of capital flows has since turned. Net capital flows to EMDEs turned negative in the second quarter of 2014. Net outflows were about US$656 billion in 2015 and US$185 billion in the first quarter of 2016 (ibid.). These amounts are significant: the 2015 outflows alone amounted to more than 25% of the capital inflows that EMDEs had received during the previous six years (Stiglitz and Rashid 2016a). The Institute of International Finance (IIF, an industry group), which takes account of previously unrecorded capital flows captured by errors and omissions, reports much larger net outflows of US$735 billion in 2015 (IIF 2016). Although several large EMDEs experienced net outflows in 2015 (e.g., Korea, Russia, and South

Africa), the bulk of the outflows (US$676 billion) came from China (ibid.).[14] China's net capital flow deficit for 2015 was equal to 4.5% of its GDP (UNCTAD 2016, chap.1). After moderating in the middle of 2016, capital outflows from China accelerated sharply. In the third quarter of 2016, net outflows of FDI reached US$31 billion (as Chinese firms engaged in overseas mergers and acquisitions) (Wildau 2016c). In the same period, US$176 billion in financial capital flows not linked to trade or FDI left China, the largest net outflows from the country since the fourth quarter of 2015 (ibid.). By comparison, net outflows from all East Asian economies during the Asian crisis in 1997 were just US$12 billion (Stiglitz and Rashid 2016a).

In this context, several EMDEs have abandoned or loosened inflow controls, and some have implemented new controls, particularly on outflows. The new controls have been introduced in response to the accelerating pace of outflows and the combined effects of slowing growth, falling commodity and asset prices, weakening currencies, and dramatic reserve reduction.[15] Stock markets in many EMDEs closed 2015 with double-digit losses, a reversal of the long boom in many markets during much of the global crisis (Akyüz 2016). The excess of cheap liquidity and asset bubbles have inevitably given way to sovereign and private debt overhangs, which are aggravated by the locational mismatch, which is made worse by the weakening of EMDE currencies.

The unsettled state of international financial markets, and the spillover effects of monetary policy in AEs, have also aggravated pressures and volatility in EMDEs. In 2013, the U.S. Federal Reserve began to discuss eventual "policy tapering," which refers to a gradual move away from the quantitative easing (QE) that constituted its policy stance during much of the global crisis. The talk of tapering spawned reversals of capital flows from EMDE markets, equity market losses, currency depreciations, and increases in bond yields. These trends incited what became known as the "taper tantrum" of May and June 2013. The decision by the Fed to begin actual tapering in December 2015 induced further disruption in EMDE markets, which was subsequently compounded by large capital outflows in late 2016 following the U.S. presidential election—what came to be termed the "Trump tantrum."[16] The flight of capital to U.S. markets was triggered by expectations that the new administration would increase infrastructure spending and reduce taxes on large firms and the wealthy. Fiscal expansion is widely seen as the harbinger of restrictive monetary policy aimed at containing inflation and growth pressures. In this context, the currencies of many EMDEs depreciated sharply against the dollar in anticipation of higher U.S. interest rates, increased debt-service costs borne by EMDE borrowers, and tightening credit market conditions worldwide. There is good reason to expect additional volatility in global financial markets in 2017 and beyond owing to uncertainty associated with the implementation of "Brexit" and to economic conflict and instability that may be fueled by nationalist governments and an erratic economic policy environment in the United States and several European nations. In this challenging environment, there is good reason to expect vicious macroeconomic cycles and capital flow volatility in EMDEs. The ability of EMDE policymakers to respond to the disturbances via strategic deployment and adjustment of capital controls will be severely tested.

We now consider a spectrum of experiences with capital controls during the global crisis and reflect on their significance and implications for developmental finance and financial governance.

"Too Much of a Good Thing"

Policymakers in a large set of EMDEs deployed capital controls to mitigate the financial fragility and vulnerabilities induced by the large capital inflows that they received during much of the global crisis. In several countries, controls were "dynamic," such that policymakers tightened, broadened, or layered new controls over existing measures as new sources of financial fragility and channels of evasion were identified and/or when existing measures proved inadequate to discourage undesirable financial activities (see Epstein, Grabel, and Jomo K. S. 2004). Controls were also removed as circumstances changed.

Brazil exemplifies the use of dynamic capital controls. Its case is interesting because the government (particularly former finance minister Mantega) staked out a strong position on policy space for controls throughout the crisis, and because the IMF's response to the country's controls reveals the evolution and equivocation in the views of Fund staff.[17]

In late October 2009, Brazil imposed a tax on inflows of portfolio investment. The controls were intended to slow the appreciation of the currency in the face of significant capital inflows. Brazil imposed a 2% tax on money entering the country to invest in equities and fixed-income investments and later a 1.5% tax on certain trades involving American Depository Receipts, while leaving FDI untaxed. The IMF's initial reaction to Brazil's inflow controls was mildly disapproving. A senior official said, "These kinds of taxes provide some room for maneuver, but it is not very much, so governments should not be tempted to postpone other more fundamental adjustments. Second it is very complex to implement those kinds of taxes, because they have to be applied to every possible financial instrument," adding that such taxes have proven "porous" over time in a number of countries. In response, Arvind Subramanian and John Williamson indicted the IMF for its doctrinaire and wrongheaded position, taking the institution to task for squandering the opportunity to think reasonably about capital controls (Subramanian and Williamson 2009). A week later, the IMF's Strauss-Kahn reframed the message on Brazil's controls. The new message was stunning: "I have no ideology on this"; capital controls are "not something that come[s] from hell" (quoted in Guha 2009).

Brazil continued to strengthen and layer new controls over existing measures in 2010 and 2011. These included controls that specifically targeted derivative transactions and others that closed identified loopholes as they became apparent. In October 2010, the tax charged on foreign purchases of fixed-income bonds was tripled (from 2% to 6%), the tax on margin requirements for foreign exchange derivatives was increased, and some loopholes on the tax on margin requirements for foreign investors were closed. In January 2011, Brazil introduced curbs on short selling in foreign exchange markets through the requirement that Brazilian financial institutions deposit the equivalent of 60% of their short dollar positions in a non–interest-bearing account at the central bank. In March 2011, it increased to 6% a tax on repatriated funds raised through international bond sales and foreign loans with a maturity of up to a year. In April 2011, a 6% tax was placed on new and renewed foreign loans with maturities of up to two years. And in July 2011, a 1% tax was placed on bets against the dollar in futures markets (with the government signaling that it could increase the tax to 25% if circumstances warranted), while it also imposed several new measures that targeted derivatives market trading. Despite this array of tightening controls, IMF economists called its strategies "appropriate" in an August 2011 review of Brazil (Ragir 2011).[18]

In 2011 and 2012, Brazilian policymakers began to narrow some capital controls even as they extended others. In December 2011, the tax on equity and fixed-income portfolio inflows was reduced to zero while the tax authority was retained, in March 2012 the hedge operations of exporters were exempted (up to a specified limit) from the tax on inflows, and the tax on new and renewed foreign loans was extended to loans with a maturity of up to five years.

Other EMDEs implemented and adjusted controls as circumstances warranted. Some strengthened existing controls, while others introduced new measures. For some countries (such as Argentina, Ecuador, Venezuela, China, and Taiwan), these measures were part of broader statist approaches to policy. For most other countries (e.g., Brazil, South Korea, Indonesia,

Costa Rica, Uruguay, the Philippines, Peru, and Thailand), controls were central features of a pragmatic, dynamic, multipronged effort to respond to the challenges of attracting too much foreign investment and speculative activity.

Peru began to impose inflow controls in early 2008. The country's central bank raised the reserve requirement tax four times between June 2010 and May 2012. The May 2012 measures included a 60% reserve ratio on overseas financing of all loans with a maturity of up to three years (compared with two years previously) and curbs on the use of a particular derivative (Yuk 2012). What is particularly interesting about Peru's measures is the way in which they were "branded" by the central bank. In numerous public statements, the central bank's president maintained that the country did not need capital controls even while it implemented and sustained its reserve requirement tax (Quigley 2013).

In August 2012, Uruguay imposed a reserve requirement tax of 40% on foreign investment in one type of short-term debt (Reuters 2012b). Like Peru, a bilateral agreement with the United States could have made this control actionable. Currency pressures also induced Costa Rica to use capital controls for the first time in twenty years. The country began to use controls in September 2011, when it imposed a 15% reserve requirement tax on short-term foreign loans received by banks and other financial institutions (LatinDADD-BWP 2011). In January 2013, the Costa Rican president sought congressional approval to raise the reserve requirement tax to 25% and to increase from 8% to 38% a levy on foreign investors transferring profits from capital inflows out of the country.

In another sign of changing sentiments during the crisis, the rating agency Moody's recommended that South East Asian countries use controls to temper currency appreciation (Magtulis 2013). Indeed, numerous Asian countries deployed new controls or strengthened existing ones during periods of large capital inflows. For instance, in November 2009, Taiwan imposed new inflow restrictions that precluded foreign investors from placing funds in time deposits. At the end of 2010, controls on currency holdings were strengthened twice (Gallagher 2011). In 2010, China added to its existing and largely quantitative inflow and outflow controls (ibid.). In 2013, China's SAFE (unit of the PBOC) took new steps to control "hot money" flows to manage the appreciation of the currency, reduce external risks, and curb efforts to bring capital into the country via trade misinvoicing (Monan 2013).

In June 2010, Indonesia announced what its officials termed a "quasi capital control" via a one-month holding period for central bank money market securities. At the same time, it introduced new limits on the sales of central bank paper by investors and on the interest rate on funds deposited at the central bank. During 2011, the holding period on central bank securities was raised to six months, a 30% cap on short-term foreign exchange borrowing by domestic banks was reintroduced, and a reserve requirement on foreign currency deposits was raised twice (from 1% to 5%, and then to 8%) (Batunanggar 2013; Manurung and Utami 2010). The awkward labeling of controls in Indonesia reflected the fact that its government was still afraid of the stigma that had long been attached to capital controls.[19]

Thailand introduced a 15% withholding tax on capital gains and interest payments on foreign holdings of government and state-owned company bonds in October 2010. In December 2012, the Philippines announced limits on foreign currency forward positions by banks and restrictions on foreign deposits (Aquino and Batino 2012).

As in Brazil, Korean authorities took a dynamic, layered approach to capital controls while also targeting the particular risks of derivatives. But unlike in Brazil, Korean authorities reframed these measures as "macroprudential" and not as capital controls (see Chwieroth 2015). In 2010, Korean regulators began to audit lenders working with foreign currency derivatives, placed a ceiling on the use of this instrument, and imposed a levy on what it termed "noncore" foreign currency liabilities held by banks. In 2011, Korea also levied a tax of up to 0.2% on holdings of short-term foreign debt by domestic banks, banned "naked" short selling, and reintroduced a 14% withholding tax on foreign investment in government bonds sold abroad and a 20% capital gains tax on foreign purchases of government bonds (Lee 2011; AsDB 2011).

"Stopping the Bleeding"

Some countries have been and are using capital controls during the global crisis for the more customary reason of stemming a financial or economic collapse. In these cases, the IMF has tolerated controls on capital outflows. This is notable insofar as the Fund and the neoclassical heart of the economics profession have long seen outflow controls as far more damaging than inflow controls.

Iceland's policymakers put outflow controls in place to slow the implosion of the economy before signing an SBA with the IMF in October 2008. The SBA made a very strong case for the extension of these controls as means to restore stability and protect the krona (IMF 2012d; Sigurgeirsdóttir and Wade 2015). In public statements, the IMF's staff repeatedly said that the country's outflow controls were crucial to prevent a collapse of the currency, that they were temporary, and that it was a priority to end all restrictions as soon as possible. The IMF's mission chief in the country commented that "capital controls as part of an overall strategy worked very, very well" (Forelle 2012), and the institution's deputy managing director stated that "unconventional measures (as in Iceland) must not be shied away from when needed" (IMF 2011b). The Fitch rating agency praised Iceland's "unorthodox crisis policies" while announcing that it had raised the country's credit rating to investment grade in February 2012 (Valdimarsson 2012). It should be said that neoliberals in the country did not share this enthusiasm for the unorthodox response or the IMF's advice (Danielsson and Arnason 2011).[20]

The IMF's characterization of and role in strengthening Iceland's outflow controls marked a dramatic precedent and revealed a fundamental change in thinking. The December 2008 SBA with Latvia allowed for maintenance of preexisting restrictions arising from a partial deposit freeze at the largest domestic bank (IMF 2009d). Soon thereafter, an IMF report acknowledged that Iceland, Indonesia, the Russian Federation, Argentina, and Ukraine all put outflow controls in place to "stop the bleeding" related to the crisis (IMF 2009a). In a sign of destigmatization, the report provided no commentary on their ultimate efficacy or warnings against their use. Outflow controls in Cyprus and Greece also precipitated measured reactions by the IMF, and by the EU and the ECB. Indeed, the IMF's IEO (2015) takes note of the institution's greater tolerance for outflow controls during the global crisis as exemplified by its support for outflow controls in Iceland, Cyprus, and Latvia (though not in Ukraine).[21]

Cyprus was the first country in the Eurozone to implement capital controls during the global crisis. The IMF and the EU did not flinch when stringent outflow controls were implemented as the country's economy imploded in March 2013.[22] Cypriot controls evolved in the months that followed and after Cyprus began to receive IMF support in May 2013. Banks temporarily closed, and cash withdrawal limits were placed on individuals and businesses; it was illegal to carry out more than €3000 on departing flights; and a ceiling was placed on funds transferred abroad by individuals and businesses, with central bank approval required for transfers above the ceiling. Capital controls began to be removed in March 2014, and the remaining controls were lifted in April 2015. Standard and Poor's upgraded Cyprus's sovereign debt rating to BB– in September 2015, and in doing so cited the removal of capital controls (Zikakou 2015).

Greece became the second Eurozone country to implement capital controls. These were put in place at the end of June 2015, when the government was locked in a pitched battle with the Troika over the referendum on a third assistance package. Stringent outflow controls were put in place once Eurozone leaders announced that they would not extend Greece's then current assistance package beyond June 30 (when it was scheduled to expire) and that the ECB would cap emergency liquidity assistance to Greek banks. In that context, Prime Minister Tsipras announced an emergency shutdown of banks and the stock exchange (which were closed for three weeks), a €60 daily cap on cash withdrawals from ATMs, and a ban on international money transfers abroad without prior approval and documentation (Yardley 2015; Chrysoloras and Ziotis 2015).[23]

Several Latin American countries also implemented controls on capital outflows when they were deemed necessary to manage instability. In December 2008, Ecuador doubled its tax on currency outflows, established a monthly tax on the funds and investments that firms kept overseas, discouraged firms from transferring dollar holdings abroad by granting tax reductions to firms that reinvest their profits domestically, and established a reserve requirement tax (Tussie 2010). In October 2010, Venezuela implemented outflow controls and new restrictions on access to foreign currency and tiered exchange rates. Capital and currency controls in the country remain in force as of this writing. In October 2010, Argentina implemented outflow controls that placed stricter limits on dollar purchases. Argentina's controls were strengthened in October 2011, requiring that all dollar purchases be authorized by tax authorities and that the country's oil and gas companies repatriate all export proceeds and convert them to pesos (Webber 2011). Unlike controls implemented elsewhere, Argentina's 2011 measures were associated with a ratings downgrade (on oil and gas companies by Moody's). However, this had far more to do with nationalization of YPF, a Spanish oil company, and the long-running conflict with foreign investors and the IMF, than with capital controls (Gill 2011). Argentina's capital and exchange controls were lifted in December 2015 following the election of President Mauricio Macri, and the new government settled with foreign investors in February 2016. Moody's and Fitch upgraded the country's debt rating in April 2016. Moody's cited the removal of capital controls as among the factors in the ratings upgrade, and both credit rating agencies highlighted the settlement with foreign investors (Moody's 2016a).

"Taper Tantrums," "Trump Tantrums," and the New Outflow Rout

Beginning in 2013, EMDEs again began to introduce and adjust diverse types of capital controls against the backdrop of growing financial fragility, weakening economic performance, depreciating currencies, and turmoil induced by international policy spillovers. The taper and Trump tantrums exacerbated EMDE fragility in 2015 and 2016. At the same time, however, controls that had been put in place to deal with challenges associated with large capital inflows were loosened or abandoned. Taken together, the new activism represents a dramatic turn toward widespread pragmatic adjustment and experimentation.

Examples of ad hoc adjustment and experimentation abound. In June 2013, Brazil eliminated some of the capital controls it had introduced just a few years earlier. It reduced the tax on overseas investments in domestic bonds from 6% to zero and removed a 1% tax on bets against the dollar in the futures market (Leahy and Pearson 2013; Biller and Rabello 2013). In January 2016, the governor of the Bank of Mexico, Agustín Carstens, a longtime critic of capital controls, announced that it might soon be time for central bankers in EMDEs "to become unconventional" to stem the vast tide of capital outflows (Wheatley and Donnan 2016).

Even in the face of mounting capital outflows, Costa Rica anticipated and planned for an eventual reversal of fortunes. In March 2014, Costa Rica put in place a framework for new capital controls intended to give the central bank the ability to curb speculative money inflows from abroad. The measures would allow the country's central bank to require special deposits to be held against any foreign capital flows that it determines are speculative and also would allow it to levy increased taxes on foreign remittances (Reuters 2014).

China's strategy of "managed convertibility" has become increasingly difficult for officials to navigate in the wake of growing national and global economic turbulence and missteps by national policymakers, particularly involving decisions to devalue the currency in August 2015 and again in late December and early January 2016.[24] Managed convertibility involves a complex mix of liberalizing capital controls so as to increase the convertibility of the renminbi (without making it fully convertible) and facilitate its flow and use across borders while also tightening existing controls and implementing new ones to protect the economy and the currency from volatile capital flows (Subacchi 2015; 2017).[25] Liberalizing capital controls was also necessitated by policymakers' long-held (and now realized) goal of having the IMF include the renminbi in the SDR. Against this backdrop and in a series of announcements in 2014, the country's policymakers eased some capital controls, such as those that restricted domestic investors from investing in foreign stocks and properties and restricted firms from selling renminbi-denominated shares abroad, and doubled the daily trading range of the renminbi (Barboza 2014; Bloomberg 2014).

After the surprise decision to allow the renminbi to devalue in August 2015, SAFE expended up to US$200 billion in reserves defending the currency during the next month, increased monitoring and controls on foreign exchange transactions, and imposed a 20% reserve on currency forward positions in hopes of curbing intense speculation against the currency (Anderlini 2015). Following another round of large capital outflows in January 2016, SAFE implemented several new, stringent capital controls. These restrict purchases of U.S. and Hong Kong dollars by individuals and businesses (by limiting annual and daily purchases and requiring increased documentation for purchases above the annual trading limit); require that those seeking to buy or sell foreign exchange demonstrate that the transaction is linked to trade, FDI, or other approved purposes; restrict banks from conducting certain types of foreign exchange transactions; and temporarily suspend operations of some foreign banks (Wildau 2016a). China still had more than US$3 trillion in reserves in early 2016 despite having depleted nearly US$500 billion in reserves in the previous year when trying to stem outflows and protect the currency (Stiglitz and Rashid 2016a). Nonetheless, in a widely reported speech at the 2016 World Economic Forum in Davos, the governor of the Bank of Japan, Haruhiko Kuroda, suggested that China tighten or use new capital controls to support its currency and economy against growing pressure. The IMF's Lagarde deflected requests for comment on this suggestion but admitted that it would be a mistake for China to deplete too much of its reserves to support the currency (Wheatley and Donnan 2016).

Chinese authorities again intervened to support the renminbi against the backdrop of large outflows in the third quarter of 2016. The currency depreciated by about 7% during 2016. It is estimated that US$88 billion in reserves were used to support the currency in September and October 2016, leading reserves to fall to US$3.05 trillion in November of that year (Wildau 2016c; Reuters 2017). Reserves fell further to US$2.99 trillion in January 2017 (Bradsher 2017). While still vast, the country's reserves fell to their lowest level since March 2011. In late 2016, the government implemented new restrictions to protect reserves, reduce outflows, and dampen financial and currency instability. The measures curb mergers and acquisitions (particularly since some are used to hide capital outflows) and limit investment in overseas markets through vetting of money transfers of US$5 million or more by SAFE, compared with the previous threshold of US$50 million (*Economist* 2016a; Wildau 2016b). Additional measures were put in place in 2017. These involve new scrutiny and reporting requirements on transfers by individuals, banks, and other financial institutions (*Economist*

2017a). Taking a page from other countries, China's state news agency announced that these measures were "not controls" (Reuters 2017). Irrespective of labeling, the pace of outflows from the country slowed in the first quarter of 2017 and by April 2017 reserves had risen to US$3.03 trillion (Bloomberg 2017).

In August 2013, India introduced capital controls on the amount that Indian-domiciled companies and residents could invest abroad (*Financial Times* 2013). These steps were taken in the context of a weakening rupee, growth in the current account deficit, and the Federal Reserve's talk of eventual tapering. Duvvuri Subbarao, then governor of the Reserve Bank of India, took pains to explain that these measures should not be labeled capital controls. In his last speech as central bank governor, he said of these measures, "I must reiterate here that it is not the policy of the Reserve Bank to resort to capital controls or reverse the direction of capital account liberalization," and he emphasized that the measures did not restrict inflows or outflows by nonresidents (Reuters 2013c). His subterfuge was only partly successful: market observers dubbed the measures "partial capital controls." When the new central bank governor, Raghuram Rajan, took his place in September 2013, he promptly rolled back the new outflow controls (Ray 2013).

Tajikistan deployed several types of outflow controls during 2015 and 2016 in the context of turmoil induced by falling oil prices. These involved administrative measures to stabilize the currency, closure of private currency exchange offices, the requirement that ruble-denominated remittances be converted to the national currency, restrictions on foreign currency transactions, and termination of the direct sale of foreign currency to the population (IntelliNews 2016; UNCTAD 2015a; National Bank of Tajikistan 2015). Here, too, authorities attempted to brand these measures as something other than capital controls. In an interview with the *Financial Times*, first deputy chairman of the country's central bank Nuraliev Kamolovich denied that these moves amounted to capital controls (Farchy 2016b).

In December 2014, the Russian government put outflow controls in place, though these were referred to in the country's press as "informal" capital controls. The government set limits on net foreign exchange assets for state-owned exporters and required large state exporting companies to report to the central bank on a weekly basis and reduce their net foreign exchange assets to the lower level that had prevailed earlier in the year. Concurrently, the central bank installed supervisors at the currency trading desks of top state banks (Kelly, Korsunskaya, and Fabrichnaya 2014).

Ukraine deployed several outflow controls in February 2014 in the context of a highly unstable political backdrop, significant weakening of the currency, depletion of official reserves, and fears of default on external debt (much of which is denominated in foreign currencies). Measures included a ceiling on foreign currency purchases by individuals, a ban on buying foreign exchange to invest overseas or prepay foreign debt, a five-day waiting period before companies could receive the foreign exchange that they have purchased, and a limit of about US$1500 per day on foreign currency withdrawals from bank deposits (Strauss 2014).[26]

The case of Azerbaijan is illustrative of the continued tensions over capital controls and also of the rating agencies' new, measured response to them. In January 2016, the country's parliament passed a bill that would impose a 20% tax on foreign currency outflows and allow repayment of dollar loans up to US$5000 at the exchange rate that had prevailed prior to the currency's devaluation. The country's president, Ilham Aliyev, rejected the bill the next month. In doing so, the president said that "it was a mistake to tax foreign-currency outflows as it would scare away foreign investors . . . [and] cause problems for large companies like BP" (Agayev 2016). In the period between the parliament's passage and the president's rejection, the rating agencies had a subdued reaction to the prospect of outflow controls in the country. Standard and Poor's lowered the country's rating, but cited low oil prices in doing so, while Fitch maintained its rating, stating that "the introduction of the capital controls does not 'automatically' have consequences for the country's sovereign rating" (Eglitis 2016; *Financial Times* 2016a).

Beginning in late 2014, Nigeria began to implement outflow controls as falling oil prices and a concomitant drop in foreign reserves destabilized its economy. In December 2014, limits on currency trading were imposed. Then, in April 2015 and continuing through the year, new outflow controls were put in place. These included limits on what Nigerians could spend on credit cards abroad; restrictions on access to hard currency and cross-border payments; limits on dollar-denominated transactions using ATM cards and daily limits on foreign ATM withdrawals; and foreign currency quotas and restrictions on access to dollars (Ferro 2014; Reuters 2015b; Johnson 2015). In February 2016, the IMF's Lagarde began to urge the government to remove capital and exchange controls, abandon the currency peg, and pursue fiscal discipline and structural reforms to bolster growth (Reuters 2016b). The country's economy (and reserve holdings) continued a downward spiral, and Nigeria's president allowed the currency to float in June 2016.

Similar Pressures, Dissimilar Responses, and Legal Constraints

Not all policymakers have responded or are responding to the pressures induced by large inflows, outflows, and policy spillovers with capital controls. Policymakers in some countries that enjoyed high inflows during much of the global crisis, such as Turkey, Chile, Mexico, and Colombia, publicly rejected inflow controls. Instead, they increased their purchases of dollars and used expansionary monetary policy to stanch currency appreciation. Divergent responses to similar pressures reflect many factors, not least of which are differing internal political economies, the continued sway of neoliberal ideas, and the long shadow cast by the belief that central banks must signal their commitment to neoliberalism in order to maintain international credibility.

There is more to the matter of resisting capital controls than the long half-life of neoliberalism, however. Some countries simply cannot introduce capital controls—either on inflows or outflows—because of bilateral or multilateral trade and investment treaties with the United States, such as the North American Free Trade Agreement (NAFTA) and the Dominican Republic–Central American Free Trade Agreement, or because of commitments embedded in EU and OECD membership (Gallagher 2014, chap. 8; 2012; Shadlen 2005; Wade 2003). The failed Trans-Pacific Partnership (TPP), a multilateral trade agreement, would have made it more difficult for signatory countries to utilize capital controls (Public Citizen 2015).[27]

Governments also face restrictions on controls stemming from obligations to liberalize financial services under the World Trade Organization (WTO) (Gallagher 2012). Article 63 of the Lisbon Treaty of the EU enforces open capital accounts across the union and requires that members not restrict capital transactions with other countries.[28] However, EU members Cyprus and Greece did deploy stringent outflow controls in 2013 and 2015, respectively, when their banking systems imploded. The EC and the ECB gave their blessing to these capital controls on the grounds that they were temporary and essential to preventing large-scale capital flight and the collapse of the banking system.[29] This suggests that EU strictures can be less binding than is usually thought, at least when countries avail themselves of the treaty's temporary safeguard measures during crises. Other restrictions appear in the OECD's Code of Liberalisation of Capital Movements, though since it is not a treaty, the obligations are not actionable (Abdelal 2007; Gallagher 2012).

At the time when many of these agreements were negotiated, the restrictions on capital controls no doubt seemed redundant since controls were effectively blocked by the effective constraints imposed by the IMF, rating agencies, and investors. Today, however, in the face of reversals by the previous enforcers of neoliberalism, the provisions are consequential. Chile's refusal to use capital controls during the global crisis has far more to do with its 2004 trade agreement with the United States than with neoliberal ideology. In the negotiations with the United States, Chile in fact sought a "carve-out" for the kind of inflow controls it used in the 1990s, when it was a pioneer in regard to reserve requirement taxes (Grabel 2003a). The United States refused to grant the exception. The resulting U.S.-Chile trade agreement exposes the country to lawsuits by investors who are able to demonstrate that they have been harmed by controls.[30] Mexico's situation is similar. Here neoliberal views are backed up by the strictures in NAFTA that threaten to punish any change in its policy stance.[31] By contrast, Brazil has been free to utilize controls during the global crisis because it has not signed bilateral treaties with the United States.

Reframing capital controls as something other than controls seems to be one viable avenue in cases where policymakers do not have the appetite to push the limits of trade/investment agreements (as with Peru and Uruguay) or where they otherwise fear the stigma that attaches to dirigisme; hence Korea's macroprudential measures, Indonesia's quasi-controls, Russia's informal controls, Tajikistan's outright denial that its measures amount to controls, and India's partial controls.[32] When policymakers are not confident of their ability to sell reframed controls to foreign investors, they are sometimes led, like Azerbaijan's president, to block capital controls altogether.

Revising the Rule Book

Since 2008, many EMDEs have implemented controls without seeking permission from the IMF. For many countries, controls were a response to the side effects of their relative economic success during much of the global crisis. It is highly unlikely that capital controls could have been rebranded as legitimate policy tools as quickly and deeply as has been the case had it not been for the divergent effects of the crisis across the globe, and the initiatives of many of the winners from the crisis to assert control over financial flows. Just as history is written by the victors, so may it be the case that the rebranding and relegitimizing of a forbidden policy tool depends primarily on the practices and strategies of those countries whose success grants them the latitude, confidence, and influence over other countries not just to "cheat" in a policy domain but to rewrite the rule book. Whether the IMF and the economics profession have fundamentally changed their view of capital controls, then, may matter less than the altered global economic and political context in which they are being utilized.

It is clear that outflow controls are still seen in a different light than inflow controls, but the crisis has catalyzed rethinking on this controversial instrument as well. This may prove to be important in the near future, if the present economic turbulence deepens. A new round of crises might very well feature increased use of outflow controls, which may test the limits of the new policy space surrounding capital controls.

The rebranding of controls has also been facilitated by the fact that carry trade pressures in some AEs caused central bankers to reconsider their long-held opposition to currency interventions and even to capital controls. For example, in 2013, a top official of Germany's Bundesbank signaled a softening of its traditional position, stating that "limited use of controls could sometimes be appropriate" to counter currency pressures (Reuters 2013a). In 2015, the Swiss National Bank intervened aggressively and repeatedly to curb the Swiss franc's appreciation (Moschella 2015a). At that time, the head of the country's central bank, Thomas Jordan, announced that it would even consider implementing controls on foreign deposits to respond to pressure on the currency, though these measures were not introduced (Ross and Simonian 2012). These attitudes and actions should be expected to spread in the future as a consequence of the broadening mission of central banks in the AEs and EMDEs during the crisis. Today, central banks are targeting financial stability and the reduction of systemic risk through macroprudential policies rather than simply price stability (Benlialper and Cömert 2016; Moschella 2015a).

The Economics Profession, the IMF, and the New Pragmatism on Capital Controls

Today IMF staff economists and leading academic economists have taken steps toward elaborating a theoretical and empirical case for capital controls. The rapid succession of financial crises over the past two decades may be encouraging those economists at the IMF with reservations about capital liberalization to give voice to their concerns and to assert themselves more effectively and consistently, particularly now that views on capital controls by prominent academic economists are in flux. Economists at the Fund are not immune to the loss of confidence by many economists in the theories, models, and policy tools that have long dominated professional practice. A 2012 statement by the IMF's chief economist, Olivier Blanchard, is instructive in this regard: "We have entered a brave new world. The economic crisis has put into question many of our beliefs. We have to accept the intellectual challenge" (Blanchard et al. 2012, 225).

Neoclassical Economics and Capital Controls

Two views on capital controls have predominated among academic economists who advocate neoliberalism. The first, and minority view, is associated with libertarian thought. The libertarian case against capital controls is a principled rather than a welfare consequentialist argument. From the libertarian perspective, controls are a violation of investor rights. The case against them is therefore impervious to new empirical evidence or a change in economic conditions. In contrast, neoclassical welfarist critics have long held that capital controls are counterproductive.

Although the neoliberal case against capital controls began to fray during the global crisis, some ardent defenders remain. For instance, in a discussion of inflow controls at an IMF conference in 2015, Mexico's central bank governor Carstens said: "I have only eight seconds left to talk about capital controls. But that's OK. I don't need more time than that to tell you: they don't work, I wouldn't use them, I wouldn't recommend them" (Carstens 2015). In the same speech, he indicted outflow controls: "When investors come in [to a new country] they first look to see where the exit is and if it doesn't exist, they won't come in."[33] Prominent economists such as William Cline (2010) rebuked the IMF for its new tolerance of controls and for its outright support of controls in Brazil and Iceland. The Heritage Foundation, a conservative U.S. think tank, has been sharply critical of the IMF's recent acceptance of capital controls as embodied in its "Institutional View" (to be discussed), while a Heritage "Issue Brief" highlights with horror praise by the IMF's Lagarde for Malaysia's 1998 controls (Olson and Kim 2013).

Prior to the global crisis, neoclassical economists had almost universally held that controls raised the cost of capital, especially for small and medium-sized firms, and generated costly evasion strategies (Forbes 2005; Edwards 1999). Capital controls were therefore imprudent since EMDEs could hardly afford to introduce new sources of inefficiency.

Research in neoclassical economics during the global crisis challenges the critique by emphasizing the negative externalities associated with highly liberalized international financial flows, particularly in the absence of international coordination of monetary policies. The research has helped to legitimize capital controls, particularly those that are targeted and intended to be temporary. The research also offers support for international policy coordination and/or regulations on capital flows in both source and recipient countries.

There are three dimensions to the new academic research. The first strand, called the "new welfare economics of capital controls," is associated with the work of Anton Korinek.[34] It assumes that in an environment of uncertainty, imperfect information, and volatility, unstable capital flows generate negative externalities in recipient economies (Korinek 2011; Aizenman 2009).[35] In this approach, liberalized short-term capital flows are understood to induce ambient risk that can destabilize economies. Contemporary Pigouvians argue that unregulated capital flows induce externalities because individual investors and borrowers do not know, or find it advantageous to ignore, the effects of their decisions on the aggregate level of stability in a particular nation. Capital controls are then theorized as a second-best strategy that can reduce risk and dampen instability. What were formerly recognized as unwarranted interventions into otherwise efficient capital markets have now been rebranded as prudential financial regulation in an uncertain world. Inflow controls are conceptualized as a Pigouvian tax that corrects for a market failure rather than as a cause of market distortions. Inflow controls induce borrowers to internalize the externalities of risky capital flows, and thereby promote macroeconomic stability and enhance welfare (Korinek 2011).

A second strand of research, associated with Korinek (2011; 2014) and Hélène Rey (2015; 2016), has also contributed to a mainstreaming of capital controls within the profession. This work emphasizes the way in which capital controls protect EMDEs from the international spillover effects of monetary policy in AEs, and it explicitly takes up the absence of multilateral mechanisms to coordinate monetary, capital control, and other prudential policies. Korinek's and Rey's research provide rigorous academic support for the claims of Brazil's Mantega and India's Rajan (among others) regarding currency wars and spillover effects. Similarly, it provides support for the view of Hyun Song Shin, head of research at the BIS, who has highlighted the destabilizing spillover effects and speculative investment flows induced by Federal Reserve policy (Shin 2015). An article in the *Economist* put the connection between these spillover effects and capital controls quite clearly: "QE has helped to make capital controls intellectually respectable again" (*Economist* 2013).

The negative international spillover effects of expansionary monetary policy during the global crisis highlight the need for multilateral coordination (Korinek 2013). An IMF Staff Discussion Note (in which Korinek is one of the authors) extends these themes (Ostry, Ghosh, and Korinek 2012).

Citing Keynes and White, the report argues that spillovers in the absence of coordinating mechanisms justify regulating capital flows at both ends. In this view, coordination of capital controls between source and recipient countries improves welfare since unilateral action requires more intensive measures than coordinated action, and since the cost of controls increases at an increasing rate with the intensity of controls. Thus, international coordination or cooperation achieves globally more efficient outcomes and helps to prevent what Ghosh, Qureshi, and Sugawara (2014) term costly "capital control wars" (see also Korinek 2014; Korinek and Sandri 2015; Davis and Presno 2014).[36]

Rey's (2015) work is also motivated by the unwelcome international spillover effects of monetary policy in AEs. These spillover effects necessitate using targeted capital controls on inflows and outflows, particularly since she sees international coordination on monetary policy spillovers as being "out of reach." Capital controls are necessary to protect EMDEs from what Rey terms the "global financial cycle," the instability triggered by large, sudden inflows associated with carry trade activity and their equally sudden exit (ibid.). In a 2014 lecture at the IMF, Rey argued that the negative spillover effects of the global financial cycle affect countries with floating and pegged exchange rate systems alike (Rey 2016). In a lecture at the IMF the next year, former Federal Reserve chairman Ben Bernanke criticized Rey and Mantega by name for portraying policymakers in EMDEs as "passive objects of the effects of Fed policy decisions" (Bernanke 2015, 24, 30, 33, 36, 44). Moreover, he argued that the EMDEs that experienced the most turbulence already had fragile economies because of domestic economic problems. Thus, international cooperation on monetary policy was neither necessary nor appropriate. Instead, Bernanke called for increased communication among central bankers. Bernanke nonetheless endorsed the use of targeted capital controls to tackle the unwelcome international spillover effects of monetary policy, even while emphasizing the primary importance of domestic regulatory and other macroprudential measures.

Other neoclassical economists have wrestled with the international spillover effects of monetary policy and capital controls during the crisis. Nobel laureate Michael Spence (and co-author Richard Dobbs) wrote of the troubling "financial protectionism" that was occasioned by expansionary monetary policy in AEs, and expressed worry that protectionism would accelerate as the era of "cheap capital" came to a close (Dobbs and Spence 2011). Despite characterizing controls as financial protectionism, however, Spence spoke favorably about their utility in EMDEs during a 2010 speech at the Reserve Bank of India. There he stated that capital controls are "essential as part of the process of maintaining control," and he also noted that most high-growth EMDEs have had such controls (Spence 2010b).

A third strand of new neoclassical research is empirical and substantiates the theoretical claims of the welfarist approach.[37] For example, Qureshi et al. (2011) found that capital controls and prudential measures relating to foreign currency in 51 EMDEs from 1995 to 2008 were associated with a lower proportion of foreign currency lending in total domestic bank credit and a lower proportion of portfolio debt in total external liabilities. The study concludes that capital controls and foreign-currency measures in place during the boom enhanced resilience during the bust of 2008. Ghosh and Qureshi (2016) review a large body of empirical evidence that shows that inflow controls change the composition of capital inflows and do not discourage investors. They argue that evidence on the efficacy of outflow controls is more mixed. Even Forbes, a long-standing critic of controls, found that Brazilian taxes on foreign purchases of fixed-income assets between 2006 and 2011 achieved one of its key goals by reducing the purchase of Brazilian bonds (Forbes et al. 2011). Recent "meta-analysis" of existing studies likewise finds evidence of the utility of controls. Magud and Reinhart extended their 2006 work to encompass a larger number of studies, including some that focus on the global crisis (Magud, Reinhart, and Rogoff 2011). They found that inflow controls enhanced monetary policy independence, altered the composition of inflows, and reduced real exchange rate pressures, but did not reduce the aggregate volume of net inflows. Finally, Jeanne, Subramanian, and Williamson (2011) show that free capital mobility has little benefit to long-run growth. On this basis, they conclude that the international community should not promote unrestricted financial flows, and they call for an international code of good practices for controls under the auspices of the IMF in coordination with the WTO.

Empirical findings by economists outside the profession's mainstream sustain deeper support for controls than we find in the recent work of neoclassical economists (e.g., Epstein 2012; Erten and Ocampo 2013; Gallagher 2014; Grabel 2015b). Erten and Ocampo (2013) provide what is perhaps the most expansive evidence of the achievements of a range of capital controls, including those on outflows. Using data from 51 EMDEs from 1995 to 2011, they find that capital controls that target inflows, outflows, and measures related to foreign exchange were associated with lower foreign exchange pressures. They also find that outflow regulations had larger effects than inflow regulations. They conclude that these three types of measures have enhanced monetary policy autonomy, that increasing their restrictiveness in the run-up to the global crisis reduced the growth decline during the crisis (and thereby enhanced crisis resilience), and that countries using these measures experienced less overheating during postcrisis recovery when a new surge in capital inflows occurred.

The Global Crisis, the IMF, and Capital Controls

The evolution in thinking by academic economists on capital controls is reflected in and reinforced by developments at three overlapping levels of practice at the IMF: research, official statements by key officials, and policy recommendations by its staff.[38] We find continued discomfort and tension around capital controls during the global crisis, which is reflected in efforts to develop a hierarchy among types of capital controls and the circumstances under which they are most acceptable.

There is ample evidence of change and tension in recent IMF research on capital controls. An IMF report drafted early in the crisis found that the use of capital controls protected the banking systems in low-income countries, stating that "the existence of capital controls in several countries . . . helped moderate the direct and indirect effects of the financial crisis" (IMF 2009c, 9, fn9). An Article IV report on Bangladesh credits the effective closure of its capital account for its ability to avoid the global "flight to safety" early in the crisis (IMF 2010a).

In February 2010, a team of IMF economists, led by Jonathan Ostry, published a thorough survey of econometric evidence that commended inflow controls for preventing crises and reducing the risk and severity of crisis-induced recessions, while reducing fragility by lengthening the maturity structure of external liabilities and improving the composition of inflows (Ostry et al. 2010). The findings refer to the experience with controls prior to and after the Asian crisis, as well as during the global crisis. The study indicates that "such controls, moreover, can retain their potency even if investors devise strategies to bypass them. . . . The cost of circumvention strategies acts as 'sand in the wheels'" (ibid., 5). The study hedges in the expected ways—identifying the restrictive conditions under which controls can work. But in stark comparison with earlier IMF reports, the qualifications are just that—considerations to take into account but not insuperable obstacles to the use of controls. That, in itself, represents a major advance in IMF open-mindedness.

After the Ostry report was released, prominent IMF watchers praised the Fund for finally embracing a sensible view of controls. Ronald McKinnon stated, "I am delighted that the IMF has recanted" (quoted in Rappeport 2010); former IMF official Eswar Prasad asserted that the paper represented a "marked change" in the IMF's advice (quoted in Wroughton 2010); and Rodrik concluded that "the stigma on capital controls [is] gone" and that the report "is a stunning reversal—as close as an institution can come to recanting without saying, 'Sorry, we messed up'" (Rodrik 2010). Rodrik also noted that "just as John Maynard Keynes said in 1945—capital controls are now orthodox" (quoted in Thomas 2010). Equally telling is the sharp rebuke to Ostry et al. (2010) by Cline, an unrepentant advocate of capital liberalization, who viewed the new IMF embrace of controls as troubling and wrongheaded (Cline 2010).

Research on controls spilled out from the IMF from 2011 through 2016. Findings appeared in reports of its research departments and in Staff Position Notes and Staff Discussion Notes. The reports continue to illustrate the growing legitimation of controls while also providing a window into the endurance of the dissenters.[39] The IMF's crisis-induced research on controls culminated in a December 2012 report of the Executive Board, which the IMF terms the "Institutional View" (IMF 2012e; 2012f). The Institutional View is an official board-endorsed view that IMF staff are expected to incorporate into surveillance activities (Gallagher 2015a). The report makes clear that inflow and outflow surges induce instability; that countries should not consider capital liberalization prematurely; that temporary, targeted, and transparent inflow and even outflow controls may be warranted during turbulence, though they should not discriminate against foreign investors; that countries retain the right under Article VI to put controls in place; and that the IMF's new, more permissive stance on controls may conflict with and be subsumed by trade and other agreements. Particularly notable is the fact that the report refrains from dismissing capital controls as a "last resort" measure—a theme that had recurred throughout IMF research in 2010 and 2011—and that it sanctions the deployment of outflow controls during crises.[40]

The Institutional View provides ample evidence of the IMF's continued effort to "domesticate" the use of controls. We see this in the language around targeted, transparent, temporary, and nondiscriminatory measures. Moreover, arguments in the report continue to be guided by the view that capital liberalization is ultimately desirable, though claims to this effect are more nuanced than in the past.[41] Not least, the report rejects the presumption that capital account liberalization is the right policy for all countries at all times. Tensions over these and other matters among members of the IMF's Executive Board were given an oblique airing in a Public Information Notice released by the IMF, and more directly in press accounts, many of which focused on criticisms of the report by Paulo Nogueira Batista Jr., then IMF executive director for Brazil and ten other countries (IMF 2012e; Beattie 2012). Nogueira Batista focused on the failure of the Institutional View to consider the role of push factors from AEs and the IMF's lack of evenhandedness (Prasad 2014, 195). That said, the fact that the IMF shifted the discussion of capital controls away from circa-1980s neoclassical economics and toward the legal and institutional conditions required for their success is further evidence that the most stubborn resistance to controls on economic grounds has been overcome.[42]

The IMF continues to wrestle with the interpretation and practical implications of its own Institutional View. An April 2013 Staff Guidance Note sought to provide clarification regarding how IMF staff should interpret the Institutional View (IMF 2013c). The note reiterates that "staff advice should not presume that full liberalization is an appropriate goal for all countries at all times," and it made allowance for "a temporary re-imposition" of capital flow measures under certain circumstances (ibid., 9–10, 16). But it also reiterates that controls should be "transparent, targeted, temporary, and preferably non-discriminatory" (ibid.). Despite increasing acknowledgment of spillover effects, the note rejects the view that capital source countries should be expected to take spillover effects into account when pursuing policies in line with their "primary domestic objectives" (ibid., 17). A December 2015 report prepared for IMF staff (IMF 2015d) probes what the Institutional View and the Staff Guidance Note entail specifically for outflow controls. The 2015 report insists that outflow controls (like inflow controls) should be transparent, temporary, lifted once the crisis conditions abate, and nondiscriminatory, though it does acknowledge that sometimes residency-based measures may be hard to avoid (ibid., fn1). The report also observes that, unlike controls on inflows, temporary outflow controls generally need to be comprehensive and adjusted to avoid circumvention (ibid., 3) and that "re-imposition of [controls] on outflows can be appropriate and consistent with an overall strategy of capital flow liberalization . . . even in non-crisis-type circumstances if premature or improperly sequenced liberalization . . . outpaced the capacity . . . to safely handle the resulting flows" (ibid., 4).

The messiness of the Institutional View and the Talmudic process of interpretation that has followed its release reflect deep internal conflicts within and outside the IMF. The IEO reports that the Institutional View was the "furthest some Directors (mainly from major AEs) were prepared to go in condoning the use of CFMs [capital flow management] and the minimum other Directors (mainly from major emerging market economies) were willing to accept as a repudiation of full capital account liberalization

as a desirable goal" (IEO 2015, 9, fn15). Notwithstanding board endorse-
ment of the Institutional View, the same report notes that it is uncertain
whether IMF advice on capital controls will be consistent, owing to the
fragile nature of the consensus around this view, the presence of internal
conflict, and the constraints on controls in trade and investment agreements. Preliminary evidence suggests a basis for cautious optimism. The
2015 IEO report that reviews the IMF's Article IV reports from January 2006
to August 2014 finds that staff advice on capital controls was more discouraging in the early part of this period and more supportive and even encouraging of such measures from 2010 on (ibid., 12). Today the IMF continues
to study country experiences and what it terms "emerging issues" in connection with capital flow management.[43]

Public statements by current and former officials at the BWIs beginning
in 2009 further illustrate the normalization, lingering ambivalence, and
attempt to domesticate the use of controls. IMF first deputy managing
director John Lipsky acknowledged in a December 2009 speech that "capital controls also represent an option for dealing with sudden surges in
capital flows" (Lipsky 2009). In the address, he argues that controls should
be used when capital inflow surges are temporary (though we have to won-
der when sudden surges would not be temporary), and he emphasizes that
controls likewise should be temporary. Despite these caveats, he argues that
"above all, we should be open-minded." Public statements by the IMF's
Strauss-Kahn illustrate particularly clearly the grudging evolution in the
IMF's views. In public statements in 2009, Strauss-Kahn emphasized the
costs of capital controls, claiming that they tend to lose effectiveness over
time (IEO 2015, box 3). But, in a July 2010 speech, he reframed his message,
saying "it is just fair that these [EMDEs] countries would try to manage the
inflows" as a last resort against inflow-induced asset bubbles (Oliver 2010),
and later in the year he reiterated what was by then the new mantra that
capital controls are a legitimate part of the toolkit (Strauss-Kahn 2010c; IEO
2015, 16). In 2010, the director of the IMF's Western Hemispheric department made a case (unsuccessfully) for the utility of controls in Colombia,
owing to the appreciation of its currency (Crowe 2010). The IMF's Lagarde
spoke in 2012 and 2014 of the utility of temporary, targeted capital controls
(IEO 2015, box 3), and in March 2015 she observed that there is scope for
greater cooperation in connection with monetary policy spillovers (Lagarde
2015a).

The World Bank, too, amended its public position on capital controls
during the global crisis. A 2009 World Bank report concludes cautiously that
"capital controls might need to be imposed *as a last resort* to help mitigate

financial crisis or stabilize macroeconomic developments" (World Bank 2009, 48, emphasis added). In a similar spirit, commenting on the reemergence of controls in Asia, World Bank president Robert Zoellick offered qualified support for capital controls by stating that they are "not a silver bullet . . . they may help at the margin" (quoted in Gallagher 2010). A World Bank report issued after the IMF's Institutional View (and reports related to it) captures well the continued hedging on the matter. It cautions that "there is potential danger for policymakers to err on the side of overly strict capital controls, choking off access to finance, when what is really needed is careful reform of regulatory institutions and greater institutional regulatory coordination" (World Bank 2013a).

Given the inconsistency of the IMF's position on capital controls after the Asian crisis, the research, policy advice, and statements coming from key officials during the global crisis mark, by its standards, a minor revolution.[44] Change at the Fund has been uneven, to be sure, with one step back for every two steps forward. None of this should be surprising. We should expect that deeply established ideas hang on despite their apparent disutility (Grabel 2000; 2003b). We should expect to find continuing evidence of tension and equivocation in research by academic economists and in future IMF reports and practices that preclude a clear and decisive verdict on capital controls. But for now, at least, welfarist arguments for controls have been embraced at the top of the profession, and this will surely continue to influence the IMF and other critical actors—even if just by validating views that they have come to hold independent of developments within academia. More importantly, and as I have argued throughout this book, change at the IMF and in the economics profession is only one of a larger set of factors that have legitimated capital controls.

The Struggle to Control Capital Controls

At several key moments, the IMF, the G-20, and the G-24 turned their attention to, and sometimes sparred on, the matter of standards for capital controls, which body should adjudicate the appropriateness of controls, and the right of nations to experiment with them. Beginning in late 2010, the IMF and the G-20 discussed the development of standards for the appropriate use of controls (Habermeier, Kokenyne, and Baba 2011; IMF 2010c; 2011c; Ostry et al. 2011; Ostry, Ghosh, and Korinek 2012). This project was also given life by the French government, which tried to use its leadership of the G-20 and G-8 in early 2011 to authorize the IMF to pursue this project (Hollinger and Giles 2011).[45] Indeed, capital flows figured prominently on the G-20 agenda during France's leadership of the network. The matter of capital controls and a code of conduct to manage their use fell off the G-20 agenda shortly thereafter, perhaps because of a leadership change, the exigencies of the Eurozone crisis, and, per Chwieroth (2014; 2015), because of enduring U.S. influence.

At the same time that the IMF was developing its Institutional View, the G-20 approved an expansive statement on controls that reflected the work of a fractious G-20-appointed committee co-chaired by Germany and Brazil (G-20 2011a). The G-20 statement goes beyond the IMF's Institutional View by taking an unambiguous, firm stand against "one size fits all" approaches to controls, rejecting the idea of developing a set of conditions for their use, and calling on nations to develop their own approaches to their use. The IMF's Institutional View report includes the G-20 document as an appendix and notes the importance of building on it, though it acknowledges that the G-20 document is nonbinding and is the product of a "hard-won consensus" (read: conflict that pitted the United States and other AEs against Brazil and other EMDE members).[46]

The IMF's 2013 Staff Guidance Note obliquely takes up the matter of the IMF's role in adjudicating capital controls. This note invokes many times a refrain along the lines of "this will require staff judgment" in connection with country policies. This reflects continued efforts by the IMF to try to secure for itself a leading role in managing the use of controls. However, equally instructive is the fact that Brazil and other EMDEs working through the G-24, G-20, and even the IMF have consistently, unequivocally, and publicly rejected such a role for the Fund (G-24 2011; Reddy 2011; Wagsty 2011). The opponents of IMF oversight have pressed to maintain the right to deploy capital controls that are expansive, blunt, lasting, and discriminatory, so long as internal or external economic conditions warrant. Newly enjoying policy autonomy in this domain, EMDEs are not anxious to succumb to IMF codes, sanctions, or guidance that could tie their hands in the face of destabilizing flows of hot money and the unwelcome spillover effects of monetary policy in AEs.[47]

China had indicated that it would use its position at the helm of the G-20 in 2016 to resurrect dormant discussions of international capital flows, capital controls, and global financial architecture (G-20 2016b, para. 5). But the September 2016 communiqué released after the final Leaders' Summit of the year contained only general diplomatic language to the effect that the group looks forward to the release of the IMF's latest study of experiences with managing capital flows by year-end 2016, supports more effective cooperation between the IMF and regional financial arrangements, welcomes the upcoming CMIM-IMF test run, and endorses a strengthened global financial safety net with a strong, quota-based, and adequately resourced IMF at its center (G-20 2016c). China may have passed on the opportunity to take the lead on capital flow management because its officials were occupied with domestic financial volatility during 2016 and the launch of new institutions, such as the AIIB.

Conclusion

The ultimate outcome of the rethinking of capital controls is uncertain, of course. It is possible that the pre-2008 view of controls may reestablish itself, not least because its advocates have proven remarkably adept at "paradigm maintenance" over the last three decades—as Wade (1996), Mirowski (2010), and Hodgson (2009) have noted, and as Polanyi (2001[1944], 143) argued long ago. As with most rebranding exercises, there is also uncertainty about whether the new framing will prove sufficiently sticky, especially in the context of tensions and countervailing impulses at the IMF and elsewhere, a resilient bias within economics against state management of economic flows, and new attempts to assert outflow controls in times of distress that would run counter to the interests of powerful financial actors.

That said, it seems most unlikely that the pendulum will swing back in the direction of reifying capital liberalization. The myriad changes that I have examined here (and throughout the book)—especially the pragmatic turn in global financial governance, along with the growing exigencies occasioned by the latest turbulence in the world economy—portend continuing interest in and experimentation with capital controls.[48]

In the end, whether the IMF's new openness on capital controls fades with the crisis may not matter much insofar as the institution has been rendered less relevant as it faces increasingly autonomous and assertive EMDE members, on which it now depends. The fact that many economies that performed relatively well during the crisis successfully utilized controls has eliminated the instrument's long-standing stigma. That the Fund has also acknowledged the utility of outflow controls in countries in crisis also makes it harder to envision a return to pre-2008 views.

For now, there seems to be substantial momentum propelling increasing use of and experimentation with the flexible deployment of capital controls, in some cases with IMF support and in most other cases without IMF resistance. The fact that support for capital controls stems from such diverse quarters today increases the likelihood that the new thinking will be sustained. Prominent neoclassical economists have used the tools and language of their discipline to make a theoretical case for controls and to highlight the costs of policy spillover effects. Neoclassical and heterodox economists have added ample empirical evidence that controls have had important beneficial macroeconomic effects during the crisis. Former and current central bankers such as Bernanke and Kuroda have spoken in favor of controls. Key officials of the BWIs have argued in favor of some types of capital controls (under some conditions). National policymakers in many of the most assertive EMDEs are committed to controls. And rating agencies have come to accept capital controls in many contexts as reasonable policy responses to financial threats. Such widespread support not only makes possible the continued use of capital controls but also creates the opportunity for the construction of a viable, flexible, and permissive capital control regime that is consistent with the goals of mitigating negative international spillovers and financial instability while promoting development and enhancing national policy space.

The widening of policy space and the practical experience with capital controls gained during the global crisis may prove consequential in the immediate future, if as we might expect the emerging financial fragility continues to deepen. Even as the problems of "doing too well" fade across EMDEs, earlier experiments with controls on capital inflows may pay important dividends in what are likely to be challenging times ahead. A critical test of recent and ongoing experiences with capital controls will occur in future crises, as states rely on and adjust fledgling practices and policies in hopes of dampening instability and otherwise managing turbulence better than they had over the course of previous crises. The coming period may test—sooner rather than later—the resilience of the new openness to controls, especially on outflows. It may also test the ability of states and institutions to capitalize on the opportunities that they have had for learning by doing and learning from others that have thus far been afforded by the crisis.

One reason for cautious optimism is found in the effects of the enormous capital outflows from the EMDEs in 2015 and early 2016. Taken in isolation, the numbers are bleak. In the past, outflows of this magnitude would inevitably have induced an immediate, severe, and sustained crisis and touched off crisis contagion across the EMDEs. It is notable, then, that despite the intensity of EMDE capital flow reversals since 2015, EMDEs have not imploded. In comparison with the past, EMDEs are demonstrating significant financial resilience (UNCTAD 2016, chap. 1, fn14). China's experience is particularly notable. Although China has suffered extraordinary outflows, it continues to possess the largest international reserve holdings in the world (ibid.).

In my view, it is critical that efforts be made to maintain and expand the opportunity that has emerged in the crisis environment for national policymakers to experiment with capital controls and to adjust them as circumstances warrant. The pressing policy challenge today, then, is to construct regimes that expand national policy autonomy to use capital controls while managing cross-border spillover effects. This certainly suggests abandoning or, at the very least, renegotiating the restrictions on capital controls in existing and pending bilateral and multilateral trade and investment agreements. It also suggests the need to develop global and/or regional frameworks for burden sharing and regional and international cooperation in the case of spillover effects. Recent and ongoing experimentation with subregional, regional, and transregional arrangements and institutions during the global crisis might therefore generate significant benefits in regard to developing strategies to manage the spillover effects from capital controls or currency fluctuations. Moreover, historical and recent experience indicates that capital controls on inflows and outflows should be thought of not as a last resort but rather as a permanent and dynamic part of a broader prudential, countercyclical toolkit to be deployed as internal and external conditions warrant, and that there are circumstances where controls may need to be blunt, comprehensive, significant, lasting, and discriminatory rather than modest, narrowly targeted, and temporary (Epstein, Grabel, and Jomo K. S. 2004; Erten and Ocampo 2013; Fritz and Prates 2014; Grabel 2003c; 2004; 2017; Rodrik 2015b).[49]

Any governance regime that seeks to develop a framework for capital controls should err on the side of generality, flexibility, and permissiveness; should involve and promote cooperation by both capital source and recipient countries; and should embody an evenhanded acknowledgment that monetary policies, like capital controls, have positive and negative global spillover effects that necessitate some type of burden sharing. It is therefore heartening that the crisis appears to have occasioned the rediscovery of the relevant views of Keynes and White[50] and that these views have been given new life by the widespread use and rebranding of capital controls across diverse national contexts and by the related attention to currency wars and policy spillovers.

The spread of capital controls and the conflict over spillovers highlights the problems associated with the absence of regional and/or global policy coordination. Brazil's former finance minister raised the matter of unwelcome spillover effects on many occasions. More recently, in October 2015,

Rajan began to be openly critical of IMF support of the easy money policies in AEs, and the institution's failure to flag the negative spillover effects of such measures (*Times of India* 2015). Echoing Mantega's concerns, Rajan has drawn attention to the tide of competitive and nationalist monetary easing among central banks in AEs, and the related absence of consideration of the negative financial and political spillover effects for EMDEs (ibid.).

Rajan's proposals warrant attention here because they focus attention on the right kinds of issues. He calls on the IMF (and possibly the G-20 and BIS) to develop a system for assessing the net effects of policy spillovers, in which spillovers would be graded on a color-coded traffic light type of system. "Green-rated" policies are those that are beneficial to domestic and foreign economies, have few adverse spillovers, or only have temporary negative spillover effects on foreign economies. "Orange" are those policies that should be used only temporarily and only with care. In contrast, "red" policies are those that should be avoided at all times because they are likely to have significant adverse spillover effects on foreign economies (even if they have small positive effects on the domestic economy) (Rajan 2016a; 2016b). For reasons of expediency, a group of globally representative "eminent academics" (appointed by the IMF, G-20, and/or BIS) would measure, analyze, and grade policies in terms of their spillover effects. The next step would involve discussions within international organizations (such as the IMF Executive Board and the BIS) that would be based on background papers on spillovers prepared by the IMF, academics, and central banks in EMDEs. Following these discussions, policymakers would be asked to defend their policy choices when they are deemed to have spillover effects that are sufficiently detrimental so as to be graded red. Rajan notes that it would be necessary to consider how and if consideration of international spillovers aligns with the domestic mandates of individual central banks. He also observes that his approach might necessitate either a new international agreement or, at the very least, a change in the IMF's Articles of Agreement. One might expect a renewed attention to policy spillovers in 2017 if EMDEs, as expected, continue to experience fallout from a strengthening dollar and tightening U.S. monetary policy (or more generalized volatility in U.S. markets).

We have thus far focused on the negative spillover effects of capital controls and monetary policies. But capital controls can also have beneficial political and economic spillovers. In particular, they can enhance democracy, state capacity, and national policy autonomy. Returning to Hirschman's exit and voice, capital controls can to some degree rebalance political voice by limiting the entrance and exit options available to the holders of capital. As the 2016 release of the "Panama Papers" makes clear, massive offshore money holdings facilitate tax avoidance by the world's super-rich, a practice that both deprives states of badly needed tax revenues and enhances the political voice of investors vis-à-vis states and less wealthy groups within national economies.[51]

Capital controls can also enhance financial stability. Thus, they may protect intraregional trade relationships while also reducing the likelihood of cross-border financial contagion and the need for IMF involvement in domestic governance. Of course, destabilizing capital flows may be diverted from an economy with capital controls to one that does not have them, and this can export financial instability. Here again, there are benefits to cross-border coordination of capital flows or, at the very least, ex ante discussions of possible negative spillovers.

In this environment of disruption, economic and institutional change, intellectual aperture, and uncertainty, we find a productive expansion of policy space for experimentation with capital controls. We also find a grudging movement away from the idealization of financial liberalization within neoclassical economics, something that may ultimately be seen as a consequential legacy of the global crisis. Taken together, the change, messiness, aperture, and uncertainty exemplify the productive incoherence of the present conjuncture.

IV   Where from Here?

8 Conclusion: Opportunities, Challenges, and Risks

The evidence advanced in previous chapters demonstrates the degree to which transformations in central features of global financial governance that bear on EMDEs are under way. The focus throughout has been on those institutional and policy innovations that, in one way or another, enhance the possibilities for national policy autonomy and policy space for economic and human development, financial stability and resilience in the face of disturbances, and financial inclusion. These transformations should be understood as experimental, messy, ad hoc, uneven, and inconsistent. Together, they are generating what I have called an incoherent system of global financial governance—but one that is nevertheless productive. I am guided in this assessment by Hirschman, who emphasized the value of "development processes *in the small*" (Hirschman 1969[1958], ix, emphasis in original) and stressed that development projects "should be developed as much as possible in an experimental spirit, in the style of a pilot project gathering strength and experience gradually" (Hirschman 1967a, 19).

The emergent incoherence features an uncertain relationship to the hegemonic neoliberalism that constrained the material, ideational, institutional, and policy domains over the past several decades, especially across the global south and east. Neoliberalism has not been abandoned—far from it. No compelling utopian vision stands ready to contest it. Instead, the challenge has emerged from pragmatic practice rather than high theory. It remains largely inchoate and unarticulated. The turn away from neoliberal hegemony is not of the kind that many observers and especially many critics of neoliberalism, including myself, have long hoped for. We certainly do not seem to be at the dawn of a new epoch of global prosperity, stability, and economic justice.

It bears repeating that, to date, neither a new twenty-first-century theoretical champion nor any recycled twentieth-century model has emerged to rival neoliberalism in the domain of global financial governance. The present moment is characterized instead by contestation and uncertainty at the ballot box and within the economics profession, the BWIs, and across many levels of economic policy and institutional formation in the EMDEs over the nature of international integration in general and financial governance in particular. In the absence of a new consensus, policymakers in EMDEs are pursuing ad hoc, pragmatic adjustments in response to current and anticipated problems they confront—such as financial instability, the scarcity of long-term finance (for infrastructure and other capital investments), the myriad vagaries of international capital flows, and limited voice in institutions and networks of global financial governance. These responses draw on both neoliberal and non-neoliberal visions but also represent unscripted adjustments that are not consistent with any overarching theoretical framework. Today utopian visions are threatened by a pragmatic orientation in which necessity drives invention.[1]

The roots of the innovations now under way lie in an escalating series of economic crises of the neoliberal era—most importantly, the Asian crisis. The crises reminded careful observers of Polanyi's (2001[1944]) powerful insight that what he called the "self-regulating market economy" is far too dangerous and damaging not just for EMDEs but for the AEs as well. The crises had contradictory effects on neoliberalism—chipping away at the neoliberal consensus while at the same time locking some countries into the neoliberal agenda. Lock-in occurred through radical reforms that were tied to IMF assistance, a range of bilateral and multilateral trade and investment agreements, strictures of WTO membership, and the judgments of credit rating agencies and investors. But the crises motivated policymakers in the EMDEs to search for pathways forward that would free them from dependence on the BWIs. As we have seen (in chapters 1 and 3), the most ambitious proposals were never realized. Disappointed observers, then and since, cite these failures as evidence that neoliberalism has survived more or less intact and that any apparent discontinuities in global financial governance can be dismissed as either trivial or as papering over fundamental continuities. But as I have argued throughout, the crises planted the seeds for the gradual fracturing of neoliberal orthodoxy and for a corresponding increase in policy autonomy and financial resilience in many EMDEs. Leading EMDEs pursued escape strategies that entailed reserve accumulation under the particularly fortuitous global economic conditions that followed the Asian crisis and the beginnings of institutional, policy, and ideational innovations. When the crisis of 2008 broke out, these initiatives began to bear fruit, and indeed policymakers continued to deepen them. The crisis spurred significant expansion of financial governance networks while shoring up the confidence and determination to create opportunities for forum shopping and expanded autonomy that could be exploited to pursue new experiments (as we have seen in chapters 4–7).

The IMF itself was affected by these events (as we saw in chapter 5). Change in IMF practices was modest in the period following the Asian crisis, to be sure, but became more significant during and following the crisis of 2008. As we have seen, the IMF came to accept the legitimacy of capital controls, generally acceding to their use and in some cases actually proposing their introduction in response to domestic crisis tendencies while protecting economies from external financial instability. The reorientation on capital controls has been accompanied by other shifts at the IMF. The IMF's behavior during the conflict over the Greek bailout, in which it pushed back against the most severe austerity demands by its Troika partners until its capitulation in the spring of 2016, is just one notable example of IMF drift away from its prior uncompromising commitment to neoliberalism.[2] In its research and rhetoric, the institution has come to emphasize the need to protect the most vulnerable communities and highlight the costs of inequality and extreme austerity, even while it often directed countries to pursue contractionary economic policies. The IMF has adopted largely symbolic reforms of its formal governance structure, as leading EMDEs began to lend to the Fund and to press long-standing criticisms of various dimensions of IMF decision making. At the same time, changes that are more meaningful are under way regarding informal governance norms that bear on the role of rising powers, particularly China, at the IMF.

One of the most important features of the current period is the extent to which EMDE policymakers now enjoy and are taking advantage of increasing freedom to act autonomously to establish new institutions and practices of financial governance and developmental finance. As we explored at length in chapter 6, the crisis of 2008 motivated policymakers to establish entirely new subregional, regional, and transregional institutions; to build out existing institutions, substantially increasing their funding and capacity; to expand their mandates into new activities; and, in some cases (and with the support of the IMF), to explore ways in which these institutions might link to and coordinate with one another in various ways. Here we have surveyed just the most advanced and promising institutional innovations. But the overview should suffice to demonstrate the degree to which global financial governance has evolved and is likely to continue to evolve in the near future. To date, these developments do not threaten the BWIs, and, indeed, they are explicitly not intended to do so. Nor do they amount to a potent challenge to the financial hegemony of the United States and other leading AEs. But displacement is the wrong standard against which to measure their significance. The emerging pluripolar regime of financial governance—where the BWIs continue to play central roles in crisis avoidance and response, and in providing developmental finance, but where a wide range of new institutions provide these and other services both in conjunction with the Bretton Woods and related institutions and also relatively autonomously—is meaningfully different from one where the BWIs do their work unencumbered by alternative institutions. A dense, heterogeneous, pluripolar system of financial governance has the potential to promote experimentation and the deepening of networks, which may be of particular benefit to policymakers in smaller economies; more extensive policy autonomy; greater opportunities for inclusion of less powerful actors, not least through possibilities for forum shopping; wider scripted and unscripted institutional and policy innovation; more adequate mechanisms for delivering long-term development and infrastructure finance; better surveillance of crisis tendencies and quicker and more adequate responses to emergent crises (such as through liquidity provision); and more effective and autonomy-protecting strategies to ameliorate a crisis when it does in fact emerge. That none of these benefits are guaranteed does not amount to a sufficient indictment of the emerging constellation of institutions and policies. In the world of economic development, at least, we should keep in view what Hirschman argued so convincingly: guarantees are few and far between, and almost always illusory.

Hirschmanian Lessons . . .

Where does all this leave us? What are the implications for both development theory and practice, academic and applied economists, and for the BWIs? And what are the limitations and risks of institutional and policy incoherence in the domain of global financial governance in general and developmental finance in particular?

By now it should be evident that I am committed to the idea that development economics would be well served by a full appreciation of and engagement with Hirschmanian perspectives on economic development; social change; the role of development economists, practitioners, and institutions; and the influence of rhetoric in enabling or stifling beneficial reform. Reflecting Hirschman's commitments, I have attempted to make sense of the crosscutting and even what appear to be chaotic institutional and policy developments of the current period as productive. This follows from what I take to be a Hirschmanian understanding of the nature of development as largely consisting of unplanned processes of institutional change that entail perpetual experimentation yielding learning by doing and from others and pragmatic adjustment. Like Hirschman, we need to embrace more nuanced understandings of progressive social change as path dependent, contingent, and dependent on the evolution of economic and political institutions, practices, and norms as public and private actors respond to the myriad challenges and obstacles they face. Rejected here is the more common view of development as the asymptotic approach of real economies to the pristine models that economists have so long embraced. Development does not occur through the elimination of this or that key obstacle to the functioning of the market mechanism when it is seen to be undermined by some impediment or other. The challenge is to wean ourselves from the view that the most useful interventions emerge first on the economist's blackboard. Instead, useful innovations occur when economists and other development practitioners and civil society actors "muddle through," searching for solutions via unruly practices that appear to the fastidious economist in possession of a tidy, buttoned up worldview as irredeemably messy, insignificant, partial, and ad hoc.

Hirschman urges us to loosen the grip of grand theoretical accounts on our imaginations and conceptions of what is possible in the world we engage and on our interpretations of change. Emphasis is to be placed on epistemic inadequacy and on expert humility (DeMartino 2011). Freed from the narrative fallacy (Taleb 2007) that grand theory generates, the hope is that development economists will come to appreciate the unyielding complexity of the ever-evolving world. In the Hirschmanian vision, ignorance is to be recognized not just as restrictive but also as emancipatory since it substantially widens the field where opportunistic engagement might generate real advances.[3] Pushing back against grand theory allows us to recognize and helps to sustain meaningful change in prosaic, small, particular, context-dependent adjustments, the significance of which tends to be dismissed by the habit of theorizing real change only as systemic and complete, as an overhaul or displacement that entails the installation of new, expansive, consistent models of economic or social organization.

. . . And Hirschmanian Risks

But aren't there real dangers in a Hirschmanian world that comprises and is even defined by unscripted institutional and policy innovations? Aren't there substantial risks when decision making is relatively unconstrained by a coherent model that gives direction and provides criteria for distinguishing progress from regress? Lacking such a model, aren't decisionmakers prone to paralysis or, alternatively, to self-interested behavior for which they can't be held accountable owing to the absence of a consensus around the social good and the best means for achieving it?

The answer to all these questions is most certainly "yes." It needs to be emphasized that institutional heterogeneity and policy diffusion are hardly panaceas—neither in the domains of financial governance and developmental finance nor in the domain of development more generally. Instead, they are fraught with grave risks. In the context of a pluripolar financial governance architecture, one marked by policy and institutional diversity but also by inconsistency and contradiction, the old development economics conversation about how to ensure conformity with an overarching model—how to get to true Keynesianism, neoliberalism, structuralism, or democratic socialism—must give way to a new discussion about the acute challenges and even dangers facing development practitioners that derive from the relative autonomy of distinct actors. For the sake of exposition, I collect these risks under three headings: "innocent" spillovers, beggar-thy-neighbor strategies, and systemic risk.

"Innocent" but Damaging Spillovers

Development decisions made by one or more states or nonstate actors, fully in the spirit of experimentation and pragmatic adjustment to challenges and risks, may induce unintended spillovers that harm others. There are myriad examples in the domain of economic development, especially in a highly integrated world economy. Policy choices in one jurisdiction, pursued simply as means to address a domestic problem or in pursuit of legitimate, valued goals, may cause substantial disturbances abroad.

It would be disingenuous to claim that a system with greater policy autonomy would not generate substantial spillovers. But it is naïve to believe that *any* global regime, no matter how pristine or coherent, resolves this problem. All systems are fraught with anticipated and unanticipated spillovers—partly because of the complexity and interdependence of economic and social systems and partly because all economic and social systems constantly evolve in unanticipated and unpredictable ways.

Many spillovers may not be preventable. Alternatively, prevention may entail too high a price when measured in terms of forgone opportunities for development. Rather than seek to prevent all spillovers that are the consequence of increased policy autonomy, it is better to accept that new spillovers will continue to appear, which will need to be managed or ameliorated. The point is simple and yet important: the claim that a world of substantially increased institutional and policy autonomy will be characterized by unwelcome spillovers is not a compelling basis for rejecting autonomy since all regimes face this problem. Nor is it always useful to try to lay blame for emerging spillovers—as though such spillovers could be avoided if all countries behaved properly. They can't be.

The crisis of 2008 provides guidance in this connection. The extraordinarily expansive monetary policy undertaken by the United States and other AEs arguably represented a legitimate and even necessary (though by no means sufficient) response that reduced the degree of financial distress in those countries and beyond.[4] But that policy choice caused severe problems for many EMDEs. Rapid capital inflows generated asset price bubbles and inflation while at the same time inducing sharp currency appreciation that threatened trade performance and financial stability. In that context, is it useful to demonize the loose monetary policy in the AEs, *or* the consequent EMDE reliance on capital inflow restrictions, on grounds that either or both initiatives imposed an unacceptable risk for others? Or is it more reasonable to accept that states must perforce pursue strategies that in an integrated world will necessarily induce spillovers; that these strategies will evolve as the world economy evolves; and that multilateral institutions of financial governance, particularly the IMF, must be centrally concerned with anticipation, amelioration, and evenhanded discussion and management of these spillovers?

Beggar-Thy-Neighbor Policies

What I have called innocent spillovers can easily bleed into explicit beggar-thy-neighbor stratagems in the context of zero-sum scenarios where policymakers in one country engage in competitive innovations that are designed to or are likely to monopolize benefits while offloading risks and harms onto others. While there is always temptation to pursue such strategies, one could plausibly argue that the opportunities for beggar-thy-neighbor initiatives increase with the extent of institutional and policy autonomy. Indeed, the BWIs sought to constrain policy autonomy in substantial part to thwart the ability of states to design and implement such stratagems. The same can be said of the neoliberal regime, whose theoretical architects (if not the interested parties neoliberalism came to serve) saw in domestic and international market mediation of economic affairs the ascendance of enlightened self-interest of internationalism over the naked self-interest associated with nationalist impulses (see DeMartino 2000, especially introduction).

As with spillovers, it is naïve to think that coherent regimes avoid this problem. As many have by now argued convincingly, for instance, the "coherent" classical gold standard, the postwar Bretton Woods gold standard, and the post–gold standard dirty float regime all entail special privileges for the hegemons (the United Kingdom and the United States, respectively) at the expense of less powerful countries. In the same vein, global neoliberalism has been rightly derided by many critics for the degree to which it most benefits the AEs and very few EMDEs, and especially the economic elites and large industrial and financial firms within both types of countries, despite its purported neutral and fair rules of economic engagement. In this regard, neoliberalism exemplifies the kinds of power asymmetries that Hirschman worried about. The point is that the most coherent economic regimes of the past century have arguably been both nationalist (and, in the case of neoliberalism, elitist) in substance despite their internationalist form.

That said, those advocating Hirschmanian principles can't dodge the nationalist risks associated with a weakening of the authority of the institutions at the center of global financial governance. Especially today, in the wake of Brexit, and the election of Donald Trump as U.S. president and the strengthening of nationalist parties in Europe, it is not at all difficult to imagine a deglobalized world of increased autonomy marked by the proliferation of nationalist initiatives that generate economic and geopolitical rivalry and that challenge the legitimacy and threaten the effectiveness of the BWIs. I will argue momentarily that managing this problem—and the problem of innocent spillovers—ought to be among the principal responsibilities of the BWIs in a world of enhanced policy autonomy. Given the complexity of the problem, the BWIs will need to cultivate allies among new institutions and networks of financial governance, especially those across the EMDEs.

Systemic Risk

One could also argue that a world lacking tight, centralized, organized financial governance according to a theoretical script might be particularly prone to systemic risk emanating from the disconnected decisions of private and public actors. For instance, if in the context of looming instability national governments are relatively free to pursue risk-shifting strategies, we might expect locally rational crisis responses that generate regionally or even globally damaging outcomes. Productive redundancy could also generate uncertainties about crisis response and impair coordination when it is most necessary. Productive redundancy could also generate uncertainties such as over whether, when, and by whom support will be provided—especially during crisis moments, when policymakers and private actors are most in need of certainty. Forum shopping could very well exacerbate this problem.

It is not self-evident, however, that the kind of global financial architecture now emerging would be prone to greater systemic risk. First, the fully coherent neoliberal project, with centralized monetary and financial authority, has proven itself to be particularly rife with systemic risk—indeed, more prone to risk than its Keynesian and statist predecessors. A lesson of the neoliberal period is that regimes with tightly coordinated and centralized financial governance pose substantial systemic risk. This is especially true when the system is largely designed to achieve just the one normative criterion of efficiency. Blackboard economics ought to warn us that efficiency of the sort neoclassical economists prize can only be achieved if all goes just as theorized, in the presence of a Walrasian auctioneer, as we have seen (see Crotty 2009; Kirman 2016). Increased risk follows from the closed-minded pursuit of perfection in a world that does not permit its achievement (Taleb and Blyth 2011; Best 2014; 2016). As DeMartino (2011) argues, in advancing the neoliberal prescription, an overconfident economics profession fell under the spell of the "maxi-max decision rule," which directs decisionmakers to pursue the highest possible payoff even when the probability of achieving it is minimal, and when the costs of failure are extreme. There are additional reasons why a fully coherent regime of monetary governance (were it achievable) would be prone to crisis, as we will see. It can be claimed with some assurance, then, that a decentralized, pluripolar, and even inconsistent regime of financial governance is not uniquely prone to systemic risk. Indeed, there is good reason to believe it is more robust as the burdens of responding to financial instability are borne by a greater number of actors marked by a diverse range of experiences, sensibilities, capabilities, and instruments.

That said, it is not my claim that a Hirschmanian world would be largely free of systemic risk. It would be better to presume the likelihood of systemic risk and to refocus attention previously targeted toward policy and institutional convergence around some presumed ideal toward emerging sources of risk with an eye toward devising a rich portfolio of strategies and a proliferation of networks of institutions to manage them.

Toward Hirschmanian Mandates

Innocent spillovers, beggar-thy-neighbor stratagems, and systemic risk are and will be features of all global economic regimes of financial governance. They are not unique to the emerging Hirschmanian world, but neither are they resolved by it.

What new mandates arise for the existing and emerging institutions that are engaged in global financial governance and developmental finance? The Hirschmanian answer should by now be apparent. These institutions must facilitate the opportunity for wide-ranging unscripted experimentation at the local, national, and regional levels. If they are not successful in this mandate, they have little chance of promoting inclusive, sustainable, and relatively stable development. The institutions of global financial governance must also learn to better manage growth—attending to sustainability, stability, and equity—and not just crises. But, at the same time, institutions that provide project finance and liquidity support must look to anticipate and manage the cross-border transmission of unintended or undesirable spillovers and any sources of systemic risk that present themselves in a world of institutional and policy heterogeneity. In this world, policy autonomy at once mediates and is mediated by the need to prevent or ameliorate spillovers and systemic risk. A potential tension between autonomy and risk must be acknowledged as central to the development enterprise. The tension must be recognized and confronted by decisionmakers, but not by sacrificing either autonomy or risk prevention and amelioration. Instead, the mandate facing policymakers is to search for reasonable, evolving compromises that fit the shifting development contexts they face.

It is vital to note that in this scheme the salience and role of the BWIs are not diminished in the least. Instead, their roles are substantially reformed from what they were understood to be during the height of the neoliberal era. *Managing and protecting diversity rather than imposing homogeneity* is perhaps the most direct way of putting the matter. Rodrik (2011, 45) has effectively made the case for managing policy and regulatory diversity in the context of international trade: "The WTO should be conceived of not as an institution devoted to harmonization and the reduction of national institutional differences, but as an institution that manages the interface between different national systems."

Rodrik does not tell us just how the WTO should manage the trade-off between autonomy and spillovers, and with good reason. There is no formula that lends itself to this problem, especially once we reject any simplistic criterion like efficiency to guide policy formation. Rodrik similarly argues that coordination and cooperation in the realm of financial governance should manage and protect national diversity, policy autonomy, and experimentation. Policymakers must be free to design strategies that are most suitable to their national economic and political conditions and institutional capacities.[5] More generally, Rodrik (2011, 205–206, 280) makes a case against global standards and global regulations. Instead, he makes a case for a "thin version of globalization," which accepts a collection of diverse national strategies whose interactions are regulated by a set of simple, transparent, and commonsense rules. In the same vein, the BWIs should look to balance the desirability of institutional and policy autonomy and the need for coordination to prevent spillovers and systemic risk. This is not an easy task, to be sure, but it is one that can be confronted with Hirschmanian sensibilities that recognize fundamental uncertainty and the consequent need for BWI support of experimentation, learning by doing, learning from others via new networks, the importance of making space for policymakers to engage in opportunistic problem solving (as per Hirschman's Hiding Hand), and pragmatic adjustments that are not constrained by fealty to any particular theoretical vision.

In the heyday of the neoliberal revolution, neoclassical economists argued that states could not and should not "pick winners" among sectors or firms. Government officials simply lacked the information necessary to direct the economy in that way. Instead, winners should and would emerge from fair competition among private market actors. Paradoxically, however, neoliberal social engineers were in fact and at the very same time picking winners among institutional forms and policy options. The Hirschmanian alternative (echoed by Rodrik 2011; see also Ellerman 2005) directs us instead to permit institutional and policy innovation, and to find out what works through the unending experience of trial and error.

Leading observers of the global financial governance architecture have begun to articulate visions for the BWIs that are consistent with this mandate. Ocampo has long argued that a reformed IMF should sit at the apex of a pyramid-like system in which it coordinates its strategies with the new and existing regional, subregional, and transregional institutions rather than dictate that they all march in lockstep, while also serving as a backstop in times of systemic crisis (e.g., Ocampo 2006, chap. 1; Ocampo 2010b; 2010c). More recently, Rajan has advanced the idea that the IMF, the G-20, or some other entity should evaluate national monetary and exchange rate policies in hopes of raising awareness of their unintended spillover consequences abroad, warn those that might be affected, and provide forums for the relevant parties to discuss alternative policies that might prevent or mitigate substantial harms for others (Rajan 2016a; 2016b). Relatedly, Spence has called for the IMF to play a role in coordinating diverse national policies (Spence 2010a).

In the view of some observers, the IMF is already beginning to redefine its mission in terms of a vague "new multilateralism" (Nissan 2015). The reorientation might entail just these kinds of coordinating roles, but they could be defined in ways that either protect autonomy and diversity or constrain them. In the context of newly assertive EMDEs, there is reason for hope that IMF thinking and practice will evolve in the former rather than the latter direction. At the same time, the proliferation of alternate forums is establishing new opportunities for knowledge sharing, coalition building, and relationship deepening that might ultimately prove more valuable than IMF reform in anticipating and responding to harmful spill-overs associated with national policy autonomy. These include the G-20, the FSB, new networks of EMDE policymakers and finance officials, such as the BRICS, and other networks that are forming around and among the institutions discussed in chapter 6.[6] In this context, we should take note of the success of EMDEs in transforming the conversation around capital controls within the G-20 and the IMF. The EMDE intervention, still in its infancy, could generate constructive norms regarding which spillovers are and are not legitimate to impose on others, and what strategies are and are not required by those countries inducing the spillovers to ameliorate their effects.

The kind of shift envisioned here, away from the imposition of insti-tutional conformance and toward the management of diversity, draws on distinct criteria for assessing policy and institutional innovations that are already emerging in the context of the erosion of neoliberal hegemony. I note in this regard the multifaceted criteria that are codified in the UN's SDGs. We find today greater emphasis on the goals of fairness, sustain-ability, targeting the benefits of economic growth toward those most dis-advantaged, and genuine opportunities for participation by those largely excluded from decision making during the neoliberal era.[7] This normative transformation is long overdue. Equally important, the stultifying and exceedingly risky imperative to achieve efficiency, especially in the EMDEs, must give way to criteria that reflect humility about what economists can know and control (see DeMartino 2011). Development economists should seek institutional arrangements and policies that confer redundancy, resil-ience, and even antifragility (Taleb 2012). For instance, "excess" reserve accumulation by EMDEs is typically theorized simply as a cost associated with underdeveloped financial markets—as a deflection of funds away from efficient allocations or as a source of global imbalances. This one-sided view fails to recognize that large reserves carry the potential to generate greater stability and resiliency in the face of instability, which in turn per-mit greater policy autonomy. Outsized reserves may be a necessary cost to ensure greater space for perpetual learning and pragmatic adjustment even and perhaps especially in the face of a crisis. In addition, the one best way that the efficiency criterion imposes in the minds of development economists must give way to an affirmative commitment to the virtues of policy and institutional heterogeneity, which must be preserved even at the risk of some degree of spillover. To reiterate, spillovers must be anticipated and managed, to be sure, but in ways that don't undermine policy entrepreneurship or Hirschmanian experimentation.

These criteria may help us to view pluripolarity in a new light. Rather than focus simply on its potential inefficiencies and inconsistencies, we should understand that pluripolarity is a vital means to achieve important development goals. First, pluripolarity can be a vehicle for giving voice to nations that have largely been silenced within the BWIs; not least, pluripolarity can enhance their bargaining power. At the same time, the proliferation of new institutions of financial governance provides an opportunity for capacity building as EMDE practitioners develop their ability to manage their affairs and to represent their national interests at the BWIs. Proliferation also facilitates forum shopping so that states that cannot secure adequate voice in the BWIs can at least partially escape the BWIs' orbit of influence. All of this is potentially conducive to the enhancement and sustenance of policy autonomy.

It bears repeating that pluripolarity, with its overlapping architectures of financial governance, generates institutional density that may yield robustness and antifragility. This kind of architecture may entail greater opportunity for rapid, appropriate, innovative responses in times of instability and crisis that better meet the acute and long-term needs of member states. Pluripolarity might generate institutions with greater capacity to adjust effectively to changing circumstances and challenges than is exhibited by large, centralized institutions. Institutional nimbleness was already becoming apparent during the crisis of 2008, despite the relative immaturity of many of the new institutions that were called on to provide assistance and stability. There is good reason to hope for improved performance over time in these respects, as the fledgling and maturing institutions surveyed in chapter 6 continue to expand their capacities, missions, and the trust of their members.

Finally, pluripolarity has the potential to facilitate experimentation to a degree that is typically unattainable when the financial architecture is organized around a central authority that is driven in turn by a uniform ideology. The two can and often do go together. Unipolarity of institutions and authority lends itself to the embrace of an organizing theoretical vision that ensures consistency across the strategies it employs and across its vast regions of influence. There is no doubt that the vision can simplify the work of policymakers, but the cost can be and generally is a failure to achieve the goal of genuine, inclusive, sustainable development. Achieving that goal may require a loosening of the institutional and ideological grip of unipolarity, and substantial relaxation of the fastidiousness that requires deep uniformity and extensive harmonization.

In my view, the chief lesson of the neoliberal era and the series of crises it induced is not just that one policy regime, be it neoliberalism or some competitor, is inappropriate for all contexts (as argued in, for example, Chang 2002b; 2007; 2012; 2014; Chang and Grabel 2014[2004]; DeMartino 2000; Rodrik 2007–2008; 2009b; 2011). That is certainly true, as even many mainstream development economists now understand. The chief lesson may be that placing just one institutional complex at the center of global financial governance and developmental finance puts too much demand on it; gives it too much power to shape policy but also to influence preferences of subordinate actors; constrains pragmatic adjustments and experimentation; and substantially amplifies the effects of any of the inevitable mistakes that it will make. Centralized institutional authority also risks closed-minded, discouraging, dangerous "there is no alternative" thinking that prevents learning by doing since there's only one principal doer, doing only one principal thing—especially, as is so often the case, when its work is driven by some totalizing "ism" or other.

A Closing Thought

The dismissal of recent and ongoing changes in global financial governance and developmental finance that I have explored here can have real, concrete effects. As Hirschman argues so forcefully in his insightful work on rhetoric, how social scientists theorize and speak of the world influences that world (Hirschman 1991; see also Hirschman 1965; 1967b; 2013[1971]). Our rhetorical choices and scholarly dispositions—whether we search for possibilities or let ourselves be buried in obstacles—can enable and encourage or prevent genuine human progress. For Hirschman, a "passion for the possible" is recognized as a "vital actor" in the development enterprise (Hirschman 2013[1971], 30; see also Hirschman 2013[1970], 147; Adelman 2013a, xii).

Guided by Hirschman, I interpret contemporary developments as propitious for the reorientation of development thinking and practice, reorientation away from practice driven by faithfulness to an overarching model and toward practice that features what I have called throughout the book *unscripted* innovations that do not cohere around any particular model and that arise in the context of persisting and emerging challenges. This model of development is uncomfortable and unruly, to be sure. Hirschman would have us push past our professional impulse toward theoretical closure and systemic engineering so that we can instead embrace the small, the ad hoc, the context-dependent, and the experimental as perhaps the only avenue toward genuine development.

Today we look out on a decidedly unsettled world. It is marked by substantial shuffling in regional and global economic, political, and geopolitical alignments, such as Brexit; rising nationalism in some contexts alongside resurgent neoliberalism in others; hostility by the Trump administration toward international organizations and networks and the public goods they provide; enduring macroeconomic imbalances; escalating economic inequalities that in some countries are reaching historic proportions; and climate change. At the same time, a recurrent confluence in EMDEs of weak commodity prices, slowing economic growth, instability of international capital flows, currency fluctuations, and high leverage rates threatens renewed volatility and even crisis. These developments represent severe challenges that the emerging global financial governance architecture will be asked to manage. By now it is both prudent and sensible to assume that there will always be new financial crises and that the most vulnerable nations and economically disadvantaged and politically disenfranchised groups within them will bear the heaviest burdens.

The Hirschmanian regime now emerging provides no guarantees against crises. *We should always expect things to fall apart.* The chief test of the Hirschmanian regime, then, will be neither whether it can prevent all financial crises nor how well it does in responding to the next crisis. The chief test will be whether it permits and indeed encourages learning, problem solving, pragmatic adjustments, and autonomy in the face of successes and failures in the context of an ever-evolving torrent of challenges. There is good reason to hope that it will. In my view, much depends on whether, when the challenges hit, the myriad institutions and networks that are now emerging across the globe respond in the spirit of Hirschmanian possibilism.

Notes

Preface

1. Later I encountered the use of the phrase "immensely productive incoherence" in Gibson-Graham (1996), invoking the work of Eve Sedgwick (1993). At the time I was relieved to find other theorists who recognized the potential virtue of incoherence.

Chapter 1

1. On architectural failings and the Asian crisis, see Feldstein (1998) and Stiglitz (2002). On new architectures, see Best (2003), Chin (2014b), Eichengreen (1999), and Kirshner (2014b).

2. The acronym BRICs (lower case "s") refers to Brazil, Russia, China, and India. In 2011 South Africa joined the group, at which point it was renamed the BRICS.

3. Representatives of Brazil and China made these points most vocally. On China, see Chin (2014b) and Kirshner (2014a; 2014b).

4. Ocampo (2015b) and others term it a "non-system."

5. I've benefited from engagement with Best's work (2005; 2012), which discusses the centrality and even desirability of ambiguity in global financial governance. She argues insightfully that the international political and economic stability of the post–World War II era depended on a carefully maintained balance between coherence and ambiguity, and that ambiguity can be both functional and necessary. Monolithic models of economic integration, such as neoliberalism, are intended in part to banish ambiguity—to generate clear, unambiguous institutional and policy directives that will yield fully coherent economic systems. One of my central contentions is that elimination of ambiguity represents a dangerous impediment to prudent financial governance.

6. See Chin (2010), which was written early in the crisis, before many of the most important discontinuities emerged. Chin has since moved toward a discontinuity view (Chin 2014b; 2015; 2016).

7. In contrast, James (2014) views the central role of the Federal Reserve as representing discontinuity (rather than continuity) insofar as the institution took responsibility for global stabilization, a burden traditionally borne by the IMF. Note that Helleiner's views have evolved over the course of the crisis (as we will see later in this chapter and elsewhere in the book).

8. See Cohen and Benney (2014) for a discussion of continuity in the international currency system.

9. Germain's (2009) intervention is more nuanced than most continuity contributions. He rightly emphasizes the importance of taking the long view of evolutionary change and continuity, and he identifies modest rebalancing of power among states in the period before the global crisis. But he ultimately emphasizes continuity and complex evolution rather than rupture, and he suggests that this is the most likely outcome in the years ahead. In my view, he undersells the significance of his findings, owing to an implicit notion that change must be abrupt and decisive.

10. On continuity and the ASEAN+3 countries, see Cohen (2012), Grimes (2015), and Haggard (2013). On the BRICS, see Bond (2016), Gray and Murphy (2013), Nel and Taylor (2013), and Rodrik (2013). On rising powers, see Peruffo and Prates (2016). Unlike most in this tradition, Gray and Murphy allow for some uncertainty regarding an emerging "regime change," though it is not likely to be what they see as "emancipatory."

11. Conflicting visions about development and the voices of EMDE representatives were a more important feature of discussions around the Bretton Woods order than most observers appreciate (Helleiner 2014a).

12. Political movements across the world continue to wrestle over the desirability of neoliberal policies. Recent political developments in some AEs threaten to promote a dangerous mix of neoliberalism and economic nationalism.

13. Kirshner (2014a) argues that the global crisis is a turning point for the United States, reflected in the relative erosion in its hard and soft powers, including the credibility of its liberalized financial model as a global ideal. He emphasizes the unevenness of this intellectual transformation, comparing its resilience in the United States to its loss of credibility elsewhere. More broadly, I note here that a range of traditions in political science examine how crises can open space for change. These studies pay particular attention to uneven, gradual evolution (e.g., see Blyth 2002; Gourevitch 1986). We return to this matter very briefly later in this chapter and more deeply in subsequent chapters.

14. The only area where the G-20 has taken a bold, though largely rhetorical, step concerns capital controls (see chapter 7).

15. See Lütz and Kranke (2014) on tension in some Eastern European and Central European cases.

16. Some work within "historical institutionalism" also approaches institutional change as a gradual, evolutionary process (most notably Mahoney and Thelen 2010). See chapter 5.

17. Some observers, such as José Antonio Ocampo (2016), use the term North Atlantic crisis since this region was the epicenter of the crisis.

Chapter 2

1. Following Ellerman (2005), I use the (admittedly awkward) term "Hirschmanian" to refer to scholarly work and policy and institutional innovations that are consistent with Hirschman's key theoretical and epistemic commitments. Others refer to "Hirschmanesque" impulses (Kirshner 1997; 2014a; Abdelal and Kirshner 1999–2000).

2. The most useful of these contributions are Drezner (2013), Fukuyama (2013), Gladwell (2013), Alacevich (2014; 2015; 2016), and a collection of papers published in the journal *Humanity* (Adelman et al. 2015). Drezner argues that Hirschman developed "some of the key building blocks of how to think about political economy"; that his ideas upended long-standing shibboleths in economics, political science, economic history, and sociology; and that some of his most important ideas (particularly insights in his books *The Passions and the Interests*, *National Power and the Structure of Foreign Trade*, and *Exit, Voice, and Loyalty*) became touchstones for scholars and prefigured what became critical areas of research in the decades that followed their publication. Gladwell (2013) describes Hirschman as one of the "twentieth century's most extraordinary intellectuals" and, like Adelman, finds it impossible to separate Hirschman's distinct life trajectory from the content of his writings. See also Lepenies (2008).

3. See Adelman (2013a, introduction; 2013b) and Alacevich (2014; 2015; 2016).

4. I thank Michele Alacevich for this point.

5. Hirschman is used as a foil in the essay. The history of development economics serves as a backdrop for Krugman's observations about methodology in economics more broadly.

6. The title of Krugman's essay, "The Fall and Rise of Development Economics," is a play on the title of Hirschman's 1981 essay "The Rise and Decline of Development Economics."

7. See Adelman (2013b, 343–344) for a more charitable reading of the same matter, and see Alacevich (2014; 2015) for a discussion of the context of the move away from high development theory.

8. In Krugman's (1994) view, the publication of Murphy, Shleifer, and Vishny (1989) helped resurrect development economics. See Herrera (2006) for a critique of

Krugman's essay, and a discussion of what he sees as the absorption of development theory and policy by neoclassical economics.

9. As will become clear in what follows, this claim, though not incorrect, is misleading. Hirschman was very much interested in small-scale initiatives and microresults, and his big concepts involved the need to appreciate diminutive, mundane policy interventions.

10. In a similar vein, Picciotto (1994), then director general of operations evaluation at the World Bank, optimistically argued in 1994 that the World Bank's development agenda, specifically its work in development evaluation, had become more Hirschmanian in response to past failures and criticisms.

11. *A Bias for Hope* is the title of a 1971 book of Hirschman's essays. Rodrik restricts himself, in his otherwise characteristically open-minded contribution *One Economics, Many Recipes* (2007b, 3), to "neoclassical economic analysis." "One Economics" signals from the outset that Rodrik seeks to rescue neoclassical economic theory from itself rather than propose that we embrace many paradigms within economic theory. That said, Rodrik's book, and indeed much of his work, is profoundly consistent with Hirschman's insights. We find in Rodrik an embrace of unbalanced growth (i.e., selective, strategic interventions), deep engagement with local context, pragmatism, humility, and experimentation (Alacevich 2016). Rodrik's 2015 book *Economics Rules: The Rights and Wrongs of the Dismal Science* is both a celebration of what he identifies as the discipline's movement toward "many and context-specific models" and a call for it to move further in this direction. By way of contrast, Ha-Joon Chang's *Economics: The User's Guide* (2014) argues for a greater degree of theoretical pluralism in economics.

12. See Chang (1994; 1997; 2002a; 2002b; 2007; 2012; 2014), Chang and Grabel (2014[2004]), Easterly (2001; 2014), Wade (1976; 2003[1990]; 2004), and, as previously noted, Rodrik (1991; 2007b; 2011; 2015a) and Hausmann, Rodrik, and Velasco (2008). The dedication to Wade's *Governing the Market* (2003[1990]) invokes Hirschman's "art of trespassing," a play on the title of Hirschman's 1981 book *Essays in Trespassing*. Though Alice Amsden's major books, *Asia's Next Giant* (1992) and *The Rise of the Rest* (2001), do not cite Hirschman, their emphasis on the importance of trial and error and learning clearly give them a Hirschmanian flavor. See also Lepenies (2008) for a reflection on Hirschman's numerous contributions to social science. The author focuses on what he sees as Hirschman's general approach to problem solving as embodied in his commitment to "possibilism" (to which we will return later).

13. See, for example, Kirshner (1997, chap. 4; 2014a), Abdelal and Kirshner (1999–2000), and Blyth (2011; 2013a).

14. As Drezner (2013) notes, Hirschman's book underscored his long-held commitment to the view that dialogue between economists and political scientists could be mutually beneficial. In this connection, Hirschman noted that, "In developing [exit

and voice] . . . I hope to demonstrate to political scientists the usefulness of economic concepts *and to economists the usefulness of political concepts*" (1970, 19, emphasis in original).

15. Gerald Helleiner (2010) employs Hirschman's exit, voice, and loyalty framework to explain why the Asian and especially the global crisis renewed interest among EMDE policymakers in ways to escape IMF control through the creation of alternative institutions of financial governance.

16. "Cult of exit" is drawn from the essay "Exit Albert Hirschman" published shortly after his death (*Economist* 2012).

17. The idea that linkage effects would induce unbalanced growth represented a stark alternative to the idea of "balanced growth" that was in vogue at the time. See also Paul Streeten (1959) for a critique of the balanced growth orthodoxy.

18. See Hirschman (2013[1970], 144) for an examination of the professional sociology that contributed to the tendency toward grand theories and paradigms.

19. Herbert Simon's (1990) conception of "bounded rationality" stems from a related recognition that the social world is inherently complex and only partly intelligible. Hirschman's approach is more closely aligned with the inferences drawn by contemporary students of complexity, such as Kirman (2016), than with the less radical inferences drawn by Colander and Kupers (2016), who try to retain a notion of equilibrating mechanisms.

20. Hirschman (2013[1970], 144) wondered whether such efforts were "inspired primarily by compassion or by contempt" for the lot of poorer countries. The failure to appreciate complexity and the limits of knowledge also underpins Popper's rejection of grand plans and social engineering (see McMillan 2008).

21. The commitments inform the analysis in *The Strategy of Economic Development*, *Journeys toward Progress: Studies of Economic Policy-Making in Latin America*, and *Development Projects Observed*, and are treated in particular depth in several of his essays, including "Obstacles to Development: A Classification and a Quasi-Vanishing Act" (1965), "The Principle of the Hiding Hand" (1967a, chap. 1), "The Search for Paradigms as a Hindrance to Understanding" (2013[1970]), "Political Economics and Possibilism" (2013[1971]), and "Against Parsimony: Three Easy Ways of Complicating Some Categories of Economic Discourse" (2013[1986a]).

22. Alacevich (2014; 2015) explores this episode, and I draw on his work in the following paragraphs.

23. The terms in quotation marks appear in Hirschman (1967a) and are discussed in Alacevich (2014).

24. Alacevich (2014, 140) cites Judith Tendler's related observations. In a book on Brazil (for which Hirschman authored a foreword), Tendler (1968) highlighted the

strong tensions that can "arise among the intrinsically uncertain nature of the knowledge acquired on development issues, the limits of knowledge transmission between donors and domestic recipients, and the status of 'development experts.'"

25. Alacevich (2014, 161–162) notes that the chilly reception of Hirschman's work may also have reflected an organizational culture that made outside evaluation unwelcome. Hirschman might have expected as much: he wrote insightfully about the mutual distrust that often emerged between foreign experts and their clients (discussed later).

26. Hirschman (1967a, xvii) acknowledges that the Hiding Hand was "the most speculative chapter of the book, was close to a provocation [to the World Bank]. Nothing could be less 'operationally useful.'" Nevertheless, he argued that the chapter was meant to function as a prologue to the more mundane, practical aspects of the book and that it was intended to reinforce his view that uncertainty, creativity, and learning are intrinsic to an understanding of development.

27. Highlighting the lyrical nature of Hirschman's prose in this and other essays, Gladwell (2013) writes: "Remember, this is an *economist* who's writing" (emphasis in original). Gladwell (2013) also discusses the roots of the Hiding Hand in Hirschman's deep reading in psychology and psychoanalysis, which contributed to his interest in the productive value of negative emotions—namely, frustration, aggression, and anxiety (see Adelman 2013b, 340–342). The Hiding Hand illustrates the value of adversity as a teacher.

28. In this respect, again, it is striking how much Hirschman anticipates the turn in economics away from theorizing the economy as an essentially simple, self-contained system toward recognizing it as an adaptive, complex system. For instance, teasing out the implications of complexity theory, Kirman (2016, 547) argues that this conception requires the economist to abandon the "benchmark model in which there are clear causal relationships, and in which the consequences of modifying parameters can be predicted, albeit with some uncertainty." See also Colander (2003).

29. George Soros's notion of reflexivity also focuses attention on the ways in which economic theory influences the world (Soros 2013). I thank Jerry Epstein for this point.

30. I thank an anonymous referee who pointed out parallels between Hirschman's work and that of another underappreciated theorist of global social change, Robert Cox. Both were iconoclastic thinkers who rejected the "problem solving" positivist bent of social science and were deeply committed to understanding the continuing process of historical change. That said, Cox was more sympathetic to grand narratives than was Hirschman.

31. See also Hirschman (2013[1971]). These themes are developed most fully and elegantly in his essays "Obstacles to Development" (1965), "The Search for Paradigms" (2013[1970]), and "Political Economics and Possibilism" (2013[1971]).

32. These themes are echoed in contemporary feminist thought, especially the work of theologian Sharon Welch (see Welch 1990).

33. In this respect, Hirschman anticipated the work of scholars working on "wicked" and "super wicked" problems (see Levin et al. 2012). I thank Matthew Paterson for pointing me in the direction of both Levin et al. and complexity theory (discussed later).

34. The rejection of utopianism had deep roots in Hirschman's personal and professional life—including his practical experiences working on the Marshall Plan and European reconstruction under the auspices of the U.S. Federal Reserve Board; his work as a consultant in Colombia, and deep connections to Latin America more broadly; his two experiences with the World Bank, first as its adviser to the Colombian government from 1952 to 1956 and later as a consultant studying project design, management, and appraisal; and his personal history as a refugee from fascism. The latter, in the view of his biographer, led Hirschman to appreciate the likelihood that grand utopian projects will yield horrific outcomes (Adelman 2013b).

35. The argument finds an echo in the work of Gibson-Graham (2008), who pushes back against the academic need for "strong theory" that purports to know too much and forecloses too readily on economic experiments. In a maneuver that is consistent with Hirschman's oeuvre, Gibson-Graham advocates instead "weak theory" that acknowledges what is not and cannot be known, writing that "experimental forays . . . are often judged as inadequate before they are explored in all their complexity and incoherence" (6).

36. The trend lamented in Krugman (1994), as we saw earlier. Hirschman's rejection of top-down social engineering resonates with the work of other critics, including Hayek (1974; 2014[1944]), Popper (1957; 1971), and Smith (1976[1759], 233–234) (who ridiculed the "man of system"), and contemporary critics such as DeMartino (2011, 9–11, 17, fns1, 5, 141–150), Easterly (2001; 2006; 2008; 2014), Ellerman (2004; 2005; 2014), McCloskey (1990), McMillan (2008), and Rodrik (2007b; 2009a; 2011). Ellerman (2005), a former World Bank economic advisor to the chief economist, indicts the institution (and similar institutions) for the hubris that characterizes its approach. Rodrik (2007b; 2009a; 2009b; 2011) has long written of the need for gradualism over abrupt institutional revolution, the importance of trial and error and practical innovation over fidelity to a scripted plan, and the related virtues of what he terms a "thin" version of globalization that protects national policy space in place of uniform and inflexible global rules and norms.

37. Colander (2003) likewise relies on the concept of muddling through in his examination of economic policy making. He simultaneously connects himself to and distances himself from Lindblom's (and, by extension, Hirschman's) conception of the process. Colander (2003, 198) dismisses early approaches to muddling through as applications of "armchair heuristics." That said, Colander's approach

retains a Hirschmanian flavor, particularly because he sees the economy as a complex system in which policymakers necessarily face limits on their ability to anticipate the effects of policy. This follows from Colander's rejection of what he sees as the economics profession's attachment to the "economics of control," a path that he traces to the long shadow cast by Abba Lerner (1944). Colander's notion of muddling through shares with Hirschman an appreciation of learning by doing, an embrace of the diminutive over the grand plan, and a return to what Colander (2003) terms "blended reasoning," by which he means economic policy analysis that draws broadly on social science and humanistic disciplines.

38. In this connection, Hirschman commends theorist Louis Althusser, even if he ironically notes that, as a Marxist, Althusser should be an "inveterate paradigm lover" (Hirschman 2013[1970], 151–152). What Althusser terms "overdetermination" in his account of transformative experiences, such as revolutions, Hirschman notes should more accurately be termed uniqueness.

39. Hirschman's work anticipates or, at the very least, resonates with contemporary work in complexity theory in regard to its emphasis on the inherent messiness and necessity of experimentation in climate governance (Hoffmann 2011).

40. Sabel and Reddy (2003) argue that pooled experience, learning, experimentation, and pragmatism are basic to any alternative to the command and control model of development. See the discussion of open learning in Ellerman (2004; 2005, 164–165, 218, 237–239), and see Schön (1994) for an examination of what he terms Hirschman's "underlying, elusive" model of social learning in development. Mazzucato (2013; 2015) draws on Hirschman (1967a, chap. 1) in a discussion of the messiness of the policymaking process and the benefits of trial and error.

41. See also the discussion in McMillan (2008).

42. Rodrik (2009a) identifies all of these as features of the "new" development economics, which in important respects is consistent with key features of Hirschman's "old" development economics. See also Ravallion (2008) on the process of evaluation in development.

43. Polanyi (2001[1944], 143) wrote of precisely this phenomenon when discussing the propensity of advocates of economic liberalism to explain its failure as stemming from insufficient liberalization rather than from the inherent failure of the utopian project itself: "Its apologists are repeating in endless variations that but for the policies advocated by its critics, liberalism would have delivered the goods; that not the competitive system and the self-regulating market but interference with that system and interventions with that market are responsible for our ills."

44. See McCloskey's (1990) scathing critique of economic planners.

45. Angus Deaton has been critical of RCTs on methodological and ethical grounds that resonate with Hirschman's sensibilities, particularly in connection with the lat-

ter's distaste for the hubris of development experts, the drive to generalize from and export what is inherently particular, and the complicated relationship between experts and affected populations. Deaton (2010) focuses on methodological concerns but includes a brief discussion of ethical matters (e.g., 447). The ethical critique is developed much further in Deaton (2015), where he notes that RCTs are generally conducted on the poor by researchers who are not themselves poor and that these RCTs reflect an underlying paternalism that he rejects.

46. Lepenies (2008) argues that possibilism constitutes what he terms Hirschman's "general method of analysis." He correctly sees possibilism as an approach that is useful outside of the development context, and he argues that it should be understood as a "valid and multidisciplinary tool for unorthodox contemporary social analysis" (439, 444).

47. This theme reappears in certain contributions to poststructuralist political economy (see DeMartino 2013b).

48. "Reverence for life" appears in Hirschman (2013[1970], 147).

49. Though this book focuses on conservative rhetoric, Hirschman argues that progressives are apt to deploy similar rhetorical strategies.

50. This theme remains relevant today. As Blyth (2011) argues, Hirschman's theses on conservative rhetoric provide insight into the justifications advanced by neoliberals since 2008 against regulation of the behaviors and practices that led to the global financial crisis. Hirschman's theses are also relevant to understanding claims that there was no meaningful change in financial governance or developmental finance in EMDEs during the crisis and that whatever innovations have occurred in fact make matters worse.

51. On refusing to know too much, see Gibson-Graham (2006, 6) and DeMartino (2013b).

52. Note that some see Hirschman as strictly a "state-centric" thinker. This implies that Hirschman's approach may not be the most appropriate frame for understanding the types of changes that I am discussing in this book, some of which are below the level of states and others above it. More generally and relatedly, some might assume that Hirschman's work is less relevant today in a world of sub- and transnational actors. Admittedly, Hirschman's best-known work, which is the work on exit and voice and on international trade and national interest, is often understood as statist. But in fact these works have readily apparent implications for sub- and transnational actors. Moreover, Hirschman's development trilogy (Hirschman 1967a; 1969[1958]; 1973[1963]) focuses explicitly on processes and change at levels below the state. I thank Randall Germain for raising this line of discussion.

53. If the monetary tightening in the United States that began in December 2016 were to continue, it would likely renew debate over the harmful international spillover

effects of AE policies. So might the uncertain policy environment that has emerged in the immediate wake of the election of Donald Trump as President of the United States.

Chapter 3

1. For etiologies of the Asian crisis, see citations in note 4 of this chapter. On the Mexican financial crisis, see Grabel (1996a; 1996b).

2. See Mishkin (2006) for an example of this kind of treatment.

3. Chinese authorities continued to advocate radical architectural reform in the years that followed the Asian crisis despite the absence of a sympathetic audience (Chin 2014b). The proposals advanced by the governor of the country's central bank in 2009 should be understood in this historical context (ibid.). Notwithstanding the longevity of its interest in architectural reform, China's dollar holdings supported the system and sustained U.S. current account deficits (Helleiner and Kirshner 2014). After 2009, China's policy moved more firmly in the direction of seeking greater autonomy from the dollar and fundamental adjustment to the international monetary system (Chin 2014b; Kirshner 2014b).

4. For explanations of the Asian crisis that "have the added advantage of being true," see Chang (2000), Crotty and Lee (2002; 2005), Grabel (1999a; 1999b; 2002; 2007), Noble and Ravenhill (2000), Wade (1998a; 1998b; 2003[1990], introduction), and Wade and Veneroso (1998). The phrase in quotation marks is drawn from Wade (2003[1990], xxiv, borrowing from former U.S. president Richard Nixon).

5. Papers in Kenen (1996) discuss the recommendations of the Rey Committee (formed at Halifax) and the decisions made at the next G-7 summit in Lyons, which tightly linked crisis prevention to information dissemination.

6. See Best (2006), Grabel (2003d), Helleiner (2014b, chap. 4), and Mosley (2003). Best (2006) discusses the underlying power dynamics behind the IMF's stance on universal standards and codes.

7. SBAs are the IMF's basic short-term loan agreement.

8. Many observers make this point. Examples include Crotty and Lee (2002; 2004; 2005; 2006), Grabel (2003a; 2007), Harvey (2005, chaps. 3 and 4), Singh (1999), and Wade (2007).

9. The same logic prevailed in the United States during the 1990s as neoliberals dominated discussions of how to respond to home-grown financial turbulence. For example, the Enron, Long-Term Capital Management, and other financial implosions were resolved on the side of those favoring more information, transparency, and market discipline in lieu of increased financial regulation.

10. See, for example, Bhagwati (1998), Chang, Park, and Yoo (1998), Chang (2000), Crotty and Lee (2002; 2005; 2009), Feldstein (1998), Noble and Ravenhill (2000), Kirshner (2014b), Pempel (1999), Stiglitz (2002), Wade (1998b), Wade and Veneroso (1998), and Winters (1999).

11. See citations in the previous note.

12. Ukraine returned to borrower status during the global crisis, when it signed a US$16.4 billion SBA with the Fund in November 2008, followed by additional support packages in July 2010, April 2014, and March 2015.

13. As the global crisis unfolded, demands on a now leaner staff increased just as the institution enjoyed an increase in its financial resources. By May 2009, the institution's hiring freeze was reversed, and it began an aggressive process of recruiting new staff, particularly economists and others with expertise in financial sector issues (IEO 2014, Annexes 1 and 2). See chapter 5.

14. Discussion of the evolution of the IMF's role draws on Blyth (2013a, 162–165), Broome (2010), and Eichengreen (2000).

15. But see Nelson (2014a), who argues that the institution never faced a legitimacy crisis and was never in danger of losing its unique position as the crucial catalytic lender during complex financial crises (see also Henning 2009a).

16. The World Bank was critical of the IMF's failure to consider the effects of its SAPs on poverty and inequality during the 1980s (e.g., in relation to IMF programs in Africa, as noted by Noble and Ravenhill 2000). Under the leadership of Camdessus (who assumed office in 1987), the IMF attempted to respond to these criticisms. However, efforts by Camdessus and his successors bore little practical fruit despite vigorous rhetoric and numerous policy directives concerning poverty and inequality (Momani 2010; IEO 2007).

17. See, for example, Best (2007), Momani (2005; 2010), Reinold (2016), reports of the institution's IEO, and chapter 5 on the gap between IMF rhetoric and practice.

18. MacIntyre, Pempel, and Ravenhill (2008) argue that the Asian crisis served as a powerful catalyst for wide-ranging change across several dimensions of Asian political economy, though they nonetheless recognize important continuities.

19. The latter was doubled to US$58 billion in October 2011. The Bank of Korea also had bilateral swaps in place with the central bank of Japan, which predated the global crisis (Obe and Jun 2015).

20. Official reserves and sovereign wealth fund data use the designation for AEs and EMDEs as reported by the IMF.

21. Many observers have claimed that excess reserve accumulation also generates global imbalances that contribute to global financial instability. Paradoxically, while

reserve accumulation enhances policy autonomy, it also reflects the structural power of the United States—or what Susan Strange calls its "super-exorbitant privilege" (Germain 2009, 684–685; Strange 1987).

22. Total global SWF assets of US$7.4 trillion (as of December 2016) dwarf the US$2.94 trillion managed by hedge funds as of the first quarter of 2015 (Hedge Fund Research Institute 2015). Global SWF assets in 2016 represent 2.5% of total global financial assets, which were estimated to be US$294 trillion in 2014 (global financial assets reported in Ro 2015).

23. There is evidence that during the global crisis China deployed official reserves to stabilize AE financial markets and that SWF assets supported foreign and domestic markets (see chapters 5 and 7).

24. Discussion of the AMF draws on Cumings (1999), Grimes (2009a; 2009b), Holroyd and Momani (2012), and Noble and Ravenhill (2000).

25. See Holroyd and Momani (2012) on the Japanese government's frustrations with the IMF.

Chapter 4

1. The term "network of networks" is drawn from Slaughter (2004). See also Drezner (2007) and Woods and Martinez (2009, introduction).

2. Networks therefore contribute to the development of "soft law."

3. The Finance G-20 (discussed later) included a small number of EMDEs from the start.

4. Discussion in this paragraph draws on several critical analyses of the G-20, including Blyth (2013a), Helleiner (2014b), Payne (2010), and Vestergaard and Wade (2011; 2012b).

5. The discussion in this paragraph and the next draws on Helleiner (2014b, chap. 2), Helleiner and Pagliari (2009; 2010), Moschella and Tsingou (2013), and Viola (2014).

6. The EU is represented by the European Commission and the European Central Bank.

7. See Viola (2014) and Helleiner (2011a; 2011b; 2014b; 2016b) for an accounting of accomplishments, failures, and missed opportunities.

8. Guerrieri and Lombardi (2010) cite the speed with which the Basel Committee reached agreement on the Basel 3 accord as an achievement of the G-20. They also praise the G-20 for its role in the IMF governance reforms of 2010. After their paper was published, the U.S. Congress stalled these reforms for five years (see chapter 5). During that time, the Finance G-20 and the G-20 pressed Congress to end the gridlock (see G-20 2015).

9. Henning and Walter (2016) see the expansion of membership in networks such as the FSB as a key achievement in the G-20's scant record. Among academics, Cooper (2010; 2011) is perhaps the most bullish on the G-20, though he acknowledges its limitations, such as the lack of regional representation.

10. For cautiously pessimistic views, see Helleiner (2011a) and Woods (2010).

11. See Vestergaard and Wade (2011; 2012a) and Wade (2011) on an alternative to the G-20, which they term a Global Economic Council, and see Ocampo and Stiglitz (2011) on a Global Economic Coordination Council.

12. Discussion of governance reform began at the November 2008 G-20 meeting in Washington, DC. In the spirit of the moment, then British prime minister Gordon Brown, host of the April 2009 G-20 summit in London, declared that "the old Washington consensus is over. Today we have . . . a new consensus—that we take global action together to deal with the problems we face. . . . A new world order is emerging and with it the foundations of a new and progressive era of international cooperation" (quoted in Prasad 2014, 171–172). Despite this rhetoric, the stimulus programs undertaken by some national governments reflected "distinct national choices . . . in response to domestic pressures" rather than the G-20's call for bold, coordinated action (Helleiner 2014b, 51).

13. The Keynesian moment was cut short by many factors, including the dismissal of Keynesian sensibilities by the European Central Bank and the German government (Blyth 2013a, 55–58). The IMF's rediscovery and abandonment of Keynes paralleled that of the G-20. However, some Keynesian ideas were sustained within the institution, as we explore in chapters 5 and 7.

14. See Skidelsky (2011) on renewed interest in Keynes in 2009, and Farrell and Quiggin (2017) on "foxhole Keynesianism" in academia. The latter refers to Robert Lucas's famous quip that "everyone is a Keynesian in a foxhole" (quoted in Fox 2008).

15. The IMF acceded to China's wishes in 2015 (see chapter 5).

16. Several arguments in this paragraph are advanced in Helleiner (2011a; 2011b; 2014b, chap. 2).

17. Today, the World Bank and the OECD are similarly captivated by infrastructure and private infrastructure finance.

18. In this role, infrastructure has displaced microfinance and property rights.

19. See Alexander (2014, 9) for critical examinations of these and other infrastructure initiatives.

20. Much the same could be said about a recent infrastructure initiative by the World Bank (see chapter 6). Similarly, in 2012, African heads of state adopted the Programme for Infrastructure Development in Africa. Its main source of funding will

be the African Development Fund of the African Development Bank (AfDB), though it will also utilize public, private, and public-private partnerships. As of this writing, financing has not yet been secured.

21. The loose commitments on exchange rates were reaffirmed in March 2017 when Germany assumed leadership of the G-20, although U.S. Treasury secretary Steven Mnuchin insisted on striking from the resulting communiqué the G-20's longstanding pledge to "resist all forms of protectionism" (*Economist* 2017b).

22. Of particular importance are those networks that involve only EMDE policy-makers, such as the Commission for Africa, the BRICS Leaders' Summits, the Heavily Indebted Poor Countries' Finance Ministers' Network, Central Bankers' Network of the Centre for Latin American Monetary Studies, and the Central Eastern and South Eastern Europe Senior Budget Officials Network.

23. The discussion of the FSB draws on Pagliari (2014) and also on Griffith-Jones, Helleiner, and Woods (2010, 6–7) and Helleiner (2010; 2014b, chap. 5).

24. The European Central Bank was already a member of the FSB. See Helleiner (2014b, 137) for a discussion of pressure for this membership expansion.

25. Helleiner has written critically of the limited achievements of these networks, but on occasion he has taken a more encouraging view of their potential, as noted in chapter 1. In particular, in recent work he is encouraged by G-20 and FSB efforts in 2015 to address over-the-counter derivatives, though he recognizes difficulties in coordinating regulations and sharing information, which may lead to "greater fragmentation of global derivatives markets along territorial lines" (Helleiner 2016b, 6).

Chapter 5

1. See Grabel (2011) for an early elaboration of some of these arguments.

2. The continuity view of the IMF is reflected in Gabor (2010; 2015), Güven (2012), Islam et al. (2012), Kentikelenis, Stubbs, and King (2016), Muchhala (2011), Nelson (2014a; 2017), Ortiz and Cummins (2013), Rowden (2009), UNICEF (2010), Van Waeyenberge, Bargawi, and McKinley (2011), and Vernengo and Ford (2014). Reinold (2016) argues for continuity in one dimension of IMF practice; Güven (2012) and Vestergaard and Wade (2013a) find continuity at the World Bank; and Hanieh (2015) concludes that continuity marks BWI practice in Tunisia, Morocco, and Egypt.

3. On the BWIs, see Park and Vetterlein (2010). On the IMF, see Abdelal (2007, chap. 6), Babb (2003), Ban (2015), Barnett and Finnemore (2004, chap. 3), Best (2005; 2006; 2012), Broome and Seabrooke (2007; 2012), Chwieroth (2010), Lütz and Kranke (2014), Momani (2005; 2010), Moschella (2010), Nelson (2017), and

Woods (2006). On the World Bank, see Weaver (2008). On the role of local inter-locutors, see Ban (2016) and Woods (2006). Another tradition in political sci-ence, historical institutionalism, also emphasizes the complex interaction of the economic and social realms and focuses on the mutually constitutive relation-ship between agents and the ideational, material, and political conditions that open and restrict their fields of action (see, e.g., Mahoney and Thelen 2010, 6–7).

4. See related discussions in Abdelal (2007, chap. 6), Broome and Seabrooke (2007; 2012), Moschella (2012), and Weaver (2008). Mahoney and Thelen's (2010, 8) treat-ment of "ambiguous compromises" echoes key constructivist themes.

5. Wade's (1996; 2002) and Weaver's (2008) work on the World Bank are taken as seminal. Wade advances the idea of "paradigm maintenance"; Weaver's concept of organized hypocrisy is an extension of Brunsson (1989; 2003; see Weaver 2008, chap. 2). See Kentikelenis, Stubbs, and King (2016) on the related idea of "orga-nizational facades."

6. Broome and Seabrooke (2012) offer Fine (2001) as an example of analysis that fails to resist this temptation. Another example can be found in Vernengo and Ford's (2014) treatment of the IMF. Relatedly, Palley (2013) focuses on the public relations value and political cover provided by economists' strategy of asserting change in economic ideas when none has actually occurred. See also Vollmann (2015) on image and political cover in recent IMF research on inequality and labor unions.

7. Historical institutionalist analysis has tended to emphasize institutional con-tinuity over long periods. New contributions push the boundaries of the approach, taking account instead of the ways in which institutions evolve endoge-nously, incrementally, and in subtle ways that can add up to consequential shifts in identity and practice. Piecemeal adjustments tend to be overlooked and underap-preciated by those who focus on momentous exogenous shocks leading to radical, abrupt institutional transformation. See Mahoney and Thelen (2010, chap. 1) (and essays therein) on modalities of gradual institutional change.

8. Seabrooke (2010, 139) focuses on another type of gap at the IMF—the gap between the IMF's "reform 'talk' and borrowers' reform 'walk.'" The gap between IMF dictate and borrower practice has grown since the Asian crisis, as more EMDEs achieve greater relative autonomy from the IMF (discussed later).

9. See Barnett and Finnemore (2004, chap. 3), Chwieroth (2007a; 2007b; 2010), and Nelson (2014b; 2017) on the shared neoliberal worldview, selection, training, and socialization of IMF staff, and related work by Best (2007) and Momani (2005).

10. Several key contributions focus on the way that exogenous shocks undermine the capacity of predominant ideas to explain events while creating opportunities for new ideas to gain traction, either rapidly or incrementally, and stick (Best 2003; Blyth

2002; Broome and Seabrooke 2007; Chwieroth 2014; 2015; Moschella 2010; 2014; Widmaier, Blyth, and Seabrooke 2007), while others focus on the interaction between ideas and external interests in driving ideational change (Blyth 2003; Kirshner 2003; Moschella 2010). McNamara (1999) illustrates how ideas influence economic policy formation, Widmaier (2007) shows that similarities in crisis conditions facing policy-makers can yield dramatically divergent interpretations of interests and crisis responses, owing to their respective understandings of monetary trends (see also Widmaier 2014), and Widmaier (2016) demonstrates how ideas that initially reduce uncertainty can ultimately breed misplaced certainty and crisis.

11. See citations in note 3 of this chapter.

12. See Wade (2010; 2013a) on the World Bank.

13. There was also a very modest increase in IMF resources through gold sales and other means. The NAB was established in 1997 and activated in 1998 to finance an SBA for Brazil. The NAB was not utilized again until April 2011. It has been activated ten times since its 2011 enlargement.

14. See McElhiny (2009) for a description of how the IADB's holiday party in 2008 celebrated the increased demand for infrastructure packages. See Kulish (2009) on reinvigoration of the European Bank for Reconstruction and Development (EBRD). See chapter 6 for a broader discussion.

15. See Helleiner (2014b, 40, fn58), Henning (2016), and Prasad (2014). On bank exposure, see Broz (2014).

16. See also Harding (2014), Reuters (2013b), and Yukhananov (2013).

17. After the Fed, the PBOC provided the second-largest set of swaps to EMDEs (Gallagher 2014, 75). Together, the two provided over US$200 billion in swaps to EMDEs during the global crisis (ibid., 76). McDowell (2017) notes that EMDE central banks have been key actors in the spread of the international swap network, which was motivated by recognition of the risks of international capital flows and of dollar dependence in trade.

18. European officials were initially reluctant to involve the IMF, but by March 2010 they were forced to acknowledge the necessity of doing so (Eichengreen 2015, 134).

19. The ESM is a crisis-resolution mechanism that was created by euro area coun-tries during the global crisis. The ESM can raise funds from numerous sources, including private markets, and can provide support to Eurozone countries, subject to conditions (Schadler 2014, fn8). It is to replace the temporary European Financial Stability Facility (EFSF).

20. The preference for internal devaluation over external devaluation by national authorities reflected what Kattel and Raudla (2013) identify as a hardening of neo-liberal resolve in the Baltics during the crisis. Troika members apparently feared that

external devaluation would induce severe instability in Baltic capital markets and capital flight, and would have negative spillovers in Central and Eastern Europe.

21. See also Ban (2016) and Moschella (2016).

22. The levy was ultimately rejected by the Cypriot Parliament.

23. Strauss-Kahn, a small group of IMF staff, and officials from the German and French finance ministries quietly explored Greek debt restructuring in 2010. Debt relief was not granted until March 2012 (Blustein 2015, 1).

24. The report also contains self-indictment: it acknowledges that the IMF underestimated the negative effects of spending cuts and tax increases, and misjudged the government's capacity to implement structural reforms. Nevertheless, it concludes that the IMF's "overall thrust of policies" was "broadly correct" (IMF 2013a, 32).

25. The IEO takes note of EU discomfort with the IMF's Ex Post Evaluation (IEO 2016, 3). The IEO (ibid., 16) also notes that senior IMF officials were divided and that staff were generally skeptical regarding its involvement in Greece.

26. One of the main goals of the second SBA was to protect European banks that bought Greek bonds in the hopes of making a profit (Ewing and Alderman 2015).

27. Discussion in this paragraph relies on Taylor (2015).

28. The Eurogroup is an informal body comprising Eurozone finance ministers, the EC, and the ECB.

29. The primary budget excludes interest payments on debt.

30. As of May 2017 the IMF remains non-committal about whether it will participate in the disbursal to Greece that is scheduled for July 2017.

31. Despite much evidence to the contrary, a 2016 IEO report rejects the view that the IMF had a "muted voice" in Troika programs in Portugal, Ireland, and (the first program in) Greece (IEO 2016). The report does note that the institution lost its "characteristic agility" as a crisis manager and that the technical judgments of staff were potentially subjected to political pressure. It also faults the fragmented nature of euro-area decision making. News reports suggest that IMF staff, some executives, members of the European Department, and some European executive directors unsuccessfully tried to obstruct production of and remove passages from the IEO report (Thomas 2016).

32. Additional support to Ireland also came in the form of bilateral loans of €3.8 billion from the United Kingdom, €0.6 billion from Sweden, and €0.4 billion from Denmark; €17.7 billion from Euro-area member states/EFSF; and from the Irish government itself, which contributed €17.5 billion from its own cash reserves and liquid assets. Reporting on IMF participation in European packages is complicated

by program suspensions, renewals, replacement of programs by new ones, and the rapid evolution of European support mechanisms. Figures here are drawn from IMF press releases and Miyoshi (2013, 19–21).

33. For example, at the end of December 2015, the notional amount of outstanding over-the-counter derivatives contracts was valued at US$493 trillion (BIS 2016).

34. Some analysts disagree, arguing that the IMF would likely not consent to being a junior partner in arrangements with regional financial actors outside Europe (Mohan and Kapur 2015, 51).

35. Disbursal of the larger loan by the World Bank has been delayed until at least 2017, owing to a dispute between the government and the institution over macro-economic reforms. Nigeria did receive disbursement of the US$500 million IDA loan in 2016.

36. See Yukhananov (2013) for comments along these lines by other BRICS country leaders.

37. The Intergovernmental Group of Twenty-Four on International Monetary Affairs and Development (known as the G-24) is an informal organization estab-lished in 1971. It has a permanent secretariat in Washington and is housed within the IMF's building, though it does not operate on the IMF board level (Woods and Lombardi 2006). The G-24 coordinates the positions of a collection of EMDEs at the BWIs and advocates on their behalf in discussions of global financial reform (G-24 2014).

38. See Woods (2010) on BRICs positions on governance reform, financial support to the Fund, and instruments through which support would be provided.

39. The agreement abolishes the right of the five largest quota holders to appoint their own members of the Executive Board. Instead, all board members are to be elected by groups of countries (Eichengreen and Woods 2016, 48).

40. Executive directors are civil servants appointed by their home governments. They sit on the IMF's Executive Board and are apportioned voting rights on it. The Executive Board is the institutional venue where member states most directly exer-cise their national interests (Nelson 2014a, 167). The Executive Board is the IMF's day-to-day governing council. Countries with more voting power have their own representatives on the board, while other countries share a representative (Eichen-green and Woods 2016).

41. Mohan and Kapur (2015, 3) note that U.S. Treasury officials had called for IMF governance reform since at least 2005. The United States was the principal architect of the 2010 agreement (Truman 2015). See Vestergaard and Wade (2015) on the politics of the gridlock, and see Lesage et al. (2013) on why the U.S. executive branch was willing to approve the 2010 agreement.

42. Vestergaard and Wade (2014; 2015) show that governance reforms at the World Bank in 2010 had an even more microscopic, perverse effect on EMDE voice than reforms at the IMF.

43. This matter is explored extensively by Lesage et al. (2013), and I draw on their discussion.

44. As noted in chapter 1, South Africa formally joined the group at its April 2011 meeting, leading to the adoption of the new acronym BRICS to replace the previous acronym BRICs.

45. See Wade (2012) on the politics of this episode.

46. So did the practice (rather than formal rule) of requiring a supermajority of votes. The norm maintains U.S. veto power (Wade 2012).

47. The divisiveness among the BRICS is proof for some analysts that they are unlikely to challenge prevailing patterns of global governance (Bond 2013).

48. Members can still enjoy exceptional access absent an upfront debt restructuring operation so long as other official creditors provide loans on sufficiently concessional terms to make the debt sustainable (Ellmers 2016).

49. Article IV consultations are carried out annually for nearly every member country, result in a paper on each country's economy and economic policy, and provide recommendations on a range of issues. Recommendations become influential only when countries require IMF assistance (Lombardi and Woods 2008).

50. Jiang (2014) takes a different view. She sees China's actions and rhetoric as symbolic, self-interested, and not indicative of a significant break with the past.

51. SDR-bond arrangements were to be folded into the expanded NAB, which was to be unwound once the 2010 agreement went into effect (Lesage et al. 2013, 561).

52. Some analysts suggest that China's decision to contribute this second tranche of funds was related to Japan's mid-April 2012 announcement that it would contribute an additional US$60 billion to the IMF (Jiang 2014, 174). Japan's announcement apparently came as a surprise to China. Since February 2012, and in a rare instance of solidarity, China and Japan have raised the issue of increasing the EMDEs' voice at the IMF while also pressing the Eurozone to lift a €500 billion cap on bailout funds if it hoped to secure additional funding from non-European G-20 members (ibid., 173). China's second tranche also reflected its "responsible great power" ambitions, its commitment to provide funds through the safety of the IMF, and broader BRICS demands to increase EMDEs' voice at the Fund (ibid.).

53. Civil society organizations protested these contributions on two grounds. First, there were far better domestic uses for these funds than helping the IMF assist European banks. Second, long-standing objections to Fund governance had not been

addressed. See Bond (2013) on opposition by South African trade unions to the government's commitment.

54. Recall that Mantega began raising this threat in 2007.

55. Abdelal (2007) highlights informal, though effective, influence exercised by France in relation to U.S. interests at the IMF prior to the global crisis.

56. The last time the Treasury Department labeled China as such was in 1994 (though it presently has the country on a "currency monitor list" along with Germany, Japan, and South Korea).

57. The discussion in the balance of this paragraph and the next draws on Armijo, Katada, and Roberts (2015, 17–18).

58. The IEO acknowledged that the IMF contributed to the crisis by promoting financial liberalization (IEO 2011) and missing signs of banking system fragility in several countries (IEO 2016, vii).

59. The IEO takes the IMF to task in noting that the "call for fiscal consolidation proved . . . premature," that the policy mix was "not appropriate," and that the negative consequences of European austerity were foreseeable in light of the institution's precrisis research (IEO 2014, 11, 33).

60. See also findings in Molina (2010), Muchhala (2011), Rowden (2009), and Van Waeyenberge, Bargawi, and McKinley (2011).

61. More broadly, Vreeland argues that IMF conditionality provides the political leverage to advance unpopular domestic policy changes: "The moment it demands that deficits be cut . . . the IMF has entered into domestic politics" (Vreeland 2008, 367).

62. Country reports include Article IV consultations, reviews conducted as part of lending operations, consultations under nonlending arrangements, and publicly available IMF reports.

63. Momani and Lanz (2014) see the impact of the Arab Spring on the IMF differently. They find that there has been significant change in the cases of Tunisia, Egypt, and Morocco. In their reading, the content of IMF policy advice is "visibly different" in these cases (i.e., the IMF gave greater attention to inclusive growth, income inequality and redistribution, and health and education spending). They acknowledge, however, that the quality of the IMF's advice on social targets is vague, particularly in comparison with advice in other policy realms. While the authors do not address the factors that drove change, their analysis suggests that political turmoil and social pressures led to increased IMF focus on the social dimensions of economic policy.

64. Egypt's currency was devalued by 50% in anticipation of the IMF agreement.

65. Some countries, such as Nigeria, have continued to turn away from the Fund and have sought support from other multilateral institutions and investment from China.

66. The IMF continued to highlight the need to contain the wage bill around the September 2016 disbursement of a loan tranche.

67. Several self-congratulatory reports written early in the crisis by Fund staff conclude that the policy content of new IMF programs is fundamentally different from that of the Asian crisis era (IMF 2009b; 2009d; 2011a).

68. For example, in public statements on the November 2016 program with Egypt, the IMF emphasized its "homegrown" character (IMF 2016e). Best (2014) links the IMF's emphasis on country ownership to its efforts to manage policy failure. In earlier work, she argued that the IMF's efforts to promote borrower ownership of reforms and revise conditionality were at the heart of its struggles to reinvent and "re-legitimize" itself prior to the global crisis (Best 2007).

69. The creation of the IEO after the Asian crisis and the office's willingness to issue reports critical of IMF performance even in areas that are central to the IMF's mission themselves represent vitally important ruptures in IMF conduct. The reports contribute to ambiguity at the IMF. They often validate the critiques of less influential IMF members and external IMF watchers but do not dictate changes in IMF practices. The latter point was underscored in an early external evaluation of the IEO, which concluded that there is "little evidence that findings and recommendations . . . are being systemically taken up and followed by senior management and the Board" (Lissakers, Husain, and Woods 2006, 4). Nevertheless, IEO reports have legitimized a range of dissenting voices within the IMF and beyond, and have contributed to an environment where it is increasingly respectable for key actors to criticize and/or discount the Fund's policy positions.

70. The remainder of this paragraph draws on Kentikelenis, Stubbs, and King (2016).

71. The Fund developed precautionary facilities after the Asian crisis. It introduced several precautionary facilities during the global crisis. It launched the Short-Term Liquidity Facility in October 2008, replaced it with the FCL in March 2009, and introduced the Precautionary Credit Line (PCL) in 2010. Macedonia was the only country that applied for and received support under the PCL (in January 2011). In November 2011, the PCL was replaced by the Precautionary and Liquidity Line, which has only been used by Morocco. The replacement of one program by another is indicative of the IMF's inability to develop the right instrument and to appreciate the stigma and market signals associated with its support (Henning 2016, 123).

72. Mexico was the first to apply for an FCL. It was approved for US$47 billion in April 2009. In May 2009, Poland and Colombia were approved for US$20.5 billion and US$10.5 billion, respectively. These three countries have not drawn on the FCL,

and each has several times requested and been approved for new, larger lines as old ones expired.

73. One scholarly study of social spending targets in IMF concessional lending programs early in the global crisis concludes that there has been nearly universal incorporation of these targets into concessional loans (Clegg 2014).

74. Lütz and Kranke (2014, 320, 324) argue that in Hungary, Latvia, and Romania the IMF was more sensitive than its European partners to social protection. See Kattel and Raudla (2013) on conflict between the IMF and EU partners over internal devaluation in the Baltics.

75. Reinold (2016) identifies the same dynamic in explaining the IMF's failure to mainstream what it terms "social issues" (e.g., human rights and the right to food and shelter) despite much rhetoric about doing so. She also identifies this dynamic in the failure to act on Lagarde's frequent attention to income inequality and gender equity (discussed later).

76. As Mody (2016) observes, estimation of fiscal multipliers is arguably one of the IMF's areas of "core competency," so this failure is particularly damaging to its credibility. The IMF has a long history of issuing overly optimistic forecasts only to downgrade them later.

77. See also Ban (2015) on modest changes at the IMF regarding fiscal consolidation, and see also the discussion earlier in this chapter.

78. Other IMF research during the crisis is indicative of a new discomfort with "big finance." Gabor (2015) traces the emergence after 2010 of the IMF's view that transnational banks were, in its words, "super spreaders" of systemic risk and tended to engage in regulatory and tax arbitrage. Here, too, there is a gap between IMF research and practice, as Gabor demonstrates. Another high-profile IMF study expresses reservations about the size of the financial sector in several large AEs (Sahay et al. 2015). The authors argue that these economies suffer from "too much finance" and that banks and financial institutions that assume too big a share in the economy contribute more to economic and financial volatility than to growth.

79. The IMF also toyed with new ideas on tax policy. It issued tepid support in 2010 and 2013 for taxation of large financial institutions and more general progressive taxation (Claessens, Kean, and Pazarbasioglu 2010; IMF 2010b; 2013c). Some observers saw the Fund's *Fiscal Monitor Report* of October 2013 as advancing a case for a wealth tax (IMF 2013b). After the report was released, the institution quickly issued a press release to distance itself from this interpretation (IMF 2013d). The reversal illustrates the continued internal contestation over new ideas, and also the influence of key member states that sought to reframe what they saw as the IMF's message on taxation.

80. Though an advocate of strong continuity, Nelson (2017, 205) acknowledges discontinuity around IMF research (and capital controls).

81. Monetary and exchange rate policies have not figured into the European programs since most of these countries do not have independent monetary policy and several post-communist countries chose not to break their currency peg.

82. For citations of what I have called the continuity literature, see note 2 of this chapter.

83. Scattered throughout this chapter are references to the salient literature, such as Ban (2015), Ban and Gallagher (2015), Best (2014; 2016), Broome (2015), Clegg (2014), Grabel (2011), and Moschella (2010; 2014; 2016).

84. On change in other international organizations, see, for example, Sharma (2013) on discontinuities at the World Bank and Chorev (2013) on the World Health Organization. See Babb (2013) on change surrounding the Washington Consensus.

85. The essay does not address capital flow liberalization, though this is an area where IMF research and practice has evolved most unambiguously.

Chapter 6

1. Chin (2015, 307) advances a subtle interpretation of the kinds of changes examined in this chapter. He argues that, on the surface, the "rising powers" appear to have a status quo orientation toward and effect on the global financial architecture. But he urges a deeper, more patient treatment, highlighting the potential significance of their increased commitment to bilateralism and the renewal of interest in regional and subregional arrangements that respond to transnational economic (and security) problems. See also Armijo and Roberts (2014) and Fritz and Mühlich (2014).

2. See also Helleiner (2010), Ocampo (2006, chap. 1; 2010a; 2010b; 2011), and essays in Volz and Caliari (2010).

3. I thank Luis Rosero for this point.

4. Eichengreen (2015) proposes principles regarding the relationship between the IMF and regional financial arrangements.

5. On Asia, see Chin (2012); on Latin America, see Riggirozzi and Tussie (2012) and Armijo (2012); and for surveys, see Fritz and Mühlich (2014; 2015), Grabel (2013a), McKay, Volz, and Wölfinger (2011), Miyoshi (2013), Mühlich and Fritz (2016), Rana (2013), Rhee, Sumulong, and Vallée (2013), and Volz and Caliari (2010). For an examination that pre-dates the crisis see the essays in Ocampo (2006), especially Culpeper (2006). Peter Katzenstein's (2005) *A World of Regions* is a seminal contribution to the political science literature on regionalism. He argues that diverse regionalism(s) reshaped but did not displace a globalized world, an observation that resonates with the discussion of regional and other institutional innovations in this chapter.

6. See treatments along these lines by Chin (2015), Golub (2013), Grabel (2013a; 2015a), Helleiner (2016b), Huotari and Hanemann (2014), Mittelman (2013), Rana (2013), Sohn (2012), Tussie (2010), and Woods (2010).

7. See Culpeper (2006) and Ocampo (2006, chap. 1) on regional payment systems and regional macroeconomic and monetary integration in EMDEs prior to the global crisis.

8. Some of the reserve pooling entities described in this chapter are formally considered "arrangements," while others are considered "institutions." In the text, I will use each term as appropriate, though nothing of significance is implied by the terminological choice.

9. The discussion of the CMI/CMIM draws from AsDB (2010), Capannelli (2011), Ciorciari (2011), Cohen (2012), Eichengreen (2010; 2012), Fritz and Mühlich (2014), Grabel (2013a), Grimes (2009a; 2011; 2015), Henning (2009a), Kim and Yang (2014), Lombardi (2010), Miyoshi (2013), Rhee, Sumulong, and Vallée (2013), and Sussangkarn (2011), and personal communications with officials.

10. See Eichengreen (2012) and Haggard (2013) on the challenges of regional surveillance.

11. Given China's long-standing discomfort with the IMF, and its own commitment to policy autonomy, its insistence on an IMF link reveals the wariness with which many policymakers approach regional surveillance mechanisms. Of course, China did not expect to need assistance, so the IMF link was not expected to compromise *its* autonomy.

12. The Asian Bond Market Initiative was also expanded. CMIM was not given the capacity to issue its own bonds.

13. China and Japan each contribute 32%; Korea supplies 16%.

14. In order to address the latter issue, some have called for expanding the swap pool through broader membership, including India, Australia, and New Zealand (Lombardi 2010).

15. Personal communications with officials.

16. Kim and Yang (2014) are optimistic on this score; Eichengreen (2012) is pessimistic, especially in light of the ASEAN tradition of noninterference.

17. Katada and Sohn (2014) argue that the CMIM allows Japan and China to increase their bargaining power in global and regional financial governance without directly confronting Western powers.

18. Even some skeptics note that another crisis may propel further development; see Cohen (2012) and Grimes (2015).

19. Personal communication with official.

20. The AsDB and AMRO signed a memorandum of understanding to strengthen cooperation in May 2017.

21. Discussion of the FLAR draws on the institution's website and annual reports, and Eichengreen (2012), Fritz and Mühlich (2014), Grabel (2013a), McKay, Volz, and Wölfinger (2011), Miyoshi (2013), Mühlich and Fritz (2016), Ocampo and Titelman (2009–2010; 2012), Perry (2015), Rhee, Sumulong, and Vallée (2013), Rosero (2011; 2014), Titelman et al. (2014), Urrutia (2015), and personal communications with officials.

22. In 1984, the FLAR created a subregional currency, the Andean peso, which is an accounting unit created to facilitate payment among central banks and other authorized holders (Ocampo and Titelman 2012, 18).

23. Members are Bolivia, Colombia, Costa Rica, Ecuador, Paraguay, Peru, Uruguay, and Venezuela.

24. The FLAR has 52 permanent staff members (Miyoshi 2013, 33).

25. Lending to Peru was delayed in the late 1980s, however, while the country negotiated its arrears with other international institutions (Ocampo and Titelman 2012, 26).

26. The only exception involved two loans to Ecuador. A loan was approved in October 2005 but not disbursed until 2006, on the condition that newly elected president Palacio meet FLAR requirements that the government maintain a primary budget surplus of at least 2% of GDP during 2006–2008 and that a new central bank board be installed (Rosero 2014, 75). In 2009, the FLAR approved a US$480 million balance of payments credit to the country. But when the government rejected conditions that the FLAR usually attaches to loans, credit was extended to the central bank on the stipulation that it deposit US$250 million of reserves with the FLAR (Haggard 2013, 271).

27. This is also the case with Treasury credit lines.

28. The FLAR contributed just 7% of the resources to a Colombian rescue package in 1999. Its loan was part of a larger package from the IMF, IADB, World Bank, and the Andean Development Corporation (Rosero 2014, 70). FLAR members have on ten occasions drawn on the institution's resources while also receiving support from the IMF, though one was not conditioned on the other (Mühlich and Fritz 2016, 21). This happened most frequently in the 1980s and 1990s and involved Bolivia, Colombia, Ecuador, and Peru (ibid.).

29. During the global crisis, the IMF disbursed only one loan to a FLAR member, and that was to Ecuador. It disbursed an emergency loan to the country under the Rapid Financing Instrument following the 2016 earthquake. The IMF extended an SBA to FLAR member Costa Rica, though it was treated as precautionary and was not disbursed. In general, the IMF made relatively few traditional loans to Latin America

during the crisis, though it did make a number of loans to Caribbean countries. In addition, the IMF extended FCLs to Colombia and Mexico. The former is a FLAR member, while the latter is not.

30. Under the latter, each country would hold equal basic votes, and additional votes would be allocated based on contributions to a common fund and in proportion to claims on particular credit lines (Ocampo 2015a).

31. In the view of Titelman et al. (2014), an expanded FLAR should be sized to cope with "most likely" scenarios. See also Ocampo and Titelman (2012, 26) and Kawai and Lombardi (2012).

32. See Truman (2010) and especially Eichengreen (2015) on the problems of subordinating the IMF to regional financial arrangements.

33. Discussion of the ArMF draws on the institution's website and annual reports, and Ciorciari (2011), Corm (2006), Fritz and Mühlich (2014), Grabel (2013a), McKay, Volz, and Wölfinger (2011, 20–22), Miyoshi (2013), Mühlich and Fritz (2016), Rhee, Sumulong, and Vallée (2013), Titelman et al. (2014), and UNCTAD (2007,122).

34. Members include Jordan, United Arab Emirates, Bahrain, Tunisia, Algeria, Djibouti, Saudi Arabia, Sudan, Syria, Somalia, Iraq, Oman, Qatar, Kuwait, Lebanon, Libya, Egypt, Morocco, Mauritania, Yemen, Comoros, and the Palestinian Authority.

35. The technical staff comprises about 50 employees (McKay, Volz, and Wölfinger 2011, 21).

36. Data in this paragraph are from ArMF annual reports, except where noted.

37. The discussion of the EFSD draws on the institution's website and annual reports, and Fritz and Mühlich (2014), Miyoshi (2013), Mühlich and Fritz (2016), Rhee, Sumulong, and Vallée (2013), and personal communications with officials.

38. The countries include Armenia, Belarus, Kazakhstan, the Kyrgyz Republic, the Russian Federation, and Tajikistan.

39. The Russian government has committed not to borrow from the EFSD. The second-largest member in the EFSD, Kazakhstan, is not likely to draw on financial credits since (like Russia) it has oil reserves.

40. The Eurasian Development Bank was founded in 2006 by Russia, and the country contributes about two-thirds of its resources.

41. A member may elect to reallocate a portion of its access to another member state. Russia's decision to do so in 2011 made the large financial credit to Belarus possible (Miyoshi 2013, 43).

42. The discussion in this and the following paragraph draws on Armijo and Echeverri-Gent (2014), Armijo, Katada, and Roberts (2015), Chin (2014a), Ghosh

(2012), HKEx (2012), Mielniczuk (2013), Stuenkel (2013, 619–620, 626), Ustinova (2012), and Wade (2011, 365).

43. Details on the CRA drawn from BRICS (2014c). See Montes (2014) for examination of the treaty that establishes the CRA, including voting procedures and prioritization of creditors based in BRICS countries.

44. See Armijo and Roberts (2014), Chin (2015), and Stuenkel (2016a) on evolving thinking on the BRICS and other rising powers in relation to the global financial architecture.

45. Examples of arguments along these lines include Bond (2016), Chandrasekhar (2014), Eichengreen (2014), Patnaik (2015), Roy (2014), and Steil (2014).

46. See, for example, Ban and Blyth (2013), Fourcade (2013), Huotari and Hanemann (2014), and Palacio (2015).

47. On the new imperialism, see Bond (2016, 615–617; 2015) and Ferrando (2014); on the BRICS' significance, see Palacio (2015).

48. Examples of arguments along these lines include Armijo (2017), Bello (2014), Desai (2013), Grabel (2013a; 2015a), Griffith-Jones, Fritz, and Cintra (2014), Mielniczuk (2013), Montes (2014), Stuenkel (2016b), Ugarteche (2014), and Weisbrot (2014).

49. Henning (2016, 126, 134) examines the question of whether the CRA (and other regional or transregional reserve pooling arrangements) will or even should develop surveillance capacities and concludes that the IMF is the better institution to handle surveillance.

50. Economic historian Alexander Gerschenkron (1962) examined the important role of specialized financial institutions in overcoming the shortage of long-term capital in late industrializing nations in the late nineteenth century. For analyses and surveys of development banks, see Chandrasekhar (2015b; 2016), de Luna-Martínez and Vicente (2012), and Humphrey (2015b). See Amsden (1992; 2001) and Wade (2003[1990]) on development banks in a range of Asian countries; Mazzucato and Penna (2016) on the "market-correcting" and "market-shaping" roles of development banks; Humphrey (2015b) for comparisons between newly created banks and older ones; and Humphrey (2015a) on a range of multilateral development banks.

51. Trends in infrastructure finance at the IADB and AsDB are similar to those at the IBRD/IDA (Humphrey 2015a).

52. A study of the infrastructure gap by the AsDB (2017) estimates that "developing Asia" will need to invest US$26 trillion between 2016 and 2030—or more than double the US$750 billion that the AsDB estimated in 2009 (AsDB 2009). To put the figure in context, loan approvals by the AsDB in 2015 were US$15 billion.

53. The vast infrastructure investment gap and the need for sustainable infrastructure is reflected in the SDGs. Infrastructure figures explicitly in SDG number 19, which focuses on infrastructure. But it also figures in several others, such as goals 6, 7, 11, 13, and 17, which focus (respectively) on water, energy, sustainable cities, climate change, and partnerships for development. See Alexander (2014) and Bhattacharya, Oppenheim, and Stern (2015) for discussions of how infrastructure investment can facilitate inclusive, green development.

54. The acronym CAF is still used for legal reasons, so it will be used in what follows. Discussion of the CAF draws on the institution's website and annual reports, and Griffith-Jones, Griffith-Jones, and Hertova (2008), Humphrey (2014), Ocampo and Titelman (2012), and personal communications with officials.

55. Members include Argentina, Barbados, Bolivia, Brazil, Chile, Colombia, Costa Rica, the Dominican Republic, Ecuador, Jamaica, Mexico, Panama, Paraguay, Peru, Portugal, Spain, Trinidad and Tobago, Uruguay, and Venezuela. Fourteen private banks have ownership positions in the CAF.

56. Data in the balance of this paragraph draw from Ocampo and Titelman (2009–2010, 252; 2012).

57. Data in this paragraph and the next two are from the annual reports of the CAF and the IADB, except where noted.

58. The discussion in this paragraph draws from Griffith-Jones, Griffith-Jones, and Hertova (2008), except where noted.

59. I thank Luis Rosero for information on bond issuance by the CAF.

60. Discussion of the NDB draws from BRICS (2014a, 2014b), Chin (2014a), Griffith-Jones (2014), and especially Humphrey (2015b). Data on the World Bank and MRDBs are drawn from the institutions' websites and annual reports.

61. In September 2016, the institution's representatives announced that they were pursuing a credit rating (NDB 2016b).

62. See Alexander (2014) and Chandrasekhar (2015a) for critical examinations of the infrastructure boom.

63. The World Bank established a Global Infrastructure Facility in October 2014 as an entity outside the World Bank. The facility was launched in April 2015 with an initial capitalization of US$100 million. To date, outcomes have lagged aspirations. Various problems have limited the scope of this facility to pilot projects and preparatory work (Arezki et al. 2016).

64. In addition to the arguments advanced against the CRA, critics argue that the NDB represents the "old development as infrastructure view" (Rodrik 2013). Others argue that the NDB is not inherently progressive insofar as it does not mark a break with traditional powers and that it is neither green, democratic, nor inclusive of

EMDEs beyond the BRICS themselves. See Bond (2015; 2016), Chandrasekhar (2014), Ferrando (2014), Patnaik (2015), and Steil (2014). Possibilists acknowledge these risks but nevertheless recognize the NDB as an evolving institutional experiment with potential, even if with no guarantees. For this view, see Armijo (2017), Bello (2014), Chin (2014a), Desai (2013), Eichengreen (2014), Grabel (2013a; 2015a), Griffith-Jones (2014), and Stuenkel (2016a).

65. Japan and the United States are the AsDB's largest shareholders, followed by China. The United States and Japan each have voting rights that are nearly equal to one another and well over twice those of China. The president of the AsDB is always from Japan.

66. The discussion of these and other financial initiatives led by China draws on the AIIB website, Chin (2016), Dollar (2015), Elgin-Cossart and Hart (2015), Gallagher, Kamal, and Wang (2016), Griffith-Jones, Xiaoyun, and Spratt (2016), He (2016), and Humphrey (2015b).

67. In April 2017 the AIIB and the World Bank signed a memorandum of understanding that signals increasing cooperation and promises increased lending capacity for both institutions.

68. In the lead-up to the launch of the bank, China was apparently willing to reduce its voting rights and forgo veto power if the United States and Japan joined. It appears that the matter of China's voting rights remains negotiable should new members join (Chin 2016, 13; Humphrey 2015b, 26).

69. Chin (2016, 17) suggests that this board structure may have a demonstration effect for the World Bank and that it is notable that the World Bank recently began a review of its governance.

70. This contrasts with the NDB, where discussion of a similar document was confined to founding member countries.

71. A final round of public comment on a revised energy strategy document concluded in March 2017.

72. It is unclear if this commitment is more or less solid than that of the World Bank. Following U.S. president Obama's lead in 2013, the World Bank announced in the same year that it would lend for coal-fired electricity generation projects only in "rare circumstances" (Chin 2016, 19).

73. For instance, a 2016 report by an advocacy organization finds that the World Bank's International Finance Corporation has supported institutions that have funded at least 41 new coal projects since the 2013 decision on coal-fired plants (IDI 2016).

74. The Belt and Road initiative was announced in late 2013 and is articulated in a detailed document released in early 2015 (Ministries of Foreign Affairs and Commerce 2015).

75. The "S" for social was added in 1982.

76. The discussion of BNDES draws on the institution's website and annual reports, and Armijo (2017), Armijo and Echeverri-Gent (2014), Hochstetler (2014a), Hochstetler and Montero (2012; 2013), Studart and Ramos (2016), Tavares de Araujo (2013), and Torres Filho (2011).

77. As of this writing, it is uncertain whether BNDES will continue to play as central a role, given Brazil's economic and political turmoil, scandals that have damaged the institution, and the current government's decided tilt toward the market.

78. Another controversy concerns the dependence of BNDES on transfers from the national treasury, especially after 2009 (Studart and Ramos 2016, 21–22).

79. The discussion of the CDB draws on the institution's website and annual reports, Bräutigam and Gallagher (2014), Gallagher, Kamal, and Wang (2016), Gallagher, Koleski, and Irwin (2012), and Wang (2016).

80. Data in this paragraph and the next are drawn from the annual reports of the CDB and World Bank. The combined assets of the CDB and the country's Export-Import Bank are over US$2 trillion, whereas the combined assets of the World Bank Group and the MRDBs are just over US$700 billion (Gallagher, Kamal, and Wang 2016).

81. The CDB has also been promoting the cross-border use of the country's currency for international trade and investment through a variety of means, such as selling renminbi-denominated bonds outside the Chinese mainland beginning in 2007. Armijo, Katada, and Roberts (2014, 16) note that "by 2014, more than 22% of China's trade was being settled in renminbi, up from almost nothing five years previously." China's central bank also used currency swaps during the global crisis as an alternative mechanism of financing and trade settlement. Ultimately it established a network of 23 bilateral local currency swap agreements at a total value of RMB2.57 trillion with Asian and non-Asian central banks. The network facilitated trade settlements by providing access to the renminbi, boosted the role of the renminbi by increasing the share of China's trade invoiced and settled in renminbi, and promoted market confidence during a period of fragility (Chin 2014b; Henning 2016, 129; Huotari and Hanemann 2014; Jiang 2014).

82. The discussion in this paragraph summarizes research by Bräutigam and Gallagher (2014). See Bräutigam (2009) on the country's loans (and other financial flows) to Africa prior to the crisis. See Gallagher (2016) on China's role as a dominant lender to Latin America.

83. The World Bank and the MRDBs provided about US$118 billion in energy-related financing in the same period (Gallagher, Kamal, and Wang 2016).

84. The discussion in this paragraph draws on Hochstetler (2014b).

85. I do not discuss two European banks, the European Bank for Reconstruction and Development (EBRD) and the European Investment Bank (EIB). The EBRD operates more like a commercial bank than a development bank (insofar as around 80% of its loans are to the private sector). The EIB operates mainly in industrialized European countries, and only a small share of its operations are outside the EU (Humphrey 2015a, table 1). See Babb (2009, chap. 1) on the EBRD, and Griffith-Jones, Griffith-Jones, and Hertova (2008) and Ocampo et al. (2012) on the EIB. See Babb (2009) and Strand (2014) for analyses of the MRDBs.

86. Data and discussion in this paragraph and the next two draw on Ocampo et al. (2012, especially 65–69), except where noted.

87. Data for the World Bank are from 2016, data for the IADB are from 2013, and data for the AsDB and AfDB are from 2012 (World Bank Group 2016; Humphrey 2015a, 13, figure 14).

88. Gross disbursements by the EIB of US$69.7 billion during 2015 exceeded those of the World Bank Group. World Bank Group data are reported on a fiscal year basis; AfDB, AsDB, EIB, and IADB data are as of December 31, 2015. Data are from the institutions' annual reports.

89. In contrast, China has been increasing the paid-in capital for both the CDB and its Export-Import Bank (Gallagher, Kamal, and Wang 2016).

90. See Bradlow and Humphrey (2016) for a survey of development banks in Africa, which they argue are mostly quite small, have limited access to finance, and insufficient capacity.

91. ALBA members include Venezuela, Bolivia, Ecuador, Cuba, Nicaragua, Dominica, St. Vincent and the Grenadines, Antigua and Barbuda, St. Kitts and Nevis, St. Lucia, and Grenada. In 2006, ALBA expanded to include the Peoples' Trade Treaty (Spanish acronym TCP), and in 2009 it accordingly became ALBA-TCP. ALBA members Antigua and Barbuda, St. Kitts and Nevis, St. Lucia, and Grenada are not members of the Bank of ALBA.

92. The most widely known of ALBA's projects involves the Unitary System for Regional Compensation (Spanish acronym SUCRE), which is a regional payment system created in October 2009 (see Fritz and Mühlich 2014). ALBA's portfolio of projects broadened beyond the SUCRE and the Bank of ALBA during the time that Venezuela enjoyed large oil revenues and several members had populist governments. ALBA moved into South-South aid and concessional financing via Petrocaribe, a Venezuelan program to provide oil to Haiti at preferential prices; exchanges with Cuba in which subsidized oil is bartered for medical services, education, and pharmaceuticals; and a variety of human development and capacity-building programs (Baranyi, Feldmann, and Bernier 2015; Riggirozzi 2012a; 2012b).

93. The discussion of ALBA draws on Armijo (2012), Baranyi, Feldmann, and Bernier (2015), Fritz and Mühlich (2014), Riggirozzi (2012a; 2012b), and Rosales (2013).

94. SUCRE officials report in personal communications that as of the end of November 2016, the payment system was still operating despite the challenges facing Venezuela's economy.

95. Members of the BDS include Argentina, Bolivia, Brazil, Ecuador, Paraguay, Uruguay, and Venezuela. The discussion of the BDS draws on Armijo (2012), Marshall (2010), Marshall and Rochon (2009), Riggirozzi (2012a), Rosales (2013), Rosero and Erten (2010), and personal communications.

96. See Rosales (2013) and Bond (2016, 614) on Brazil's role in reshaping the BDS vision.

97. Many of the participants (myself included) at a simultaneous meeting at the same venue where the BDS reached and announced this agreement were consequently surprised by the news.

98. Personal communication with official.

99. Disbursal criteria for both forms of support available from the CMIM and CRA are currently under consideration.

100. In a related vein, Weller and Zulfiqar (2013) show that greater financial market diversity (i.e., different types of institutions serving different constituencies) can contribute to stability.

Chapter 7

1. See Ghosh and Qureshi (2016), Helleiner (1994), and Neely (1999). The turn away from capital controls began at the IMF during the 1970s (Chwieroth 2010).

2. On broader programs of financial liberalization, see Grabel (1995) and Arestis (2017). On complementary central bank reforms, see Epstein (2006).

3. Investor antipathy toward capital controls continued through the next decade. Controls in Thailand were reversed by the central bank within a few days after their implementation in December 2006 (following a coup) after they triggered massive capital flight (Adam and Kate 2010).

4. On Keynesian support for capital controls prior to the global crisis, see, for example, Chang and Grabel (2014[2004]), Crotty (1983; 1990), Crotty and Epstein (1996), Epstein, Grabel, and Jomo K. S. (2004), Epstein (2005), and Grabel (2003a; 2003c; 2003d; 2004).

5. Other observers remained skeptical about the lessons of Malaysia's outflow controls. Magud and Reinhart (2006) argue that outflow controls succeeded in Malaysia

but had inconclusive effects elsewhere, and Abdelal and Alfaro (2003) conclude that Malaysia's experience holds few lessons for other countries. Research by IMF staff during the global crisis supports what is by now a sanguine consensus view on Malaysia's controls (Saborowski et al. 2014, 5–6). The IMF's Lagarde in a 2012 speech even commended the country for "being ahead of the curve in this area" (Lagarde 2012).

6. The IEO report (IEO 2005, 48) finds that during and after the Asian crisis, the IMF "displayed sympathy with some countries in the use of capital controls and . . . even suggested that market-based measures could be introduced as a prudential measure." The report documents that the IMF supported the use of capital controls in 7 of the 12 countries it assisted, that in 2 of these countries it advised policymakers to deploy controls as part of their overall reform recommendations, and that on balance its support for controls increased following the Asian crisis. That said, the report rightly acknowledges that there was a lack of consistency in the IMF's advice regarding controls in the years following the Asian crisis.

7. In addition to the constructivist insights introduced in the discussion of the IMF (see chapter 5), we should take note here of others that are relevant for the rebranding of capital controls. Chwieroth (2015) offers the useful idea of "stigma management." Elsewhere he explores the informal, internal norm entrepreneurship within the IMF (Chwieroth 2010), and relatedly the layering of new policies over old ones (Chwieroth 2014). Abdelal (2007) explores processes by which leaders of international organizations sought to rewrite formal rules around capital liberalization; Moschella (2009; 2012; 2014) examines the incremental change around capital controls and the interaction between ideas and the political environment; and Nelson (2014a) and Kirshner (2003) highlight the pragmatism of actors at the IMF who may abandon sanctified views of liberalization during crises when they come to obstruct what is perceived to be effective intervention. See also Mahoney and Thelen (2010, chap. 1) on messy, incremental processes of change.

8. Five factors play critical roles in the extraordinary evolution regarding capital controls (see Grabel 2015b). These include: (1) the rise of increasingly autonomous EMDEs, largely as a consequence of their successful response to the Asian crisis and the fortuitous economic conditions that followed; (2) the increasing confidence and assertiveness of their policymakers, in part as a consequence of their relative success during the early years of the global crisis, when many AEs stumbled; (3) a pragmatic adjustment by the IMF to an altered global economy in which the geography of its influence was severely restricted and in which it became financially dependent on its former clients; (4) the intensification of the need for capital controls by countries facing a range of economic circumstances; and (5) the evolution in the ideas of academic economists and IMF staff concerning the trade-offs involved in capital flow liberalization and the consequences of this liberalization. I have discussed the first

three of these factors in chapters 3 and 5. The fourth and fifth factors are the subject of the discussion that follows.

9. Some scholars reject the idea of incoherence and discontinuity regarding controls (Gabor 2012; Güven 2012, 875; Helleiner 2014b; Nelson 2014a). In recent work, Nelson (2017) and Helleiner (2016b) see the matter differently.

10. Though I do not explore the matter here, the range of countercyclical macroeconomic policies adopted during the global crisis represent another indicator of increased EMDE policy space. Ocampo et al. (2012) provide an extensive examination of countercyclical policies in EMDEs, and we draw on this work here. China deployed the most ambitious countercyclical support—equivalent to about 14% of its GDP in 2009 and 2010. Sub-Saharan African countries (i.e., Kenya, Mauritius, South Africa, and Tanzania) adopted more modest programs. In Latin America, the picture was more mixed. This record represents a radical departure from the recent past, when EMDE policymakers generally had no alternative but to implement strongly procyclical policies in the context of liberalized international capital flows, most often per the conditions of IMF assistance. EMDE policymakers could implement countercyclical strategies because of the enabling effects of prior reserve accumulation strategies and the related growth in SWFs. SWF resources were used inter alia to stabilize domestic stock markets and banking systems, and even foreign economies (BIS 2009, 153; Campanella 2012, 20; Park and van der Hoorn 2012).

11. The G-20 did not explicitly address capital controls as a protective response to the crisis until late in 2010 at its Seoul summit, when it charged the IMF with examining the matter. Chwieroth (2014; 2015) suggests that the G-20's timid and late focus on capital flows reflects U.S. policy preferences and influence.

12. The process of setting negative interest rates was triggered by the ECB in June 2014. The central banks of Japan, Sweden, Switzerland, and Denmark followed suit, and the ECB itself undertook three additional rounds of rate cutting. Lagarde's support of negative interest rates reflects the desperation of the times. Of these, she said: "If we had not had those negative rates, we would be in a much worse place today, with inflation probably lower than where it is, with growth probably lower than where we have it" (Jaffe 2016).

13. The difference in interest rates between nations is known as the "carry." The practice of borrowing at low rates and investing at high rates is accordingly referred to as "carry trade" activity.

14. The figure for China includes US$216 billion in unrecorded outflows in errors and omissions.

15. See Akyüz (2016) on the end of the "super commodity cycle," which he and others see as partly resulting from the slowdown in China and massive excess supply in many markets.

16. Compared with the previous five years, EMDE currencies experienced their second-largest daily sales volume a few days after the U.S. election; foreign investors withdrew approximately US$7 billion from EMDE markets in the week following the election (*Economist* 2016c).

17. See Chwieroth (2015) on the country's successful "counter-stigmatization" of controls, and Gallagher (2014) and especially Fritz and Prates (2014) on the political economy of its controls.

18. In an example of the stickiness of old views, in August 2010, Canadian prime minister Harper used some of his time in Brazil to lecture the government about dismantling controls (Mayeda 2011).

19. Personal communication with a former Indonesian central bank staff member.

20. Iceland's "temporary" outflow controls have turned out to be rather long lived—indeed the central bank and the Finance Ministry did not begin to remove them until October 2016, in a gradual process set to continue into 2017. As recently as June 2016, the central bank introduced a new capital control to protect the economy from inflows driven by exchange rate fluctuations and differences between the country's interest rates and those elsewhere. This new control took the form of a reserve requirement against certain foreign currency inflows (and involved a one-year holding period) (Central Bank of Iceland 2016). In a statement announcing an upgrade in the country's sovereign debt rating in 2016, Moody's favorably noted the cautious nature of the liberalization program while also highlighting the continued risks of removing controls (Moody's 2016b). The new inflow control was tightened in March 2017 at the same time as the country's remaining outflow controls were eliminated (*Economist* 2017c).

21. In late 2008, Ukraine attempted to stem outflows and defend the currency by implementing a five-day waiting period for nonresident conversions of domestic currency into foreign currency (IEO 2015, 13). According to the IEO, the IMF recommended removal of the country's controls as quickly as possible in the context of an SBA, and the Fund noted that Ukraine's controls did not work (IEO 2015, 13; Saborowski et al. 2014).

22. Fitch downgraded Cyprus's Hellenic Bank, but this seems to reflect the surprisingly sudden observation that the country's banking system was bloated with laundered Russian money.

23. Greek officials removed some controls in July 2016 in hopes of attracting deposits. However, restrictions on many types of cash transactions remain in place as of May 2017 and are expected to stay in effect through 2018 (*Financial Times* 2016b; Chrysopoulos 2017).

24. Subacchi (2016; 2017) argues that managed convertibility has thus far been associated with the very problems that it was designed to avoid; namely, outflows

that have necessitated sustained currency intervention, depleted reserves, and an erosion of confidence in the currency. These problems were predictable, and indeed were predicted (Bayoumi and Ohnsorge 2013).

25. Increased renminbi convertibility has been a goal since 1993, and was reiterated in 2013 (Wildau 2015).

26. Some of these measures were loosened in 2015.

27. A separate annex (i.e., a "carve-out") to the TPP would have allowed Chile to maintain or enact capital controls consistent with its own domestic laws to ensure financial stability, but such a carve-out was not negotiated for other TPP signatories.

28. Lisbon Treaty obligations precluded the use of capital controls by countries on the European periphery during the crisis (with the important exceptions noted earlier). On paper, such countries enjoy less policy space than many EMDEs.

29. On the EC's approval of capital controls in Cyprus, see Higgins (2013). On Greece, see Reuters (2015a).

30. Chile had to settle for a "cooling off" provision that prevents a U.S. investor from filing a claim for damages related to the use of controls until one year after they are deployed. By contrast, Korea's 2007 trade agreement with the United States allows temporary controls under certain circumstances. The greater leeway granted to Korea reflected the country's greater bargaining power with U.S. negotiators, who sought access to particular sectors of Korea's economy (see Gallagher 2014, chap. 8, 181, 192–195). The U.S. concession proved consequential: although Korea is an OECD member, it was nevertheless able to implement capital controls (labeled as macroprudential regulations) during the global crisis without raising the ire of other members.

31. NAFTA includes a balance of payments exception that allows capital controls when the host states "experience serious balance of payments difficulties, or the threat thereof," but use of this exception must be temporary and nondiscriminatory (Gallagher 2014, 181).

32. The renormalization of capital controls may involve rebranding, the focus of this chapter, and/or the reframing of capital controls as something other than capital controls. The former represents a more direct assault on the preexisting neoliberal ideology and is expected where states have achieved substantial policy autonomy. The latter amounts to "cheating"—attempting to use a strategy that is not permitted under the neoliberal rules of the game without admitting it. We should expect this strategy in cases where states have not achieved significant policy autonomy. In a case like Korea, it is difficult to discriminate between the two strategies. Capital controls are taken to be valuable policy instruments that are central to Korean economic governance, which suggests rebranding, but the

government has been very careful to refer to its strategies as macroprudential measures while avoiding altogether the use of the term capital controls, suggesting reframing. See Chwieroth (2015) on Korea's policies.

33. Recall that (as noted earlier) Carstens spoke more pragmatically about controls in January 2016.

34. See also Heathcoate and Perri (2016).

35. That this work is marketed as "new" says much about the state of economics.

36. Ghosh, Qureshi, and Sugawara (2014) also cite Keynes and White in arguing for international coordination, but they also recognize the impediments to coordination, including administrative deficiencies and treaty obligations.

37. Adair Turner, former chair of the United Kingdom's Financial Services Authority, takes note of the staying power of the liberalization ideal despite empirical evidence against it (Turner 2014).

38. We should of course not presume that developments at these three levels necessarily unfold in a lockstep manner. What is remarkable about the current conjuncture, however, is the degree to which there have been parallel developments on all three levels concerning capital controls.

39. Even though they do not represent the IMF's official position (and do not require member state approval), Staff Discussion Notes (such as Ostry et al. 2011) are nevertheless authorized for distribution. Thus, they are important documents in tracking the evolution of thinking at the IMF. Indeed, Ostry et al. (2011) and Ostry, Ghosh, and Korinek (2012) were authorized by no less than Olivier Blanchard.

40. See Gallagher (2015a, 14) on conflict over last resort language.

41. See Fritz and Prates (2014) for a critique of the Institutional View on these and other grounds.

42. Chwieroth (2014) argues that the greater equivocation on controls in the Institutional View reflects the fact that official documents require member state approval, whereas reports such as Staff Position Notes and Staff Discussion Notes do not.

43. An IMF review of experiences with the Institutional View issued at the end of 2016 reiterates findings from the previous studies discussed, while making oblique reference to differing opinions among IMF executive directors (IMF 2016a).

44. Notably, Kentikelenis, Stubbs, and King (2016, 15) did not find in the last decade a single instance of IMF conditionality that required capital account liberalization.

45. Managing capital controls through multilateral rules has long been a French preoccupation (Abdelal 2007).

46. See Gallagher (2014, chap. 6) on the ability of the BRICS and other EMDEs to move the IMF on capital controls by working within the institution and through leverage gained by working in the G-20.

47. See Moschella (2015b) on codes of conduct around capital controls and the broader "legalization" trend.

48. Another possibility is that conflict over controls has decisively shifted from the economic to the legal arena of investment and trade agreements, as I suggested earlier.

49. On the matter of blunt versus targeted controls, Rodrik (2015b) argues that "limited controls that target specific markets . . . do not have a significant impact on key outcomes—the exchange rate, monetary independence, or domestic financial stability." He argues that "capital controls may need to be blunt and comprehensive, rather than surgical and targeted, to be truly effective." By contrast, Stiglitz and Rashid (2016a) advocate a more cautious (and, in my view, less helpful) approach, arguing that turbulence in EMDEs may necessitate quick action that includes targeted and time-bound capital controls, especially on outflows.

50. On these views, see Horsefield (1969, 31, 65) and Steil (2013, 134, 150).

51. I thank Roy Culpeper for this point and for reference to Chakrabortty (2016), who linked the tax avoidance revealed in the Panama Papers to Hirschman's exit and voice.

Chapter 8

1. The paramount exception to the new pragmatism is the reactionary political movement that now appears to be spreading across the AEs, which is rooted in a romanticized longing for a utopian past.

2. As of this writing, the IMF is again pushing back against the position taken by Eurozone officials (see chapter 5).

3. See DeMartino (2011; 2013b), Gibson-Graham (2011), and Gibson-Graham and Roelvink (2010) for poststructuralist accounts of the "productiveness of ignorance" that accord well with Hirschman's view and with the arguments I advance here.

4. One can concede the point while also recognizing that a better response would have entailed expansionary and redistributive fiscal policies and new measures that placed more stringent controls over the financial sector (such as on capital outflows from AEs and on the activities of lenders and other financial actors).

5. Rodrik develops this point most explicitly in his essay "A Plan B for Global Finance" (Rodrik 2009b) and elaborates on it in other work (e.g., Rodrik 2001; 2007b; 2007–2008; 2011).

6. See the discussion of other EMDE networks in Woods and Martinez-Diaz (2009).

7. That said, the SDGs also call for a greater role for private financial flows than is desirable given the inherent instability and "short-termism" that marks liberalized financial markets.

References

Abdelal, Rawi. 2007. *Capital Rules: The Construction of Global Finance.* Cambridge, MA: Harvard University Press.

Abdelal, Rawi, and Laura Alfaro. 2003. "Capital and Control: Lessons from Malaysia." *Challenge* 46 (4): 36–53.

Abdelal, Rawi, Mark Blyth, and Craig Parsons, eds. 2010. *Constructing the International Economy.* Ithaca, NY: Cornell University Press.

Abdelal, Rawi, and Jonathan Kirshner. 1999–2000. "Strategy, Economic Relations, and the Definition of National Interests." *Security Studies* 9 (1–2): 119–156.

Achebe, Chinua. 1992[1958]. *Things Fall Apart.* New York: Knopf.

Adam, Shamin, and Dan Ten Kate. 2010. "Asia Should Consider Capital Controls to Stem Asset-Bubble Risks, UN Says." Bloomberg, May 6. http://www.bloomberg.com /news/articles/2010-05-06/asia-should-consider-capital-controls-to-stem-asset -bubble-risks-un-says.

Adelman, Jeremy. 2013a. *The Essential Hirschman.* Princeton, NJ: Princeton University Press.

Adelman, Jeremy. 2013b. *Worldly Philosopher: The Odyssey of Albert O. Hirschman.* Princeton, NJ: Princeton University Press.

Adelman, Jeremy, Michele Alacevich, Victoria de Grazia, Ira Katznelson, and Nadia Urbinati. 2015. "Albert Hirschman and the Social Sciences: A Memorial Roundtable." *Humanity* 6 (2): 265–286. doi: 0.1353/hum.2015.0022.

African Development Bank (AfDB). 2016. "Annual Reports." Accessed December 20. https://www.afdb.org/en/knowledge/publications/annual-report/annual-report -2016/.

Agayev, Zulfugar. 2016. "Azeri Leader Rejects Bill to Tax Outflows of Foreign Currency." Bloomberg, February 10. http://www.bloomberg.com/news/articles/2016-02 -10/azeri-leader-rejects-bill-to-tax-outflows-of-foreign-currency.

Agosin, Manuel. 2001. "Strengthening Regional Financial Cooperation." *CEPAL Review*, no. 73:31–50.

Aizenman, Joshua. 2009. "Hoarding International Reserves versus a Pigouvian Tax-cum-Subsidy Scheme: Reflections on the Deleveraging Crisis of 2008–09, and a Cost Benefit Analysis." NBER Working Paper No. 15484. Cambridge, MA: National Bureau of Economic Research. http://www.nber.org/papers/w15484.

Akyüz, Yilmaz. 2013. "Waving or Drowning: Developing Countries after the Financial Crisis." South Centre Research Paper No. 48. Geneva: South Centre. http://g24.org /wp-content/uploads/2014/03/RP48_Waving-or-drowning_EN.pdf.

Akyüz, Yilmaz. 2016. "Grim Economic Situation Calls for Bold Measures." *Third World Resurgence*, nos. 307–308:15–18.

Alacevich, Michele. 2014. "Visualizing Uncertainties, or How Albert Hirschman and the World Bank Disagreed on Project Appraisal and What This Says about the End of 'High Development Theory.'" *Journal of the History of Economic Thought* 36 (2): 137–168.

Alacevich, Michele. 2015. "Albert Hirschman Observed: Afterword," afterword to *Development Projects Observed*, by Albert O. Hirschman, 175–190. Washington, DC: Brookings Institution Press.

Alacevich, Michele. 2016. "Albert O. Hirschman." In *Handbook of Alternative Theories of Economic Development*, edited by Erik Reinert, Jayati Ghosh, and Rainer Kattel, 456–474. Cheltenham: Edward Elgar.

Alesina, Alberto, and Silvia Ardagna. 2009. "Large Changes in Fiscal Policy: Taxes versus Spending." NBER Working Paper No. 15438. Cambridge, MA: National Bureau of Economic Research.

Alexander, Nancy. 2014. *The Emerging Multi-polar World Order: Its Unprecedented Consensus on a New Model for Financing Infrastructure Investment and Development.* Washington, DC: Heinrich Böll Foundation North America. http://us.boell.org/sites /default/files/alexander_multi-polar_world_order_1.pdf.

Amsden, Alice. 1992. *Asia's Next Giant: South Korea and Late Industrialization.* Oxford: Oxford University Press.

Amsden, Alice. 2001. *The Rise of "the Rest": Challenges to the West from Late Industrializing Countries.* Oxford: Oxford University Press.

Amyx, Jennifer. 2008. "Regional Financial Cooperation in East Asia since the Asian Financial Crisis." In *Crisis as Catalyst: Asia's Dynamic Political Economy*, edited by Andrew Macintyre, T. J. Pempel, and John Ravenhill, 117–139. Ithaca, NY: Cornell University Press.

Anderlini, Jamil. 2015. "Beijing Clamps Down on Forex Deals to Stem Capital Flight." *Financial Times*, September 9. http://www.ft.com/intl/cms/s/0/0f825e12-56cf-11e5 -a28b-50226830d644.html.

Aquino, Norman, and Clarissa Batino. 2012. "Philippines Joins Korea in Restraining Currency Gains: Economy." Bloomberg, December 26. http://www.bloomberg.com /news/articles/2012-12-26/philippines-imposes-currency-forward-caps-to-restrain -peso-surge.

Arab Monetary Fund (ArMF). 2016. "Annual Reports." Accessed December 20. http:// www.amf.org.ae/en/annual_reports.

Arab Monetary Fund (ArMF). 2017. Website. Accessed January 10. http://www.amf .org.ae/en.

Arestis, Philip. 2017. "Financial Liberalization, the Finance-Growth Nexus, Financial Crises and Policy Implications." In *Financial Liberalisation: Past, Present and Future*, edited by Philip Arestis and Malcolm Sawyer, 1–42. Basingstoke: Palgrave Macmillan.

Arezki, Rabah, Patrick Bolton, Sanjay Peters, Frederic Samama, and Joseph Stiglitz. 2016. "From Global Savings Glut to Financing of Infrastructure." IMF Working Paper No. 18. Washington, DC: International Monetary Fund. https://www.imf.org /external/pubs/cat/longres.aspx?sk=43689.0.

Armijo, Leslie Elliott. 2012. "Equality and Multilateral Financial Cooperation in the Americas." desiguALdades.net Working Paper Series No. 29. Berlin: Research Network on Interdependent Inequalities in Latin America. http://www.desigualdades .net/Working_Papers/Search-Working-Papers/Working-Paper-29-_Equality-and -Multilateral-Financial-Cooperation-in-the-Americas_/index.html.

Armijo, Leslie Elliott. 2017. "The Public Bank Trilemma: Brazil's New Developmentalism and the BNDES." In *Democratic Brazil Ascendant*, edited by Peter Kingstone and Timothy Power, 230–247. Pittsburgh, PA: University of Pittsburgh Press.

Armijo, Leslie Elliott, and John Echeverri-Gent. 2014. "Brave New World? The Politics of International Finance in Brazil and India." In *Financial Statecraft of Emerging Powers: Shield and Sword in Asia and Latin America*, edited by Leslie Eliot Armijo and Saori N. Katada, 47–76. Basingstoke: Palgrave Macmillan.

Armijo, Leslie Elliot, and Saori N. Katada. 2015. "Theorizing the Financial Statecraft of Emerging Powers." *New Political Economy* 20 (1): 42–62.

Armijo, Leslie Elliott, Saori N. Katada, and Cynthia Roberts. 2015. "The Collective Financial Statecraft of the BRICS: Hanging Together, but Why and How?" Paper presented at the International Studies Association Annual Convention, New Orleans, LA, February 16–21.

Armijo, Leslie Elliott, and Cynthia Roberts. 2014. "The Emerging Powers and Global Governance: Why the BRICS Matter." In *Handbook of Emerging Economies*, edited by Robert Looney, 503–524. London: Routledge.

ASEAN+3. 2016. "Joint Statement of the 19th ASEAN+3 Finance Ministers' and Central Bank Governors' Meeting, 3 May 2016, Frankfurt, Germany. May 3. http://asean

.org/joint-statement-19th-asean3-finance-ministers-central-bank-governors-meeting
-3-may-2016-frankfurt-germany/.

ASEAN+3 Macroeconomic Research Office (AMRO). 2016a. "Key Points for Strengthening the CMIM, Annex 1." AMRO, April. http://www.amro-asia.org/key-points-for
-strengthening-the-cmim/.

ASEAN+3 Macroeconomic Research Office (AMRO). 2016b. "Strengthening a Multilayered Global Financial Safety Net Is Critical to Secure Macroeconomic and Financial
Stability." AMRO, October 6. http://www.amro-asia.org/strengthening-a-multi-layered
-global-financial-safety-net-is-critical-to-secure-macroeconomic-and-financial-stability/.

ASEAN+3 Macroeconomic Research Office (AMRO). 2017. Website. Accessed January 10.
http://www.amro-asia.org.

Asian Development Bank (AsDB). 2009. *Infrastructure for a Seamless Asia*. Manila:
AsDB and Asian Development Bank Institute. https://www.adb.org/sites/default
/files/publication/159348/adbi-infrastructure-seamless-asia.pdf.

Asian Development Bank (AsDB). 2010. *Institutions for Regional Integration: Towards
an Asian Economic Community*. Manila: AsDB.

Asian Development Bank (AsDB). 2011. *Asian Capital Markets Monitor*. Manila: AsDB,
August. http://www.adb.org/publications/asia-capital-markets-monitor-august-2011.

Asian Development Bank (AsDB). 2016. "Annual Reports." Accessed December 20.
https://www.adb.org/documents/series/adb-annual-reports.

Asian Development Bank (AsDB). 2017. "Meeting Asia's Infrastructure Needs."
Manila: AsDB, February. https://www.adb.org/sites/default/files/publication/227496
/special-report-infrastructure.pdf.

Asian Development Bank (AsDB) and Inter-American Development Bank (IADB).
2012. *Shaping the Future of Asia—Latin America and the Caribbean Relationship*. Manila:
AsDB, IADB, and Asian Development Bank Institute.

Asian Infrastructure Investment Bank (AIIB). 2016a. *AIIB Energy Strategy: Sustainable
Energy for Asia. Issues Note for Discussion*. Beijing: AIIB, October. https://www.aiib.org
/en/news-events/news/2016/_download/aiib-energy-strategy-sustainable-energy-for
-asia-issues-note-for-discussion.pdf.

Asian Infrastructure Investment Bank (AIIB). 2016b. *Articles of Agreement*. Beijing: AIIB.
Accessed October 6. https://www.aiib.org/en/about-aiib/basic-documents/articles-of
-agreement/index.html.

Asian Infrastructure Investment Bank (AIIB). 2017. Website. Accessed January 10.
http://www.aiib.org.

Azis, Iwan. 2011. "Assessing Asian Economic Integration with Cautionary Notes."
Journal of Northeast Asia Development 13:17–42. http://iwanazis.com/files/documents

/Iwan-Azis-Paper-Assessing-Asian-Economic-Integration-with-Cautionary-Notes
2011.pdf.

Babb, Sarah. 2003. "The IMF in Sociological Perspective: A Tale of Organizational
Slippage." *Studies in Comparative International Development* 38 (2): 3–27.

Babb, Sarah. 2009. *Behind the Development Banks*. Chicago: University of Chicago
Press.

Babb, Sarah. 2013. "The Washington Consensus as Transnational Policy Paradigm:
Its Origins, Trajectory and Likely Successor." *Review of International Political Economy*
20 (2): 268–297.

Ban, Cornel. 2013. "On the Road to Damascus: Ambiguity and Continuity at the IMF."
Triple Crisis, April 18. http://triplecrisis.com/on-the-road-to-damascus-ambiguity-and
-continuity-at-the-imf/.

Ban, Cornel. 2015. "Austerity versus Stimulus? Understanding Fiscal Policy Change
at the International Monetary Fund since the Great Recession." *Governance* 28 (2):
167–183.

Ban, Cornel. 2016. *Ruling Ideas: How Global Neoliberalism Goes Local*. Oxford: Oxford
University Press.

Ban, Cornel, and Mark Blyth. 2013. "The BRICs and the Washington Consensus: An
Introduction." *Review of International Political Economy* 20 (2): 241–255.

Ban, Cornel, and Kevin Gallagher. 2015. "Recalibrating Policy Orthodoxy: The IMF
since the Great Recession." *Governance* 28 (2): 131–146.

Bank for International Settlements (BIS). 2009. "Capital Flows and Emerging Market
Economies." Committee on the Global Financial System Paper No. 33. Basel: BIS.
http://www.bis.org/publ/cgfs33.pdf.

Bank for International Settlements (BIS). 2016. "OTC Derivatives Statistics at End-
December 2015." Monetary and Economic Department of the BIS. Basel: BIS, May.
https://www.bis.org/publ/otc_hy1605.pdf.

Baranyi, Stephen, Andreas E. Feldmann, and Lydia Bernier. 2015. "Solidarity Forever? ABC, ALBA and South-South Cooperation in Haiti." *Third World Quarterly* 36
(1): 162–178.

Barboza, David. 2014. "China's Central Bank Allows Its Currency More Volatility." *New
York Times*, March 15. http://www.nytimes.com/2014/03/16/business/international
/chinas-central-bank-raises-the-volatility-of-its-currency.html.

Barnett, Michael, and Martha Finnemore. 2004. *Rules for the World: International
Organizations in Global Politics*. Ithaca, NY: Cornell University Press.

Batunanggar, Sukarela. 2013. "Macroprudential Framework and Measures: The
Indonesian Experience." In *Macroprudential Frameworks in Asia*, edited by Rodolfo

Maino and Steven Barnett, 121–129. Washington, DC: International Monetary Fund.

Bayoumi, Tamim, and Franzisk Ohnsorge. 2013. "Do Inflows or Outflows Dominate: Global Implications of Capital Account Liberalization in China." IMF Working Paper No. 189. Washington, DC: International Monetary Fund. https://www.imf.org /external/pubs/cat/longres.aspx?sk=40901.0.

Beattie, Alan. 2009. "Geithner Demands 'Forceful' Action." *Financial Times*, March 12. http://www.ft.com/intl/cms/s/0/dcd02646-0ea7-11de-b099-0000779fd2ac.html.

Beattie, Alan. 2012. "IMF Drops Opposition to Capital Controls." *Financial Times*, December 3. http://www.ft.com/intl/cms/s/0/e620482e-3d5c-11e2-9e13-00144feabdc0 .html.

Bello, Walden. 2014. "The BRICS: Challengers to the Global Status Quo." *Foreign Policy in Focus*, August 29. http://fpif.org/brics-challengers-global-status-quo/.

Benlialper, Ahmet, and Hasan Cömert. 2016. "Central Banking in Developing Countries after the Crisis: What Has Changed?" IDEAS Working Paper Series No. 1. http:// www.networkideas.org/working/jan2016/01_2016.pdf.

Bernanke, Ben. 2015. "Federal Reserve Policy in an International Context." Mundell-Fleming Lecture at the International Monetary Fund, Washington, DC, November 5. http://www.imf.org/external/np/res/seminars/2015/arc/pdf/Bernanke.pdf.

Bernes, Thomas. 2014. "IMF Leadership and Coordination Roles in the Response to the Global Financial and Economic Crisis." IEO Background Paper 14/06. Washington, DC: IEO. http://www.ieo-imf.org/ieo/files/completedevaluations/BP1406 - Bernes. pdf.

Best, Jacqueline. 2003. "From the Top Down: The New Financial Architecture and the Re-embedding of Global Finance." *New Political Economy* 8 (3): 363–384.

Best, Jacqueline. 2005. *The Limits of Transparency: Ambiguity and the History of International Finance.* Ithaca, NY: Cornell University Press.

Best, Jacqueline. 2006. "Civilizing through Transparency: The International Monetary Fund." In *Global Standards of Market Civilization*, edited by Brett Bowden and Leonard Seabrook, 134–145. London: Routledge.

Best, Jacqueline. 2007. "Legitimacy Dilemmas: The IMF's Pursuit of Country Ownership." *Third World Quarterly* 28 (3): 469–488.

Best, Jacqueline. 2012. "Ambiguity and Uncertainty in International Organizations: A History of Debating IMF Conditionality." *International Studies Quarterly* 56 (4): 674–688.

Best, Jacqueline. 2014. *Governing Failure: Provisional Expertise and the Transformation of Global Development Finance.* Cambridge: Cambridge University Press.

Best, Jacqueline. 2016. "When Crises Are Failures: Contested Metrics in International Finance and Development." *International Political Sociology* 10 (1): 39–55.

Bhagwati, Jagdish. 1998. "The Difference between Trade in Widgets and Dollars." *Foreign Affairs* 77 (3): 7–12.

Bhattacharya, Amar, and R. Holt. 2017 "Assessing the Changing Infrastructure Needs in Emerging Markets and Developing Countries." Global Green Growth Institute and G-24 Paper Series on Infrastructure Finance in the Developing World. Seoul: Global Green Growth Institute. http://gggi.org/infrastructure-financing-in-the-developing-world-working-paper-series/.

Bhattacharya, Amar, Jeremy Oppenheim, and Nicholas Stern. 2015. "Driving Sustainable Development through Better Infrastructure: Key Elements of a Transformation Program." Global Economy and Development@Brookings Working Paper No. 91. Washington, DC: Brookings Institution, July. http://www.brookings.edu/~/media/Research/Files/Papers/2015/07/sustainable-development-transformation-program/07-sustainable-development-infrastructure-v2.pdf?la=en.

Bhattacharya, Amar, and Mattia Romani. 2013. "Meeting the Infrastructure Challenge: The Case for the New Development Bank." Presentation at the G-24 Technical Committee Meeting. Washington, DC: Group of Twenty-Four, March 21. http://g24.org/events/technical-group- meetings/.

Biller, David, and Maria Luiza Rabello. 2013. "Brazil Dismantles Capital Control as Real Drops to Four Year Low." Bloomberg, June 12. http://www.bloomberg.com/news/articles/2013-06-13/brazil-dismantles-capital-control-as-real-drops-to-four-year-low.

Bird, Graham. 2009. "Reforming IMF Conditionality." *World Economics* 10 (3): 81–104.

Blanchard, Olivier J., Florence Jaumotte, and Prakash Loungani. 2013. "Labor Market Policies and IMF Advice in Advanced Economies during the Great Recession." IMF Staff Discussion Note No. 2. Washington, DC: International Monetary Fund, March 29. https://www.imf.org/external/pubs/ft/sdn/2013/sdn1302.pdf.

Blanchard, Olivier J., and Daniel Leigh. 2013. "Growth Forecast Errors and Fiscal Multipliers." IMF Working Paper No. 1. Washington, DC: International Monetary Fund. https://www.imf.org/external/pubs/ft/wp/2013/wp1301.pdf.

Blanchard, Olivier J., David Romer, Michael Spence, and Joseph E. Stiglitz. 2012. *In the Wake of the Crisis: Leading Economists Reassess Economic Policy.* Cambridge, MA: MIT Press.

Bloomberg. 2014. "China Outlines Plan to Ease Capital Curbs, Push Yuan." October 10. http://www.bloomberg.com/news/articles/2014-10-09/china-outlines-plans-to-ease-capital-controls-boost-use-of-yuan.

Bloomberg. 2017. "China Reserves Rise a Third Month Amid Tighter Capital Controls," May 6. https://www.bloomberg.com/news/articles/2017-05-07/china-reserves-rise-a-third-month-amid-tighter-capital-controls

Blustein, Paul. 2015. "Laid Low: The IMF, the Eurozone and the First Rescue of Greece." CIGI Working Paper No. 61, April. Waterloo: Center for International Governance Innovation. https://www.cigionline.org/publications/laid-low-imf-euro-zone-and-first-rescue-of-greece.

Blyth, Mark. 2002. *Great Transformations: Economic Ideas and Institutional Change in the Twentieth Century.* Cambridge: Cambridge University Press.

Blyth, Mark. 2003. "The Political Power of Financial Ideas." In *Monetary Orders: Ambiguous Economics, Ubiquitous Politics,* edited by Eric Helleiner and Jonathan Kirshner, 239–259. Ithaca, NY: Cornell University Press.

Blyth, Mark. 2011. "Albert Hirschman, Alan Greenspan, and the Problem of Intellectual Capture." *Triple Crisis,* April 4. http://triplecrisis.com/the-problem-of-intellectual-capture/.

Blyth, Mark. 2013a. *Austerity: The History of a Dangerous Idea.* Oxford: Oxford University Press.

Blyth, Mark. 2013b. "Paradigms and Paradox: The Politics of Economic Ideas in Two Moments of Crisis." *Governance* 26 (2): 197–215.

Bond, Patrick. 2013. "Sub-imperialism as Lubricant of Neoliberalism: South African 'Deputy Sherrif' Duty Within the BRICS." *Third World Quarterly* 34 (2): 251–270.

Bond, Patrick. 2015. "BRICS and the Sub-imperial Location." In *BRICS: An Anti-capitalist Critique,* edited by Patrick Bond and Ana Garcia, 15–26. London: Pluto.

Bond, Patrick. 2016. "BRICS Banking and the Debate over Sub-imperialism." *Third World Quarterly* 37 (4): 611–629.

Boughton, James M. 2012. *Tearing Down Walls: The International Monetary Fund 1990–1999.* Washington, DC: International Monetary Fund.

Bradlow, Daniel, and Chris Humphrey. 2016. "Sustainability and Infrastructure Investment: National Development Banks in Africa." Boston University Global Economic Governance Initiative Working Paper No. 4, July. Boston: Boston University. https://www.bu.edu/pardeeschool/files/2016/07/Bradlow.Final_.pdf.

Bradsher, Keith. 2017. "China Shed $1 Trillion in Reserves, Should the World Be Worried?" *New York Times,* February 8, B2.

Bräutigam, Deborah. 2009. *The Dragon's Gift: The Real Story of China in Africa.* Oxford: Oxford University Press.

Bräutigam, Deborah, and Kevin Gallagher. 2014. "Bartering Globalization: China's Commodity-Backed Finance in Africa and Latin America." *Global Policy* 5 (3): 346–352.

Brazilian Economic and Social Development Bank (BNDES). 2017. Website. Accessed January 10. http://www.bndes.gov.br/SiteBNDES/bndes/bndes_en/.

Bretton Woods Project (BWP). 2010a. "Debt Crisis in Europe: Beware of IMF Bearing Gifts." BWP Update No. 71, June–July. http://www.brettonwoodsproject.org/2010 /06/art-566356/.

Bretton Woods Project (BWP). 2010b. "Implementing IMF Governance Reform: Baby Steps in Slow Motion." BWP Update No. 73, November 29. http://www.bretton woodsproject.org/2010/11/art-567219/.

Bretton Woods Project (BWP). 2012. "Building Alternatives BRICS by BRICS." BWP Update No. 80, April 5. http://www.brettonwoodsproject.org/2012/04/art -569947/.

BRICS (Brazil, Russian Federation, India, China, and South Africa). 2012. "Fourth Summit: Delhi Declaration." Delhi, India, March 29. http://www.cfr.org/brazil/brics -summit-delhi-declaration/p27805.

BRICS. 2014a. "Agreement on the New Development Bank—Fortaleza Declaration of the Sixth BRICS Summit." Fortaleza, Brazil, July 15. http://ndb.int/download/Agree ment on the New Development Bank.pdf.

BRICS. 2014b. "Sixth Summit: Fortaleza Declaration and Action Plan. Fortaleza, Brazil, July 15." http://brics.itamaraty.gov.br/category-english/21-documents/223 -sixth-summit-declaration-and-action-plan.

BRICS. 2014c. "Treaty for the Establishment of a BRICS Contingent Reserve Arrangement." Fortaleza, Brazil, July 15. http://brics6.itamaraty.gov.br/media2/press -releases/220-treaty-for-the-establishment-of-a-brics-contingent-reserve-arrange ment-fortaleza-july-15.

Broome, André. 2010. "The International Monetary Fund, Crisis Management and the Credit Crunch." *Australian Journal of International Affairs* 64 (1): 37–54.

Broome, André. 2015. "Back to Basics: The Great Recession and the Narrowing of IMF Policy Advice." *Governance* 28 (2): 147–165.

Broome, André, and Leonard Seabrooke. 2007. "Seeing Like the IMF: Institutional Change in Small Open Economies." *Review of International Political Economy* 14 (4): 576–601.

Broome, André, and Leonard Seabrooke. 2012. "Seeing Like an International Organisation." *New Political Economy* 17 (1): 1–16.

Brown, Kevin. 2011. "Inside Asia: Currency Co-operation Creeps on to Asian Agenda." *Financial Times*, January 12. https://www.ft.com/content/dcde5e22-1da6-11e0-aa88 -00144feab49a.

Broz, Lawrence J. 2014. The Politics of Rescuing the World's Financial System: The Federal Reserve as a Global Lender of Last Resort. SSRN Research Paper. http://papers .ssrn.com/sol3/papers.cfm?abstract_id=2531108.

Brunsson, Nils. 1989. *The Organization of Hypocrisy: Talk, Decisions, and Actions in Organizations*. New York: John Wiley and Sons.

Brunsson, Nils. 2003. "Organized Hypocrisy." In *The Northern Lights: Organizational Theory in Scandanavia*, edited by Barbara Czarniawska and Guje Sevon, 201–222. Oslo: Copenhagen Business School Press.

Calmes, Jackie. 2016. "Deal to Overhaul IMF May Give US Image a Vital Lift." *New York Times*, January 7, B1.

Campanella, Miriam. 2012. "Where Is the Big Money Going? SWFs: A Balancing Act or a Game-Changer of the Globalization Story." Unpublished paper.

Campbell, John L. 2004. *Institutional Change and Globalization*. Princeton, NJ: Princeton University Press.

Capannelli, Giovanni. 2011. "Institutions for Economic and Financial Integration in Asia: Trends and Prospects." ADBI Working Paper No. 308. Tokyo: Asian Development Bank Institute. https://www.adb.org/sites/default/files/publication/156163/adbi -wp308.pdf.

Caraballo, Mayvelin. 2017. "PH Seeks Japan Backing on Higher Drawing Rights under Chiang Mai Initiative." *Manila Times*, May 17. http://www.manilatimes.net/ph-seeks -japan-backing-higher-drawing-rights-chiang-mai-initiative/327627/.

Carin, Barry, Paul Heinbecker, Gordon Smith, and Ramesh Thakur. 2010. "Making the G-20 Summit Process Work: Some Proposals for Improving Effectiveness and Legitimacy." CIGI G-20 Paper No. 2. Waterloo: Center for International Governance Innovation. http://www10.iadb.org/intal/intalcdi/PE/2011/08274.pdf.

Carrasquilla, Ana María. 2015. "The Last Ten Years and the Future of FLAR." In *Building a Latin American Reserve Fund: 35 Years of FLAR*, edited by Guillermo Perry, 205–213. Bogotá: Latin American Reserve Fund.

Carstens, Agustín 2015. "Capital Inflows, Exchange Rate Management and Capital Controls." Speech at the Conference on Rethinking Macro Policy III, International Monetary Fund, Washington, DC, April 15. http://www.imf.org/external/mmedia /view.aspx?vid=4176918093001.

Central Bank of Iceland. 2016. "Capital Flow Measures." Reykjavík: Central Bank of Iceland, June. http://www.cb.is/foreign-exch/questions-answers/capital-flow-measures/.

Chakrabortty, Aditya. 2016. "The 1% Hide Their Money Offshore—Then Use It to Corrupt Our Democracy." *Guardian*, April 10. http://www.theguardian.com /news/commentisfree/2016/apr/10/money-offshore-corrupt-democracy-political -influence.

Chandrasekhar, C. P. 2014. "Banking with a Difference." *Economic and Political Weekly* 49 (32): 10–12.

Chandrasekhar, C. P. 2015a. "Infrastructure Financing as Power Politics." *Triple Crisis*, April 27. http://triplecrisis.com/infrastructure-financing-as-power-politics/.

Chandrasekhar, C. P. 2015b. "Introduction: Development Banking in Comparative Perspective." In *Development Finance in BRICS Countries*, edited by Heinrich Böll Stiftung Foundation, 11–22. New Delhi: Heinrich Böll Stiftung Foundation.

Chandrasekhar, C. P. 2016. "National Development Banks in a Comparative Perspective." In *Country Studies and International Comparisons*. Vol. 2 of *Rethinking Development Strategies after the Financial Crisis*, edited by Alfredo Calcagno, Sebastian Dullien, Alejandro Márquez-Velázquez, Nicolas Maystre, and Jan Priewe, 21–30. Geneva: UNCTAD.

Chang, Ha-Joon. 1994. *The Political Economy of Industrial Policy*. London: Macmillan.

Chang, Ha-Joon. 1997. "The Economics and Politics of Regulation." *Cambridge Journal of Economics* 21 (6): 703–728.

Chang, Ha-Joon. 2000. "The Hazard of Moral Hazard: Untangling the Asian Crisis." *World Development* 28 (4): 775–788.

Chang, Ha-Joon. 2002a. "Breaking the Mould: An Institutional Political Economy Alternative to the Neo-liberal Theory of the Market and the State." *Cambridge Journal of Economics* 26 (5): 539–559.

Chang, Ha-Joon. 2002b. *Kicking Away the Ladder: Policies and Institutions for Economic Development in Historical Perspective*. London: Anthem.

Chang, Ha-Joon. 2007. *Bad Samaritans: The Myth of Free Trade and the Secret History of Capitalism*. London: Random House.

Chang, Ha-Joon. 2012. *23 Things They Don't Tell You about Capitalism*. New York: Bloomsbury.

Chang, Ha-Joon. 2014. *Economics: The User's Guide*. New York: Bloomsbury.

Chang, Ha-Joon, and Ilene Grabel. 2014[2004]. *Reclaiming Development: An Alternative Economic Policy Manual*. London: Zed.

Chang, Ha-Joon, Hong-Jae Park, and Chul Gyue Yoo. 1998. "Interpreting the Korean Crisis: Financial Liberalisation, Industrial Policy and Corporate Governance." *Cambridge Journal of Economics* 22 (6): 735–746.

Chin, Gregory. 2010. "Remaking the Architecture: The Emerging Powers, Self-Insuring and Regional Insulation." *International Affairs* 86 (3): 693–715.

Chin, Gregory. 2012. "Responding to the Global Financial Crisis: The Evolution of Asian Regionalism and Economic Globalization." ADBI Working Paper No. 343. Tokyo: Asian Development Bank Institute.

Chin, Gregory. 2014a. "The BRICS-Led Development Bank: Purpose and Politics beyond the G20." *Global Policy* 5 (3): 366–373.

Chin, Gregory. 2014b. "China's Rising Monetary Power." In *The Great Wall of Money*, edited by Eric Helleiner and Jonathan Kirshner, 184–263. Ithaca, NY: Cornell University Press.

Chin, Gregory. 2015. "The State of the Art: Trends in the Study of the BRICS and Multilateral Organizations." In *Rising Powers and Multilateral Institutions*, edited by Dries Lesage and Thijs Van de Graaf, 19–41. Basingstoke: Palgrave MacMillan.

Chin, Gregory. 2016. "Asian Infrastructure Investment Bank: Governance, Innovation and Prospects." *Global Governance* 22 (1): 11–25.

China Development Bank (CDB). 2017. Website. Accessed January 10.

Chorev, Nitsan. 2013. "Restructuring Neoliberalism at the World Health Organization." *Review of International Political Economy* 20 (4): 627–666.

Chorev, Nitsan, and Sarah Babb. 2009. "The Crisis of Neoliberalism and the Future of International Institutions: A Comparison of the IMF and the WTO." *Theory and Society* 38 (5): 459–484.

Chowla, Peter. 2012. "Does BRICS Money for the IMF Mean They Are Bailing Out Europe?" *Triple Crisis*, June 21. http://triplecrisis.com/spotlight-g-20-does-brics-money -for-the-imf-mean-they-are-bailing-out-europe/.

Chrysoloras, Nikos, and Christos Ziotis. 2015. "Greek Capital Controls Halt Exodus after Banks Lose $48 Billion." Bloomberg, September 25. http://www.bloomberg .com/news/articles/2015-09-25/greek-capital-controls-halt-exodus-after-banks-lose -48-billion.

Chrysopoulos, Philip. 2017. "Capital Controls to Stay in Effect Until End of 2018 at Least." *Greek Reporter*, May 10. http://greece.greekreporter.com/2017/05/10/capital -controls-to-stay-in-effect-until-end-of-2018-at-least/

Chwieroth, Jeffrey. 2007a. "Neoliberal Economists and Capital Account Liberalization in Emerging Markets." *International Organization*, no. 61:443–463.

Chwieroth, Jeffrey. 2007b. "Testing and Measuring the Role of Ideas: The Case of Neoliberalism in the International Monetary Fund." *International Studies Quarterly* (51):5–30.

Chwieroth, Jeffrey. 2010. *Capital Ideas: The IMF and the Rise of Financial Liberalization*. Princeton, NJ: Princeton University Press.

Chwieroth, Jeffrey. 2014. "Controlling Capital: The International Monetary Fund and Transformative Incremental Change from Within International Organizations." *New Political Economy* 19 (3): 445–469.

Chwieroth, Jeffrey. 2015. "Managing and Transforming Policy Stigmas in International Finance: Emerging Markets and Controlling Capital Inflows after the Crisis." *Review of International Political Economy* 22 (1): 44–76.

Ciorciari, John. 2011. "Chiang Mai Initiative Multilateralization: International Politics and Institution-Building in Asia." *Asian Survey* 51 (5): 926–952.

Claessens, Stijn, Michael Kean, and Ceyla Pazarbasioglu. 2010. *Financial Sector Taxation: The IMF's Report to the G-20 and Background Material*. Washington, DC: International Monetary Fund, September. http://www.imf.org/external/np/seminars/eng/2010/paris/pdf/090110.pdf.

Clegg, Liam. 2014. "Social Spending Targets in IMF Concessional Lending: US Domestic Politics and the Institutional Foundations of Rapid Operational Change." *Review of International Political Economy* 21 (3): 735–763.

Clements, Benedict, Sanjeev Gupta, and Masahiro Nozaki. 2013. "What Happens to Social Spending in IMF-Supported Programmes?" *Applied Economics* 45 (28): 4022–4033.

Clements, Benedict, Sanjeev Gupta, and Masahiro Nozaki. 2014. "What Happens to Public Health Spending in IMF-Supported Programs." *IMF Direct*, December 21. https://blog-imfdirect.imf.org/2014/12/21/what-happens-to-public-health-spending-in-imf-supported-programs-another-look/.

Clift, Ben. 2014. "'Productive Incoherence' at the Heart of the Troika? Economic Ideas and IMF/European Commission/ECB Dissonance in Addressing the Eurozone Crisis." Paper presented at the Networking Europe and the IMF Research Workshop, University of Warwick, October 8–10.

Cline, William. 2010. "The IMF Staff's Misleading New Evidence on Capital Controls." *Peterson Institute for International Economics Realtime Economic Issues Watch*, February 24. http://blogs.piie.com/realtime/?p=1351.

Clover, Charles, and Lucy Hornby. 2015. "China's Great Game: Road to a New Empire." *Financial Times*, October 12. https://www.ft.com/content/6e098274-587a-11e5-a28b-50226830d644.

Coalition for Human Rights in Development. 2016. "What You Need to Know about the BRICS New Development Bank." Washington, DC: Coalition for Human Rights in Development, October. http://rightsindevelopment.org/wp-content/uploads/2015/08/BRICS-NDB-Factsheet-Final-1.pdf.

Cohen, Benjamin J. 2012. "Finance and Security in East Asia." In *The Nexus of Economics, Security, and Finance in East Asia*, edited by Avery Goldstein and Edward D. Mansfield, 39–65. Palo Alto, CA: Stanford University Press.

Cohen, Benjamin J., and Tabitha M. Benney. 2014. "What Does the International Currency System Really Look Like?" *Review of International Political Economy* 21 (5): 1017–1041.

Colander, David. 2003. "Muddling Through and Policy Analysis." *New Zealand Economic Papers* 37 (2): 197–215.

Colander, David, and Roland Kupers. 2016. *Complexity and the Art of Public Policy: Solving Society's Problems from the Bottom Up*. Princeton, NJ: Princeton University Press.

Cooper, Andrew F. 2010. "The G20 as an Improvised Crisis Committee and/or a 'Contested Steering' Committee for the World." *International Affairs* 86 (3): 741–757.

Cooper, Andrew F. 2011. "The G-20 and Its Regional Critics: The Search for Inclusion." *Global Policy* 2 (2): 203–209.

Corm, Georges. 2006. "The Arab Experience." In *Regional Financial Cooperation*, edited by José Antonio Ocampo, 291–328. Washington, DC: Brookings Institution.

Coy, Peter, Manjeet Kripalani, and Mark Clifford. 1998. "Capital Controls: Lifeline or Noose?" *Bloomberg Business Week*, September 28, 37.

Crotty, James. 1983. "On Keynes and Capital Flight." *Journal of Economic Literature* 21:59–65.

Crotty, James. 1990. "Keynes on the Stages of Development of the Capitalist Economy: The Institutional Foundation of Keynes' Methodology." *Journal of Economic Issues* 24 (3): 761–780.

Crotty, James. 2009. "Structural Causes of the Global Financial Crisis: A Critical Assessment of the 'New Financial Architecture.'" *Cambridge Journal of Economics* 33 (4): 563–580.

Crotty, James, and Gerald Epstein. 1996. "In Defence of Capital Controls." In *Are There Alternatives? Socialist Register 1996*, edited by Leo Panitch, 118–149. London: Merlin.

Crotty, James, and Kang-Kook Lee. 2002. "A Political-Economic Analysis of the Failure of Neo-liberal Restructuring in Post-crisis Korea." *Cambridge Journal of Economics* 26 (5): 667–678.

Crotty, James, and Kang-Kook Lee. 2004. "Was the IMF's Imposition of Economic Regime Change in Korea Justified?: A Critique of the IMF's Economic and Political Role in Korea before and after the Crisis." PERI Working Paper No. 77. Amherst, MA:

University of Massachusetts, Political Economy Research Institute. http://scholarworks
.umass.edu/cgi/viewcontent.cgi?article=1063&context=peri_workingpapers.

Crotty, James, and Kang-Kook Lee. 2005. "From East Asian 'Miracle' to Neoliberal
'Mediocrity': The Effects of Liberalization and Financial Opening on the Post-crisis
Korean Economy." *Global Economic Review* 34 (4): 415–434.

Crotty, James, and Kang-Kook Lee. 2006. "The Effects of Neoliberal Reforms on the
Post-crisis Korean Economy." *Review of Radical Political Economics* 38 (4): 669–675.

Crotty, James, and Kang-Kook Lee. 2009. "Was IMF-Imposed Economic Regime
Change in Korea Justified?: The Political Economy of IMF Intervention." *Review of
Radical Political Economics* 41 (2): 149–169.

Crowe, Darcy. 2010. "Colombia Central Bank Rules Out Capital Controls." *Colombia
Reports*, October 19. http://colombiareports.com/colombia-central-bank-rules-out
-capital-controls/.

Culpeper, Roy. 1997. *Titans or Behemoths?* Vol. 5 of *The Multilateral Development
Banks*. Boulder, CO: Lynne Rienner.

Culpeper, Roy. 2006. "Reforming the Global Financial Architecture: The Potential of
Regional Institutions." In *Regional Financial Cooperation*, edited by José Antonio
Ocampo, 40–67. Washington, DC: Brookings Institution.

Cumings, Bruce. 1999. "The Asian Crisis, Democracy, and the End of 'Late' Development." In *The Politics of the Asian Economic Crisis*, edited by T. J. Pempel, 17–44.
Ithaca, NY: Cornell University Press.

Dabilis, Andy. 2014. "Troika Wants More Salary Slashes." *Greek Reporter*, March 8.
http://greece.greekreporter.com/2014/03/08/troika-wants-more-salary-slashes/.

Dadush, Uri, and Bennett Stancil. 2011. "Why Are Reserves So Big?" Vox.eu, May 9.
http://vox.eu/index.php?q=node/6471.

Danielsson, Jon, and Ragnar Arnason. 2011. "Capital Controls Are Exactly Wrong
for Iceland." Voxeu.org, November 14. http://www.vox.eu/org/article/iceland-and
-imf-why-capital-controls-are-entirely-wrong.

D'Arista, Jane, and Gerald Epstein. 2011. *Dodd-Frank and the Regulation of Dangerous
Interconnectedness, the Future of Financial Reform: Will It Work? How Will We Know?
The Future of Financial Reform*. New York: Roosevelt Institute, October 4.

Davis, Scott, and Ignacio Presno. 2014. "Capital Controls as an Instrument of Monetary Policy." Federal Reserve Bank of Dallas Working Paper No. 171. Dallas, TX:
Federal Reserve. http://www.dallasfed.org/assets/documents/institute/wpapers/2014
/0171.pdf.

Deaton, Angus. 2010. "Instruments, Randomization, and Learning about Development." *Journal of Economic Literature* 48 (2): 424–455.

Deaton, Angus. 2015. Interview conducted by Timothy Ogden (October 14) with Angus Deaton in conjunction with *Experimental Conversations*. Cambridge, MA: MIT Press, 2017. https://medium.com/@timothyogden/experimental-conversations-angus -deaton-b2f768dffd57.

de Luna-Martínez, José, and Carlos Leonardo Vicente. 2012. "Global Survey of Development Banks." World Bank Policy Research Working Paper No. 5969. Washington, DC: World Bank, February. http://www-wds.worldbank.org/external/default/WDS ContentServer/WDSP/IB/2012/02/15/000158349_20120215153214/Rendered/PDF /WPS5969.pdf.

DeMartino, George F. 2000. *Global Economy, Global Justice: Theoretical and Policy Alternatives to Neoliberalism*. London: Routledge.

DeMartino, George F. 2011. *The Economist's Oath: On the Need for and Content of Professional Economic Ethics*. Oxford: Oxford University Press.

DeMartino, George F. 2013a. "Epistemic Aspects of Economic Practice and the Need for Professional Economic Ethics." *Review of Social Economy* 71 (2): 166–186.

DeMartino, George F. 2013b. "Ethical Engagement in a World beyond Control." *Rethinking Marxism* 25 (4): 483–500.

Desai, Radhika. 2013. "The BRICS Are Building a Challenge to Western Economic Supremacy." *Guardian*, April 2. http://www.theguardian.com/commentisfree/2013 /apr/02/brics-challenge-western-supremacy.

Desai, Raj, and James Raymond Vreeland. 2014. "What the New Bank of BRICS Is All About." *Washington Post, Monkey Cage*. http://www.washingtonpost.com/blogs /monkey-cage/wp/2014/07/17/what-the-new-bank-of-brics-is-all-about/.

Development Bank of Latin America (CAF). 2017. Website. Accessed January 10. https://www.caf.com/en.

Dobbs, Richard, and Michael Spence. 2011. "The Era of Cheap Capital Draws to a Close." *Financial Times*, January 31. http://www.ft.com/cms/s/0/1478bc50-2d70 -11e0-8f53-00144feab49a.html - axzz41OPv4o3d.

Dollar, David. 2015. "China's Rise as a Regional and Global Power: The AIIB and the 'One Belt, One Road.'" *Horizons*, (4):162–172. https://www.brookings.edu/research /chinas-rise-as-a-regional-and-global-power-the-aiib-and-the-one-belt-one-road/.

Donnan, Shawn. 2016a. "Christine Lagarde Wants Softer, Kinder IMF to Face Populist Anger." *Financial Times*, July 13. https://next.ft.com/content/0fc06c9e-4877-11e6 -8d68-72e9211e86ab.

Donnan, Shawn. 2016b. "IMF Economists Put 'Neoliberalism' under Spotlight." *Financial Times*, May 26. http://www.ft.com/cms/s/0/4b98c052-238a-11e6-9d4d -c11776a5124d.html - axzz4Dxn2tCUe.

Donnan, Shawn. 2016c. "World Bank Lending at Record since Aftermath of Financial Crisis." *Financial Times*, April 10. http://www.ft.com/cms/s/0/2fecc550-fed3-11e5 -9cc4-27926f2b110c.html?siteedition=intl - axzz4EydexQoH.

Donnan, Shawn. 2017. "IMF Under Pressure in Washington over Greek Bailout." *Financial Times*, March 16. https://www.ft.com/content/e77f3c0c-0abc-11e7-97d1 -5e720a26771b.

Donnan, Shawn, and Chris Giles. 2016. "IMF Urges Shake-up of Greek Bailout." *Financial Times*, April 14. https://next.ft.com/content/13bf85c0-0261-11e6-99cb -83242733f755.

Drezner, Daniel. 2007. *All Politics Is Global: Explaining International Regulatory Regimes.* Princeton, NJ: Princeton University Press.

Drezner, Daniel. 2013. "The Purest Political Economist of Them All: Albert Hirschman's Legacy." *Monkey Cage*, June 12. http://themonkeycage.org/2013/06/12 /the-purest-political-economist-of-them-all-albert-hirschmans-legacy/.

Easterly, William. 2001. *The Elusive Quest for Growth: Economists' Adventures and Misadventures in the Tropics.* Cambridge, MA: MIT Press.

Easterly, William. 2006. *The White Man's Burden: Why the West's Efforts to Aid the Rest Have Done So Much Ill and So Little Good.* New York: Penguin.

Easterly, William. 2008. "Introduction: Can't Take It Anymore?" In *Reinventing Foreign Aid*, edited by William Easterly, 1–44. Cambridge, MA: MIT Press.

Easterly, William. 2014. *The Tyranny of Experts: How the Fight against Global Poverty Suppressed Individual Rights.* New York: Basic Books.

Economist. 2012. "Exit Albert Hirschman." December 22. http://www.economist .com/news/business/21568708-great-lateral-thinker-died-december-10th-exit-albert -hirschman.

Economist. 2013. "Just in Case." October 12, 10–12. http://www.economist.com /news/special-report/21587383-capital-controls-are-back-part-many-countries -financial-armoury-just-case.

Economist. 2016a. "A Harder Call." December 3, 61–62. https://www.economist.com /news/finance-and-economics/21711073-china-among-many-countries-see-its -currency-quail-strengthening.

Economist. 2016b. "Our Bulldozers, Our Rules." July 2. http://www.economist.com /news/china/21701505-chinas-foreign-policy-could-reshape-good-part-world -economy-our-bulldozers-our-rules.

Economist. 2016c. "Reversal of Fortune." November 19, 61–62. http://www.economist .com/news/finance-economics/21710244-american-election-has-added-new-source -uncertainty.

Economist. 2017a. "China's Currency Upsets Forecasts by Beginning the New Year Stronger." January 14. http://www.economist.com/node/21714258/print.

Economist. 2017b. "Closer to Centre-Stage," March 15, 61. http://www.economist .com/news/finance-and-economics/21719498-america-retreats-china-advances -chinas-growing-clout-international-economic.

Economist. 2017c. "The End of a Saga," March 18. http://www.economist.com/news /finance-and-economics/21718889-last-country-marks-symbolic-recovery-its -financial-meltdown-iceland.

Edwards, Kim, and Wing Hsieh. 2011. "Recent Changes in IMF Lending." *Reserve Bank of Australia Bulletin*, December quarter. http://www.rba.gov.au/publications /bulletin/2011/dec/8.html.

Edwards, Sebastian. 1999. "How Effective Are Capital Controls?" *Journal of Economic Perspectives* 13 (4): 65–84.

Eglitis, Aaron. 2016. "Azerbaijan Credit Rating Cut to Junk by S&P after Oil Plunge." Bloomberg, January 29. http://www.bloomberg.com/news/articles/2016-01-29 /azerbaijan-credit-rating-cut-to-junk-by-s-p-after-oil-s-collapse.

Eichengreen, Barry. 1999. *Toward a New International Financial Architecture: A Practical Post-Asia Agenda*. Washington, DC: Peterson Institute for International Economics.

Eichengreen, Barry. 2000. "The International Monetary Fund in the Wake of the Asian Crisis." In *The Asian Crisis and the Architecture of Global Finance*, edited by Gregory W. Noble and John Ravenhill, 170–191. Cambridge: Cambridge University Press.

Eichengreen, Barry. 2009. "Out of the Box Thoughts about the International Financial Architecture." IMF Working Paper No. 116. Washington, DC: International Monetary Fund, Strategy, Policy, and Review Department, May. https://www.imf .org/external/pubs/ft/wp/2009/wp09116.pdf.

Eichengreen, Barry. 2010. "The International Financial Architecture and the Role of Regional Funds." Paper prepared for the Fifth Annual FLAR Economic Studies Conference, Cartagena, August. http://eml.berkeley.edu/~eichengr/intl_finan _arch_2010.pdf.

Eichengreen, Barry. 2012. "Regional Financial Arrangements and the International Monetary Fund." ADBI Working Paper No. 394. Tokyo: Asian Development Bank Institute. http://www.adbi.org/working-paper/2012/11/06/5328.regional.financial .arrangements.imf/.

Eichengreen, Barry. 2014. "Banking on the BRICS." *Project Syndicate*, August 13. http://www.project-syndicate.org/commentary/barry-eichengreen-is-bullish-on

-the-group-s-new-development-bank—but-not-on-its-contingent-reserve
-arrangement.

Eichengreen, Barry. 2015. "Regional Financial Arrangements and the IMF: What Have We Learned from Europe?" In *Building a Latin American Reserve Fund: 35 Years of FLAR*, edited by Guillermo Perry, 133–142. Bogotá: Latin American Reserve Fund.

Eichengreen, Barry, and Ngaire Woods. 2016. "The IMF's Unmet Challenges." *Journal of Economic Perspectives* 30 (1): 29–51.

Elgin-Cossart, Molly, and Melanie Hart. 2015. "China's New International Financing Institutions." Center for American Progress, September 22. https://www.american progress.org/issues/security/report/2015/09/22/121668/chinas-new-international -financing-institutions/.

Ellerman, David. 2004. "Autonomy-Respecting Assistance: Toward an Alternative Theory of Development Assistance." *Review of Social Economy* 62 (2): 149–168.

Ellerman, David. 2005. *Helping People Help Themselves*. Ann Arbor: University of Michigan Press.

Ellerman, David. 2014. "Parallel Experimentation: A Basic Scheme for Dynamic Efficiency." *Journal of Bioeconomics* 16 (3): 259–287.

Ellmers, Bodo. 2016. "Reform of the IMF Lending Framework: The IMF Bails Out from Bailouts." Committee for the Abolition of Illegal Debt, Liege, February 3. http://cadtm.org/Reform-of-the-IMF-lending.

El Telégrafo. 2016. "Con Elección de Presidente, el Banco del Sur Inicia Su Fase Preoperativa." December 1. http://www.eltelegrafo.com.ec/noticias/economia/8/con -eleccion-de-presidente-el-banco-del-sur-inicia-su-fase-preoperativa.

Emmers, Ralf, and John Ravenhill. 2011. "The Asian and Global Financial Crises: Consequences for East Asian Regionalism." *Contemporary Politics* 17 (2): 133–149.

Epstein, Gerald, ed. 2005. *Capital Controls in Developing Countries*. Cheltenham: Edward Elgar.

Epstein, Gerald. 2006. "Central Banks as Agents of Economic Development." UNU-WIDER Research Paper No. 54. Helsinki: United Nations University—World Institute for Development Economics Research. http://hdl.handle.net/10419/63574.

Epstein, Gerald A. 2012. "Capital Outflow Regulation: Economic Management, Development and Transformation." In *Regulating Global Capital Flows for Long-Run Development, Pardee Center Task Force Report*, edited by Kevin P. Gallagher, Stephany Griffith-Jones, and José Antonio Ocampo, 47–58. Boston: Boston University, Pardee Center for the Study of the Longer-Range Future.

Epstein, Gerald, Ilene Grabel, and Jomo K. S. 2004. "Capital Management Techniques in Developing Countries: An Assessment of Experiences from the 1990s and Lessons for the Future." G24 Discussion Paper No. 27, Intergovernmental Group of Twenty Four. Geneva: United Nations Conference on Trade and Development, March. http://policydialogue.org/files/publications/Capital_Mgmt_Epstein.pdf.

Erten, Bilge, and José Antonio Ocampo. 2013. "Capital Account Regulations, Foreign Exchange Pressures, and Crisis Resilience." Initiative for Policy Dialogue Working Paper Series, New York: Columbia University, October. http://policydialogue.org/files/publications/CAR_Erten_Ocampo_withCS.pdf.

Eurasian Fund for Stabilization and Development (EFSD). 2016. "Annual Reports." Accessed December 20. http://efsd.eabr.org/e/documents_acf_e/Reports_acf_e/.

Eurasian Fund for Stabilization and Development (EFSD). 2017. Website. Accessed January 10. http://efsd.eabr.org/e/.

European Commission (EC). 2012. "Autumn Economic Forecast: Sailing through Rough Waters." *European Economy* 7. http://ec.europa.eu/economy_finance/eu/forecasts/2012_autumn_forecast_en.htm.

European Union (EU). 2015. "Euro Summit Statement." SN 4070/15. Brussels: European Union, July 12. http://www.consilium.europa.eu/press-releases-pdf/2015/7/40802200528_en_635732421000000000.pdf.

Evans-Pritchard, Ambrose. 2010. "Bundesbank Attacks Greek Rescue as a Threat to Stability." *Telegraph*, April 8. http://www.telegraph.co.uk/finance/financialcrisis/7569358/Bundesbank-attacks-Greek-rescue-as-a-threat-to-stability.html.

Evripidou, Stefanos. 2013. "Cyprus' Fate 'A Path of Inevitability': The IMF's Internal Views on Cyprus Bailout." *Cyprus Mail*, May 26. http://cyprus-mail.com/2013/05/26/cyprus-fate-a-path-of-inevitability-the-imfs-internal-views-on-cyprus-bailout/.

Ewing, Jack, and Liz Alderman. 2015. "Bailout Money Goes to Greece, Only to Flow Out Again." *New York Times*, July 31, B1.

Farchy, Jack. 2016a. "Azerbaijan Hits Out at IMF's Response to Oil Price Drop." *Financial Times*, July 17. http://www.ft.com/cms/s/0/843a5ff6-4c2a-11e6-88c5-db83e98a590a.html.

Farchy, Jack. 2016b. "Tajikistan and IMF in Talks over Bailout." *Financial Times*, February 23. http://www.ft.com/intl/cms/s/0/3dd384b0-da48-11e5-98fd-06d75973fe09.html - axzz43lSYfpkX.

Farrell, Henry, and John Quiggin. 2017. "Consensus, Dissensus and Economic Ideas: Economic Crisis and the Rise and Fall of Keynesianism." *International Studies Quarterly*, forthcoming.

Feldstein, Martin. 1998. "Refocusing the IMF." *Foreign Affairs* 77 (2): 20–33.

Ferrando, Tomaso. 2014. "Land Grabbing under the Cover of Law: Are BRICS-South Relationships Any Different?" In *Shifting Power: Critical Perspectives on Emerging Economies*, edited by Nick Buxton and Nicola Bullard, 150–173. Amsterdam: Transnational Institute.

Ferro, Shane. 2014. "Nigeria Brings on Capital Controls." *Business Insider*, December 19. http://www.businessinsider.com/nigeria-imposes-capital-controls-2014-12.

Financial Nigeria. 2016. "Nigeria to Receive $3.5 Billion Loans from the World Bank and AfDB." January 31. http://www.financialnigeria.com/nigeria-to-receive-3-5 -billion-loans-from-the-world-bank-and-afdb-news-331.html.

Financial Stability Board (FSB). 2014. "FSB Review of the Structure of Its Representation." Basel: Financial Stability Board, November 14. http://www.financialstabilityboard .org/2014/11/fsb-review-of-the-structure-of-its-representation/.

Financial Times. 2013. "India's Capital Crisis." August 15. http://www.ft.com/intl/cms /s/0/d469362e-05af-11e3-8ed5-00144feab7de.html - axzz40jfKd1Ev.

Financial Times. 2016a. "Fitch Keeps Wary Eye on Azerbaijan after Controls." January 22. http://www.ft.com/fastft/2016/01/22/fitch-keeps-wary-eye-on-azerbaijan -after-capital-controls/.

Financial Times. 2016b. "Greece Loosens Capital Controls to Win Back Deposits." July 25. https://www.ft.com/content/ecf7012a-527e-11e6-befd-2fc0c26b3c60.

Fine, Ben. 2001. "Neither the Washington nor the Post-Washington Consensus: An Introduction." In *Development Policy in the Twenty-First Century: Beyond the Post-Washington Consensus*, edited by Ben Fine, Costas Lapavitsas, and Jonathan Pincus, 1–27. London: Routledge.

Fischer, Stanley. 1997. "Asia and the IMF." IMF Seminar, Hong Kong, September 19. https://www.imf.org/external/np/apd/asia/FISCHER.HTM.

Forbes, Kristin. 2005. "Capital Controls: Mud in the Wheels of Market Efficiency." *Cato Journal* 25 (1): 153–166.

Forbes, Kristin, Marcel Fratzscher, Thomas Kostka, and Roland Straub. 2011. "Bubble Thy Neighbor: Direct and Spillover Effects of Capital Controls." Paper presented at the 12th Jacques Polak Annual Research Conference. Washington, DC: International Monetary Fund, November 10–11. https://www.imf.org/external/np/res/seminars /2011/arc/pdf/forbes.pdf.

Forelle, Charles. 2012. "In European Crisis Iceland Emerges as an Island of Recovery." *Wall Street Journal*, May 21. http://www.wsj.com/articles/SB10001424052702304203 604577396171007652042.

Fourcade, Marion. 2013. "The Material and Symbolic Construction of the BRICs: Reflections Inspired by the RIPE Special Issue." *Review of International Political Economy* 20 (2): 256–267.

Fox, Justin. 2008. "Bob Lucas on the Comeback of Keynesianism." *Time*, October 28. http://business.time.com/2008/10/28/bob-lucas-on-the-comeback-of-keynesianism/.

Foy, Henry. 2015. "Charities Struggle to Plug Gaps in Gutted Welfare State." *Financial Times*, June 24. http://www.ft.com/intl/cms/s/0/7a6a2e38-1978-11e5-a130-2e7db721 f996.html - axzz3e57O18T0.

Fritz, Barbara, and Laurissa Mühlich. 2014. "Regional Monetary Cooperation in the Developing World: Taking Stock." Paper for the UNCTAD project Strengthening Pro-Growth Macroeconomic Management Capacities for Enhanced Regional and Monetary Cooperation among Selected Countries of Latin America and the Caribbean, and West and Central Africa. http://www.lai.fu-berlin.de/homepages/fritz /publikationen/Paper-Stocktaking-Regional-Monetary-Cooperation-Fritz-Muehlich -22-07-14-end.pdf.

Fritz, Barbara, and Laurissa Mühlich. 2015. "Varieties of Regional Monetary Cooperation: A Tool for Reducing Volatility in Developing Economies?" *Contemporary Politics* 21 (2): 127–144.

Fritz, Barbara, and Daniela Magalhães Prates. 2014. "The New IMF Approach to Capital Account Management and Its Blind Spots: Lessons from Brazil and South Korea." *International Review of Applied Economics* 28 (2): 210–239.

Fukuyama, Francis. 2013. "Albert O. Hirschman, 1915–2012." *American Interest*, January 6. http://blogs.the-american-interest.com/2013/01/06/albert-o-hirschman-1915 -2012/.

G-20. 2009a. "Declaration on Strengthening the Financial System, London Summit." Group of Twenty, April 2. http://www.treasury.gov/resource-center/international/g7 -g20/Documents/London April 2009 Fin_Deps_Fin_Reg_Annex_020409_-_1615_final .pdf.

G-20. 2009b. "G-20 Leaders' Statement, Pittsburgh Summit." Group of Twenty, September 24–25. http://www.treasury.gov/resource-center/international/g7-g20 /Documents/pittsburgh_summit_leaders_statement_250909.pdf.

G-20. 2010. "Communiqué, Gyeongju Summit." Meeting of Finance Ministers and Central Bank Governors of the Group of Twenty, October 23. http://www.treasury .gov/resource-center/international/Documents/Final G-20 FM Gyeongju Communique October 23.pdf.

G-20. 2011a. "G-20 Coherent Conclusions for the Management of Capital Flows Drawing on Country Experiences." Group of Twenty, October 15. http://www.g20 .utoronto.ca/2011/2011-finance-capital-flows-111015-en.pdf.

G-20. 2011b. "G-20 Principles for Cooperation between the IMF and Regional Financial Arrangements." Group of Twenty, October 15. http://www.g20.utoronto.ca /2011/2011-finance-principles-111015-en.pdf.

G-20. 2014. "G20 Global Infrastructure Initiative, Brisbane Leaders' Summit." Group of Twenty, November 16. http://www.g20.utoronto.ca/2014/g20_note_global_infra structure_initiative_hub.pdf.

G-20. 2015. "Communiqué, Istanbul Summit." Meeting of Finance Ministers and Central Bank Governors of the Group of Twenty. Istanbul, February 9–10. http:// www.g20.utoronto.ca/2015/150210-finance.pdf1

G-20. 2016a. "Communiqué, Meeting of Finance Ministers and Central Bank Governors of the Group of Twenty." Washington, DC, April 14–15. http://wjb.mof.gov.cn /pindaoliebiao/gongzuodongtai/201604/t20160416_1952794.html.

G-20. 2016b. "Communiqué, Meeting of Finance Ministers and Central Bank Governors of the Group of Twenty." Shanghai, February 27. http://www.g20.utoronto.ca /2016/160227-finance-en.html.

G-20. 2016c. "G-20 Leaders' Communique, Hangzhou Summit." Group of Twenty, September 4–5. http://www.g20.org/English/Documents/Current/201609/t20160906 _3395.html.

G-20. 2016d. "Global Infrastructure Connectivity Alliance Initiative." Group of Twenty, September. http://www.g20chn.org/English/Documents/Current/201608 /P020160815370070969702.pdf.

G-24. 2011. "Intergovernmental Group of Twenty-Four on International Monetary Affairs and Development Communiqué." Washington, DC: International Monetary Fund, April 14. https://www.imf.org/external/np/cm/2011/041411.htm.

G-24. 2014. "Mandate." Intergovernmental Group of Twenty Four. http://www.g24 .org/mandate/.

Gabor, Daniela. 2010. "The International Monetary Fund and Its New Economics." *Development and Change* 41 (5): 805–830.

Gabor, Daniela. 2012. "Managing Capital Accounts in Emerging Markets: Lessons from the Global Financial Crisis." *Journal of Development Studies* 48 (6): 714–731.

Gabor, Daniela. 2015. "The IMF's Rethink of Global Banks: Critical in Theory, Orthodox in Practice." *Governance* 28 (2): 199–218.

Galbraith, James K. 2016. *Welcome to the Poisoned Chalice: The Destruction of Greece and the Future of Europe.* New Haven, CT: Yale University Press.

Gallagher, Kevin P. 2010. "Obama Must Ditch Bush-Era Trade Deals." *Guardian*, July 1. http://www.theguardian.com/commentisfree/cifamerica/2010/jun/30/obama -bush-us-trade.

Gallagher, Kevin P. 2011. "Regaining Control? Capital Controls and the Global Financial Crisis." Political Economy Research Institute Working Paper No. 250.

Amherst: University of Massachusetts-Amherst, Political Economy Research Institute. http://www.ase.tufts.edu/gdae/policy_research/KGCapControlsPERIFeb11.html.

Gallagher, Kevin P. 2012. "The Global Governance of Capital Flows: New Opportunities, Enduring Challenges." Political Economy Research Institute Working Paper No. 283. Amherst: University of Massachusetts-Amherst, Political Economy Research Institute. http://www.peri.umass.edu/236/hash/5177c19e45bd73aaf9ae065db58a72 cb/publication/512/.

Gallagher, Kevin P. 2014. *Ruling Capital: Emerging Markets and the Reregulation of Cross-Border Finance.* Ithaca, NY: Cornell University Press.

Gallagher, Kevin P. 2015a. "Contesting the Governance of Capital Flows at the IMF." *Governance* 28 (2): 185–198.

Gallagher, Kevin P. 2015b. "Obama Abandons Allies on China's Marshall Plan." *Globalist*, March 18. http://www.theglobalist.com/obama-abandons-allies-on-chinas -marshall-plan/.

Gallagher, Kevin P. 2016. *The China Triangle: Latin America's China Boom and the Fate of the Washington Consensus.* Oxford: Oxford University Press.

Gallagher, Kevin P., Rohini Kamal, and Yongzhong Wang. 2016. "Fueling Growth and Financing Risk: The Benefits and Risks of China's Development Finance in the Global Energy Sector." Global Economic Governance Initiative Working Paper No. 2. Boston: Boston University, Frederick S. Pardee School of Global Studies, May. https://www.bu.edu/pardeeschool/files/2016/05/Fueling-Growth.FINAL_.version .pdf.

Gallagher, Kevin P., Katherine Koleski, and Amos Irwin. 2012. "The New Banks in Town: Chinese Finance in Latin America." Washington, DC: Inter-American Dialogue, February. http://ase.tufts.edu/gdae/Pubs/rp/GallagherChineseFinanceLatin AmericaBrief.pdf.

Gallagher, Kevin P., and Elen Shrestha. 2012. "The Social Cost of Self-Insurance: Financial Crisis, Reserve Accumulation, and Developing Countries." *Global Policy* 3 (4): 501–509. doi: 10.1111/j.1758-5899.2011.00150.x.

Gallagher, Kevin P., and Sarah Sklar. 2016. "Nationalizing Development Finance: Putting National Development Banks in Context." Boston: Boston University, Global Economic Governance Initiative, Frederic S. Pardee School of Global Studies.

Germain, Randall. 2009. "Financial Order and World Politics: Crisis, Change and Continuity." *International Affairs* 85 (4): 669–687.

Gerschenkron, Alexander. 1962. *Economic Backwardness in Historical Perspective.* Cambridge, MA: Harvard University Press.

Ghosh, Atish, Jonathan Ostry, and Charalambos Tsangarides. 2012. "Shifting Motives: Explaining the Buildup in Official Reserves in Emerging Markets since the 1980s." IMF Working Paper No. 34. Washington, DC: International Monetary Fund, Research Department. http://www.imf.org/external/pubs/cat/longres.aspx?sk=25683.

Ghosh, Atish R., and Mahvash S. Qureshi. 2016. "What's in a Name? That Which We Call Capital Controls." IMF Working Paper No. 25. Washington, DC: International Monetary Fund, February. https://www.imf.org/external/pubs/ft/wp/2016/wp1625.pdf.

Ghosh, Atish R., Mahvash S. Qureshi, and Naotaka Sugawara. 2014. "Regulating Capital Flows at Both Ends: Does It Work?" IMF Working Paper No. 188. Washington, DC: International Monetary Fund, October. https://www.imf.org/external/pubs/ft/wp/2014/wp14188.pdf.

Ghosh, Jayati. 2012. "Using the Potential of BRICS Financial Cooperation." *Triple Crisis*, April 16. http://triplecrisis.com/using-the-potential-of-brics-financial-cooperation/.

Gibson-Graham, J. K. 1996. *The End of Capitalism (as We Knew It): A Feminist Critique of Political Economy*. Oxford: Blackwell.

Gibson-Graham, J. K. 2006. *A Postcapitalist Politics*. Minneapolis: University of Minnesota.

Gibson-Graham, J. K. 2008. "Diverse Economies: Performative Practices for 'Other Worlds.'" *Progress in Human Geography* 32 (5): 613–632.

Gibson-Graham, J. K. 2011. "A Feminist Project of Belonging for the Anthropocene." *Gender, Place and Culture* 18 (1): 1–21.

Gibson-Graham, J. K., and Gerda Roelvink. 2010. "An Economic Ethics for the Anthropocene." *Antipode* 41 (s1): 320–346.

Giles, Chris. 2012. "Brics to Create Financial Safety Net." *Financial Times*, June 18. http://www.ft.com/intl/cms/s/0/bfd6adfe-b9bb-11e1-a470-00144feabdc0.html.

Gill, Nathan. 2011. "Moody's Cuts Argentine Oil Companies on Capital Control Law." Bloomberg, October 31. http://www.bloomberg.com/news/articles/2011-10-31/moody-s-cuts-argentine-oil-companies-on-capital-control-law-1-.

Gladwell, Malcolm. 2013. "The Gift of Doubt: Albert O. Hirschman and the Power of Failure." *New Yorker*, June 24, 74–79. http://www.newyorker.com/magazine/2013/06/24/the-gift-of-doubt.

Golub, Philip. 2013. "From the New International Economic Order to the G20: How the 'Global South' Is Restructuring World Capitalism from Within." *Third World Quarterly* 34 (6): 1000–1015.

Gottschalk, Ricardo. 2016. "The Role of Development Banks in Promoting Growth and Sustainable Development in the South." Geneva: United Nations Conference on Trade and Development, December, mimeo.

Gourevitch, Peter. 1986. *Politics in Hard Times: Comparative Responses to International Economic Crises.* Ithaca, NY: Cornell University Press.

Grabel, Ilene. 1995. "Speculation-Led Economic Development: A Post-Keynesian Interpretation of Financial Liberalization Programmes in the Third World." *International Review of Applied Economics* 9 (2): 127–149.

Grabel, Ilene. 1996a. "Marketing the Third World: The Contradictions of Portfolio Investment in the Global Economy." *World Development* 24 (11): 1761–1776.

Grabel, Ilene. 1996b. "Stock Markets, Rentier Interest and the Current Mexican Crisis." *Journal of Economic Issues* 30 (2): 443–449.

Grabel, Ilene. 1999a. "Mexico Redux? Making Sense of the Financial Crisis of 1997–98." *Journal of Economic Issues* 33 (2): 375–381.

Grabel, Ilene. 1999b. "Rejecting Exceptionalism: Reinterpreting the Asian Financial Crises." In *Global Instability: The Political Economy of World Economic Governance*, edited by Jonathan Michie and John Grieve Smith, 37–67. London: Routledge.

Grabel, Ilene. 2000. "The Political Economy of 'Policy Credibility': The New-classical Macroeconomics and the Remaking of Emerging Economies." *Cambridge Journal of Economics* 24 (1): 1–19.

Grabel, Ilene. 2002. "Neoliberal Finance and Crisis in the Developing World." *Monthly Review* 53 (11): 34–46.

Grabel, Ilene. 2003a. "Averting Crisis? Assessing Measures to Manage Financial Integration in Emerging Economies." *Cambridge Journal of Economics* 27 (3): 317–336.

Grabel, Ilene. 2003b. "Ideology, Power and the Rise of Independent Monetary Institutions in Emerging Economies." In *Monetary Orders: Ambiguous Economics, Ubiquitous Politics*, edited by Jonathan Kirshner, 25–52. Ithaca, NY: Cornell University Press.

Grabel, Ilene. 2003c. "International Private Capital Flows and Developing Countries." In *Rethinking Development Economics*, edited by Ha-Joon Chang, 324–345. London: Anthem.

Grabel, Ilene. 2003d. "Predicting Financial Crisis in Developing Economies: Astronomy or Astrology?" *Eastern Economic Journal* 29 (2): 243–258.

Grabel, Ilene. 2004. "Trip Wires and Speed Bumps: Managing Financial Risks and Reducing the Potential for Financial Crises in Developing Economies." G-24

Discussion Paper No. 33. Geneva: United Nations Conference on Trade and Development, November. http://www.unctad.org/en/docs/gdsmdpbg2420049_en .pdf.

Grabel, Ilene. 2007. "One Step Forward, Two Steps Back: Policy (In)coherence and Financial Crises." In *Ten Years After: Revisiting the Asian Financial Crisis*, edited by Bhumika Muchhala, 95–104. Washington, DC: Wilson Center Press.

Grabel, Ilene. 2011. "Not Your Grandfather's IMF: Global Crisis, 'Productive Incoherence' and Developmental Policy Space." *Cambridge Journal of Economics* 35 (5): 805–830.

Grabel, Ilene. 2013a. "Financial Architectures and Development: Resilience, Policy Space, and Human Development in the Global South." Human Development Report Office Occasional Paper No. 7. New York: United Nations Development Programme. http://hdr.undp.org/sites/default/files/hdro_1307_grabel.pdf.

Grabel, Ilene. 2013b. "Global Financial Governance and Development Finance in the Wake of the 2008 Financial Crisis." *Feminist Economics* 19 (3): 32–54.

Grabel, Ilene. 2015a. "Post-crisis Experiments in Development Finance Architectures: A Hirschmanian Perspective on 'Productive Incoherence.'" *Review of Social Economy* 73 (4): 388–414.

Grabel, Ilene. 2015b. "The Rebranding of Capital Controls in an Era of Productive Incoherence." *Review of International Political Economy* 22 (1): 7–43.

Grabel, Ilene. 2017. "Capital Controls in a Time of Crisis." In *Financial Liberalisation: Past, Present and Future*, edited by Philip Arestis and Malcolm Sawyer, 177–223. Basingstoke: Palgrave Macmillan.

Grabel, Ilene, and Kevin P. Gallagher. 2015. "Capital Controls and the Global Financial Crisis: An Introduction." *Review of International Political Economy* 22 (1): 1–6.

Gray, Kevin, and Craig N. Murphy. 2013. "Introduction: Rising Powers and the Future of Global Governance." *Third World Quarterly* 34 (6): 183–193.

Griffith-Jones, Stephany. 2014. "A BRICS Development Bank: A Dream Coming True?" UNCTAD Discussion Paper No. 215. Geneva: United Nations Conference on Trade and Development, March. http://unctad.org/en/PublicationsLibrary/osgdp20141 _en.pdf.

Griffith-Jones, Stephany, Barbara Fritz, and Marcos Antonio Cintra. 2014. "The BRICS Contingent Reserve Arrangement Is a Step Towards More Financial Stability." recoveryhumanface.org, July 24. http://www.recoveryhumanface.org/e-discussion -2013/archives/07-2014.

Griffith-Jones, Stephany, David Griffith-Jones, and Dagmar Hertova. 2008. "Enhancing the Role of Regional Development Banks." G-24 Discussion Paper No. 50. Geneva:

United Nations Conference on Trade and Development, July. http://unctad.org/en /Docs/gdsmdpg2420081_en.pdf.

Griffith-Jones, Stephany, Eric Helleiner, and Ngaire Woods. 2010. "The Financial Stability Board: An Effective Fourth Pillar of Global Economic Governance?" Special Report. Waterloo: Center for International Governance Innovation, June. https:// www.cigionline.org/publications/financial-stability-board-effective-fourth-pillar -global-economic-governance.

Griffith-Jones, Stephany, Li Xiaoyun, and Stephen Spratt. 2016. "The Asian Infra-structure Investment Bank: What Can It Learn From, and Perhaps Teach To, the Multilateral Development Banks?" IDS Evidence Report No. 179. Brighton: Insti-tute for Development Studies, March. http://opendocs.ids.ac.uk/opendocs/handle /123456789/9701.

Griffiths, Jesse, and Konstantinos Todoulous. 2014. "Conditionally Yours: An Analy-sis of the Policy Conditions Attached to IMF Loans." Brussels: European Network on Debt and Development, April. http://eurodad.org/files/pdf/533bd19646b20.pdf.

Grimes, William. 2009a. *Currency and Contest in East Asia: The Great Power Politics of Financial Regionalism.* Ithaca, NY: Cornell University Press.

Grimes, William. 2009b. "The Global Financial Crisis and East Asia: Testing the Regional Financial Architecture." EAI Fellows Program Working Paper No. 20. Seoul: East Asia Institute. http://www.eai.or.kr/data/bbs/eng_report/2009070210204477 .pdf.

Grimes, William. 2009c. "Japan Confronts the Global Economic Crisis." *Asia-Pacific Review* 16 (2): 42–54.

Grimes, William. 2011. "The Asian Monetary Fund Reborn? Implications of Chiang Mai Initiative Multilateralization." *Asia Policy* 11 (1): 79–104.

Grimes, William. 2015. "East Asian Financial Regionalism: Why Economic Enhancements Undermine Political Sustainability." *Contemporary Politics* 21 (2): 145–160.

Gros, Daniel. 2016. "IMF Go Home." *Project Syndicate*, June 8. https://www.project -syndicate.org/commentary/imf-greek-debt-reduction-deal-by-daniel-gros-2016-06.

Guerrieri, Paolo, and Domenico Lombardi. 2010. "US Politics after Seoul: The Reality of International Cooperation." Washington, DC: Brookings Institution, November 23. http://www.brookings.edu/research/opinions/2010/11/23-g20 -outcomes-lombardi.

Guha, Krishna. 2009. "IMF Refuses to Rule Out Use of Capital Controls." *Finan-cial Times*, November 2. http://www.ft.com/intl/cms/s/0/80201cce-c7ef-11de-8ba8 -00144feab49a.

Güven, Ali Burak. 2012. "The IMF, the World Bank, and the Global Economic Crisis: Exploring Paradigm Continuity." *Development and Change* 43 (4): 869–898.

Habermeier, Karl F., Annamaria Kokenyne, and Chikako Baba. 2011. "The Effectiveness of Capital Controls and Prudential Policies in Managing Large Inflows." IMF Staff Discussion Note No. 14. Washington, DC: International Monetary Fund, August 5. https://www.imf.org/external/pubs/ft/sdn/2011/sdn1114.pdf.

Haggard, Stephen. 2013. "Regional Responses to Financial Crises: The Americas, East Asia, and Europe." In *Responding to Financial Crisis: Lessons from Asia Then, the United States and Europe Now*, edited by Changyong Rhee and Adam Posen, 249–275. Washington, DC: Peterson Institute for International Economics.

Hale, David D. 1998. "Dodging the Bullet—This Time." *Brookings Review* 16 (3): 22–25.

Hamanaka, Shintaro. 2016. "Insights to Great Powers' Desire to Establish Institutions: Comparison of ADB, AMF, AMRO and AIIB." *Global Policy* 7 (2): 288–292. doi: 10.1111/1758-5899.12304.

Hanieh, Adam. 2015. "Shifting Priorities or Business as Usual? Continuity and Change in the Post-2011 IMF and World Bank Engagement with Tunisia, Morocco and Egypt." *British Journal of Middle Eastern Studies* 42 (1): 119–134.

Harding, Robin. 2014. "US Fails to Approve IMF Reforms." *Financial Times*, January 14. http://www.ft.com/intl/cms/s/0/8d4755ee-7d43-11e3-81dd-00144feabdc0.html -axzz31oWxFc4Z.

Harmes, Adam. 2001. "Institutional Investors and Polanyi's Double Movement: A Model of Contemporary Currency Crises." *Review of International Political Economy* 8 (3): 389–437.

Harvey, David. 2005. *A Brief History of Neoliberalism*. Oxford: Oxford University Press.

Hausmann, Ricardo, Lant Pritchett, and Dani Rodrik. 2005. "Growth Accelerations." *Journal of Economic Growth*, no. 10:303–329.

Hausmann, Ricardo, Dani Rodrik, and Andrés Velasco. 2008. "Growth Diagnostics." In *The Washington Consensus Reconsidered: Towards a New Global Governance*, edited by Narcís Serra and Joseph Stiglitz, 324–355. Oxford: Oxford University Press.

Hayek, Friedrich. 1974. "The Pretence of Knowledge." Nobel Prize Lecture in Economic Sciences, December 11. http://www.nobelprize.org/nobel_prizes/economic -sciences/laureates/1974/hayek-lecture.html.

Hayek, Friedrich. 2014[1944]. *The Road to Serfdom*. London: Routledge.

He, Alex. 2016. "China in the International Financial System A Study of the NDB and the AIIB." CIGI Working Paper No. 106. Waterloo: Center for International Governance Innovation, June. https://www.cigionline.org/publications/china -international-financial-system-study-ndb-and-aiib.

Heathcoate, Jonathan, and Fabrizio Perri. 2016. "On the Desirability of Capital Controls." *IMF Economic Review* 64 (1): 75–102.

Hedge Fund Research Institute. 2015. "Hedge Fund Assets Approach US$43 Trillion Milestone as Investors Return to Macro." April 20. https://www.hedgefundresearch .com/pdf/pr_20150420.pdf.

Heinbecker, Paul. 2011. "The Future of the G-20 and Its Place in Global Governance." CIGI G-20 Paper No. 5. Waterloo: Center for International Governance Innovation, April. http://www.cigionline.org/publications/2011/4/future-g20-and-its-place-global -governance.

Helleiner, Eric. 1994. *States and the Reemergence of Global Finance.* Ithaca, NY: Cornell University Press.

Helleiner, Eric. 2009. "Reregulation and Fragmentation in International Financial Governance." *Global Governance* 15 (1): 16–22.

Helleiner, Eric. 2010a. "A Bretton Woods Moment? The 2007–2008 Crisis and the Future of Global Finance." *International Affairs* 86 (3): 619–636.

Helleiner, Eric. 2010b. "What Role for the New Financial Stability Board? The Politics of International Standards after the Crisis." *Global Policy* 1 (3): 282–290. doi: 10.1111/j.1758-5899.2010.00040.x.

Helleiner, Eric. 2011a. "The Limits of Incrementalism: The G20, the FSB, and the International Regulatory Agenda." *Journal of Globalization and Development* 2 (2): Article 11. doi: 10.1515/1948-1837.1242.

Helleiner, Eric. 2011b. "Should We Be Feeling More Secure?" thestar.com, September 24. http://www.thestar.com/opinion/editorialopinion/2011/09/24/should_we _be_feeling_more_secure.html.

Helleiner, Eric. 2014a. *Forgotten Foundations of Bretton Woods: International Development and the Making of the Postwar Order.* Ithaca, NY: Cornell University Press.

Helleiner, Eric. 2014b. *The Status Quo Crisis: Global Financial Governance after the 2008 Meltdown.* Oxford: Oxford University Press.

Helleiner, Eric. 2016a. "Incremental Origins of Bretton Woods." In *Oxford Handbook of Historical Institutionalism*, edited by Orfeo Fioretos, Tulia G. Falleti, and Adam Sheingate, 627–641. Oxford: Oxford University Press.

Helleiner, Eric. 2016b. "Legacies of the 2008 Crisis for Global Financial Governance." *Global Summitry* 2 (1): 1–12.

Helleiner, Eric, and Jonathan Kirshner. 2014. "Introduction: The Politics of China's International Monetary Relations." In *The Great Wall of Money*, edited by Eric Helleiner and Jonathan Kirshner, 1–22. Ithaca, NY: Cornell University Press.

Helleiner, Eric, and Stefano Pagliari. 2009. "Towards a New Bretton Woods? The First G20 Leaders Summit and the Regulation of Global Finance." *New Political Economy* 1 (2): 275–287.

Helleiner, Eric, and Stefano Pagliari. 2010. "Crisis and the Reform of International Financial Regulation." In *Global Finance in Crisis: The Politics of International Regulatory Change*, edited by Eric Helleiner, Stephen Pagliari, and Hubert Zimmerman, 1–17. London: Routledge.

Helleiner, Eric, and Stefano Pagliari. 2011. "The End of an Era in International Financial Regulation? A Postcrisis Research Agenda." *International Organization* 65:169–200.

Helleiner, Gerald K. 2010. "Towards Realistic Governance Reform in International Financial Institutions." *Global Economy Journal* 10 (3): 1–4.

Henning, C. Randall. 2009a. *Future of the Chiang Mai Initiative: An Asian Monetary Fund?* Washington, DC: Peterson Institute for International Economics.

Henning, C. Randall. 2009b. "US Interests and the International Monetary Fund." Peterson Institute for International Economics Policy Brief No. PB09-12. Washington, DC: Peterson Institute for International Economics. http://www.iie.com/publica tions/pb/pb09-12.pdf.

Henning, C. Randall. 2016. "The Global Liquidity Safety Net: Precautionary Facilities and Central Bank Swaps." In *Global Financial Governance Confronts the Rising Powers*, edited by C. Randall Henning and Andrew Walter, 119–150. Waterloo: Center for International Governance Innovation.

Henning, C. Randall, and Andrew Walter. 2016. "Global Financial Governance and the Changing Structure of International Finance." In *Global Financial Governance Confronts the Rising Powers: Emerging Perspectives on the New G20*, edited by C. Randall Henning and Andrew Walter, 1–28. Waterloo: Center for International Governance Innovation.

Herrera, Rémy. 2006. "The Neoliberal 'Rebirth' of Development Economics." *Monthly Review* 58 (1). http://monthlyreview.org/2006/05/01/the-neoliberal-rebirth -of-development-economics/.

Higgins, Andrew. 2013. "Currency Controls in Cyprus Increase Worry about Euro System." *New York Times*, July 9. http://www.nytimes.com/2013/07/10/world /europe/currency-controls-in-cyprus-increase-worry-about-euro-system.html?_r=0.

High Level Panel on Infrastructure Investment (HLP). 2011. "Recommendations to G-20 Final Report." High Level Panel on Infrastructure Investment, October 26.

https://us.boell.org/sites/default/files/downloads/HPL_Report_on_Infrastructure_10 -26-2011.pdf.

Hirschman, Albert O. 1965. "Obstacles to Development: A Classification and a Quasi-Vanishing Act." *Economic Development and Cultural Change* 13 (4): 385–393.

Hirschman, Albert O. 1967a. *Development Projects Observed*. Washington, DC: Brookings Institution.

Hirschman, Albert O. 1967b. "The Principle of the Hiding Hand." *The Public Interest* 6:10–23.

Hirschman, Albert O. 1969[1958]. *The Strategy of Economic Development*. New Haven, CT: Yale University Press.

Hirschman, Albert O. 1970. *Exit, Voice, and Loyalty: Responses to Decline in Firms, Organizations and States*. Cambridge, MA: Harvard University Press.

Hirschman, Albert O. 1971. *A Bias for Hope: Essays on Development and Latin America*. New Haven, CT: Yale University Press.

Hirschman, Albert O. 1971[1957]. "Economic Policy in Underdeveloped Countries." In *A Bias for Hope: Essays on Development and Latin America*, edited by Albert O. Hirschman, 255–269. New Haven, CT: Yale University Press.

Hirschman, Albert O. 1973[1963]. *Journeys toward Progress: Studies of Economic Policy-making in Latin America*. New York: Norton Library, Twentieth Century Fund.

Hirschman, Albert O. 1980[1945]. "Preface to the Expanded Paperback Edition." In *National Power and the Structure of Foreign Trade*, v–xii. Berkeley: University of California Press.

Hirschman, Albert O. 1981. *Essays in Trespassing: Economics to Politics and Beyond*. Cambridge: Cambridge University Press.

Hirschman, Albert O. 1981[1978]. "Exit, Voice, and the State." In *Essays in Trespassing: Economics to Politics and Beyond*, edited by Albert O. Hirschman, 246–265. Cambridge: Cambridge University Press.

Hirschman, Albert O. 1991. *The Rhetoric of Reaction: Perversity, Futility, Jeopardy*. Cambridge, MA: Harvard University Press.

Hirschman, Albert O. 1995. *A Propensity to Self-Subversion*. Cambridge, MA: Harvard University Press.

Hirschman, Albert O. 2013[1968a]. "The Political Economy of Import-Substituting Industrialization in Latin America." In *The Essential Hirschman*, edited by Jeremy Adelman, 102–136. Princeton, NJ: Princeton University Press.

Hirschman, Albert O. 2013[1968b]. "Underdevelopment, Obstacles to the Perception of Change, and Leadership." In *The Essential Hirschman*, edited by Jeremy Adelman, 35–48. Princeton, NJ: Princeton University Press.

Hirschman, Albert O. 2013[1970]. "The Search for Paradigms as a Hindrance to Understanding." In *The Essential Hirschman*, edited by Jeremy Adelman, 137–154. Princeton, NJ: Princeton University Press.

Hirschman, Albert O. 2013[1971]. "Political Economics and Possibilism." In *The Essential Hirschman*, edited by Jeremy Adelman, 1–34. Princeton, NJ: Princeton University Press.

Hirschman, Albert O. 2013[1981a]. "A Generalized Linkage Approach to Development, with Special Reference to Staples." In *The Essential Hirschman*, edited by Jeremy Adelman, 155–194. Princeton, NJ: Princeton University Press.

Hirschman, Albert O. 2013[1981b]. "The Rise and Decline of Development Economics." In *The Essential Hirschman*, edited by Jeremy Adelman, 49–73. Princeton, NJ: Princeton University Press.

Hirschman, Albert O. 2013[1986a]. "Against Parsimony: Three Easy Ways of Complicating Some Categories of Economic Discourse." In *The Essential Hirschman*, edited by Jeremy Adelman, 248–264. Princeton, NJ: Princeton University Press.

Hirschman, Albert O. 2013[1986b]. "Rival Views of Market Society." In *The Essential Hirschman*, edited by Jeremy Adelman, 214–247. Princeton, NJ: Princeton University Press.

Hirschman, Albert O., and Charles Lindblom. 1971[1962]. "Economic Development, Research and Development and Policy Making: Some Converging Views." In *A Bias for Hope: Essays on Development and Latin America*, edited by Albert O. Hirschman, 63–84. New Haven, CT: Yale University Press.

HKEx. 2012. "The BRICS Securities and Derivatives Markets." HKEx Research and Corporate Development, December 31. https://www.hkex.com.hk/chi/stat/research/rpaper/Documents/HKEx_BRICS.pdf.

Hochstetler, Kathryn. 2014a. "The Brazilian National Development Bank Goes International: Innovations and Limitations of BNDES' Internationalization." *Global Policy* 5 (3): 360–365. doi: 10.1111/1758-5899.12131.

Hochstetler, Kathryn. 2014b. "Development Banks of the Developing World." *Global Policy* 5 (3): 344–345. doi: 10.1111/1758-5899.12161.

Hochstetler, Kathryn, and Alfred Montero. 2012. "Inertial Statism and the New Developmentalist State in Brazil." Paper presented at a meeting of the Latin American Studies Association, San Francisco, May 23–26. https://www.yumpu.com/en

/document/view/19283861/inertial-statism-and-the-new-developmentalist-state-in
-brazil-co-.

Hochstetler, Kathryn, and Alfred Montero. 2013. "The Renewed Developmental State: The National Development Bank and the Brazilian Development Model." *Journal of Development Studies* 49 (11): 1484–1499.

Hodgson, Geoffrey. 2009. "The Great Crash of 2008 and the Reform of Economics." *Cambridge Journal of Economics* 33 (6): 1205–1221.

Hoffmann, Matthew J. 2011. *Climate Governance at the Crossroads: Experimenting with a Global Response after Kyoto.* Oxford: Oxford University Press.

Hollinger, Peggy, and Chris Giles. 2011. "Sarkozy Seeks Capital Flow Code." *Financial Times,* January 24. http://www.ft.com/intl/cms/s/0/30e9ca28-27b2-11e0-a327 -00144feab49a.html#axzz3YRnyq3aK.

Holroyd, Karin, and Bessma Momani. 2012. "Japan's Rescue of the IMF." *Social Science Japan Journal* 15 (2): 201–218.

Horsefield, J. Keith. 1969. *The International Monetary Fund, 1945–65,* vol. 3. Washington, DC: International Monetary Fund.

Humphrey, Chris. 2014. "The Politics of Loan Pricing in Multilateral Development Banks." *Review of International Political Economy* 21 (3): 611–639.

Humphrey, Chris. 2015a. "Challenges and Opportunities for Multilateral Development Banks in 21st Century Infrastructure Finance." Working Paper Series Infrastructure Finance in the Developing World. Seoul: Intergovernmental Group of Twenty-Four and Global Green Growth Institute, June. http://g24.org/wp-content /uploads/2016/05/MARGGK-WP08.pdf.

Humphrey, Chris. 2015b. "Development Revolution or Bretton Woods Revisited?" ODI Working Paper No. 418. London: Overseas Development Institute, April. https:// www.odi.org/sites/odi.org.uk/files/odi-assets/publications-opinion-files/9615.pdf.

Huotari, Mikko, and Thilo Hanemann. 2014. "Emerging Powers and Change in the Global Financial Order." *Global Policy* 5 (3): 298–310. doi: 10.1111/1758-5899.12133.

Inclusive Development International (IDI). 2016. "Behind the Fumes: The Dirty Truth behind the World Bank's Commitments on Climate Change, Part I." Asheville, NC: Inclusive Development International, October. http://www.inclusive development.net/wp-content/uploads/2016/09/Outsourcing-Development -Climate.pdf.

Independent Evaluation Office (IEO). 2003. "The IMF and Recent Capital Account Crises: Indonesia, Korea, and Brazil." Washington, DC: IEO of the International Monetary Fund. https://www.imf.org/external/np/ieo/2003/cac/pdf/all.pdf.

Independent Evaluation Office (IEO). 2005. *Report on the Evaluation of the IMF's Approach to Capital Account Liberalization.* Washington, DC: IEO of the International Monetary Fund. http://www.ieo-imf.org/ieo/files/completedevaluations /04202005report.pdf.

Independent Evaluation Office (IEO). 2007. *Structural Conditionality in IMF-Supported Programs.* Washington, DC: IEO of the International Monetary Fund. http://www.ieo-imf.org/ieo/files/completedevaluations/01032008SC_main _report.pdf.

Independent Evaluation Office (IEO). 2009. IMF Interactions with Member Countries. Washington, DC: IEO of the International Monetary Fund. http://www.ieo-imf.org /ieo/files/completedevaluations/A.%20%20Full%20Text%20of%20Main%20Report .pdf.

Independent Evaluation Office (IEO). 2011. *IMF Performance in the Run-up to the Financial and Economic Crisis: IMF Surveillance in 2004–2007.* Washington, DC: IEO of the International Monetary Fund. http://www.imf.org/ieo/files/completedevaluations /Crisis- Main Report (without Moises Signature).pdf.

Independent Evaluation Office (IEO). 2013. *The Role of the IMF as Trusted Advisor.* Washington, DC: IEO of the International Monetary Fund. http://www.ieo-imf.org /ieo/pages/CompletedEvaluation157.aspx.

Independent Evaluation Office (IEO). 2014. *IMF Response to the Financial and Economic Crises.* Washington, DC: IEO of the International Monetary Fund. http://www .ieo-imf.org/ieo/pages/EvaluationImages227.aspx.

Independent Evaluation Office (IEO). 2015. *IMF's Approach to Capital Account Liberalization, Revisiting the 2005 IEO Evaluation.* Washington, DC: IEO of the International Monetary Fund. http://www.ieo-imf.org/ieo/files/whatsnew/The IMFs Approach to Capital Account Liberalization Revisiting the 2005 IEO Evaluation3.pdf.

Independent Evaluation Office (IEO). 2016. *The IMF and the Crises in Greece, Ireland, and Portugal: An Evaluation by the Independent Evaluation Office.* Washington, DC: IEO of the International Monetary Fund. http://www.ieo-imf.org/ieo/pages/Completed Evaluation267.aspx.

Institute of International Finance (IIF). 2016. "Capital Flows to Emerging Markets." Washington, DC: IIF, January 19. https://images.magnetmail.net/images/clients/IIF _2/attach/CF_0116_Press(3).pdf.

IntelliNews. 2016. "Tajik Central Bank Denies Termination of Ruble Transfers." February 8. http://www.intellinews.com/tajik-central-bank-denies-termination-of-ruble -transfers-90219/.

Inter-American Development Bank (IADB). 2016. "Annual Reports." Accessed December 20. http://www.iadb.org/en/about-us/annual-reports,6293.html.

International Financial Institution Advisory Commission. 2000. "Report of the Meltzer Commission: The Future of the IMF and World Bank." Hearing before the Committee on Foreign Relations, United States Senate, One Hundred Sixth Congress, Senate Hearing 106-657, Second Session, May 23, 2000. Washington, DC: US Government Printing Office. http://0-congressional.proquest.com.bianca .penlib.du.edu/congressional/docview/t29.d30.hrg-2000-for-0016?accountid =14608.

International Monetary Fund (IMF). 2008. "World Leaders Launch Action Plan to Combat Financial Crisis." IMF Survey. Washington, DC: IMF, November 15. https:// www.imf.org/external/pubs/ft/survey/so/2008/NEW111508A.htm.

International Monetary Fund (IMF). 2009a. *Annual Report on Exchange Rate Arrangements and Exchange Restrictions.* Washington, DC: IMF. http://www.elibrary.imf.org /page/AREAER/www.imfareaer.org.

International Monetary Fund (IMF). 2009b. *Creating Policy Space—Responsive Design and Streamlined Conditionality in Recent Low-Income Country Programs.* Washington, DC: IMF, Strategy, Policy and Review Department. http://www.imf.org/external/np /pp/eng/2009/091009A.pdf.

International Monetary Fund (IMF). 2009c. *The Implications of the Global Financial Crisis for Low-Income Countries.* Washington, DC: IMF, March. https://www.imf.org /external/pubs/ft/books/2009/globalfin/globalfin.pdf.

International Monetary Fund (IMF). 2009d. *Review of Recent Crisis Programs.* Washington, DC: IMF, Strategy, Policy and Review Department. http://www.imf.org /external/np/pp/eng/2009/091409.pdf.

International Monetary Fund (IMF). 2010a. "Bangladesh: 2009 Article IV Consultation—Staff Report. Public Information Notice on the Executive Board Discussion." Washington, DC: IMF, February. https://www.imf.org/external/pubs/ft/scr /2010/cr1055.pdf.

International Monetary Fund (IMF). 2010b. *A Fair and Substantial Contribution by the Financial Sector.* Final Report for the Group of 20. Washington, DC: IMF, June. http://www.imf.org/external/np/g20/pdf/062710b.pdf.

International Monetary Fund (IMF). 2010c. *The Fund's Role Regarding Cross-Border Capital Flows.* Washington, DC: Strategy, Policy, and Review Department and the Legal Department, IMF. https://www.imf.org/external/np/pp/eng/2010/111510.pdf.

International Monetary Fund (IMF). 2010d. "Greece: First Review under Stand-by Arrangement." Country Report No. 10/286. Washington, DC: IMF, September. http://www.imf.org/external/pubs/ft/scr/2010/cr10286.pdf.

International Monetary Fund (IMF). 2010e. "Greece: Staff Report on Request for Stand-by Arrangement." IMF Country Report No. 10/110. Washington, DC: IMF, May. https://www.imf.org/external/pubs/ft/scr/2010/cr10110.pdf.

International Monetary Fund (IMF). 2010f. "IMF Executive Board Approves Major Overhaul of Quotas and Governance." Press Release No. 10/418. Washington, DC: IMF, November 5. https://www.imf.org/external/np/sec/pr/2010/pr10418.htm.

International Monetary Fund (IMF). 2011a. *Crisis Assessment: IMF Support Helping Restore Growth but Key Risks Ahead. IMF Survey.* Washington, DC: IMF, April 15. http://www.imf.org/external/np/spr/2011/crisprorev/survey/041511.pdf.

International Monetary Fund (IMF). 2011b. "How Iceland Recovered from Its Near Death Experience." *IMF Direct*, October 26. http://blog-imfdirect.imf.org/2011/10/26/how-iceland-recovered-from-its-near-death-experience/.

International Monetary Fund (IMF). 2011c. "The Multilateral Aspects of Policies Affecting Capital Flows." Background Paper. Washington, DC: IMF, Monetary and Capital Markets Department and the Strategy, Policy, and Review Department, October 13. http://www.imf.org/external/np/pp/eng/2011/102111.pdf.

International Monetary Fund (IMF). 2011d. *Recent Experiences in Managing Capital Inflows—Cross-cutting Themes and Possible Policy Framework.* Washington, DC: IMF, Strategy, Policy, and Review Department, February 14. http://www.imf.org/external/np/pp/eng/2011/021411a.pdf.

International Monetary Fund (IMF). 2012a. *2011 Review of Conditionality: Background Paper 1, Content and Application of Conditionality.* Washington, DC: IMF, Strategy, Policy and Review Department, June 18. http://www.imf.org/external/np/pp/eng/2012/061812.pdf.

International Monetary Fund (IMF). 2012b. *2011 Review of Conditionality: Overview Paper.* Washington, DC: IMF, Strategy, Policy and Review Department, June 19. http://www.imf.org/external/np/pp/eng/2012/061912a.pdf.

International Monetary Fund (IMF). 2012c. *Greece: Letter of Intent, Memorandum of Economic and Financial Policies, and Technical Memorandum of Understanding.* Washington, DC: IMF, March 9. http://www.imf.org/external/np/loi/2012/grc/030912.pdf.

International Monetary Fund (IMF). 2012d. "Iceland: Ex Post Evaluation of Exceptional Access under the 2008 Stand-by Arrangement." IMF Country Report No. 12/91. Washington, DC: IMF, April. https://www.imf.org/external/pubs/ft/scr/2012/cr1291.pdf.

International Monetary Fund (IMF). 2012e. "IMF Executive Board Discusses the Liberalization and Management of Capital Flows—An Institutional View." Public

Information Notice No. 12/137. Washington, DC: IMF, December 3. https://www
.imf.org/external/np/sec/pn/2012/pn12137.htm.

International Monetary Fund (IMF). 2012f. "The Liberalization and Management of
Capital Flows: An Institutional View." Washington, DC: IMF, November 14. http://
www.imf.org/external/np/pp/eng/2012/111412.pdf.

International Monetary Fund (IMF). 2012g. "Coping with High Debt and Sluggish
Growth." *World Economic Outlook*, October. Washington, DC: IMF. https://www.imf
.org/external/pubs/ft/weo/2012/02/.

International Monetary Fund (IMF). 2012h. "Growth Resuming, Dangers Remain."
World Economic Outlook, April. Washington, DC: IMF. http://www.imf.org/external
/pubs/ft/weo/2012/01/.

International Monetary Fund (IMF). 2013a. "Ex Post Evaluation of Exceptional Access
under the 2010 Stand-by Arrangement." IMF Country Report No. 13/156. Washington,
DC: IMF, June. http://www.imf.org/external/pubs/ft/scr/2013/cr13156.pdf.

International Monetary Fund (IMF). 2013b. *Fiscal Monitor: Taxing Times*. Washington,
DC: IMF, October. http://www.imf.org/external/pubs/ft/fm/2013/02/pdf/fm1302.pdf.

International Monetary Fund (IMF). 2013c. *Guidance Note for the Liberalization and
Management of Capital Flows*. Washington, DC: IMF, April 25. https://www.imf.org
/external/np/pp/eng/2013/042513.pdf.

International Monetary Fund (IMF). 2013d. "IMF Statement on Taxation." Press
Release No. 13/427. Washington, DC: IMF, November 5. http://www.imf.org
/external/np/sec/pr/2013/pr13427.htm.

International Monetary Fund (IMF). 2013e. "Hopes, Realities, Risks." *World Economic
Outlook*, April. Washington, DC: IMF. http://www.imf.org/external/pubs/ft/weo
/2013/01/.

International Monetary Fund (IMF). 2014a." Factsheet: IMF Conditionality." Washington, DC: IMF. http://www.imf.org/external/np/exr/facts/conditio.htm.

International Monetary Fund (IMF). 2014b. "Ghana: 2014 Article IV Consultation."
IMF Country Report No. 14/129. Washington, DC: IMF, May. https://www.imf.org
/external/pubs/ft/scr/2014/cr14129.pdf.

International Monetary Fund (IMF). 2014c. "Kenya: 2014 Article IV Consultation."
IMF Country Report No. 14/302. Washington, DC: IMF, October. https://www.imf
.org/external/pubs/ft/scr/2014/cr14302.pdf.

International Monetary Fund (IMF). 2014d. "Recovery Strengthens, Remains
Uneven." *World Economic Outlook*, April. Washington, DC: IMF. http://www.imf.org
/external/Pubs/ft/weo/2014/01/.

International Monetary Fund (IMF). 2014e. "Factsheet: The IMF's Advice on Labor Market Issues." Washington, DC: IMF, September 30. https://www.imf.org/external /np/exr/facts/labor.htm.

International Monetary Fund (IMF). 2015a. "Factsheet: Protecting the Most Vulnerable under IMF-Supported Programs." Washington, DC: IMF, April. https://www.imf .org/external/np/exr/facts/pdf/protect.pdf.

International Monetary Fund (IMF). 2015b. "Greece: An Update of IMF Staff's Preliminary Public Debt Sustainability Analysis." IMF Country Report No. 15/186. Washington, DC: IMF, July 14. https://www.imf.org/external/pubs/ft/scr/2015 /cr15186.pdf.

International Monetary Fund (IMF). 2015c. "The IMF and Europe." Washington, DC: IMF, April 10. http://www.imf.org/external/np/exr/facts/pdf/europe.pdf.

International Monetary Fund (IMF). 2015d. *Managing Capital Outflows—Further Operational Considerations. Staff Report issued to the Executive Board.* Washington, DC: IMF, December. https://www.imf.org/external/np/pp/eng/2015/120315.pdf.

International Monetary Fund (IMF). 2016a. "Capital Flows—Review of Experience with the Institutional View." Staff Report. Washington, DC: IMF, November 7. http://www.imf.org/external/pp/longres.aspx?id=5081.

International Monetary Fund (IMF). 2016b. "Chief Economist Interview, Evolution Not Revolution: Rethinking Policy at the IMF." IMF Survey. Washington, DC: IMF, June 2. http://www.imf.org/external/pubs/ft/survey/so/2016/POL060216A.htm.

International Monetary Fund (IMF). 2016c. "Historic Quota and Governance Reforms Become Effective." Press Release No. 16/25. Washington, DC: IMF, January 27. https://www.imf.org/external/np/sec/pr/2016/pr1625a.htm.

International Monetary Fund (IMF). 2016d. "The IMF and Europe." Washington, DC: IMF, March 23. http://www.imf.org/external/np/exr/facts/europe.htm.

International Monetary Fund (IMF). 2016e. "IMF Executive Board Approves US$12 Billion Extended Arrangement under the Extended Fund Facility for Egypt." Washington, DC: IMF, November 11. http://www.imf.org/en/News/Articles/2016/11/11 /PR16501-Egypt-Executive-Board-Approves-12-billion-Extended-Arrangement.

International Monetary Fund (IMF). 2017. "Currency Composition of Official Foreign Exchange Reserves (COFER)." Washington, DC: IMF. Last updated March 31. http://data.imf.org/?sk=E6A5F467-C14B-4AA8-9F6D-5A09EC4E62A4.

Islam, Iyanatul, Ishraq Ahmed, Rathin Roy, and Raquel Ramos. 2012. "Macroeconomic Policy Advice and the Article IV Consultations: A Development Perspective." ILO Research Paper No. 2. Geneva: International Labour Office, August. http://www .ilo.org/global/research/papers/WCMS_187406/lang—en/index.htm.

Jaffe, Stephen. 2016. "IMF's Lagarde: Negative Rates Benefit Global Economy." *MSN Money*, March 18. http://www.msn.com/en-ph/money/topstories/imfs-lagarde -negative-rates-benefit-global-economy/ar-BBqD8pa.

James, Harald. 2014. "The Secret History of the Financial Crisis." *Project Syndicate*, March 7. http://www.project-syndicate.org/commentary/harold-james-examines-the -real-story-behind-the-international-response-to-the-near-meltdown-in-2008.

Janike, Kiraz. 2008. "Summit of the Bolivarian Alternative Concludes in Venezuela." Venezuelananalysis.com, January 27. http://venezuelanalysis.com/news/3104.

Jeanne, Olivier, Arvind Subramanian, and John Williamson. 2011. *Who Needs to Open the Capital Account?* Washington, DC: Peterson Institute for International Economics.

Jiang, Yang. 2014. "The Limits of China's Monetary Diplomacy." In *The Great Wall of Money*, edited by Eric Helleiner and Jonathan Kirshner, 156–183. Ithaca, NY: Cornell University Press.

Johnson, Juliet. 2008. "Forbidden Fruit: Russia's Uneasy Relationship with the US Dollar." *Review of International Political Economy* 15 (3): 379–398.

Johnson, Steve. 2015. "Emerging Market Slump Raises Fears of Capital Controls." *Financial Times*, September 9. http://www.ft.com/intl/cms/s/3/72c18c2c-554a-11e5 -b029-b9d50a74fd14.html - axzz43mCKnnUk.

Jones, Bruce D. 2011. "Largest Minority Shareholder in Global Order LLC: The Changing Balance of Influence and US Strategy." Foreign Policy at Brookings Policy Paper No. 25. Washington, DC: Brookings Institution. https://www.brookings.edu /wp-content/uploads/2016/06/03_global_order_jones.pdf.

Kahler, Miles. 2000. "The New International Financial Architecture and Its Limits." In *The Asian Financial Crisis and the Architecture of Global Finance*, edited by Gregory W. Noble and John Ravenhill, 235–260. Cambridge: Cambridge University Press.

Kaplan, Ethan, and Dani Rodrik. 2001. "Did the Malaysian Capital Controls Work?" NBER Working Paper No. 8142. Cambridge, MA: National Bureau of Economic Research, February. http://www.nber.org/papers/w8142.

Kapur, Devesh, and Richard Webb. 2007. "Beyond the IMF." *Economic and Political Weekly*, February 17–23, 581–589.

Katada, Saori, and Injoo Sohn. 2014. "Regionalism as Financial Statecraft: China and Japan's Pursuit of Counterweight Strategies." In *The Financial Statecraft of Emerging Powers*, edited by Leslie Eliot Armijo and Saori N. Katada, 138–161. Basingstoke: Palgrave Macmillan.

Kattel, Rainer, and Ringa Raudla. 2013. "The Baltic Republics and the Crisis of 2008–2011." *Europe-Asia Studies* 65 (3): 426–449. doi: 10.1080/09668136.2013.779456.

Katzenstein, Peter J. 2005. *A World of Regions: Asia and Europe in the American Imperium*. Ithaca, NY: Cornell University Press.

Kawai, Masahiro. 2010. "East Asian Financial Cooperation and the Role of the ASEAN+3 Macroeconomic Research Office." In *Regional and Global Liquidity Arrangements*, edited by Ulrich Volz and Aldo Caliari, 50–56. Bonn: German Development Institute and Center of Concern.

Kawai, Masahiro, and Domenico Lombardi. 2012. "Regional Financial Arrangements Are Reshaping the International Financial Architecture and Helping Global Financial Stability." *Finance and Development* 49 (3): 23–25.

Kelly, Lidia, Darya Korsunskaya, and Elena Fabrichnaya. 2014. "Informal Capital Controls Arrest Russian Rouble's Slide." Reuters, December 24. http://uk.reuters.com /article/uk-russia-crisis-rouble-idUKKBN0K10EE20141224.

Kenen, Peter, ed. 1996. *From Halifax to Lyons: What Has Been Done about Crisis Management? Essays in International Finance*. Princeton, NJ: Princeton University, Department of Economics.

Kentikelenis, Alexander, Thomas Stubbs, and Lawrence King. 2016. "IMF Conditionality and Development Policy Space, 1985–2014." *Review of International Political Economy* 23 (4): 543–582.

Kim, Soyoung, and Doo Yong Yang. 2014. "Regional Financial Architecture beyond the Global Financial Crisis." In *The Political Economy of Asian Regionalism*, edited by G. Capannelli and M. Kawai, 85–104. Tokyo: Asian Development Bank Institute.

King, Mervyn. 2006. "Reform of the International Monetary Fund." Speech at the Indian Council for Research on International Economic Relations, New Delhi, India, Feburary 20. http://www.bankofengland.co.uk/archive/Documents/historicpubs /speeches/2006/speech267.pdf.

Kirman, Alan. 2016. "Complexity and Economic Policy: A Paradigm Shift or a Change in Perspective? A Review Essay on David Colander and Roland Kupers's *Complexity and the Art of Public Policy*." *Journal of Economic Literature* 54 (2): 534–572.

Kirshner, Jonathan. 1997. *Currency and Coercion: The Political Economy of International Monetary Power*. Princeton, NJ: Princeton University Press.

Kirshner, Jonathan. 2003. "The Inescapable Politics of Money." In *Monetary Orders: Ambiguous Economics, Ubiquitous Politics*, edited by Jonathan Kirshner, 3–24. Ithaca, NY: Cornell University Press.

Kirshner, Jonathan. 2014a. *American Power after the Financial Crisis*. Ithaca, NY: Cornell University Press.

Kirshner, Jonathan. 2014b. "Regional Hegemony and an Emerging RMB Zone." In *The Great Wall of Money*, edited by Eric Helleiner and Jonathan Kirshner, 213–240. Ithaca, NY: Cornell University Press.

Kissinger, Henry A. 1998. "How the U.S. Can End Up as the Good Guy." *Los Angeles Times*, February 8. http://articles.latimes.com/1998/feb/08/opinion/op-16725.

Knight, Frank. 1971[1921]. *Risk, Uncertainty, and Profit*. Chicago: University of Chicago Press.

Korinek, Anton. 2011. "The New Economics of Prudential Capital Controls: A Research Agenda." *IMF Economic Review* 59 (3): 523–561.

Korinek, Anton. 2013. "Capital Controls and Currency Wars." University of Maryland, February, mimeo. http://www.cepr.org/sites/default/files/Korinek_Capital Controls and Currency Wars.pdf.

Korinek, Anton. 2014. "International Spillovers and Guidelines for Policy Cooperation: A Welfare Theorem for National Economic Policymaking." Paper presented at the 15th Jacques Polak Annual Research Conference. Washington, DC: International Monetary Fund, November 13–14. https://www.imf.org/external/np/res/seminars/2014/arc/pdf/korinek.pdf.

Korinek, Anton, and Damiano Sandri. 2015. "Capital Controls or Macroprudential Regulation?" IMF Working Paper No. 2018. Washington, DC: International Monetary Fund, October. https://www.imf.org/external/pubs/ft/wp/2015/wp15218.pdf.

Kozul-Wright, Richard, and Daniel Poon. 2015. "Development Finance with Chinese Characteristics?" *Project Syndicate*, May 20. http://www.project-syndicate.org/commentary/china-silk-road-fund-development-financing-by-richard-kozul-wright-and-daniel-poon-2015-05.

Kristof, Nicholas D., and Sheryl WuDunn. 1999. "Of World Markets, None an Island." *New York Times*, February 17, A1.

Krugman, Paul. 1994. "The Rise and Fall of Development Economics." In *Rethinking the Development Experience: Essays Provoked by the Work of Albert O. Hirschman*, edited by Lloyd Rodwin and Donald Schön, 39–58. Washington, DC: Brookings Institution.

Krugman, Paul. 1998. "Saving Asia: It's Time to Get Radical." *Fortune*, September 7, 35–36. http://archive.fortune.com/magazines/fortune/fortune_archive/1998/09/07/247884/index.htm.

Kulish, Nicholas. 2009. "Global Economic Crisis Rescues European Bank." *New York Times*, October 8, B3.

Lagarde, Christine. 2012. "Asia and the Promise of Economic Cooperation." Speech in Kuala Lumpur, November 14. https://www.imf.org/external/np/speeches/2012/111412.htm.

Lagarde, Christine. 2015a. "Spillovers from Unconventional Monetary Policy—Lessons for Emerging Markets." Speech at the Reserve Bank of India, March 17. https://www.imf.org/external/np/speeches/2015/031715.htm.

Lagarde, Christine. 2015b. "Statement by IMF Managing Director Christine Lagarde on Greece." Press Release No. 15/381. Washington, DC: International Monetary Fund, August 14. http://www.imf.org/external/np/sec/pr/2015/pr15381.htm.

Landler, Mark. 2009. "Rising Powers Challenge US on IMF Role." *New York Times*, A15.

Landler, Mark, and David E. Sanger. 2009. "World Leaders Pledge $1.1 Trillion for Crisis." *New York Times*, April 3, A1.

Latin American Debt and Development Network–Bretton Woods Project (LatinDADD–BWP). 2011. *Breaking the Mould: How Latin America Is Coping with Volatile Capital Flows*. Latin American Debt and Development Network–Bretton Woods Project, December. http://www.brettonwoodsproject.org/wp-content/uploads/2013/10/breakingthemould.pdf.

Latin American Reserve Fund (FLAR). 2017. Website. Accessed January 10. https://www.flar.net.

Leahy, Joe. 2011. "Brazil: Mantega Gloats as Europe Burns." *Financial Times*, December 2. http://blogs.ft.com/beyond-brics/2011/12/02/brazil-mantega-gloats-as-europe-burns/.

Leahy, Joe, and Samantha Pearson. 2013. "Brazil Slashes Financial Transactions Tax." *Financial Times*, June 5. http://www.ft.com/intl/cms/s/0/6c113a7c-cd74-11e2-90e8-00144feab7de.html - axzz40jfKd1Ev.

Lee, Chang-ho. 2011. "S. Korea to Undertake Stress Test on Banks' FX Funding-source." Reuters, July 25. http://www.reuters.com/article/korea-banks-idUSL3E7IP0KO20110725.

Leigh, Daniel, Pete Devries, Charles Freedman, Jaime Guajardo, Douglas Laxton, and Andrea Pescatori. 2010. "Will It Hurt? Macroeconomic Effects of Fiscal Consolidation." *World Economic Outlook*, October, 93–124. Washington, DC: International Monetary Fund.

Lepenies, Philipp H. 2008. "Possibilism: An Approach to Problem-Solving Derived from the Life and Work of Albert O. Hirschman." *Development and Change* 39 (3): 437–459.

Lerner, Abba. 1944. *The Economics of Control*. London: MacMillan.

Lesage, Dries, Peter Debaere, Sacha Dierckx, and Mattias Vermeiren. 2013. "IMF Reform after the Crisis." *International Politics* 50 (4): 553–578.

Levin, Kelly, Benjamin Cashore, Steven Bernstein, and Graeme Auld. 2012. "Overcoming the Tragedy of Super Wicked Problems: Constraining Our Future Selves to Ameliorate Global Climate Change." *Policy Sciences* 45 (2): 123–152.

Lindblom, Charles. 1959. "The Science of 'Muddling Through.'" *Public Administration Review* 19 (2): 79–88.

Lindblom, Charles. 1979. "Still Muddling, Not Yet Through." *Public Administration Review* 39 (6): 517–526.

Lipsky, John. 2009. "Building a Post-crisis Global Economy." Address to the Japan Society, New York, December 10. http://www.imf.org/external/np/speeches/2009/121009.htm.

Lissakers, Karin, Ishrat Husain, and Ngaire Woods. 2006. *Report of the External Evaluation of the Independent Evaluation Office.* Washington, DC: International Monetary Fund, March 29. http://www.ieo-imf.org/ieo/files/evaluationofieo/032906.pdf.

Lombardi, Domenico. 2010. *Financial Regionalism: A Review of the Issues.* Washington, DC: Brookings Institution, Global Economy and Development. http://www.brookings.edu/research/papers/2010/11/global-economy-lombardi.

Lombardi, Domenico, and Ngaire Woods. 2008. "The Politics of Influence: An Analysis of IMF Surveillance." *Review of International Political Economy* 15 (5): 711–739.

Lütz, Susanne, and Matthias Kranke. 2014. "The European Rescue of the Washington Consensus? EU and IMF Lending to Central and Eastern European Countries." *Review of International Political Economy* 21 (2): 310–338.

Macintyre, Andrew, T. J. Pempel, and John Ravenhill. 2008. *Crisis as Catalyst: Asia's Dynamic Political Economy.* Ithaca, NY: Cornell University Press.

Magtulis, Prinz. 2013. "Moody's Backs Limited Use of Capital Controls in SEA." *Philippine Star,* February 22. http://www.philstar.com/business/2013/02/22/911570/moodys-backs-limited-use-of-capital-controls-sea.

Magud, Nicolas, and Carmen M. Reinhart. 2006. "Capital Controls: An Evaluation." NBER Working Paper No. 11973. Cambridge, MA: National Bureau of Economic Research. http://www.nber.org/papers/w11973.

Magud, Nicolas, Carmen M. Reinhart, and Kenneth Rogoff. 2011. "Capital Controls: Myth and Reality—A Portfolio Balance Approach." NBER Working Paper No. 16805. Cambridge, MA: National Bureau of Economic Research, February. http://www.nber.org/papers/w16805.

Mahoney, James, and Kathleen Thelen, eds. 2010. *Explaining Institutional Change: Ambiguity, Agency, and Power.* Cambridge: Cambridge University Press.

Mantega, Guido. 2007. Statement at the 16th Meeting of the IMFC. International Monetary and Financial Committee of the International Monetary Fund. Washington, DC, October 20. http://www.imf.org/external/am/2007/imfc/statement/eng/bra.pdf.

Manurung, Novrida, and Widya Utami. 2010. "Indonesia Tightens Rules on Foreign-Exchange Holdings." Bloomberg, December 29. http://www.bloomberg.com/news

/articles/2010-12-29/indonesia-raises-bank-foreign-currency-reserve-ratios-amid
-capital-inflows.

Marshall, Wesley C. 2010. "Banco del Sur and the Need for Downstream Linkages." *International Journal of Political Economy* 39 (3): 81–99.

Marshall, Wesley C., and Louis-Philippe Rochon. 2009. "Financing Economic Development in Latin America: The Banco del Sur." *Journal of Post-Keynesian Economics* 32 (2): 185–198.

Mayeda, Andrew. 2011. "Harper Pushing Rousseff on Currencies May Herald G-20 Spat." Bloomberg, August 8. http://www.bloomberg.com/news/articles/2011-08-08/harper-clashing-with-rousseff-on-capital-controls-may-herald-g-20-discord.

Mazzucato, Mariana. 2013. *The Entrepreneurial State: Debunking Public Vs. Private Sector Myths*. London: Anthem.

Mazzucato, Mariana. 2015. "From Market Fixing to Market-Creating: A New Framework for Economic Policy." Science Policy Research Institute Working Paper No. 25. Sussex, UK: University of Sussex, September. https://ssrn.com/abstract=2744593 or http://dx.doi.org/10.2139/ssrn.2744593.

Mazzucato, Mariana, and Caetano C. R. Penna. 2016. "Beyond Market Failures: The Market Creating and Shaping Roles of State Investment Banks." *Journal of Economic Policy Reform* 19 (4): 305–326.

McCloskey, Deirdre. 1990. *If You're So Smart: A Narrative of Economic Expertise*. Chicago: University of Chicago Press.

McDowell, Daniel. 2017. "Emergent International Liquidity Network: Central Bank Cooperation after the Global Financial Crisis." *Journal of International Relations and Development*, forthcoming.

McElhiny, Vince. 2009. "Global Crisis Is Good News for IFIs in Latin America." Americas Program Report. Washington, DC: Center for International Policy, January 27. http://www19.iadb.org/intal/intalcdi/PE/2009/03605.pdf.

McGrath, J. J. 2015. "ADB, IMF, World Bank to Cooperate with China-Led Asian Infrastructure Investment Bank, Leaders Say." *International Business Times*, March 22. http://www.ibtimes.com/adb-imf-world-bank-cooperate-china-led-asian-infrastructure-investment-bank-leaders-1855012.

McKay, Julie, Ulrich Volz, and Regine Wölfinger. 2011. "Regional Financing Arrangements and the Stability of the International Monetary System." *Journal of Globalization and Development* 2 (1): Article 5. doi: https://doi.org/10.2202/1948-1837.1139.

McMillan, John. 2008. "Avoid Hubris: And Other Lessons for Reformers." In *Reinventing Foreign Aid*, edited by William Easterly, 505–514. Cambridge, MA: MIT Press.

McNamara, Kathleen R. 1999. *The Currency of Ideas: Monetary Politics in the European Union*. Cambridge: Cambridge University Press.

Mielniczuk, Fabiano. 2013. "BRICS in the Contemporary World: Changing Identities, Converging Interests." *Third World Quarterly* 34 (6): 1075–1090.

Ministries of Foreign Affairs and Commerce. 2015. "Vision and Actions on Jointly Building Silk Road Economic Belt and 21st-Century Maritime Silk Road." People's Republic of China, March 28. http://en.ndrc.gov.cn/newsrelease/201503/t20150330 _669367.html.

Mirowski, Philip. 2010. "The Great Mortification: Economists' Responses to the Crisis of 2007– and Counting." *Hedgehog Review* 12 (3). http://www.iasc-culture.org /THR/THR_article_2010_Summer_Mirowski.php.

Mirowski, Philip. 2013. *Never Let a Serious Crisis Go to Waste: How Neoliberalism Survived the Financial Meltdown*. London: Verso.

Mishkin, Frederic S. 2006. *The Next Great Globalization*. Princeton, NJ: Princeton University Press.

Mistry, Percy S. 1999. "Coping with Financial Crises: Are Regional Arrangements the Missing Link?" In *International Monetary and Financial Issues for the 1990s*, vol. 10, edited by UNCTAD, 93–116. New York: United Nations Conference on Trade and Development (UNCTAD).

Mittelman, James H. 2013. "Global Bricolage: Emerging Market Powers and Polycentric Governance." *Third World Quarterly* 34 (1): 23–37.

Miyoshi, Toshiyuki. 2013. *Stocktaking the Fund's Engagement with Regional Financing Arrangements*. Washington, DC: International Monetary Fund, April 11. https://www .imf.org/external/np/pp/eng/2013/041113b.pdf.

Mnuchin, Steven. 2017. "IMFC Statement by Steven Mnuchin on Behalf of the United States to the 35th Meeting of the International Monetary and Financial Committee of the International Monetary Fund." Washington, DC, April 22. https:// www.imf.org/External/spring/2017/imfc/statement/eng/usa.pdf.

Mody, Ashoka. 2016. "Saving the IMF." *Project Syndicate*, April 9. https://www.project -syndicate.org/onpoint/saving-the-imf-by-ashoka-mody-2016-04?barrier=true.

Mohan, Rakesh, and Muneesh Kapur. 2015. "Emerging Powers and Global Governance: Whither the IMF?" IMF Working Paper No. 219. Washington, DC: International Monetary Fund. http://www.imf.org/external/pubs/ft/wp/2015/wp15219 .pdf.

Molina, Nuria. 2010. "Bail-out or Blow-out? IMF Policy Advice and Conditions for Low-Income Countries at a Time of Crisis." Brussels: European Network on Debt and Development, June. http://eurodad.org/3679/.

Momani, Bessma. 2005. "Limits on Streamlining Fund Conditionality: The International Monetary Fund's Organizational Culture." *Journal of International Relations and Development* 8 (2): 142–163.

Momani, Bessma. 2010. "IMF Rhetoric on Reducing Poverty and Inequality." In *Global Governance, Poverty and Inequality*, edited by Jennifer Clapp and Rorden Wilkinson, 71–89. London: Routldege.

Momani, Bessma, and Dustyn Lanz. 2014. "Shifting IMF Priorities since the Arab Uprisings." CIGI Policy Brief No. 34. Waterloo: Center for International Governance Innovation, March 6. http://www.cigionline.org/publications/shifting-imf-policies-arab-uprisings.

Monan, Zhang. 2013. "China's Cold Eye on Hot Money." *Project Syndicate*, June 10. http://www.project-syndicate.org/commentary/china-s-new-rules-for-managing-cross-border-capital-flows-by-zhang-monan?barrier=true.

Montes, Manuel. 2014. "Initial Comments on BRICS Contingent Reserve Arrangement." recoveryhumanface.org, July 21. http://www.recoveryhumanface.org/e-discussion-2013/july-21st-2014.

Moody's. 2016a. "Moody's Upgrades Argentina's Issuer Rating to B3 with a Stable Outlook." April 15. https://www.moodys.com/research/Moodys-upgrades-Argentinas-issuer-rating-to-B3-with-a-stable—PR_347279.

Moody's. 2016b. "Rating Action: Moody's Upgrades Iceland's Government Ratings to A3." September 1. https://www.moodys.com/research/Moodys-upgrades-Icelands-government-ratings-to-A3-outlook-stable—PR_351195.

Moschella, Manuela. 2009. "When Ideas Fail to Influence Policy Outcomes: Orderly Liberalization and the International Monetary Fund." *Review of International Political Economy* 16 (5): 854–882.

Moschella, Manuela. 2010. *Governing Risk: The IMF and Global Financial Crises*. Basingstoke: Palgrave Macmillan.

Moschella, Manuela. 2012. "Seeing Like the IMF on Capital Account Liberalisation." *New Political Economy* 17 (1): 59–76.

Moschella, Manuela. 2014. "Institutional Roots of Incremental Ideational Change: The IMF and Capital Controls after the Global Financial Crisis." *British Journal of Politics and International Relations* 17 (3): 442–460.

Moschella, Manuela. 2015a. "Currency Wars in the Advanced World: Resisting Appreciation at a Time of Change in Central Banking Monetary Consensus." *Review of International Political Economy* 22 (1): 134–161.

Moschella, Manuela. 2015b. "To Legalise or Not to Legalise? A Case Study on the 'Rules of the Road' for Managing Cross-Border Capital Flows." August, mimeo. https://www.rivisteweb.it/doi/10.1483/80633.

Moschella, Manuela. 2016. "Negotiating Greece: Layering, Insulation, and the Design of Adjustment Programs in the Eurozone." *Review of International Political Economy* 23 (5): 799–824.

Moschella, Manuela, and Eleni Tsingou. 2013. "Introduction: The Financial Crisis and the Politics of Reform: Explaining Incremental Change." In *Great Expectations, Slow Transformations: Incremental Change in Post-crisis Regulation*, edited by Manuela Moschella and Eleni Tsingou, 1–34. Colchester: ECPR Press.

Mosley, Layna. 2003. "Attempting Global Standards: National Governments, International Finance, and the IMF's Data Regime." *Review of International Political Economy* 10 (2): 331–362.

Mossallem, Mohammed. 2015. *The IMF in the Arab World: Lessons Unlearnt*. Bretton Woods Project, December. http://www.brettonwoodsproject.org/wp-content/uploads /2015/12/final-MENA-report.pdf.

Muchhala, Bhumika. 2011. "The IMF's Financial Crisis Loans: No Change in Conditionalities." Third World Network Global Economy Series No. 30. Penang: Third World Network. http://twn.my/title2/ge/ge30.pdf.

Mühlich, Laurissa, and Barbara Fritz. 2016. "Safety for Whom? The Scattered Global Financial Safety Net and the Role of Regional Financial Arrangements." KFG Working Paper No. 75. Berlin: The Transformative Power of Europe, Freie Universität Berlin, September. http://www.polsoz.fu-berlin.de/en/v/transformeurope/news/allgemeines /KFG-Working-Paper-No-75.html.

Murphy, Kevin, Andrei Shleifer, and Robert Vishny. 1989. "Industrialization and the Big Push." *Journal of Political Economy* 97:1003–1026.

Murrell, Peter. 1995. "The Transition According to Cambridge, Mass." *Journal of Economic Literature* 33 (1): 164–178.

Myers, Margaret, and Kevin Gallagher. 2017. "Chinese Finance to LAC in 2016." Latin America Report. Boston: Inter-American Dialogue and Global Economic Governance Initiative, February. http://www.thedialogue.org/wp-content/uploads/2017 /02/Chinese-Finance-to-LAC-in-2016-Web-and-email-res.pdf.

Myrdal, Gunnar. 1957. *Economic Theory and Under-developed Regions*. London: Duckworth.

National Bank of Tajikistan. 2015. "The Activities of Currency Exchange Offices of Physical Entities Are Suspended." Dushanbe, April 17. http://www.nbt.tj/en/news /399843.

Neely, Christopher J. 1999. "An Introduction to Capital Controls." *Federal Reserve Bank of St. Louis Review* 81 (6): 13–30.

Nel, Philip, and Ian Taylor. 2013. "Bugger Thy Neighbor? IBSA and South-South Solidarity." *Third World Quarterly* 34 (6): 1091–1110.

Nelson, Stephen C. 2014a. "The International Monetary Fund's Evolving Role in Global Economic Governance." In *Handbook of Global Economic Governance*, edited by Manuela Moschella and Catherine Weaver, 156–170. London: Routledge.

Nelson, Stephen C. 2014b. "Playing Favorites: How Shared Beliefs Shape the IMF's Lending Decisions." *International Organization* 68 (2): 297–328.

Nelson, Stephen C. 2017. *The Currency of Confidence: How Economic Beliefs Shape the IMF's Relationship with Its Borrowers*. Ithaca, NY: Cornell University Press.

New Development Bank (NDB). 2016a. "BRICS Bank to Finance Indian, Chinese Infrastructure Projects." November 24. http://ndb.int/BRICS-Bank-to-finance-Indian-Chinese-infrastructure-projects.php.

NDB. 2016b. "BRICS Nations–Led New Development Bank to Raise Up to $3 Billion in Next Three Years." September 21. http://ndb.int/BRICS-nations-led-New-Development-Bank-to-raise-up-to-3-billion-in-next-3-years.php.

NDB. 2016c. "New Development Bank Plans Rupee, Rouble Bonds." http://ndb.int/New-Development-Bank-plans-rupee-rouble-bonds.php.

New York Times Editorial Board. 2013. "The IMF Admits Mistakes. Will Europe?" *New York Times*, June 8. http://www.nytimes.com/2013/06/08/opinion/the-imf-admits-mistakes-will-europe.html?_r=0.

Nissan, Sargon. 2015. "As Obituaries Are Written for the World Bank, the IMF is Set to Become Indispensable." *Financial Times, Beyond BRICS Blog*, May 11. http://blogs.ft.com/beyond-brics/2015/05/11/as-obituaries-are-written-for-the-world-bank-the-imf-is-set-to-become-indispensable/.

Noble, Gregory W., and John Ravenhill. 2000. "Causes and Consequences of the Asian Financial Crisis." In *The Asian Financial Crisis and the Architecture of Global Finance*, edited by Gregory W. Noble and John Ravenhill, 1–35. Cambridge: Cambridge University Press.

Nogueira Batista, Paulo, Jr. 2012. "Principles for IMF Quota Formula Reform." Brookings-CIGI-G24 High Level Seminar. Speech delivered at the Brookings Institution, Washington, DC, January 12. http://inctpped.ie.ufrj.br/fordconference2011/presentations_ppt/Principles for IMF quota reform.pdf.

Nwachukwu, John Owen. 2016. "Nigeria Will Deal with Economic Challenges without Borrowing Funds—Adeosun." *Daily Post*, April 16. http://dailypost.ng/2016/04/16/nigeria-will-deal-with-economic-challenges-without-borrowing-funds-adeosun/.

Obe, Mitsuru, and Kwanwoo Jun. 2015. "Japan, South Korea to Let Currency Swap Program Expire." *Wall Street Journal*, February 16. http://www.wsj.com/articles/japan-south-korea-to-let-currency-swap-program-expire-1424088419.

Obstfeld, Maurice. 1998. "Global Capital Markets: Benefactor or Menace?" *Journal of Economic Perspectives* 12 (4): 9–30.

Obstfeld, Maurice, and Poul Thomsen. 2016. "The IMF Is Not Asking Greece for More Austerity." *IMF Direct*, December 12. https://blog-imfdirect.imf.org/2016/12/12/the-imf-is-not-asking-greece-for-more-austerity/.

Ocampo, José Antonio. 2003. "Capital Account and Counter-cyclical Prudential Regulation in Developing Countries." In *From Capital Surges to Drought: Seeking Stability for Emerging Markets*, edited by Richardo Ffrench-Davis and Stephany Griffith-Jones, 217–244. Basingstoke: Palgrave Macmillan.

Ocampo, José Antonio, ed. 2006. *Regional Financial Cooperation*. Washington, DC: Brookings Institution.

Ocampo, José Antonio. 2010a. "The Case for and Experiences of Regional Monetary Co-operation." In *Regional and Global Liquidity Arrangements*, edited by Ulrich Volz and Aldo Caliari, 24–27. Bonn: German Development Institute.

Ocampo, José Antonio. 2010b. "Reforming the International Monetary System." 14th Annual UNU-WIDER Lecture. New York: United Nations, December 9. http://www.un.org/esa/ffd/economicgovernance/WIDERAnnualLecture.pdf.

Ocampo, José Antonio. 2010c. "Rethinking Global Economic and Social Governance." *Journal of Globalization and Development* 1 (1): Article 6. http://www.degruyter.com/view/j/jgd.2010.1.1/jgd.2010.1.1.1020/jgd.2010.1.1.1020.xml.

Ocampo, José Antonio. 2010d. "Time for Global Capital Account Regulations." *Economic and Political Weekly* 45 (46): 2–33.

Ocampo, José Antonio. 2011. "A Development-Friendly Reform of the International Financial Architecture." *Politics and Society* 39 (3): 315–330.

Ocampo, José Antonio. 2015a. "FLAR and Its Role in the Regional and International Financial Architecture." In *Building a Latin American Reserve Fund: 35 Years of FLAR*, edited by Guillermo Perry, 155–174. Bogotá: Latin American Reserve Fund.

Ocampo, José Antonio. 2015b. "Reforming the Global Monetary Non-System." UNU-WIDER Working Paper No. 146. Helsinki: United Nations University—World Institute for Development Economics Research. https://www.wider.unu.edu/publication/reforming-global-monetary-non-system.

Ocampo, José Antonio. 2016. "A Brief History of the International Monetary System since Bretton Woods." UNU-WIDER Working Paper No. 97. Helsinki: United Nations University—World Institute for Development Economics Research. https://www.wider.unu.edu/sites/default/files/wp2016-97.pdf.

Ocampo, José Antonio, Stephany Griffith-Jones, Akbar Noman, Ariane Ortiz, Juliana Vallejo, and Judith Tyson. 2012. "The Great Recession and the Developing World." In *Development Cooperation in Times of Crisis*, edited by José Antonio Alonso and José Antonio Ocampo, 17–81. New York: Columbia University Press.

Ocampo, José Antonio, and Joseph E. Stiglitz. 2011. "From the G-20 to a Global Economic Coordination Council." *Journal of Globalization and Development* 2 (2): Article 9. doi: https://doi.org/10.1515/1948-1837.1234.

Ocampo, José Antonio, and Daniel Titelman. 2009–2010. "Subregional Financial Cooperation: The South American Experience." *Journal of Post-Keynesian Economics* 32 (2): 249–268.

Ocampo, José Antonio, and Daniel Titelman. 2012. "Regional Monetary Cooperation in Latin America." ADBI Working Paper No. 373. Tokyo: Asian Development Bank Institute. http://www.adbi.org/working- paper/2012/08/10/5214.regional.monetary.cooperation.latin.america/.

Oliver, Christian. 2010. "IMF Warns on Emerging Market Currency Controls." *Financial Times*, July 11. http://www.ft.com/intl/cms/s/0/5ba241aa-8ce9-11df-bad7-00144feab49a.html.

Olson, Ryan, and Anthony B. Kim. 2013. "Congress Should Query IMF Support for Capital Controls." Heritage Foundation Issue Brief No. 3949. Washington, DC: Heritage Foundation, May. http://www.heritage.org/research/reports/2013/05/congress-should-query-imf-support-for-capital-controls.

O'Neill, Jim. 2001. "Building Better Global Economic BRICs." Global Economics Paper No. 66. New York: Goldman Sachs. http://www.goldmansachs.com/our-thinking/archive/archive-pdfs/build-better-brics.pdf.

Ortiz, Isabel, and Matthew Cummins. 2013. "The Age of Austerity: A Review of Public Expenditures and Adjustment Measures in 181 Countries." Working Paper. Initiative for Policy Dialogue and the South Centre. New York: Columbia University. March. http://policydialogue.org/publications/working_papers/age_of_austerity/.

Ostry, Jonathan D., Andrew Berg, and Charalambos G. Tsangarides. 2014. "Redistribution, Inequality and Growth." IMF Staff Discussion Note No. 2. Washington, DC: International Monetary Fund, February. http://www.imf.org/external/pubs/ft/sdn/2014/sdn1402.pdf.

Ostry, Jonathan D., Atish R. Ghosh, Karl Habermeier, Marcos Chamon, Mahvash S. Qureshi, and Dennis B. S. Reinhardt. 2010. "Capital Inflows: The Role of Controls." IMF Staff Position Note No. 4. Washington, DC: International Monetary Fund, February 19. https://www.imf.org/external/pubs/ft/spn/2010/spn1004.pdf.

Ostry, Jonathan D., Atish R. Ghosh, Karl Habermeier, Luc Laeven, Marcos Chamon, Mahvash Qureshi, and Annamaria Kokenyne. 2011. "Managing Capital Inflows: What Tools to Use?" IMF Staff Discussion Note No. 6. Washington, DC: International Monetary Fund, April 5. https://www.imf.org/external/pubs/ft/sdn/2011/sdn1106.pdf. International Monetary Fund.

Ostry, Jonathan D., Atish R. Ghosh, and Anton Korinek. 2012. "Multilateral Aspects of Managing the Capital Account." IMF Staff Discussion Note No. 10. Washington, DC: International Monetary Fund, September 7. https://www.imf.org/external/pubs /ft/sdn/2012/sdn1210.pdf.

Ostry, Jonathan D., Prakash Loungani, and Davide Furceri. 2016. "Neoliberalism: Oversold?" *Finance and Development*, June. http://www.imf.org/external/pubs/ft /fandd/2016/06/ostry.htm.

Pagliari, Stefano. 2014. "The Financial Stability Board as the New Guardian of Financial Stability." In *Handbook of Global Economic Governance*, edited by Manuela Moschella and Catherine Weaver, 143–155. London: Routledge.

Palacio, Ana. 2015. "The BRICS Fallacy." *Project Syndicate*, September 29. https:// www.project-syndicate.org/commentary/brics-decline-american-leadership-by-ana -palacio-2015-09.

Palley, Thomas I. 2013. "Gattopardo Economics: The Crisis and the Mainstream Response of Change That Keeps Things the Same." *European Journal of Economics and Economic Policies*, no. 2:193–206.

Parisot, James. 2013. "American Power, East Asian Regionalism and Emerging Powers: In or against Empire?" *Third World Quarterly* 34 (7): 1159–1174.

Park, Joonkyu, and Han van der Hoorn. 2012. "Financial Crisis, SWF Investing, and Implications for Financial Stability." *Global Policy* 3 (2): 211–221. doi: 10.1111 /j.1758-5899.2011.00151.x.

Park, Susan, and Antje Vetterlein. 2010. *Owning Development: Creating Policy Norms in the IMF and the World Bank*. Cambridge: Cambridge University Press.

Parker, George, Tony Barber, and Daniel Dombey. 2008. "European Call for 'Bretton Woods II.'" *Financial Times*, October 16. http://www.ft.com/intl/cms/s/0/7cc16b54 -9b19-11dd-a653-000077b07658.html?siteedition=intl - axzz3ViaP9QQb.

Parker, George, Anne-Sylvaine Chassany, and Geoff Dyer. 2015. "Europeans Defy US to Join China-Led Development Bank." *Financial Times*, March 16. http://www.ft .com/intl/cms/s/0/0655b342-cc29-11e4-beca-00144feab7de.html - axzz3Vz8LutmO.

Patnaik, Prabhat. 2015. "The BRICS Bank." *People's Democracy*, July 27. http:// peoplesdemocracy.in/2014/0727_pd/brics-bank.

Pauly, Louis. 2010. "The Financial Stability Board in Context." In *The Financial Stability Board: An Effective Fourth Pillar of Global Economic Governance?*, edited by Stephany Griffith-Jones, Eric Helleiner, and Ngaire Woods, 13–18. Waterloo: Center for International Governance Innovation.

Payne, Anthony. 2010. "How Many Gs Are There in 'Global Governance' after the Crisis? The Perspectives of the 'Marginal Majority' of the World's States." *International Affairs* 86 (3): 729–740.

Pempel, T. J. 1999. "Conclusion." In *The Politics of the Asian Economic Crisis*, edited by T. J. Pempel, 224–238. Ithaca, NY: Cornell University Press.

Pérez Caldentey, Esteban, and Matías Vernengo. 2012. "Portrait of the Economist as a Young Man: Raúl Prebisch's Evolving Views on the Business Cycle and Money, 1919–1949." *CEPAL Review* no. 106:7–21.

Pérez Caldentey, Esteban, and Matías Vernengo. 2016. "Reading Keynes in Buenos Aires: Prebisch and the Dynamics of Capitalism." *Cambridge Journal of Economics* 40:1725–1741.

Perlez, Jane. 2015. "Hostility from US as China Lures Allies to New Bank." *New York Times*, March 20. http://www.nytimes.com/2015/03/20/world/asia/hostility-from-us -as-china-lures-allies-to-new-bank.html?_r=0.

Perry, Guillermo. 2015. "Introduction." In *Building a Latin American Reserve Fund: 35 Years of FLAR*, edited by Guillermo Perry, 15–30. Bogotá: Latin American Reserve Fund.

Peruffo, Luiza, and Daniela Magalhães Prates. 2016. "What Is Left of the Rise of the South: Sceptical Prospects for Multipolarity." *Bretton Woods Observer*, April 5. http://www.brettonwoodsproject.org/2016/04/what-is-left-of-the-rise-of-the-south-scep tical-prospects-for-multipolarity/.

Picciotto, Robert. 1994. "Visibility and Disappointment: The New Role of Development Evaluation." In *Rethinking the Development Experience: Essays Provoked by the Work of Albert O. Hirschman*, edited by Lloyd Rodwin and Donald Schön, 231–276. Washington, DC: Brookings Institution.

Pilling, David. 2016. "Bad Times Send African Borrowers Back to the IMF." *Financial Times*, May 11. https://next.ft.com/content/922195fa-175d-11e6-9d98 -00386a18e39d.

Polanyi, Karl. 2001[1944]. *The Great Transformation: The Political and Economic Origins of Our Time*. Boston: Beacon.

Popper, Karl R. 1957. *The Poverty of Historicism*. Vol. 2. London: Routledge and Kegan Paul.

Popper, Karl R. 1971. *The Open Society and Its Enemies*. Vol. 1. Princeton, NJ: Princeton University Press.

Prasad, Eswar. 2014. *The Dollar Trap: How the US Dollar Tightened Its Grip on Global Finance*. Princeton, NJ: Princeton University Press.

Prasad, Eswar, Kenneth Rogoff, Shang-Jin Wei, and M. Ayan Kose. 2003. "Effects of Financial Globalization on Developing Countries: Some Empirical Evidence." IMF Occasional Paper No. 220. Washington, DC: International Monetary Fund, September 9. https://www.imf.org/external/pubs/nft/op/220/.

Premium Times. 2016. "Presidency Lists Nigeria's Benefits from Buhari's China Visit." April 15. http://www.premiumtimesng.com/news/top-news/201873-presidency-lists -nigerias-benefits-buharis-china-visit.html.

Public Citizen. 2015. "Secret TPP Investment Chapter Unveiled: It's Worse than We Thought." Washington, DC: Public Citizen, November 5. https://www.citizen.org /documents/analysis-tpp-investment-chapter-november-2015.pdf.

Quigley, John. 2013. "Velarde Says He Doesn't See Need for Peru Capital Controls." Bloomberg, January 25. http://www.bloomberg.com/news/articles/2013-01-25 /velarde-says-he-doesn-t-see-need-for-peru-capital-controls-1-.

Qureshi, Mahvash, Jonathan Ostry, Atish Ghosh, and Marcos Chamon. 2011. "Managing Capital Inflows: The Role of Capital Controls and Prudential Policies." NBER Working Paper No. 17363. Cambridge, MA: National Bureau of Economic Research, March 22. http://www.nber.org/papers/w17363.

Rachman, Gideon. 2010. "The G20's Seven Pillars of Friction." *Financial Times*, November 8. http://www.ft.com/intl/cms/s/0/980b2040-eb43-11df-811d-00144feab49a.html - axzz1pctq2Ymg,.

Ragir, Alexander. 2011. "Brazil's Capital Controls Are 'Appropriate' Tool, IMF Says." Bloomberg, August 3. http://www.bloomberg.com/news/articles/2011-08-03/brazilian -capital-controls-are-appropriate-tool-imf-says.

Rajan, Raghuram. 2016a. "Towards Rules of the Monetary Game." Talk by Dr. Raghuram Rajan at the IMF/Government of India Conference on "Advancing Asia: Investing for the Future," New Delhi, March 12. http://www.bis.org/review /r160316a.htm.

Rajan, Raghuram 2016b. "The Global Monetary Non-System." *Project Syndicate*, January 6. https://www.project-syndicate.org/commentary/unconventional-monetary -policy-weak-growth-by-raghuram-rajan-2016-01 - r9orRFM1oKLdA2XU.99.

Rana, Pradumna. 2013. "From a Centralized to a Decentralized Global Economic Architecture: An Overview." ADBI Working Paper No. 401. Tokyo: Asian Development Bank Institute. http://www.adbi.org/files/2013.01.15.wp401.decentralized.global .economic.architecture.pdf.

Rappeport, Alan. 2010. "IMF Reconsiders Capital Controls Opposition." *Financial Times*, February 22. http://www.ft.com/intl/cms/s/0/ec484786-1fcf-11df-8deb -00144feab49a.html.

Ravallion, Martin. 2008. "Evaluation in the Practice of Development." World Bank Policy Research Working Paper No. 4547. Washington, DC: World Bank. https:// openknowledge.worldbank.org/bitstream/handle/10986/6561/wps4547.pdf ?sequence=1.

Ravenhill, John. 2010. "The 'New East Asian Regionalism': A Political Domino Effect." *Review of International Political Economy* 17 (2): 178–208.

Ray, Atmadip. 2013. "Capital Controls Needed to Insulate Economies from US." *Economic Times*, September 18. http://articles.economictimes.indiatimes.com/2013-09-18/news/42183253_1_monetary-policy-independence-raghuram-rajan-capital.

Reddy, Sudeep. 2011. "IMF under Fire over Plans for Capital Controls." *Wall Street Journal*, April 18. http://www.wsj.com/articles/SB100014240527487037020045762698980074855142.

Reichmann, Thomas. 2013. "Advice on Fiscal Policy and the Development of Trust." Background Studies to IEO Report (IMF as a Trusted Advisor). Washington, DC: Independent Evaluation Office of the International Monetary Fund, January 17, 29–40. http://www.ieo-imf.org/ieo/files/completedevaluations/RITA_-_Background_Studies.pdf.

Reinhart, Carmen M., and Christoph Trebesch. 2016. "The International Monetary Fund: 70 Years of Reinvention." *Journal of Economic Perspectives* 30 (1): 3–27.

Reinold, Theresa 2016. "The Path of Least Resistance: Mainstreaming 'Social Issues' in the International Monetary Fund." *Global Society*, 1–25. doi: 10.1080/13600826.2016.1203764.

Reuters. 2009a. "China Wants Moves on IMF Voting at G20—Officials." Reuters.com, September 15. http://www.reuters.com/article/china-imf-idUSPEK22273820090915.

Reuters. 2009b. "Russia IMF Bond Not Dependent on Reform—cbanker." Reuters.com, October 5. http://www.reuters.com/article/imf-russia-bonds-idUSL47415720091005.

Reuters. 2012a. "IMF Urges Permanent Solution for Greece." *Financial Times*/Reuters, November 18. http://www.ft.com/cms/s/0/8852edf8-3138-11e2-bb5e-00144feabdc0.html?ft_site=falcon&desktop=true&siteedition=intl - axzz4WvLEsu2Q.

Reuters. 2012b. "Uruguay Cenbank Moves to Stem Peso's Appreciation." August 16. http://in.reuters.com/article/uruguay-peso-idINL2E8JFA4720120815.

Reuters. 2013a. "Bundesbank Warms to Capital Controls in Currency War Debate." January 24. http://in.reuters.com/article/emerging-currencies-germany-idINL6N0AT3XC20130124.

Reuters. 2013b. "Impatience with I.M.F. Is Growing." *New York Times*/Reuters, October 14. http://www.nytimes.com/2013/10/14/business/international/impatience-with-imf-is-growing.html.

Reuters. 2013c. "India Cbank Chief Says Policy Not to Resort to Capital Controls." August 29. http://in.reuters.com/article/india-cbank-governor-idINI8N0EW02N20130829.

Reuters. 2014. "Costa Rica President Says to Use Capital Controls Very Selectively." April 2. http://www.reuters.com/article/costarica-capitalcontrols-idUSL1N0MU20U20140402.

Reuters. 2015a. "EU Commission Says Greek Capital Controls Seem Justified." June 29. http://www.reuters.com/article/eurozone-greece-controls-commission-idUSL 5N0ZF0RK20150629.

Reuters. 2015b. "Nigeria's Central Bank Curbs Access to Foreign Currency." June 24. http://www.reuters.com/article/nigeria-currency-idUSL8N0ZA21C20150624.

Reuters. 2016a. "Eurozone Chides IMF over Greece Blog." December 12. http://www .reuters.com/article/us-eurozone-greece-imf-esm-idUSKBN1421ED.

Reuters. 2016b. "IMF Calls on Nigeria to Lift Foreign Exchange Curbs." February 24. http://www.reuters.com/article/nigeria-economy-idUSL8N1631D5.

Reuters. 2017. "China's New Rules on Yuan Transfers Are Not Capital Controls: Xinhua." January 2. http://www.reuters.com/article/us-china-yuan-idUSKBN14M032 ?il=0.

Rey, Hélène. 2015. "Dilemma, Not Trilemma: The Global Financial Cycle and Monetary Policy Independence." NBER Working Paper No. 21162. Cambridge, MA: National Bureau of Economic Research, May. http://www.nber.org/papers/w21162.

Rey, Hélène. 2016. "International Channels of Transmission of Monetary Policy and the Mundellian Trilemma." *IMF Economic Review* 64:16–35.

Rhee, Changyong, Lea Sumulong, and Shahin Vallée. 2013. "Global and Regional Financial Safety Nets: Lessons from Europe and Asia." In *Responding to Financial Crisis: Lessons from Asia Then, the United States and Europe Now*, edited by Changyong Rhee and Adam Posen, 213–248. Washington, DC: Peterson Institute for International Economics and Asian Development Bank.

Riggirozzi, Pía. 2012a. *Reconstructing Regionalism: What Does Development Have to Do with It?*, edited by Pía Riggirozzi and Diana Tussie. The Rise of Post-hegemonic Regionalism. Dordrecht: Springer. eBook.

Riggirozzi, Pía. 2012b. "Region, Regionness and Regionalism in Latin America: Towards a New Synthesis." *New Political Economy* 17 (4): 421–443.

Riggirozzi, Pía, and Diana Tussie. 2012. "The Rise of Post-hegemonic Regionalism." In *The Rise of Post-hegemonic Regionalism*, edited by Pía Riggirozzi and Diana Tussie, 1–16. Dordrecht: Springer. eBook.

Ro, Sam. 2015. "Here's What the $294 Trillion Market of Global Financial Assets Looks Like." *Business Insider*, February 11. http://www.businessinsider.com/global -financial-assets-2015-2.

Robertson, Jamie. 2015. "The Greek Crisis Is Shaking the IMF to Its Core." *BBC World News*, July 15. http://www.bbc.com/news/business-33537445.

Rodrik, Dani. 1991. "Policy Uncertainty and Private Investment in Developing Countries." *Journal of Development Economics* 36 (2): 229–242.

Rodrik, Dani. 2001. *The Global Governance of Trade: As if Development Really Mattered.* New York: United Nations Development Programme. http://www.giszpenc.com /globalciv/rodrik1.pdf.

Rodrik, Dani. 2006a. "Goodbye Washington Consensus, Hello Washington Confusion?" *Journal of Economic Literature* 44 (4): 973–987.

Rodrik, Dani. 2006b. "The Social Cost of Foreign Exchange Reserves." *International Economic Journal* 20 (3): 253–266.

Rodrik, Dani. 2007a. "Albert O. Hirschman Prize." April 25. http://rodrik.typepad .com/dani_rodriks_weblog/2007/04/albert_o_hirsch.html.

Rodrik, Dani. 2007b. *One Economics, Many Recipes.* Princeton, NJ: Princeton University Press.

Rodrik, Dani. 2007c. "Re-reading Hirschman." November 1. http://rodrik.typepad .com/dani_rodriks_weblog/2007/11/re-reading-albe.html.

Rodrik, Dani. 2007–2008. "One Economics, Many Recipes: What We Have Learned since Albert Hirschman." *Social Science Research Council, Items and Issues* 6 (1–2): 1–7. http://www.ssrc.org/hirschman/content/2007/rodrik_transcript.pdf.

Rodrik, Dani. 2009a. "The New Development Economics: We Shall Experiment, but How Shall We Learn?" In *What Works in Development? Thinking Big and Thinking Small*, edited by Jessica Cohen and William Easterly, 24–47. Washington, DC: Brookings Institution.

Rodrik, Dani. 2009b. "A Plan B for Global Finance." *Economist*, March 12. http:// www.economist.com/node/13278147.

Rodrik, Dani. 2010. "The End of an Era in Finance." *Project Syndicate*, March 11. http://www.project-syndicate.org/commentary/the-end-of-an-era-in-finance.

Rodrik, Dani. 2011. *The Globalization Paradox: Democracy and the Future of the World Economy.* New York: Norton.

Rodrik, Dani. 2013. "What the World Needs from the BRICS." *Project Syndicate*, April 10. http://www.project-syndicate.org/commentary/the-brics-and-global-economic -leadership-by-dani-rodrik.

Rodrik, Dani. 2015a. *Economics Rules: The Rights and Wrongs of the Dismal Science.* New York: Norton.

Rodrik, Dani. 2015b. "Global Capital Heads for the Frontier." *Project Syndicate*, March 10. https://www.project-syndicate.org/commentary/frontier-market-economy -fad-by-dani-rodrik-2015-03?barrier=true.

Rogoff, Kenneth. 2011. "Will the IMF Stand Up to Europe?" *Project Syndicate*, September 1. https://www.project-syndicate.org/commentary/will-the-imf-stand-up-to -europe?barrier=true.

Rosales, Antulio. 2013. "The Banco del Sur and the Return to Development." *Latin American Perspectives* 40 (192): 27–43.

Rosenstein-Rodan, Paul. 1943. "The Problems of Industrialization of Eastern and South-Eastern Europe." *Economic Journal* 53:202–211.

Rosero, Luis. 2011. "Essays on International Reserve Accumulation and Cooperation in Latin America." PhD dissertation, Department of Economics, University of Massachusetts.

Rosero, Luis. 2014. "Regional Pooling of International Reserves: The Latin American Reserve Fund in Perspective." *Latin American Policy* 5 (1): 62–86.

Rosero, Luis, and Bilge Erten. 2010. "Delinking through Integration: A Dependency Analysis of Regional Financial Integration." *Critical Sociology* 36 (2): 221–242.

Ross, Alice, and Haig Simonian. 2012. "Swiss Eye Capital Controls if Greece Goes." *Financial Times*, May 27. http://www.ft.com/cms/s/0/d7678676-a810-11e1-8fbb-00144 feabdc0.html - axzz43pjftUkY.

Rothschild, Emma, and Amartya Sen. 2013. "Afterword." In *The Essential Hirschman*, edited by Jeremy Adelman, 363–369. Princeton, NJ: Princeton University Press.

Rowden, Rick. 2009. *Doing a Decent Job? IMF Policies and Decent Work in Times of Crisis*. SOLIDAR, October. http://cms.horus.be/files/99931/MediaArchive/GNreport _IMF and DW_MAIL.pdf.

Roy, Rathin. 2014. "Comments on the CRA." recoveryhumanface.org, July 25. http:// www.recoveryhumanface.org/e-discussion-2013/archives/07-2014.

Rozenberg, Gabriel 2007. "IMF Prepares to Shed Staff as Crisis Looms for Global Lender." *Times* (London), December 8. http://www.thetimes.co.uk/tto/business /economics/article2146931.ece.

Sabel, Charles, and Sanjay Reddy. 2003. "Learning to Learn: Undoing the Gordian Knot of Development Today." Columbia Law and Economics Working Paper No. 308. New York: Columbia University. http://www2.law.columbia.edu/sabel/papers/Learning to Lean.pdf.

Saborowski, Christian, Sarah Sanya, Hans Weisfeld, and Juan Yepez. 2014. "Effectiveness of Capital Outflow Restrictions." IMF Working Paper No. 8. Washington, DC: International Monetary Fund, January. https://www.imf.org/external/pubs/ft /wp/2014/wp1408.pdf.

Sahay, Ratna, Martin Cihak, Papa N'Diaye, Adolfo Barajas, Diana Ayala Pena, Ran Bi, Yuan Gao, Annette Kyobe, Lam Nguyen, and Christian Saborowski. 2015. "Rethinking Financial Deepening: Stability and Growth in Emerging Markets." IMF Staff Discussion Notes No. 8. Washington, DC: International Monetary Fund. http:// www.imf.org/external/pubs/ft/sdn/2015/sdn1508.pdf.

Sanger, David. 1998. "Greenspan Sees Asian Crisis Moving World to Western Capitalism." *New York Times*, February 13. http://www.nytimes.com/1998/02/13/business/greenspan-sees-asian-crisis-moving-world-to-western-capitalism.html.

Sanger, David. 1999. "World Bank Beats Breast for Failures in Indonesia." *New York Times*, February 11, A15.

Sanyal, Bishwapriya. 1994. "Social Construction of Hope." In *Rethinking the Development Experience: Essays Provoked by the Work of Albert O. Hirschman*, edited by Lloyd Rodwin and Donald Schön, 131–146. Washington, DC: Brookings Institution.

Schadler, Susan. 2014. "The IMF's Preferred Creditor Status: Does It Still Make Sense after the Euro Crisis?" CIGI Policy Brief No. 37. Waterloo: Center for International Governance Innovation, March. https://www.cigionline.org/publications/imfs-preferred-creditor-status-does-it-still-make-sense-after-euro-crisis.

Schadler, Susan. 2015. "The IMF's Ukraine Burden." CIGI Policy Brief No. 58. Waterloo: Center for International Governance Innovation, April. https://www.cigionline.org/publications/imfs-ukraine-burden.

Schön, Donald. 1994. "Hirschman's Elusive Theory of Social Learning." In *Rethinking the Development Experience: Essays Provoked by the Work of Albert O. Hirschman*, edited by Lloyd Rodwin and Donald Schön, 67–95. Washington, DC: Brookings Institution.

Seabrooke, Leonard. 2007. "Legitimacy Gaps in the World Economy: Explaining the Sources of the IMF's Legitimacy Crisis." *International Politics* 44 (2–3): 250–268.

Seabrooke, Leonard. 2010. "Bitter Pills to Swallow: Legitimacy Gaps and Social Recognition for the IMF Tax Policy Norm in East Asia." In *Owning Development: Creating Policy Norms in the IMF and the World Bank*, edited by Susan Park and Antje Vetterlein, 137–159. Cambridge: Cambridge University Press.

Sedgwick, Eve Kosofsky. 1993. *Tendencies*. Durham, NC: Duke University Press.

Shadlen, Kenneth. 2005. "Exchanging Development for Market Access? Deep Integration and Industrial Policy under Multilateral and Regional-Bilateral Trade Agreements." *Review of International Political Economy* 12 (5): 750–775.

Sharma, Patrick. 2013. "Bureaucratic Imperatives and Policy Outcomes: The Origins of World Bank Structural Adjustment Lending." *Review of International Political Economy* 20 (4): 667–686.

Shin, Hyun Song. 2015. "External Dimensions of Monetary Policy." Speech at the Board of Governors of the Federal Reserve System Conference on Monetary Policy Implementation and Transmission in the Post-crisis Period, Washington, DC, November 13. http://www.bis.org/speeches/sp151113.htm.

Sigurgeirsdóttir, Silla, and Robert H. Wade. 2015. "From Control by Capital to Control of Capital: Iceland's Boom and Bust, and the IMF's Unorthodox Rescue Package." *Review of International Political Economy* 22 (1): 103–133.

Simon, Herbert A. 1990. "Bounded Rationality." In *The New Palgrave Utility and Probability*, edited by John Eatwell, Murray Milgate, and Peter Newman, 15–18. New York: Norton.

Singh, Ajit. 1999. "'Asian Capitalism' and the Financial Crisis." In *Global Instability and World Economic Governance*, edited by Jonathan Michie and John Grieve Smith, 9–36. London: Routledge.

Siregar, Reza, and Akkharaphol Chabchitrchaidol. 2013. "Enhancing the Effectiveness of CMIM and AMRO: Selected Immediate Challenges and Tasks." ADBI Working Paper Series No. 403. Tokyo: Asian Development Bank Institute, January. https://www.adbi.org/publications/enhancing-effectiveness-cmim-and-amro-selected-immediate-challenges-and-tasks.

Skidelsky, Robert. 2010. *Keynes: The Return of the Master*. New York: Public Affairs.

Skidelsky, Robert. 2011. "The Relevance of Keynes." *Cambridge Journal of Economics* 35:1–13.

Slaughter, Anne-Marie. 2004. *A New World Order*. Princeton, NJ: Princeton University Press.

Smith, Adam. 1976[1759]. *The Theory of Moral Sentiments*. Oxford: Clarendon.

Smith, Gordon S. 2011. "G7 to G8 to G20: Evolution of Global Governance." CIGI G-20 Paper No. 6. Waterloo: Center for International Governance Innovation, May. http://www.cigionline.org/publications/2011/5/g7-g8-g20-evolution-global-governance.

Smith, Helena. 2015. "Young, Gifted and Greek: Generation G—The World's Biggest Brain Drain." *Guardian*, January 19. http://www.theguardian.com/world/2015/jan/19/young-talented-greek-generation-g-worlds-biggest-brain-drain.

Smyth, Jamie. 2013. "Ex-IMF Official Warns Austerity 'Untenable.'" *Financial Times*, April 11. http://www.ft.com/intl/cms/s/0/66ff0b2c-a29a-11e2-9b70-00144feabdc0.html - axzz32NsRoUBI.

Soederberg, Susanne. 2010. "The Politics of Representation and Financial Fetishism: The Case of the G20 Summits." *Third World Quarterly* 31 (4): 523–540.

Sohn, Injoo. 2012. "Toward Normative Fragmentation: An East Asian Financial Architecture in the Post-global Crisis World." *Review of International Political Economy* 19 (4): 586–608.

Soros, George. 2013. "Fallibility, Reflexivity, and the Human Uncertainty Principle." *Journal of Economic Methodology* 20 (4): 309–329.

Spence, Michael. 2010a. "The IMF and Global Coordination." *Project Syndicate*, September 16. http://prosyn.org/7hL2nbK.

Spence, Michael. 2010b. "Keynote Address by Professor Andrew Michael Spence." First International Research Conference of the Reserve Bank of India, Mumbai, February 12. https://rbidocs.rbi.org.in/rdocs/Content/PDFs/FST130210.pdf.

Spiegel, Peter. 2012. "EU Hits Back at IMF over Austerity." *Financial Times*, November 7. http://www.ft.com/intl/cms/s/0/35735e76-28d5-11e2-b92c-00144feabdc0 .html?siteedition=intl - axzz32NsRoUBI.

Steil, Benn. 2013. *The Battle of Bretton Woods: John Maynard Keynes, Harry Dexter White, and the Making of a New World Order*. Princeton, NJ: Princeton University Press.

Steil, Benn. 2014. "The BRICS Bank Is a Feeble Strike against Dollar Hegemony." *Financial Times*, October 1. http://www.cfr.org/international-finance/brics-bank -feeble-strike-against-dollar-hegemony/p33542.

Steinwand, Martin C., and Randall W. Stone. 2008. "The International Monetary Fund: A Review of the Recent Evidence." *Review of International Organizations* 3 (2): 123–149.

Stiglitz, Joseph. 2002. *Globalization and Its Discontents*. New York: Norton.

Stiglitz, Joseph, and Hamid Rashid. 2016a. "Closing Developing Countries' Capital Drain." *Project Syndicate*, February 18. https://www.project-syndicate.org/commentary /developing-countries-capital-outflows-by-joseph-e-stiglitz-and-hamid-rashid-2016 -02?barrier=true.

Stiglitz, Joseph, and Hamid Rashid. 2016b. "What's Ailing the World Economy?" *Third World Resurgence*, nos. 307–308:19–20.

Stone, Randall W. 2002. *Lending Credibility: The International Monetary Fund and the Post-Communist Transition*. Princeton, NJ: Princeton University Press.

Strand, Jonathan R. 2014. "Global Economic Governance and the Regional Development Banks." In *Handbook of Global Economic Governance*, edited by Manuela Moschella and Catherine Weaver, 290–303. London: Routledge.

Strange, Susan. 1987. "The Persistent Myth of Lost Hegemony." *International Organization* 41 (4): 551–574.

Strauss, Delphine. 2014. "Ukraine Capital Controls Stem Fall in Its Currency." *Financial Times*, February 10. http://www.ft.com/intl/cms/s/0/fc4e3cf2-926d-11e3-9e43 -00144feab7de.

Strauss-Kahn, Dominique. 2010a. "2010—A Year of Transformation for the World and for Asia." Address at the Asian Financial Forum, Hong Kong, January 20. https:// www.imf.org/external/np/speeches/2010/012010.htm.

Strauss-Kahn, Dominique. 2010b. "An IMF for the 21st Century." Address delivered at Bretton Woods Committee Annual Meeting. Washington, DC: International

Monetary Fund, February 26. https://www.imf.org/external/np/speeches/2010/022610.htm.

Strauss-Kahn, Dominique. 2010c. "Macro-prudential Policies—An Asian Perspective." Speech, Shanghai, October 18. http://www.imf.org/external/np/speeches/2010/101810.htm.

Streeten, Paul. 1959. "Unbalanced Growth." *Oxford Economics Papers* 11 (2): 167–190.

Stringer, Jacob. 2012. "IMF Director Praises Colombia's Economy." *Colombia Reports*, December 10. http://colombiareports.co/imf-director-praises-colombias-economy/-modal.

Studart, Rogério, and Luma Ramos. 2016. "Infrastructure for Sustainable Development: The Role of National Development Banks." Global Economic Governance Initiative Working Paper No. 7. Boston: Boston University, Frederic S. Pardee School of Global Studies, July. https://www.bu.edu/pardeeschool/files/2016/07/Studart.New_.Version.FINAL_.pdf.

Stuenkel, Oliver. 2013. "The Financial Crisis, Contested Legitimacy, and the Genesis of Intra-BRICS Cooperation." *Global Governance* 19:611–630.

Stuenkel, Oliver. 2016a. "The BRICS: Seeking Privileges by Constructing and Running Multilateral Institutions." *Global Summitry* 2 (1): 38–53.

Stuenkel, Oliver. 2016b. *Post-Western World: How Emerging Powers Are Remaking Global Order.* Cambridge: Polity.

Subacchi, Paola. 2015. "The Renminbi Goes Forth." *Project Syndicate*, December 11. https://www.project-syndicate.org/commentary/renminbi-international-currency-in-the-making-by-paola-subacchi-2015-12.

Subacchi, Paola. 2016. "Comment: China's Ambiguous Financial Liberalisation." *Financial Times*, February 3. http://www.ft.com/cms/s/0/498f7bba-c9c2-11e5-a8ef-ea66e967dd44.html - axzz436uBoHDb.

Subacchi, Paola. 2017. *The People's Money: How China Is Building a Global Currency.* New York: Columbia University Press.

Subramanian, Arvind, and John Williamson. 2009. "The Fund Should Help Brazil to Tackle Inflows." *Financial Times*, October 25. http://www.ft.com/cms/s/0/a0c04b34-c196-11de-b86b-00144feab49a.html - axzz43lSYfpkX.

Summers, Tim. 2016. "China's New 'Silk Roads': Sub-national Regions and Networks of Global Political Economy." *Third World Quarterly* 37 (9): 1628–1643.

Sussangkarn, Chalongphob. 2011. "Chiang Mai Initiative Multilateralization: Origin, Development, and Outlook." *Asian Economic Policy Review* 6 (2): 203–220.

SWF Institute. 2017. "Sovereign Wealth Fund Rankings." Sovereign Wealth Fund Institute. Accessed January 12. http://www.swfinstitute.org/sovereign-wealth-fund-rankings/.

Tabuchi, Hiroko. 2017. "As Beijing Joins Climate Fight, Chinese Companies Build Coal Plants." *New York Times*, July 2, A10.

Taleb, Nassim Nicholas. 2007. *The Black Swan: The Impact of the Highly Improbable.* New York: Random House.

Taleb, Nassim Nicholas. 2012. *Anti-Fragile: Things That Gain from Disorder.* New York: Random House.

Taleb, Nassim Nicholas, and Mark Blyth. 2011. "The Black Swan of Cairo: How Suppressing Volatility Makes the World Less Predictable and More Dangerous." *Foreign Affairs* 90 (3): 33–39.

Tavares de Araujo, José, Jr. 2013. "The BNDES as an Instrument of Long Run Economic Policy in Brazil." Rio de Janeiro: Centro de Estudos de Integracão e Desenvolvimento. http://www.ecostrat.net/files/bndes-as-an-instrument-of-long-run-economic-policy.pdf.

Taylor, Lance. 1994. "Hirschman's *Strategy* at Thirty-Five." In *Rethinking the Development Experience: Essays Provoked by the Work of Albert O. Hirschman*, edited by Lloyd Rodwin and Donald Schön, 59–66. Washington, DC: Brookings Institution.

Taylor, Paul. 2015. "Exclusive: Europeans Tried to Block IMF Debt Report on Greece." Reuters.com, July 3. http://www.reuters.com/article/2015/07/03/us-eurozone-greece-imf-idUSKCN0PD20120150703.

Tendler, Judith. 1968. *Electrical Power in Brazil: Entrepreneurship in the Public Sector.* Cambridge, MA: Harvard University Press.

Tetlock, Philip E. 2005. *Expert Political Judgment.* Princeton, NJ: Princeton University Press.

Thomas, Landon, Jr. 2010. "Countries See Hazards in Free Flow of Capital." *New York Times*, November 10. http://www.nytimes.com/2010/11/11/business/global/11capital.html?_r=0.

Thomas, Landon, Jr. 2015. "The Greek Debt Deal's Missing Piece." *New York Times*, August 15. http://www.nytimes.com/2015/08/16/business/international/the-greek-debt-deals-missing-piece.html?_r=0.

Thomas, Landon, Jr. 2016. "Infighting in Background of Internal Unit's Sharp Critique." *New York Times*, October 21, B2.

Tietmeyer, Hans. 1999. "International Cooperation and Coordination in the Area of Financial Market Supervision and Surveillance." BIS Report. Basel: Bank for International Settlements, February 11. https://www.financialstabilityboard.org/publications/r_9902.pdf.

Times of India. 2015. "RBI Chief Rajan Blasts IMF for Being Soft on Easy Money Policies of West." *Times of India*, October 19. http://timesofindia.indiatimes.com

/business/india-business/RBI-chief-Rajan-blasts-IMF-for-being-soft-on-easy-money-policies-of-west/articleshow/49456531.cms.

Titelman, Daniel, Cecilia Vera, Pablo Carvallo, and Esteban Pérez-Caldentey. 2014. "A Regional Reserve Fund for Latin America." *CEPAL Review*, no. 112:7–28. http://repositorio.cepal.org/bitstream/handle/11362/37018/RVI112Titelmanetal_en.pdf?sequence=1.

Torres Filho, Ernani Teixeira. 2011. "Lessons from the Crisis: The Experience of the Brazilian Development Bank." Conference on New Economic Thinking, Teaching and Policy Perspectives—A Brazilian Perspective within a Global Dialogue. http://www.minds.org.br/media/papers/ernanitoreslessons-from-the.pdf.

Traynor, Ian. 2012. "Eurozone Demands Six Day Work-week for Greece." *Guardian*, September 4. http://www.theguardian.com/business/2012/sep/04/eurozone-six-day-week-greece.

Truman, Edwin. 2010. "The G-20 and International Financial Institutions' Governance." Peterson Institute for International Economics Working Paper No. 10-13. Washington, DC: Peterson Institute for International Economics, September. http://dx.doi.org/10.2139/ssrn.1681547.

Truman, Edwin. 2015. "IMF Governance Reform Better Late than Never." *Peterson Institute for International Economics Real Time Economics News Watch*, December 16. https://piie.com/blogs/realtime-economic-issues-watch/imf-governance-reform-better-late-neverDecember 16, P.

Turner, Adair. 2014. "In Praise of Fragmentation." *Project Syndicate*, February 18. https://www.project-syndicate.org/commentary/adair-turner-criticizes-economists—adherence-to-the-belief-that-the-benefits-of-capital-account-liberalization-outweigh-the-costs?barrier=true.

Tussie, Diana. 2010. "Decentralizing Global Finance." *Triple Crisis*, April 9. http://triplecrisis.com/decentralizing-global-finance/.

Ugarteche, Oscar. 2014. "BRICS Bank: Part of a New Financial Architecture." ALAI net.org. http://alainet.org/.

United Nations (UN). 2002. "Monterrey Consensus of the International Conference on Financing for Development: The Final Text of Agreements and Commitments Adopted at the International Conference on Financing for Development." Monterrey, March 18–22. http://www.un.org/esa/ffd/monterrey/MonterreyConsensus.pdf.

United Nations (UN). 2009. *Report of the Commission of Experts of the President of the United Nations General Assembly on Reforms of the International Monetary and Financial System*. New York: UN, September 21. http://www.un.org/ga/econcrisissummit/docs/FinalReport_CoE.pdf.

United Nations (UN). 2014. *Report of the Intergovernmental Committee of Experts on Sustainable Development Financing*. New York: UN, August 8. https://sustainabledevelopment .un.org/content/documents/4588FINAL REPORT ICESDF.pdf.

United Nations Children's Fund (UNICEF). 2010. "Prioritizing Expenditures for a Recovery with a Human Face: Results from a Rapid Desk Review of 86 Recent IMF Country Reports." Social and Economic Policy Working Brief. New York: UNICEF, April. http://docs.escr-net.org/usr_doc/Prioritizing_Expenditures.pdf.

United Nations Conference on Trade and Development (UNCTAD). 2007. *Trade and Development Report*. Geneva: UNCTAD.

United Nations Conference on Trade and Development (UNCTAD). 2011. *The Least Developed Countries Report*. Geneva: UNCTAD.

United Nations Conference on Trade and Development (UNCTAD). 2013. *Trade and Development Report*. Geneva: UNCTAD.

United Nations Conference on Trade and Development (UNCTAD). 2015a. "Introduction of Foreign-Exchange Controls." Geneva: UNCTAD, March 13. http://invest mentpolicyhub.unctad.org/IPM/MeasureDetails?id=2673&rgn=.

United Nations Conference on Trade and Development (UNCTAD). 2015b. *Trade and Development Report*. Geneva: UNCTAD.

United Nations Conference on Trade and Development (UNCTAD). 2016. *Trade and Development Report*. Geneva: UNCTAD.

Urbinati, Nadia. 2015. "'Proving Hamlet Wrong': The Creative Role of Doubt in Albert Hirschman's Social Thought." *Humanity* 6 (2): 267–271.

Urrutia, Miguel. 2015. "Brief History of FLAR." In *Building a Latin American Reserve Fund: 35 Years of FLAR*, edited by Guillermo Perry, 197–202. Bogotá: Latin American Reserve Fund.

U.S. Congress. 2015. H.R. 2029—Consolidated Appropriations Act 2016, 114th Congress, 2015–2016, December 18, 2015. https://www.congress.gov/bill/114th-congress /house-bill/2029/text.

U.S. Treasury. 2009. "Press Briefing by Treasury Secretary Tim Geithner on the G-20 Meeting, Pittsburgh summit." September 24. http://www.whitehouse.gov/the_press _office/Press-Briefing-by-Treasury-Secretary-Geithner-on-the-G20-Meetings.

Ustinova, Anastasia. 2012. "BRICS Bank to Be Discussed at March Summit." Bloomberg .com, February 26. http://www.bloomberg.com/news/articles/2012-02-23/india-said -to-propose-brics-bank-to-finance-developing-nations-projects.

Valdimarsson, Omar. 2012. "Iceland to Apply New Rules before Capital Controls Are Removed." Bloomberg, August 27. http://www.bloomberg.com/news/articles/2012 -08-27/iceland-to-apply-new-rules-before-capital-controls-are-removed.

Van Gunten, Tod S. 2015. "Washington Dissensus: Ambiguity and Conflict at the International Monetary Fund." *Socio-Economic Review* 15 (1): 65–84.

Van Waeyenberge, Elisa, Hannah Bargawi, and Terry McKinley. 2011. "Standing in the Way of Development? A Critical Survey of the IMF's Crisis Response in Low-Income Countries." Global Economy Series No. 31. Penang: Third World Network. http://eurodad.org/uploadedfiles/whats_new/reports/standing in the way of development(1).pdf.

Varoufakis, Yanis. 2016. "Greece, Still Paying for Europe's Spite." *New York Times*, June 1, A21.

Vary, Jarad. 2011. "How the IMF Got Its Keynesian Groove Back." *New Republic*, December 2. http://www.newrepublic.com/article/economy/98051/IMF-Merkel-euro -ECB-Keynes-crisis.

Velarde, Julio. 2015. "Financial Crises and Protection Mechanisms." In *Building a Latin American Reserve Fund: 35 Years of FLAR*, edited by Guillermo Perry, 143–154. Bogotá: Latin American Reserve Fund.

Vernengo, Matías, and Kirsten Ford. 2014. "Everything Must Change So That the IMF Can Remain the Same: The World Economic Outlook and the Global Financial Stability Report." *Development and Change* 45 (5): 1193–1204.

Vestergaard, Jakob, and Robert H. Wade. 2011. "The G20 Has Served Its Purpose and Should Be Replaced." *Journal of Globalization and Development* 2 (2): Article 10. doi: 10.1515/1948-1837.1237.

Vestergaard, Jakob, and Robert H. Wade. 2012a. "Establishing a New Global Economic Council: Governance Reform at the G20, the IMF, and the World Bank." *Global Policy* 3 (3): 257–269. doi: 10.1111/j.1758-5899.2012.00169.x.

Vestergaard, Jakob, and Robert H. Wade. 2012b. "The Governance Response to the Great Recession: The 'Success' of the G20." *Journal of Economic Issues* 46 (2): 481–489.

Vestergaard, Jakob, and Robert H. Wade. 2013a. "Protecting Power: How Western States Retained Their Dominant Voice in the World Bank's Governance Reforms." *World Development* 45: 153–164.

Vestergaard, Jakob, and Robert H. Wade. 2013b. "The West Must Allow a Power Shift in International Organizations, Part I." *Triple Crisis*, December 27. http://triplecrisis .com/the-west-must-allow-a-power-shift-in-international-organizations/.

Vestergaard, Jakob, and Robert H. Wade. 2014. "Out of the Woods: Gridlock in the IMF, and the World Bank Puts Multilateralism at Risk." DIIS Report No. 6. Copenhagen: Danish Institute for International Studies. https://www.diis.dk/files/media /publications/import/extra/rp2014-06_gridlock-imf-wb_jve_wade_web_2.pdf.

Vestergaard, Jakob, and Robert H. Wade. 2015. "Still in the Woods: Gridlock in the IMF and the World Bank Puts Multilateralism at Risk." *Global Policy* 6 (1): 1–12. http://www.globalpolicyjournal.com/articles/global-governance/still-woods -gridlock-imf-and-world-bank-puts-multilateralism-risk.

Vetterlein, Antje. 2010. "Lacking Ownership: The IMF and Its Engagement with Social Development as a Policy Norm." In *Owning Development: Creating Policy Norms in the IMF and the World Bank*, edited by Susan Park and Antje Vetterlein, 93–112. Cambridge: Cambridge University Press.

Viola, Lora Anne. 2014. "The G-20 and Global Financial Regulation." In *The Handbook of Global Economic Governance*, edited by Manuela Moschella and Catherine Weaver, 115–128. New York: Routledge.

Vollmann, Carolin. 2015. "The IMF's Chameleon-Policies on Unions Are Changing Colors." Bretton Woods Project, July 6. http://www.brettonwoodsproject.org/2015 /07/the-imfs-chameleon-policies-on-unions-are-changing-colours/.

Volz, Ulrich, and Aldo Caliari. 2010. *Regional and Global Liquidity Arrangements*. Bonn: German Development Institute and Center of Concern.

Vreeland, James Raymond. 2008. "The IMF and Economic Development." In *Reinventing Foreign Aid*, edited by William Easterly, 351–376. Cambridge, MA: MIT Press.

Wade, Robert H. 1976. "Performance of Irrigation Projects." *Economic and Political Weekly* 11 (3): 63–66.

Wade, Robert H. 1996. "Japan, the World Bank, and the Art of Paradigm Maintenance: The East Asian Miracle in Political Perspective." *New Left Review*, no. 217:3–37.

Wade, Robert H. 1998a. "The Asian Debt and Development Crisis of 1997–? Causes and Consequences." *World Development* 26 (8): 1535–1553.

Wade, Robert H. 1998b. "From 'Miracle' to 'Cronyism': Explaining the Great Asian Slump." *Cambridge Journal of Economics* 22 (6): 693–706.

Wade, Robert H. 1998–1999. "The Coming Fight over Capital Controls." *Foreign Policy*, no. 113:41–54.

Wade, Robert H. 2002. "US Hegemony and the World Bank: The Fight over People and Ideas." *Review of International Political Economy* 9 (2): 215–243.

Wade, Robert H. 2003. "What Strategies Are Viable for Developing Countries Today? The World Trade Organization and the Shrinking of 'Development Space.'" *Review of International Political Economy* 10 (4): 621–644.

Wade, Robert H. 2003[1990]. *Governing the Market: Economic Theory and the Role of Government in East Asian Industrialization*. Princeton, NJ: Princeton University Press.

Wade, Robert H. 2004. "The American Economic Empire." *Challenge* 47 (1): 64–77.

Wade, Robert H. 2007. "The Aftermath of the Asian Financial Crisis: From 'Liberalize the Market' to 'Standardize the Market' and Create a 'Level Playing Field.'" In *Ten Years After: Revisiting the Asian Financial Crisis*, edited by Bhumika Muchhala, 173–194. Washington, DC: Wilson Center Press.

Wade, Robert H. 2008. "Financial Regime Change?" *New Left Review*, no. 53:5–21.

Wade, Robert H. 2010. "The State of the World Bank." *Challenge* 53 (4): 43–67.

Wade, Robert H. 2011. "Emerging World Order? From Multipolarity to Multilateralism in the G20, the World Bank, and the IMF." *Politics and Society* 39 (3): 347–378.

Wade, Robert H. 2012. "US Keeps Control of the World Bank." *Le Monde Diplomatique*, October. http://mondediplo.com/blogs/us-keeps-control-of-the-world-bank.

Wade, Robert H. 2013a. "The Art of Power Maintenance: How Western States Keep the Lead in Global Organizations." *Challenge* 56 (1): 5–39.

Wade, Robert H. 2013b. "Western States in Global Organizations." In *Global Governance at Risk*, edited by David Held and Charles Roger, 77–110. Oxford: Polity.

Wade, Robert H., and Frank Veneroso. 1998. "The Asian Crisis: The High Debt Model versus the Wall Street-Treasury-IMF Complex." *New Left Review*, no. 228:3–23.

Wagsty, S. 2011. "IMF and Capital Controls: Sauce for the Goose Should Be Sauce for the Gander." *Financial Times*, April 6. http://blogs.ft.com/beyond-brics/2011/04/06/imf-capital-controls-sauce-for-the-goose-should-be-sauce-for-the-gander/.

Wang, Yongzhong. 2016. "The Sustainable Infrastructure Finance of China Development Bank: Composition, Experience and Policy Implications." Global Economic Governance Initiative Working Paper No. 5. Boston: Boston University, Frederic S. Pardee School of Global Studies, July. https://www.bu.edu/pardeeschool/files/2016/07/Wang.New_.Final_.pdf.

Weaver, Catherine. 2008. *Hypocrisy Trap: The Rhetoric, Reality and Reform of the World Bank*. Princeton, NJ: Princeton University Press.

Webber, Jude. 2011. "Argentina Tightens Forex Controls to Prevent Dollar Exodus." *Financial Times*, October 30. http://www.ft.com/intl/cms/s/0/77c92be8-0306-11e1-b7be-00144feabdc0.html - axzz3YRnyq3aK.

Weisbrot, Mark. 2014. "BRICS' New Financial Institutions Could Break a Long-standing and Harmful Monopoly." *Al Jazeera America*. http://www.cepr.net/index.php/op-eds-&-columns/op-eds-&-columns/brics-new-financial-institutions-could-break-a-long-standing-and-harmful-monopoly.

Weisbrot, Mark. 2015. *Failed: What the "Experts" Got Wrong about the Global Economy*. Oxford: Oxford University Press.

Weisbrot, Mark, Jose Cordero, and Luis Sandoval. 2009. *Empowering the IMF: Should Reform Be a Requirement for Increasing the Fund's Resources?* Washington, DC: Center

for Economic and Policy Research, April 20. http://www.cepr.net/index.php/public
ations/reports/empowering-the-imf-should-reform-be-a-requirement-for-increasing
-the-funds-resources/.

Weisbrot, Mark, and Jake Johnston. 2009. "IMF Voting Shares: No Plans for Significant
Changes." CEPR Issue Brief. Washington, DC: Center for Economic and Policy
Research, May. http://www.cepr.net/documents/publications/imf-voting-2009-05.pdf.

Weisbrot, Mark, and Helene Jorgensen. 2013. *Macroeconomic Policy Advice and the
Article IV Consultations: A European Union Case Study*. Washington, DC: Center for
Economic Policy Research. http://www.cepr.net/documents/publications/article-IV
-2013-01.pdf.

Weisbrot, Mark, Rebecca Ray, Jake Johnston, Jose Antonio Cordero, and Juan Antonio
Montecino. 2009. *IMF-Supported Macroeconomic Policies and the World Recession: A Look
at Forty-one Borrowing Countries*. Washington, DC: Center for Economic Policy
Research. http://www.cepr.net/documents/publications/imf-2009-10.pdf.

Weisman, Steven 2007. "I.M.F. Faces a Question of Identity." *New York Times*, September 28, C1. http://www.nytimes.com/2007/09/28/business/worldbusiness/28imf
.html?_r=0.

Welch, Sharon. 1990. *A Feminist Ethic of Risk*. Augsburg, MN: Fortress.

Weller, Christian, and Ghazal Zulfiqar. 2013. "Financial Market Diversity and Macroeconomic Stability." PERI Working Paper No. 332. Amherst: University of Massachusetts—Amherst, Political Economy Research Institute, August. http://www.peri
.umass.edu/fileadmin/pdf/working_papers/working_papers_301-350/WP332.pdf.

Wheatley, Jonathan, and Shawn Donnan. 2016. "Capital Controls No Longer Taboo
as Emerging Markets Battle Flight." *Financial Times*, January 27. http://www.ft.com
/intl/cms/s/0/36cfcc66-c41b-11e5-808f-8231cd71622e.html - axzz41OPv4o3d.

Whelan, Karl. 2013. "IMF on Greece: We Screwed Up, But It's Really the Eurozone's
Fault." *Forbes*, June 5. http://www.forbes.com/sites/karlwhelan/2013/06/05/imf-on
-greece-we-screwed-up-but-its-really-the-eurozones-fault/.

Widmaier, Wesley W. 2007. "Where You Stand Depends on How You Think: Economic Ideas, the Decline of the Council of Economic Advisers and the Rise of the
Federal Reserve." *New Political Economy* 12 (1): 43–59.

Widmaier, Wesley. 2014. "From Bretton Woods to the Global Financial Crisis: Popular Politics, Paradigmatic Debates, and the Construction of Crises." *Review of Social
Economy* 72 (2): 232–252.

Widmaier, Wesley W. 2016. *Economic Ideas in Political Times: The Rise and Fall of Economic Orders from the Progressive Era to the Global Financial Crisis*. Cambridge: Cambridge University Press.

Widmaier, Wesley W., Mark Blyth, and Leonard Seabrooke. 2007. "Exogenous Shocks or Endogenous Constructions? The Meanings of Wars and Crises." *International Studies Quarterly* 51 (4): 747–759.

Wildau, Gabriel. 2015. "China's Renminbi Liberalisation Leaves Capital Controls Intact." *Financial Times*, June 22. http://www.ft.com/intl/cms/s/0/7727bfec-18a1 -11e5-a130-2e7db721f996.html - axzz41OPv4o3d.

Wildau, Gabriel. 2016a. "China Steps Up Capital Controls to Stem Outflows." *Financial Times*, January 8. http://www.ft.com/intl/cms/s/0/9e25a772-b5df-11e5-aad2 -3e9865bc6644.html - axzz41OPv4o3d.

Wildau, Gabriel. 2016b. "China to Clamp Down on Outbound M&A in War on Capital Flight." *Financial Times*, November 29. https://www.ft.com/content/2511fa 56-b5f8-11e6-ba85-95d1533d9a62.

Wildau, Gabriel. 2016c. "China's Renminbi Hits 8-Year Low." *Financial Times*, November 16. https://www.ft.com/content/94f39188-ac6e-11e6-9cb3-bb8207902122.

Winters, Jeffrey A. 1999. "The Determinant of Financial Crisis in Asia." In *The Politics of the Asian Economic Crisis*, edited by T. J. Pempel, 79–100. Ithaca, NY: Cornell University Press.

Wise, Carol, Leslie Eliot Armijo, and Saori N. Katada. 2015. *Unexpected Outcomes: How Emerging Economies Survived the Global Financial Crisis*. Washington, DC: Brookings Institution.

Woods, Ngaire. 2006. *The Globalizers: The IMF, the World Bank, and Their Borrowers*. Ithaca, NY: Cornell University Press.

Woods, Ngaire. 2010. "Global Governance after the Financial Crisis: A New Multilateralism or the Last Gasp of the Great Powers?" *Global Policy* 1 (1): 51–63. doi: 10.1111/j.1758-5899.2009.0013.x.

Woods, Ngaire, Alexander Betts, Jochen Prantl, and Devi Sridhar. 2013. "Transforming Global Governance for the 21st Century." United Nations Development Programme Occasional Paper No. 9. New York: United Nations Development Programme. http://hdr.undp.org/sites/default/files/hdro_1309_woods.pdf.

Woods, Ngaire, and Domenico Lombardi. 2006. "Uneven Patterns of Governance: How Developing Countries Are Represented at the IMF." *Review of International Political Economy* 13 (3): 480–515.

Woods, Ngaire, and Leonardo Martinez-Diaz. 2009. *Networks of Influence? Developing Countries in a Networked Global Order*. Oxford: Oxford University Press.

World Bank. 2009. *Global Monitoring Report 2009: A Development Emergency*. Washington, DC: World Bank. https://www.imf.org/external/pubs/ft/gmr/2009/eng/gmr.pdf.

World Bank. 2011. *Global Development Horizons, Multipolarity: The New Global Economy*. Washington, DC: World Bank.

World Bank. 2013a. "Capital for the Future." Washington, DC: World Bank. http://dx .doi.org/10.1596/978-0-8213-9635-3

World Bank. 2013b. "Global Financial Development Report: Rethinking the Role of the State in Finance." Washington, DC: World Bank.

World Bank. 2016. "Annual Reports and Financial Statements." Accessed December 20. https://openknowledge.worldbank.org/handle/10986/2127.

World Bank. 2017. "World Development Indicators." World Bank. Accessed January 10. http://databank.worldbank.org/data//reports.aspx?source=2&country =&series=FI.RES.XGLD.CD&period.

World Bank Group. 2016. *Corporate Scorecards*. Washington, DC: World Bank, October. http://pubdocs.worldbank.org/en/331941477328080420/World-Bank-Corporate -Scorecard-2016-full-version.pdf.

Wroughton, Lesley. 2009. "Dispute over Control Clouds IMF Expansion." Reuters .com, October 4. http://in.reuters.com/article/2009/10/04/idINIndia-42902220091004.

Wroughton, Lesley. 2010. "IMF Endorses Capital Controls as Temporary Measure." Reuters.com, February 19. http://prasad.dyson.cornell.edu/doc/media/Reuters _19Feb2010.pdf.

Wroughton, Lesley. 2012a. "BRICS Economies to Boost IMF Funds." Reuters.com, June 18. http://www.reuters.com/article/2012/06/18/us-g2o-brics-statement -idUSBRE85H1K820120618.

Wroughton, Lesley. 2012b. "Colombia's Ocampo Withdraws from World Bank Challenge." Reuters.com, April 13. http://www.reuters.com/article/us-worldbank -ocampo-idUSBRE83C1H420120413.

Yardley, Jim. 2015. "Greece Will Shut Banks in Fallout from Debt Crisis." *New York Times*, June 28. http://www.nytimes.com/2015/06/29/world/europe/greece -will-shut-banks-in-fallout-from-debt-crisis.html.

Yardley, William. 2012. "Albert Hirschman, Optimistic Economist, Dies at 97." *New York Times*, December 24, B6.

Yeats, William Butler. 1921[1919]. "The Second Coming." In *Michael Robartes and the Dancer*. Churchtown: Chuala.

Yuk, Kwan Pan. 2012. "Peru: LatAm's Latest Currency Warrior." *Financial Times, Beyond Brics*, May 1. http://blogs.ft.com/beyond-brics/2012/05/01/peru-latams-latest -currency-warrior/.

Yukhananov, Anna 2013. "Stalled IMF Reforms Could Leave Fund on Shaky Ground." Reuters.com, October 3. http://in.reuters.com/article/2013/10/02/us-imf -reforms-analysis-idINBRE9911A120131002.

Zhou, Xiaochuan. 2009. "Reform the International Monetary System." *Bank for International Settlements Review* 41:1–3. http://www.bis.org/review/r090402c.pdf.

Zikakou, Ioanna. 2015. "S&P Upgrades Cyprus after Capital Control Removal." *Greek Reporter*, September 26. http://greece.greekreporter.com/2015/09/26/sp-upgrades -cyprus-after-capital-control-removal/.

Zoellick, Robert. 2009. "Opening Address to the 2009 Meetings of the Board of Governors of the World Bank, Summary of Proceedings." Istanbul, October 6–7. http:// www-wds.worldbank.org/external/default/WDSContentServer/WDSP/IB/2010/06/09 /000333037_20100609001522/Rendered/PDF/549450BR0SecM2101Official0Use0On ly1.pdf.

Index